Routledge Revivals

The Political Nature of a Ruling Class

First published in 1981, *The Political Nature of a Ruling Class* is a study of the role played by the 'organic intellectuals', who were attached to the capitalist class in South Africa, in shaping the processes of state and class formation in the crucial decades when the foundations of modern South Africa were being laid.

The book examines how the political and ideological character of the imperialist, 'British South African', mining bourgeoisie was formed, which revolutionised southern Africa and remained dominant until the First World War, and how a national bourgeoisie emerged and later came to prevail which differed both as a political force and as the bearer of a new 'South Africanist' ideology. In both cases, the activities of the intellectuals are explained in terms of the economic imperatives of accumulation and the capitalists' conflicts with other classes, and in each case, racism is viewed in the light of the overall system of hegemony created by capital. The origins of South African capitalism are examined finally from the point of view of one group of people—the capitalists themselves.

A concrete and readable account of capitalists and their ideologies, this contribution to theories both of class and state formation and of the relationship between political, cultural, ideological and economic forces will be of importance to students and researchers of African studies and political science.

The Political Nature of a Ruling Class

Capital and Ideology in South Africa 1890–1933

Belinda Bozzoli

Routledge
Taylor & Francis Group

First published in 1981
by Routledge & Kegan Paul Ltd

This edition first published in 2024 by Routledge
4 Park Square, Milton Park, Abingdon, Oxon, OX14 4RN

and by Routledge
605 Third Avenue, New York, NY 10017

Routledge is an imprint of the Taylor & Francis Group, an informa business

© Belinda Bozzoli 1981

Publisher's Note
The publisher has gone to great lengths to ensure the quality of this reprint but points out that some imperfections in the original copies may be apparent.

Disclaimer
The publisher has made every effort to trace copyright holders and welcomes correspondence from those they have been unable to contact.

A Library of Congress record exists under LCCN: 80042142

ISBN: 978-1-032-89932-9 (hbk)
ISBN: 978-1-003-54537-8 (ebk)
ISBN: 978-1-032-89933-6 (pbk)

Book DOI 10.4324/9781003545378

The political nature
of a ruling class

Capital and ideology in South Africa
1890–1933

Belinda Bozzoli

Routledge & Kegan Paul

London, Boston and Henley

First published in 1981
by Routledge & Kegan Paul Ltd
39 Store Street, London WC1E 7DD,
9 Park Street, Boston, Mass. 02108, USA and
Broadway House, Newtown Road,
Henley-on-Thames, Oxon RG9 1EN
Printed in Great Britain by
Redwood Burn Ltd, Trowbridge and Esher
© Belinda Bozzoli 1981

British Library Cataloguing in Publication Data

Bozzoli, Belinda

The political nature of a ruling class. –
(International library of sociology)
1. South Africa – Economic conditions
2. Capitalism
I. Title   II. Series
306'.3   HC517.S7   80–42142

ISBN 0–7100–0722–1

To Charles

Contents

Acknowledgments

This study began as a DPhil thesis for the University of Sussex, and my thanks must go to Theo Mars, my supervisor there, for his great interest in, and encouraging insights into, the original topic. At Sussex and elsewhere Martin Legassick's wide-ranging understanding of both Marxist studies and Southern African history were always something of an inspiration; while Dan O'Meara lent much support and encouragement. Richard Brown and Rob Davies read and made valuable comments on the thesis. In Oxford, Stanley Trapido taught me a great deal about historical materialism, perhaps often without realising it. He and Barbara Trapido were one reason this study was ever completed, while Bill Johnson, Anne Summers, Frank and Smitty Snowden, Joan Esteban, Susana Tavera and a number of fellow students in Oxford could not have provided a warmer and more stimulating circle of friends and colleagues. In Johannesburg, Tim Couzens's close friendship and interest in my work have never wavered, while Eddie Webster and students in the University of the Witwatersrand's Industrial Sociology classes have been a spur to the improvement of this study. I also thank Jeffrey Butler, Stanley Greenberg, Tom Karis and Sam Nolotshungu for help and advice at Yale University's Southern African Research Program; Dick Sklar for a thorough and constructive critique of the first draft of this book; Margaret Bruun-Meyer for her support and friendship; Lizzie Mthembu and Florence Zikalala for their generous help with caring for Gareth and Jessica; the Ernest Oppenheimer Memorial Trust for its financial support; and St. Antony's College Oxford for its willingness to accommodate a researcher from another university over several years.

My husband, Charles van Onselen, and my parents, lent me emotional, intellectual and financial support and encouragement over a number of difficult years and cannot be adequately thanked for all they have done to make this book possible. My deepest gratitude goes to them.

Every social class, coming into existence on the original basis of an essential function in the world of economic production, creates with itself, organically, one or more groups of intellectuals who give it homogeneity and consciousness of its function not only in the economic field but in the social and political field as well. The capitalist entrepreneur creates with himself the industrial technician, the organiser of a new culture, of a new law, etc. . . . If not all capitalists, at least an elite of them must have the capacity for organising society in general, in all its complex organism of duties up to the State organism, because of the need to create the most favourable conditionsfor the expansion of their own class . . .

Antonio Gramsci, The Formation of Intellectuals in 'The Modern Prince and Other Writings', New York, 1957, p. 118.

Introduction

In spite of the fact that South Africa has been penetrated, and indeed subordinated, by industrial capitalism for many decades, the precise nature of the connection between the South African political and ideological system on the one hand, and the capitalist economy on the other, has been notoriously difficult to discover. Many writers have asked whether 'racism', for example, in both its ideological and its institutional manifestations, is a product of, a benefit to, or a hindrance to, the growth of 'capitalism'. Controversy has raged around this question in recent years, when the perfection of the instruments of race domination in South Africa has for a large part of the time been accompanied by the rapid growth of the industrial capitalist economy. Analysts have sought to discover the relationship between these two coexisting forces, and to develop methods of analysis through which it may be better understood.

On one level this is a question unique to South Africa, to which answers may be, as they are in this study and in many other studies, sought through an examination of the historical and structural roots of the modern South African system. However, the question of the relation between 'race' and 'capital' also implies a whole range of other questions of great importance not only to the understanding of other societies and systems, which are also penetrated by industrial capitalism, but also to the interpretation of aspects of the South African system of domination other than that of race. While it is true that not all modern capitalist systems take on a vividly authoritarian and racist form, as does the South African one, all possess particular, historically specific political and ideological characteristics alongside capitalist economic forms. The explanation of the connection between racism and capitalism in South Africa

may thus perhaps fruitfully be generalised to the level
where what is sought is an explanation of the connection
between capitalism itself, as an economic system, and the
political and ideological forms that accompany it.
    In the case of South Africa, among the many discussions
of the nature of the relationship between 'race' and
'capital', at least three different broad approaches
to this intractable problem have been adopted. Legassick,
in his seminal discussion of the subject, for example,
addresses himself to the problem of the explanation of
the over-arching racist ideologies *and* structures
prevalent in South Africa (he uses the term 'racism' to
refer to both) in terms of the imperatives of capital
accumulation. He provides a periodisation of the
evolution of racism in terms of the evolution of
capitalism itself, and of the interests, particularly
the economic interests, of capital as a whole. (1) By
contrast a writer such as Johnstone is concerned with
only one group of capitalists in one period of South
African development, and thus does not tackle the more
general problems of periodisation or accumulation.
Instead, he relates the creation of the specific
structures and ideologies of racism within the mining
industry between 1911 and 1924, to the particular
accumulation requirements of mining capital itself,
and the form taken by their realisation within the
historical evolution of South African society. But
because of the fact that the mining revolution was the
crucible of South African capitalism, his analysis is of
crucial structural importance to the understanding of
certain of South Africa's racist industrial structures
in general. (2)
    The third approach represents a different way of
narrowing the focus on the connection between race and
capital, and is perhaps epitomised by Wolpe. He
relates particular aspects of South African racism to
particular needs of capital. Thus the reproduction of
labour power is cited as the problem to which territorial
segregation was the solution. And once again, because
of the crucial importance of the problem of reproduction
of labour power at particular stages in capitalist
development in South Africa, and of course because
'segregation' and 'apartheid' have been the centrepieces
of South Africa's system of race division, this approach
throws a great deal of light upon a whole range of
issues. (3)
    All three of these approaches have provided
fundamental empirical and theoretical foundations for the
argument of this study. For this analysis seeks to throw

light on the same problems that have concerned these
authors. It adopts an approach which bears a basic
similarity to those already outlined, in that it, too,
considers it important to explore the nature of the
industrialising capitalist economy in South Africa in
order to understand its racial and other non-economic
characteristics. However, in certain important respects
it differs from these analyses and indeed from others
that have been made, of the relationships outlined. In
the first place, it attempts to make more explicit than
has tended to be the case in most studies of South Africa
its assumptions about the nature of the relationship
between 'economics' and 'politics/ideology'. Indeed, it
puts forward particular hypotheses about this relationship
and how we may explore it empirically. Following on from
this, it attempts to pursue simultaneously both those
issues which are specific to South Africa (be they issues
of race or of other ideological and political
expressions), and those which may be of more general
interest to students of other capitalist societies, whether
or not these societies possess 'racist' characteristics.
Finally, and most concretely, it undertakes to do so
through the examination of the origins of South African
capitalism from the point of view of one particular,
vitally important, group of people - those who are the
prime movers of industrial capitalism, the members of the
class of capitalists itself.
  The capitalist class in all capitalist societies,
because of its dominating nature, and its central place
in the economic, political and ideological system, is of
great importance to the understanding, not only of
economic matters of immediate relevance to its
interests, but of a number of social matters as well.
The prism of the 'ruling class' reflects light upon a
whole range of social, economic and political relationships and their ideological expressions and is, it will be
argued, capable of illuminating the more general interconnections between the various levels of social
existence in capitalist society. As far as the South
African example is concerned, the bourgeoisie as a class
has remained relatively neglected as a subject for
analysis. Many writers have examined aspects or parts
of the capitalist class. They have looked at one set of
its interests (and these are usually its economic
interests), one of its sections, or one of its problems,
as we have already suggested. But no systematic attempt
has been made to explore the bourgeoisie in a more
complete way, in all its various manifestations in that
complex society which is South Africa. Here we enquire

further into the overall character of the South African
'ruling class' and ask what are the relationships
between its economic needs and the political and
ideological character of the society itself.

However, a broader approach to the nature of
capital in South Africa should not imply a lack
of theoretical and historical rigour. The concept
of the 'ruling class' is an extremely wide one, while
South Africa's experience of capital's dominance has
been relatively long. There exists the danger that the
bourgeoisie may become the basis for an unfocused
analysis of capitalists in South Africa throughout the
nineteenth and twentieth centuries. Instead this study
concentrates on the character of the South African
bourgeoisie in detail during the crucial decades from
1890-1933.

These years are important for our purposes because
they were the years during which the bourgeoisie as a
class, and indeed as a 'ruling class', was being formed.
Of course, capital had existed in the Southern African
region for many years during the nineteenth century;
but its manifestations had been local rather than
regional, and its class character in many areas inchoate.
It was after the discovery of gold in 1886 that a class
of capitalists with a Southern African base, and with
ambitions to dominate the region as a whole, began to be
formed. And it is during the process of its formation,
it is suggested, that the capitalist class forges its
internal and external relationships, and comes to express
and realise its interests in the social formation at
large. This process, therefore, represents a field in
which we may explore the general questions posed above.
Furthermore, it is no coincidence that it was during
these same crucial decades that the modern South African
system itself was also in the process of being forged.
It is a reflection, perhaps, of the fact that there is
a crucial interconnection between class formation, and
system - or state - formation, when the class concerned
is the dominant one, an interconnection whose precise
character it is essential that we examine. The years
1890-1933, therefore, appear to be potentially rich
in insights in to the nature of the bourgeoisie as a
whole, its experiences of class formation, and even the
relationships between class and state formation.

Thus, with its focus on these issues and these years,
this is a study with a complex duality to it. On the one
hand it is an examination of certain of the processes
whereby classes in capitalist society in general are
formed, with special reference to the bourgeoisie itself.

It is concerned to discover what are the complexities of
the forging of the dominant class under capitalism on
the economic, political and ideological levels, and the
relationships between these levels, and what are the
interconnections between that process of class
formation, and the formation of the society as a whole.
But inseparable from this general concern is the more
specific historical one, with the example of the
formation of the capitalist class in one, highly complex,
society - that of South Africa, in the first four
decades after gold was discovered there. In this case,
we ask more concretely what the relationship was between
the bourgeoisie's economic interests and their expression
in particular ideologies (whether these be racist or
otherwise) and particular political forms, including
the form of the state itself.
    The general theoretical concerns of this work are
thus difficult to separate from the empirical or
historical examples on which it draws. The body of
the study consists of an attempt to pursue
simultaneously both conceptual and historical-empirical
issues, in the belief that their capacity to illuminate
our understanding of capitalism is thereby enhanced.
    It is neither easy, nor entirely desirable, to extract
from this study, therefore, the particular historical
and theoretical issues which it pursues and discuss them
out of the context in which they appear. Such a
separation is necessary for purposes of exposition in
this introduction however. For it is important to
consider briefly certain general propositions concerning
the nature of the capitalist class, the concept of class
formation, the way in which this study was conducted,
and some of the questions about the South African system
which it raises, before the analysis itself is embarked
upon. However, these remarks should not be regarded as
an exhaustive review of the many matters raised in the
body of this work, but rather as a pointer to some of
the major debates with which it is concerned.

1 CLASS AND CLASS FORMATION

Perhaps the most basic concept used here is that of
'class'. 'Class formation' is a meaningless term unless
we have some notion of what it is that is being formed,
and what are its essential and less essential elements.
In this work, the term 'class' is used in a wider sense
than the strictly economic one which is used by some
Marxists. For here it refers not only to the relationship

of particular groups of people to the means and the
process of economic production under capitalism, but also
to their political, cultural and ideological characteristics and their relationships in a range of economic
and non-economic spheres, to other classes and to the
state. Classes cannot be defined, indeed do not exist,
independently of the struggles between classes which are
a constant feature of capitalist society. Their economic,
political, ideological and cultural characteristics are
all thus historically located.

In our concern with the process of class formation we
need to differentiate between the economic, political
and ideological aspects of classes, and to ask in what
way these aspects come into existence in the case of
historically specific classes. Thus while the results of
the process of class formation may constitute classes
defined in all three of these social dimensions, it is
with the processes leading to those results that we are
primarily concerned; it is therefore important to define
which of these dimensions is of primary significance in
the definition of particular classes, in our case the
dominant class, and which of secondary significance.

This study works from the assumption that it is
primarily the fact of its ownership of the means of
production that defines the bourgeoisie as the dominant
class under capitalism. And the economic relationship
that capitalists have to the means of production gives
rise to a number of economic imperatives - the
imperatives of accumulation itself. Capitalists are
driven by the economic logic of the system in which they
are embedded to secure and continually increase profits,
through the extraction of surplus value from productive
workers whose interests are subordinated to their own.
And around this driving need there arises a range of
other economic interests that the capitalist class must
fulfil, as indeed individual capitalists and their
spokesmen are aware. J. E. Borain, spokesman for South
African manufacturing, sketched out some of these complex
and interlocking interests in 1929, when he referred to
such factors as:
(a) the driving competitiveness of capital, which is both
a cause and a result of the move to 'mass production',
i.e. the introduction of mechanised and highly capital
intensive forms of production;
(b) the tendency and capacity of workers to resist their
subordination (and thereby decrease the ability of
employers to maximise the amount of surplus value which
may be extracted from them); and
(c) the barriers to mass production, mechanisation and

price reduction which are confronted by late industrialisers (like South Africa) to whom world markets are either
closed or prohibitively competitive. (4) Because
capitalists seek to accumulate in the face of ongoing
obstacles, the economic processes of accumulation tend
to take a highly contradictory form, some of whose
features Borain has pinpointed. The particular pattern
taken by the process of accumulation in South Africa is
discussed in more detail in the body of this study, and
variations between the needs of mining capital and
manufacturing capital in particular are pointed out.
But in general it seems possible to say that while
capitalist production as a whole expands and reproduces
itself, it does so in ways that breed classes whose
interests are directly opposed to its own; and in ways
that give rise to grave difficulties in sustaining, let
alone increasing, the rate of profit. It is suggested
that the capitalist class in general, by virtue of its
central place in the resulting productive cycle, an
expanding, self-contradictory, often unstable cycle,
possesses an 'economic nature' which is specific to it
as a class, and which indeed is the *sine qua non* of its
existence. To survive, it must pursue certain relentless
economic goals in spite of, and in the face of,
opposing tendencies, many of which are of its own making.
   Capital accumulation, with all its economic
implications, is a concrete and empirically verifiable
process. Capital in general may be identified according
to the role it plays in this cycle. But how may we
identify the particular manifestations of this process in
real societies? And more importantly, how may we relate
'capital', as the economic force which is central to the
accumulation process, to a specific 'capitalist class'
in a real social formation? For, as we have argued,
the bourgeoisie is not simply an economic class; every
economic interest that it possesses is also,
simultaneously, a political, social and/or ideological
interest. It is the bourgeoisie's relationships to other
social groups, to political systems, to the ideological
forms prevailing at any one time, and its place in the
history of a particular society, that will determine
not only how, but in some cases whether, its primary
economic interests are realisable.
   There is in fact a gap between capital's economic
interests - the 'economic nature' of the capitalist class
- on the one hand; and its political, social and
ideological interests - the 'political nature' of the
capitalist class - on the other. It is the gap between
abstract necessities, and concrete possibilities. In

exploring the process of class formation, this study
attempts to derive a method of analysis which will enable
us to fill this gap; and to illustrate and explore the
usefulness of this method in the case of South African
capitalist development. From the basic starting point
of the 'economic nature' of the bourgeoisie, and thus of
the crucial place it has in the accumulation process,
this study seeks to analyse the processes whereby the
economic interests which arise out of the accumulation
process in the case of particular capitalists, come to
be translated into political and ideological
realities, embedded in the historical circumstances
surrounding the capitalist class as a whole.

'Class formation' in this study, therefore, is used
to refer to the multiple processes whereby a group of
people evolves not only particular economic relationships
to each other and to outsiders, but particular
ideological and political relationships as well. Some of
these relationships may not be expressed in class
terms at all - for the ideological dimension of the class
interests of capital may, as we shall be demonstrating,
be expressed in terms of such categories as 'race',
'nationality' or 'language group'; while its political
interests may be expressed through the state form itself,
or through such categories as that of 'public opinion'.
Nevertheless, the results of these aspects of class
formation are referred to here as the 'political nature'
of the class, and it is the relationship between
'economic nature' and 'political nature' that we are
concerned to identify.

2 THE SYSTEM OF INTEREST-TRANSLATION

It is hoped that to illuminate the process whereby an
economic abstraction (the owners of the means of
production) becomes a social reality (mineowners in
South Africa at the turn of the century, with all that
that implies about their class position and class
relationships), will be to illuminate the relationships
between economics, politics and ideology; or, in a
different terminology, between 'base' and 'superstructure'. With this ambition in mind, therefore, the
basic historical question that is asked here is: how did
capitalists themselves in South Africa bridge the gap
between their more or less abstract economic needs, and
the concrete social implications thereof? Was there some
automatic social process where by a 'superstructure' came
to be erected upon the economic 'base', and whereby it

came to match its social requirements to a large degree?
Surely not. What, then, was the mechanism which operated?

To find an answer to this question it is necessary to
adopt an historical as well as materialist methodological
approach, and to assume that since the bourgeoisie was
not always the 'ruling class', there must have been a
particular period during which its dominance came into
being. The search for the roots of bourgeois hegemony in
South Africa between 1890 and 1933 thus begins with a
search for this period, and for the patterns of social,
political and ideological development experienced by
capitalists during it.

In the various media in which capitalists, or those
engaged in expressing bourgeois interests, expressed
their views about their place in the evolving social
system at particular crucial stages in South African
history, certain interesting patterns do indeed become
apparent, and it is from these patterns that a method
of analysis which contains the potential to bridge the
gap between 'economic' and other interests is derived.

The media of the emerging bourgeoisie included
journals, speeches, reports, minutes and petitions, and
are themselves discussed in detail in the appropriate
parts of this study. For present purposes what is
important about these media is the extraordinary
richness of content which they displayed in certain
periods, and their relative sterility in others. In
the case of mining capital during the 1890s and 1900s,
for example, they reveal a profound concern with
fundamental social and political issues, ranging from
the destruction of pre-capitalist black family
structures, to the overthrow of the Kruger regime; from
the advocacy of the importation of tens of thousands
of Chinese labourers, to the manipulation of white
working-class employment patterns and expressions of
resistance. And accompanying, and indeed often
indistinguishable from, these expressions of concern
with large-scale social engineering was the creative
articulation of a social ideology, of a racist and
imperialist character, integrally related to the broader
concerns of the class itself.

In other periods, however, mining media appear quite
barren by contrast. By the 1920s they provide evidence
that ideologies were not being created through the
media of mining capital as much as regurgitated; while
social structures were not being 'engineered' as much
as lubricated. The same pattern is evident in the
spheres of commerce and manufacturing, but with
significantly different periodisation, as will become

clear. At certain points it seems as if the businessmen
in one or another of these economic sectors wished to
engage in fundamental social debate through a specialised
system of intra-class communication, discussion and
expression; while at other points it seems as if they
were satisfied with the broad outlines of the system
in which they were operating and wished only to sustain
and improve upon it.
   The periods in which these systems of communication
were at their most dynamic and productive are of great
importance to the larger questions with which this study
is concerned. In setting up communications systems of
a specific and directed kind, the capitalist class in
the process of formation had, it will be argued, set up
what may be called its own system of interest-
realisation, or interest-translation, its own ideology
and policy-making network within which particular,
historically specific processes seemed to be under way.
Understanding the structure of this system of interest-
translation and realisation is crucial to understanding
its functions, and so it seems essential to outline
briefly the four elements which it contained, and to
indicate how these elements are to be analysed.

(a) The organic intellectual

The media of capital were run by men who, as journalists,
speechmakers or writers played an important intellectual
role in guiding and leading certain of the processes
of class formation themselves. These individuals,
because of their role as thinkers, strategists, ideologues
and policy-makers, are called here 'intellectuals';
while because they were organically linked to the
emerging class or sub-class whose interests they
expressed, because, in other words, they communicated
directly to members of that class or sub-class, rather
than to a wider audience, the Gramscian term 'organic
intellectuals' was adopted to describe them. (5) It will
be shown that it was the 'organic intellectual' whose
task it was to bridge the gap between economic interests
and political and ideological realities; and to translate
the abstract needs of capital into real social needs.
This study asks when it was that these 'organic
intellectuals' came into being, who they were, when and
where they developed their skills, what their main fields
of creativity were, and how they related to their
audience and to the processes of class and state
formation, social change and class struggle. As we have

suggested, organic intellectuals performed their tasks
only during particular, crucial periods, periods of
crisis, of uncertainty, when capitalists were struggling
not only to establish themselves economically, but to
embed themselves firmly in the social formation itself
in ways that suited their economic interests best.
Moreover, the unique feature of these 'organic
intellectuals' lay in the fact that they were not mere
propagandists for the bourgeoisie, nor even simply the
creators of its symbols and ideologies in these periods.
They emerged as being an essential part of its
existence, consciousness and realisation as a class.
Not only did they create ideologies, but they were
strategists and policy-makers for the emerging
bourgeoisie. It was through their activities, it seems,
that the interests of the capitalist class were
discovered and a pattern set for their realisation.
The organic intellectual was an ideological and
political craftsman whose skills lay in his ability
to assess the balance of economic and political forces
with which capital had to cope, to discover the nature
of its consciousness as a class or section of a class,
and to translate its objective problems and needs into
symbolic and political terms.

(b) The audience

Ideologies gain their significance and meaning through
their ability to convey to members of an audience
certain facts and attitudes about their lives and world
which other methods of communication are unable to
depict. They are able to 'grasp, formulate and
communicate social realities that elude the tempered
language of science', (6) and the ideologist is skilled
who can perform this task effectively over long periods.
The second element in the system of interest-realisation
was the group of people for whom the ideological,
symbolic and political formulations of the intellectual
meant something. Certainly the intellectual did not
work simply for himself. The reason he expressed his
ideas in a public way was that he had an audience; and
indeed in this case it was for the exclusive
benefit of this group that his activities were undertaken; it was to them that he was thus 'organically'
linked.
    The particular audiences who constituted an integral
part of the system of interest-translation were groups
of capitalists - mineowners, manufacturers, commercial

men, capitalist farmers, or combinations of two or more
of these groups - whose objective need was not only for
the symbolic creations of intellectuals, but also for
their capacity to perceive the economic interests of the
'audience' in social and political terms. This study
is concerned to discover what it was about these
audiences that made the services of organic intellectuals
so essential to their existence, by examining such
factors as the stage of class formation they had reached,
the extent to which their interests were realisable,
and the history of their development; by asking more
precisely who constituted the audiences - whether the
bourgeoisie as a whole, or only certain parts of it;
by exploring changes in their composition over time; and
by assessing the nature of the relationship between
that part of the bourgeoisie which constituted the
audience, and the bourgeoisie as a whole.

(c) The structure of ideas

The third element in the system of interest-translation
was that of the 'ideas' and 'policies' themselves, as
well as the particular structured ways in which they
were expressed. The intellectual's grasp of language
and his ability to convey meaning to his audience
through its use, were the foundations of the intricate
symbolic and political formulations that he developed.
The choice of medium through which he worked, the
vocabulary, syntax and structure of his ideas, and
their creative content, provide the context within
which an understanding of the craftmanship of the
organic intellectual is advanced.
    Unlike many other ideologues, the organic
intellectuals did not simply engage in the craft of
symbolic formulation, as we have suggested. This makes
the analysis of their creations particularly complex
and fascinating. For they mixed 'ideology' with
'policy', embedding in their conceptual creations real
strategic and political considerations, suggestions for
the concrete furtherance of their audience's interests.
Not only did they create a world-view for the bourgeoisie,
but they sketched the broad outline of its ideal world
as well! They planned and proposed actual policies,
as well as encapsulating them in elaborate social
imagery. Media created largely for these purposes came
into being during these crucial historical periods, and
were vehicles for the intellectuals. And indeed, the
media themselves were of great importance to the under-

standing of the structure of ideas and policies. Some
audiences relied on written media of an exclusive,
'introverted' kind while others possessed media which
looked outward, to 'public opinion', for example.
  This study examines the ideas and policies created
by the organic intellectuals in considerable detail, and
attempts to construct explanations for them which are
both historically and structurally specific. It explores
the character of the media through which the ideas were
created, asking how and why they were shaped to suit the
requirements of the audience, and whether they changed
over time. It also examines the relationships between
'symbolic' formulations and 'political' and 'strategic'
ones, asking whether the symbol was a vehicle, an
expression, or a legitimation of the strategy. Perhaps
most importantly, it attempts to develop an over-arching
structure within which individual ideas may be understood
and to which simple, small-scale strategic proposals may
be related. To the extent that the aims and achievements
of groups of capitalists - the audiences - possess a
certain coherence, so their ideologies and strategies
must constitute a more or less integrated whole, with
a distinctive, identifiable shape and form.

(d) The historical context

As has already been implied in much of the preceding
discussion, none of these elements is assumed to exist
in a vacuum. The organic intellectual is not an
autonomous actor, as perhaps an 'idealist' or 'literary'
interpretation might suggest, but an historical one,
and the factors that determine whether or not his
activities are meaningful, and what sort of meaning they
convey to his audience are historical factors. While,
of course, it is difficult to reduce the category of
'history' to any simple formulation, it seems essential
to point out that the fourth element in the system of
interest-realisation must be that of the historical
context of the social formation itself. The intellectual
must not, therefore, be seen in reified and abstract
terms, but as a real historical actor, grappling with the
character of the society in which he emerges, and more or
less capable of fulfilling his functions according to
circumstances; his audience must not be seen as an
abstract category of economically defined 'capitalists',
but as a group of people whose aspirations, interrelation-
ships, social character and past experiences deeply affect
and shape the ways in which it is possible for their

interests to be realised and expressed. The ideas too,
and the media through which they are articulated, are
not 'pure' creations, but emerge out of the past
experiences of those who adhere to and use them, as well
as the prevailing social ideologies in the society at
any one time. The historical past of the Southern
African region deeply influences the character and class
capacity of its emerging bourgeoisie and must be a constant
foundation for any meaningful conception of the system of
interest-realisation. This study is concerned to explore
the ways in which the existing nature of the South African
social formation affected the capacity of the bourgeoisie
to embed itself within it, and indeed to transform it on
many levels; while it asks what the particular uses to
capital were of the system of interest-translation in
effecting its ongoing revolution.

     The system of interest-translation thus outlined, with
its four elements of intellectual, audience, ideas and
'history', constitutes the methodological core of this
work; and the organic intellectual is the central focus
within that core, because of his active and crucial
function in making the system work. The chief forum
for the activities of intellectuals - the business journal
- provided the vast majority of the material used here,
and it seems important to discuss how such journals,
and the various other media of capital which emerged at
particular stages, were used. Hopefully some of the
methodological procedures adopted here will be of
interest to other students of ideology.

     Journals belonging to distinctive sections of capital,
orientated consciously towards the definition of their
specific interests on the one hand, and the development
of ideologies and strategies on the other, have been the
chief original source for this study. Each journal
examined employed an intellectual, usually the editor,
to create strategic, political and ideological patterns
around the problems of its audience during the crucial
period of class formation. Journals of this nature -
the 'South African Mining Journal', the 'South African
Commerce and Manufacturers' Record', 'Commercial
Bulletin' and many others - are the best written sources
available, for in them are systematically set out, month
by month, or sometimes week by week, the successive,
accumulating problems and ideologies of each 'audience',
and they have been examined over crucial periods of up to
twenty years, systematically and in the proper order. This
basic ideological and historical material was supplemented
by other audience-based material, such as speeches,
annual reports, minutes of meetings, and evidence to

commissions of enquiry. From these sources the basic
evidence for the argument sustained in this work - the
quotations which form so substantial a part of the
text - was derived.
    The creations of intellectuals were carefully
assessed and interpreted as follows: in each 'run' of a
journal (the specific dates of the run having been
determined mainly by the content of the journal itself,
some journals, as we have said, being devoid of ideological and historical content at some stages and filled
with it at others) a content analysis was made of
editorials and other expressions of intellectual
activity. This content analysis took place in two
distinct categories. On the one hand, every editorial,
for example (if editorials were the chief forum for
expression in a particular journal), was broken down
into its components, into the kinds of ideas and
proposals which comprised it. On the other hand, each
idea-type was not considered in isolation. Some indication
of the problems for that group to which the ideas may be
related was also sought and usually, though not always,
found in the journal itself. A systematic attempt to
categorise the 'problems' was therefore also made.
    From performing this activity for succeeding issues
of journals, the point was reached where many 'component
ideas' on the one hand, and many 'component problems'
on the other, had been outlined. Only a rough idea,
however, could be obtained of how these two categories
of data could be linked. The links could not be made
direct simply on the basis of the fact that one idea
and one 'problem' may have appeared together in
editorials, articles or speeches. They needed to be
reconstituted in terms of a theory of their inter-
relationship.
    From an understanding of the historical circumstances
in which the journal and its editorials existed; and of
the several related problems of theory outlined here, an
explanatory structure was derived for each audience.
This explanatory structure had to cover both sets of
accumulated data, so that the 'policies' and 'ideas'
were explained in terms of the 'problems' and vice versa.
The structure was not usually generalised, but highly
specific and integrated. It was in every case a true
structure, a detailed set of explanatory concepts
related in their essence to one, organising idea. From
the explanatory structures derived for each audience
the theoretical issues discussed in this introduction
could be treated singly and together, in historical
sequence or synchronically, and conclusions about the
political nature of capital drawn from them.

These theoretical and methodological approaches to the
problem of interest-realisation hopefully are of broader
relevance to those concerned with the relationships
between 'economic' factors on the one hand, and 'political
and ideological' ones on the other. For it is often
pointed out that vulgar Marxism, which posits a somewhat
mechanical relationship between 'base' and 'superstructure', offers no more than a simple metaphor which
needs refinement and concretisation. In positing a
deterministic relationship, it fails to provide us with
an explanation of how the base actually causes, gives
rise to, results in, or manifests itself as the superstructure. We need to develop a more sophisticated,
working, dynamic hypothesis of the way in which an
ongoing relationship between base and superstructure
is created and sustained over time. As Geertz has
pointed out: (7)

> There is a good deal of talk about emotions 'finding
> a symbolic outlet' or 'becoming attached' to
> appropriate symbols - but very little idea of how
> the trick is actually done. The link between the
> causes of ideology and its effects seems
> adventitious because the connecting element - the
> autonomous process of symbolic formulation - is
> passed over in virtual silence. Both interest
> theory and strain theory go directly from source
> analysis to consequence analysis, without ever
> seriously examining ideologies as systems of
> interacting symbols, as patterns of interworking
> meanings.

By introducing the concept of 'symbolic formulation'
Geertz introduces *process* into ideology. Instead of
being the static mechanical 'end-product' of the
abstract operations of the 'base', ideologies are the
result of the activities of those formulating them.

Hopefully the four-dimensional conceptualisation of the
process of interest-realisation, articulation and
translation put forward here provides a similarly
dynamic and sophisticated hypothesis of the relationships
between 'base' and 'superstructure', albeit an historically
specific one, of central relevance mainly to the understanding of one particular class in a certain stage of
capitalist development. In this four-dimensional concept
are contained the abstract, metaphorical 'base' and
'superstructure', but they are made concrete; while the
processes whereby they are linked are rendered real and
empirically observable, embodied as they are in the
activities of social actors rather then in abstract
mechanics. If this conceptualisation of these processes

does possess heuristic value, perhaps it is not least
because the concepts it contains arose out of the
examination of the media of capitalists themselves;
because they are not abstractions, but a result of
theorising from the concrete.

3 THE STATE AND HEGEMONY

It is probably true to say that all classes in capitalist
society possess a 'political and ideological' as well as
an 'economic' nature. However, as has already been
implied by the foregoing discussion, there comes a point
at which 'class formation' defined according to these
criteria ceases to be a concept of general applicability
to ruling and subordinate classes alike. This is because
what one has to explain *is* the place of a particular
class in the system of domination and subordination that
prevails under capitalism. It is not as if classes are
first formed, and then their place in the hierarchy of
classes is decided afterwards. This kind of thinking is
a result of placing too much emphasis on the economic,
abstract, features of classes. While clearly the
economic owners of the means of production, distribution
and exchange have the potential to prevail over non-
owners of these things, one needs to ask how this
potential is realised in the spheres of the state,
ideology and class struggle. It is the way in which these
things are decided during the process of class formation
that will determine what kind of domination and what kind
of subordination is to characterise the classes
concerned, and the system in which they are lodged. In
the case of the dominant class, therefore, what needs
to be explored is not only the relationship between
economic ownership of the means of production and the
concomitant interests arising out of the process of
accumulation, on the one hand, and the political and
ideological interests of the bourgeoisie on the other;
but also the relationships between these forces and
factors and political and ideological hegemony itself.
    While the dominance of the bourgeoisie over the
working class must first be interpreted in terms of the
struggle between those classes, it must also be located
in the sphere of the state. This represents one of the
most complex and difficult aspects of this discussion,
for 'the state' is a term used in many different ways in
the literature, with many different implications.
Moreover, like the other concepts introduced here, 'the
state' is a concept which we seek not simply to use, but

to illuminate, through the historical study itself. For
purposes of this introduction, the state will, therefore,
be treated in a highly tentative and questioning manner,
until some of the findings of this study may be brought
to bear on our understanding of it.

Marxist scholarship has emphasised that the capitalist
state must be regarded as more than simply the 'executive
committee' of the bourgeoisie. Many writers have
introduced into our understanding of it notions of
ideological as well as political dominance which go
beyond the simple metaphorical relationship between
state and capital which Marx and Engels defined in their
polemical works. Since our concern is primarily with
the process of the formation of the bourgeoisie as the
ruling class, it is important to point to at least one
of the ways in which these refinements in our understanding of the relationship between the bourgeoisie
and the state have been made; as well as to state in
what ways this study itself may be able to enhance this
understanding.

Gramsci's conception of 'hegemony' represents one
avenue along which the questions of the overall nature
of capital's dominance over labour, and over the society
at large, may be pursued; and represents a major
contribution to the refinement of our understanding of the
relationship between bourgeoisie and state. For Gramsci
'the state' does not consist of the 'system of government'
alone, but also of the wider sphere of capital's
subordination of other classes in 'civil society'
itself. 'Hegemony' thus refers to: (8)

> an order in which a certain way of life and thought
> is dominant, in which one concept of reality is
> diffused throughout society in all its institutional
> and private manifestations, informing with its spirit
> all taste, morality, customs, religious and political
> principles and all social relations, particularly
> in their intellectual and moral connotations.

Gramsci locates the development of the hegemonic order
clearly in the struggle between and within classes; he
argues that, (9)

> previously germinated ideologists become 'party', come
> into confrontation and conflict, until only one of
> them, or at least a single combination of them, tends
> to prevail, to gain the upper hand, to propogate
> itself throughout society - bringing about not only
> a unison of economic and political aims, but also
> intellectual and moral unity, posing all the questions
> around which the struggle rages, not only on a
> corporate but on a 'universal' plane, thus creating

the hegemony of a fundamental social group over a
series of subordinate groups.

Gramsci's conception of hegemony refers to class rule;
and the ways in which the rule of a particular class
over others is constituted ideologically as well as in
other dimensions. We are in a position to explore
whether and how this kind of dominance comes into
being in the case of South African capitalism, through
exploring the various patterns taken by the dominance of
capital over labour, during the period of class- and
system-formation.

The interests of workers directly contradict those
of their employers; and yet what the concept of 'hegemony'
conveys is that the remarkable thing about the dominance
of the capitalist class is that it is more often sustained
through the 'acquiescence' of workers, than through the
exercise of force over them. But it would be incorrect
and ahistorical to treat the concept of 'hegemony' as a
holistic, all-embracing, reified 'thing'. Then we would
fail to capture the subtleties, complexities and
variations in capital's ability to establish such a system
of class rule, to obtain the 'acquiescence' or even the
'consent' of workers; to evolve 'one concept of reality',
and to 'pose all the questions around which the struggle
rages'. Instead what this study attempts to do is to
seek out the ways in which the development of a system of
hegemonic domination by capitalists both succeeds and
fails, and the relationships between repression, force,
and acquiescence. Because of the division of the South
African working class into two groups, distinguished by
their place in the system of domination and subordination,
the South African example provides a good opportunity
for comparison and contrast, an opportunity to examine
the proportional importance of directly coercive and less
coercive methods of control over workers at various
stages in the development of the capitalist system.
Abundant material exists for the exploration of such
processes as the development of conservative social
ideologies; the embourgeoisement of workers; the tactics
of 'divide and rule'; the creation of controlling
mechanisms and ideologies in the workplace; the
development of 'consumerism' as a controlling ideology
for certain sections of the workforce, and the ways in
which particular kinds of trade unionism are cultivated
by capital. This study explores these varied mechanisms
of class domination in 'civil society' as well as
examining the role of the central state apparatuses - the
system of direct coercion, the party system, the structure
of legislation and the creation of a social ideology - in

bringing into being a hegemonic order; while it also
touches on the role of the petty-bourgeoisie, caught
between capital and labour, in maintaining, or perhaps
undermining, the acquiescence of workers to capital's
hegemony. Instead of being a holistic, Hegelian kind
of notion, 'hegemony', when treated in this manner,
emerges as a complex, historical set of processes,
located in the struggle between classes, in which a
of repressive and non-repressive mechanisms form
particular patterns at each stage of the development
of the capitalist mode of production.

Many subsequent writers have been deeply influenced
by Gramsci's work and have sought to develop it further.
On the one hand, Althusser has echoed Gramsci's
distinction between 'government' and 'civil society'
when he put forward his notion of the distinction between
'repressive' and 'ideological' state apparatuses – the
latter being the concrete structures and systems outside
of what is normally conceived of as the state – the
school, the church, the trade union or the family – which
operate to prevent subordinate groups from challenging
their subordination in meaningful ways. (10) On the
other, both Poulantzas (11) and Miliband (12) have sought
to understand how one may relate the interests of the
bourgeoisie itself to the development of class hegemony
in both the 'narrow' and the 'wide' states. They have an
ongoing controversy over their differing approaches to
the subject. (13) Poultantzas's general concern seems
to be with discovering the ways in which the functioning
of the state's various apparatuses and structures serves
the interests of the bourgeoisie; and this leads him to
criticise what he regards as perhaps the more
conspiratorial approach of Miliband, who embarks upon an
empirical demonstration of the real (rather than abstract)
links that exist between the capitalist class and the
systems of both government and hegemony.

These three approaches, therefore, represent different
attempts to grapple with Gramsci's conceptualisations of
state, hegemony and civil society. They address
themselves to the problem of the relationships between the
needs of the ruling class on the one hand, and the
functioning of the state and civil society on the other.
Both Althusser and Poulantzas tend to resort to what
amounts to an abstract functionalism, positing in effect
that state apparatuses operate in the interests of
capital because that is their function. Miliband, on
the other hand, seeks the hidden hand of capital behind
the system of power and authority, perhaps without
taking sufficient account of the extent to which social

systems may operate in the interests of certain groups
without those groups necessarily having to be physically
represented in every sphere of the system's operation.
This study also represents an attempt to elaborate
upon the nature of the relationships between the ruling
class on the one hand, and the state - defined in both
the narrow and the wide senses - on the other. While it
does not attempt to enter into a debate with any of
these authors in any systematic way, it is important to
point out that in one central respect its concerns need
to be distinguished from those of all of these writers.
Hopefully, indeed, it is in its distinctive approach that
the contribution of this study may lie. For what is
common to all of these authors is their concern to
discover, among other things, the ways in which the
bourgeoisie controls the state in an existing, established
capitalist society. And what this study may be
able to add to their discoveries is the historical
dimension which tends to be absent, or at least
minimised, in their works.
An historical and materialist approach is also a
radical approach, for it seeks to discover the essence
of things through observing their historical and
structural roots. By focusing on the process whereby
the dominant class is formed, this study provides some
insight into the roots, the origins, the structural
beginnings, of the relationship between the bourgeoisie
as a class, and the state as a system of rule.
Hopefully such an approach places us in a position to
explore the processes involved in the inception of those
features of the capitalist state pointed to by these
writers - ranging from the various mechanisms of class
domination exerted directly over the working class, to the
indirect systems of control embodied in the ideological
state apparatuses; from the 'conspiratorial' mechanisms
whereby the bourgeoisie inserts itself in the state
machinery, to the more structured kinds of relationships
it is able to develop as the system matures. If it is
true that the state operates in the interests of the
bourgeoisie once the capitalist system has been
entrenched, then surely it is incumbent upon those seeking
to explain and understand this fact to look back in time
and down into the structures, to assume that this was
not always the case, and to ask when and how this state
of affairs came into being. This study represents a
search, therefore, for the roots of the political and
ideological hegemony which the capitalist class exerts
in one society, and seeks thereby to illuminate the
problems of class interest and its relationship to
political domination.

4 THE SOUTH AFRICAN EXPERIENCE

All of the matters discussed so far are, of course,
pursued through the examination of the South African
experience of capitalist development and class formation.
The many issues which are thereby raised and explored
are systematically presented in the text below.
As has already been implied, the concept of
the 'system of interest-translation' will itself prove
capable of illuminating some of the most intractable
problems in South African historiography, particularly
that of the relationships between 'race' and 'capitalism'.
Moreover, the questions asked here about the way
in which the relationships between 'state' and
'bourgeoisie' may fruitfully be understood will allow us
to understand better the nature of the early South
African state, the foundation for the notoriously
authoritarian, violent and racially divided modern state,
and its relationships to the needs of the capitalist
class. These are the ongoing concerns of this study, and
perhaps they need not be further elaborated upon here.
    However, there is one further theme which is pursued
explicitly in this study, and which has not yet been
touched upon. This is the question of the status of
South Africa as a 'developing' capitalist economic
system. While it may be true that South Africa was
inhibited from undertaking an early and complete
capitalist revolution of the type undergone by Britain's
other 'dominions', perhaps because of the relatively
powerful pre-capitalist systems that imperial merchant
capital had to contend with, it nevertheless did
eventually break free of the extreme underdevelopment
and dependence that characterise most third world
countries today, to occupy something of an intermediate
position between the fully industrialised systems of the
West and the old dominions, and the underdeveloped
economies of much of Africa.
    One of the questions to which this study addresses
itself is how this partial breakthrough took place, and
to what it may be attributed. And in fact the particular
approach and methodology adopted here do bear directly
upon this question, in the light of the vigorous debate
that has arisen around the issue in recent years. This
debate (much of it in unpublished or inaccessible papers)
has a clear focus upon the role of the state and the
capitalist class itself, and two broad schools of thought
have emerged in opposition to one another. On the one
hand, several authors have attempted to explain South
Africa's industrial 'take-off' within a strictly

Poulantzian framework. Through an examination of the differing interests and political power of various 'fractions of capital', these writers have derived an explanation of this take-off in terms of what, according to their definition of the term, they call a 'change in hegemony' from 'imperial' to 'national' capital in 1924. (14) Their critics have questioned the validity not only of the sort of 'fractional' analysis they have used, suggesting that it closely resembles 'interest-group' theory and possesses many of its attendant problems, (15) but also of the use of the term 'fraction of capital' to apply to such broad groups as 'imperial capital' or 'national capital' themselves. (16)

Because of its focus on the ruling class, on the nature of hegemony and on the nature of the state, this study is in a position to address itself to these questions which, it seems, are of considerable importance to those seeking to understand how and why the ruling class changes, and what the implications of such changes are for such problems as that of underdevelopment today. It questions the usefulness of 'fraction-based' accounts, and instead attempts to develop a synthesis, an integration, of the analysis of the bourgeoisie as a whole on the one hand, and of its various sections on the other; while attempting to throw light on the role of class struggle and political power in sustaining and/or undermining imperial domination. It offers the concept of 'class' - as already defined in this introduction - as an alternative to that of 'fraction', arguing that it is capable of illuminating the process of political change in a more fruitful manner; while it finally addresses itself to the question not only of how South Africa was able to initiate a process of indigenous capitalist industrialisation, but also why.

In conclusion, perhaps it should be said that this study attempts to cover a relatively long period of time and an extremely wide range of topics in any historian's terms and is clearly unable to obtain the standards of accuracy on both the empirical and the interpretative levels, that the specialist might demand. The difficulties involved in co-ordinating the study of history with that of ideology and in addition conducting both of these pursuits on a theoretical as well as an empirical plane are considerable, and it is certain that this work has not overcome them all. Furthermore these difficulties are compounded by the fact that a great deal of the research necessary to this study had not yet been undertaken by specialists in either 'history' or 'ideology', partly because of the hegemony of liberal

interpretations of South Africa's past, but also because
of the dearth of empirical studies of capitalism in South
Africa by writers of all persuasions. Much of the
research here, therefore, is my own. The chief excuse
for any failings in this respect lies in the very nature
of the subject tackled here, which demands a long, bold
and broad view. Indeed, one of its very theses is that
'hegemony' is slow to come into being, and that it
involves not only the 'ruling class' but its relationships
to the other classes and sub-classes in the system. While
it may be hoped that this study makes up in theoretical
and comparative insights what it lacks in detailed
accuracy, there is no doubt that it would have been a
better work had it been able to rely on a more substantial
body of secondary historical, economic and sociological
literature.

1 The mining revolution

Capital's dominance over the whole South African region was first manifested in the dominance of the gold mining industry at the turn of the twentieth century. No period in South Africa's history is more fascinating than that of the 1890s and 1900s, during which this dominance rapidly and violently came into being, and the mighty imperial forces which owned or buttressed gold-mining wrought transformations in every corner of the region, in every sphere of the economy, in the nature and scope of the state, and in the form and content of ideology. These were revolutionary decades in South Africa. (1)

It was during these decades that the media of gold-mining capital flourished. An ideological network was developed within the mining industry, a network of great complexity with a range of functions, the understanding of which is crucial to the analysis of the relationship between mining's revolution, its ideology, and hegemony.

To the outsider, it was the activities of the eminent millionaire mineowners that appeared to be the ideological mainspring of the gold-mining industry. The popular and academic images of the mining industry of those early years continue to reflect this perception. The industry is conceived of as having been dominated by a stratum of individualist mineowners, whose every decision and idea was transmitted downwards into the lower strata, and outwards into the society at large. Of course, the mineowners were ideologically active individuals whose concern it was indeed to impress upon the outsider the needs of the industry over which they prevailed. But they are not the focal point of this discussion of capital's ideological network in this period. The 'great individual' was the vehicle of the transmission of the needs and ideology of capital, but

was not the source of realisation of what those needs
were, or of the ideology itself. He reproduced, rather
than produced, capital's ideology. Thus the 'greatness'
of the mineowners should itself be seen as a
manifestation of the ideology of mining capital. (2)

The mineowners' exalted position was based upon a
complex system of communication from below. Because
gold-mines were scattered and often isolated, their
managers tended to perform many of the tasks which in a
small industry would be those of ownership. The eminent
mineowners were often out of touch with the problems of
each mine, and relied on managers for information. Thus
the reverse process from that which is usually depicted
took place. Managers and compound managers, and the
'organic intellectuals' who sprang from them were far
closer to the actual problems and needs of each mine,
and those common to their own and other mines. It was
they who fed the upper stratum of mine ownership with
information, policy choices, and ideology.

This was the structure within which ideology was
articulated. At annual meetings, in annual and monthly
company reports, in newspaper articles and public
speeches, and through political organisations, the mine
magnates, their employees and associates were able to
express themselves. The 'South African Mining Journal',
started in 1891, was the earliest, most central, forum
for the creation of mining ideology. (3) It related to
the industry in all its complexity, and to the outside
world. Based in Johannesburg, it was founded and
edited by E.P. Rathbone, an important figure in
mining and other circles, who consciously aimed to
represent those who saw mining as a South African, and
not simply a British, entity, evidence, perhaps of the
extent to which mining capital was forced to localise
itself in order to realise its political interests,
while still remaining an imperial force. (4) Rathbone
made the journal an influential and representative
voice and, more importantly, an ideological vanguard,
of the industry. (5) Because of its central role, the
'SAMJ', discussed in more detail below, provides the
core of evidence for this chapter and the next, which
are based on a systematic study of its varied contents,
week by week, during the years 1891-1907. (6) A range
of other media served to flesh out the ideological
skeleton provided by the journal. Those used include
evidence (if available) and reports of the major
commissions of enquiry held during the years 1891-1907;
in particular, the 1897 Commission held in the Transvaal;
the 1903 Transvaal Labour Commission; the South African

Native Affairs Commission (Sanac) 1903-5; and the
Transvaal Indigency Commission, 1908. Also used were
Annual Reports and Chairmen's speeches of Rand Mines Ltd,
the largest mining house of the time. However, it was
necessary throughout to prune rather than to extend the
source material, not only because of the sheer quantity of
data, but because of the necessity for ideology to be
analysed in the context of the appropriate audience. Thus
speeches by mining men were treated more seriously if they
were reprinted in the 'SAMJ' than if they were ignored by
it. This reinforced the centrality of journals as sources,
and assisted in the otherwise almost impossible task of
selection from the prolific output of the mining industry
in these years. Non-journal sources tended to be used to
confirm and substantiate interpretations about the nature
of ideology as it appeared in journals.

The reasons why the media of capital were bursting
with creativity in these years must first be sought in the
fundamental imperatives, or basic interests of mining.
These must be divided into two categories. First, there
were the internal mechanisms which drove mining as a
capitalist enterprise of a particular sort. Second,
there were the general factors affecting it, as a result
of the historical conditions under which it was
established. While these 'internal' and 'external'
sets of imperatives were inextricably intertwined, they
represented two different forces of history - that of
the necessity for a single, powerful capitalist industry
to achieve profitability, and that of the necessity for
that same industry, as the representative of imperial
capital itself, to achieve a place of superiority in
economic, political and ideological terms, over the
Southern African region.

Of these two aspects of its interests, it is the
former that seems to have been ultimately determinant.
The 'economic' interests of mining have been the subject
of a penetrating and cogent analysis by F.A. Johnstone. (7)
He points out that while the two internal imperatives which
drive all capitalist industries are the maximisation of
profits, and the minimisation of costs, mining in South
Africa existed somehow at the limits of these imperatives,
its threshold of profitability being that much higher than
in most industries and its threshold of costs being that
much lower. The industry could not be brought to maximum
profitability without pressing down on its running costs,
for the price of its product was internationally fixed,
the ore was of low grade, and its capital costs were
necessarily high. Because gold was the money commodity,
the industry could not pass on its costs to any consuming

population. (8) All of these factors led to the
characteristic tendency for South African gold-mining to
direct most of its cost minimisation efforts towards the
working class. (9)

However, while its economic interests may have been
determinant, and hence preceded its political interests
in theoretical terms, the mining industry of the 1890s
and 1900s cannot be understood in terms of these alone.
Chronologically and practically, its wider 'revolutionary'
interests had to be realised before its profitability
could be secured.

Mining was not simply a 'new' industry, comparable with
one in an already industrialised country. While all 'new'
industries require capital, workers, worker-training,
managerial techniques, market pricing and marketing, a
financial network through which profits may be reinvested
or saved, and a myriad of other things, in all of the
tasks which it required to be done, the mining industry
had to create the institutions, methods, ideologies and
structures, to make them possible. Labour cannot be
simply 'obtained' or even 'recruited' if the society is
agricultural and pastoral, if its existing industries
are embryonic and if most people in the society have
their own means of subsistence. One cannot train workers
if they cannot read or write, do not know or care what a
factory is, or if they have been educated in a
way suited to the needs of a labour tenancy system for a
serf-exploiting farmer. Capital cannot simply be raised
if there are no capital-raising institutions in the
society; it must come from outside and then it must be
kept somewhere. Developing a 'managerial technique'
is difficult when there is nothing on which it can build.
Supplying the industry with the materials it needs is not
simply a matter of adjusting the factories of the society
to produce more iron, steel, machinery or even food;
there may be no factories of any size or significance in
the society and even agriculture may be, as it was in
the Transvaal, unable to cope with the new demands upon
it. All of these things need to be imported - but there
may be no railway lines to the place where nature has
determined that the industry be sited.

Furthermore, South African gold-mining was not just
new, it was big and unprofitable. If the new industry
were small and profitable it could be fitted into the
already-existing society through mutual adaptation and
adjustment, and the gradual development of new
institutions could take place. Many factories, some of
them quite large, did indeed exist in Southern Africa in
general, and the Transvaal in particular, before mining

began and during its early years, and did not themselves
require political revolution or constitute the imposition
of a new mode of production upon the region, although
their cumulative effects may have done so over time. Even
diamond-mining, which disrupted but did not revolutionise
the Cape, was incorporated into the existing mercantile-
dominated system. The sheer physical size of gold mining
required a great upheaval not only in the Transvaal, but
in the Southern African region. It had to establish a
variety of institutions and new relationships to make its
operation and profitability possible; these were
incompatible with those which were already in existence.

It is for these reasons that the mining industry of the
1890s cannot be viewed simply as an individual profit-
making enterprise or economic sector. The existence,
range and significance of its external imperatives are an
indication of the fact that mining was also the leading
and pioneering representative of industrial imperial
capital itself. It embodied a new economic, political
and social order, some would say a new mode of production,
in Southern Africa. Its 'external imperatives' were
nothing less than a compelling and unique call upon the
resources of the region - both political and economic.
It is in this sense that the term 'mining revolution' is
used. And it is because of their compelling and prior
nature that the external, revolutionary interests of
mining are discussed here before its determinant, but in
this context, secondary internal, profit-seeking and
labour-exploiting interests.

The mining industry's aspirations for dominance
extended over the entire region, and in order to realise
them it clashed with the various social forms that had
come to prevail in particular areas. South Africa's
capitalist revolution was remarkable for the fact that
it resulted from the clashing not of two, nor even of
three, but of at least four distinct social, economic
and political formations. Incoming imperial capital,
spearheaded by mining, clashed first with the South
African Republic, the state where gold was found, which
was the domain of 'Boer' agriculturalists, whose mode of
agricultural production has been described as 'semi-
feudal'. Of the various complex pre-capitalist modes of
production that existed amongst the other, black,
indigenous peoples, it was perhaps the domestic, or
subsistence-based mode that was the prevailing one,
and that constituted the second force with which the
incoming revolutionaries were confronted. At the same
time, the region as a whole had been subordinated to
British economic (and in some cases political) interests

for many decades before gold was discovered. Under the
hegemony of mercantile capital, British imperialism
had wrought great changes in both the local African
economies, and the 'Boer' economies, initiating a process
of underdevelopment which the industrial capitalists
of the gold-mining industry were to continue. Thus the
mining industry found itself representing British
imperial interests in a hostile, semi-feudal, non-
British state. And yet it represented a different kind
of imperialism from that which had presided over the
Cape or Natal. If its revolution was to be carried out,
it had to perform three separate, but simultaneous
tasks: it had to alter the form, expression and scope
of the old mercantile imperialism; and it had to
subordinate both the 'Boer' and the black modes of
production to its interests. This was the nature of
the revolution that mining required to be performed
before its real economic interests - those of
profitability - could be secured.

This is the context in which mining capital's media
flourished - and not surprisingly, for while we, with
the benefit of hindsight and large quantities of
historical documents, may discern something of the
true economic and political interests of the mining
industry, it seems certain that they were not quite so
clear-cut to the mineowners themselves in the 1890s.

No hegemonic order is ever created in a vacuum, and
the first task any organic intellectual must perform is
to situate his activities against the background of
existing structures, beliefs and modes of domination.
He has to choose and discard past social ideas and
structures according to the needs of his audience.
And those he chooses to keep should not be thought to
have a life of their own just because they persist. As
far as mercantilist South Africa was concerned, mining
found itself needing to remould, reject or adapt old
social forms and ideologies for new purposes.

It was recognised under the hegemony of British
mercantile imperialism, that the 'liberal' Cape and less
liberal Natal, had produced a specific kind of
segregationist society, whose overall character could
he made compatible with mining's needs. (10) On the other
hand, there were other mercantile imperialist forms which
mining opposed vigorously. For example, it denounced
the extent to which African peasants had been allowed
to develop in the late nineteenth century, and rejected
the Cape liberal ideology accompanying this development.
(11) Both of these aspects are discussed in detail below.
But it was the diamond-mining industry in Kimberley

that provided gold capital with a model of great
importance. While it did not involve the overthrow of
pre-existing modes of production, the diamond industry,
started in 1867 in the mercantilist Cape, first
introduced into a Southern African colony a class of
capitalists willing to introduce far-reaching changes
in the relationships between class and class. And
while capital may have certain universal and
objectively-determined needs and characteristics, it has
to learn how to realise or embed these in existing
social formations. This is particularly true in the
case of imperial capital entering a strange and unknown
arena. Thus gold-mining looked to at least four of the
achievements of diamond-mining as rehearsals for its
own revolution. (12)

First, diamond mineowners demonstrated to their
gold-mining successors that it was possible to translate
pre-industrial forms of hierarchy in South Africa into
a workable industrial class structure. It was they who
established three groups: mineowners, the owners of the
means of production; below them, white workers, the
immigrant non-owners of the means of production, who
were the majority of the former diggers, who had flooded
into the diamond fields as independent fortune-seekers,
but had then themselves been fully proletarianised by
the fact of the concentration of capital and productive
means in the hands of a few wealthier diggers. They
were allowed to vote, and were incorporated into the
system of legitimacy of the existing state. And at the
bottom, were the local black workers, drawn from
subsistence farming or peasant agriculture. They had
been deprived of the opportunity to acquire the means
of production almost from the beginning of the diamond
fields. They were in various stages of proletarianisation, deprived of access to the legitimate
institutions of power, and paid the low wages of the
powerless and colonised. Thus a rough hierarchy was
forged out of digger society, a hierarchy dependent
upon the difference in power and degree of proletarianisation between blacks and whites; and on the differential
access of the two white groups to the means of production.

The diamond industry also provided gold-mining with
the important precedent of the formation of the class
of capitalist mineowners itself. Under the initiative
of Cecil Rhodes, a cohesive industry was created out
of the original conglomeration of competing pioneering
settlements. The process of syndicate-formation and
amalgamation which had begun relatively early on was
continued to the point where all claims were under one

controlling body. Not only were diamond mineowners
united, but they formed a monopoly over production,
through the incorporation of the De Beers' Company in
1888. (13)   Between 1867 and 1888, it could be said that
in Kimberley the diamond fields community underwent the
entire process of capitalist development, from petty-
commodity production, through competing individual
capitalism to monopoly. Capitalists learned a great
deal from this experience about the nature of their
interests and of monopolies, in the specific conditions
of South Africa.

The third sphere in which diamonds were a rehearsal
for gold was that of labour control. While monopoly of
production had been achieved by 1888, no monopoly is
complete without a centralised selling mechanism and
this was not achieved until 1935. The number of
diamonds reaching the market had to be regulated through
other methods, chief amongst which was labour control.
The industry imperatively needed, and obtained, tight
control over the supply, productivity, price and
organisation of the majority of its workforce. Such
control was far more feasible in the case of the weaker
black working class, and a sophisticated and effective
system of black worker control was developed, based on
the twin institutions of the compound system and the
pass system. (14) White workers too were controlled by
the use of company-owned housing and other techniques
of 'liberal' management. (15)

Finally, the diamond industry built up an expectation
for later capitalists of how their interests should and
could be realised by the state. Not only had the British
government not opposed any of the major requirements of
diamond-mining, but it had acted positively for the
mineowners by the 1871 annexation of the diamond fields,
in the use of master-and-servant laws to enforce an
effective 'pass' system upon Coloured and African diggers
and workers, and by attempting to curb illicit diamond-
buying and selling particularly before closed compounds
were established. (16) As the industry's monopoly began
to become consolidated, it ceased to be merely a matter
of the state tolerating or assisting the industry, and
began to become a matter of the industry, particularly
through Rhodes himself, influencing and even controlling
the state. It was under the Prime Ministership of Rhodes,
in the self-governing Cape of 1894, that the Glen Grey
Act was introduced, with the explicit purpose of
producing labour for the mines and other employers by
altering the system of land tenure. (17)

Kimberley's rehearsal could be seen as having provided

the foundations for the process of class formation
amongst Rand capitalists, on the economic, and political
levels. Ideologists wishing to inform capital on the
Rand of its economic interests were provided with a
relevant and effective South African model of a highly
profitable, monopolistic industry; as far as its political
interests were concerned, they were able to draw on
the example of Kimberley's hierarchical structure and
divided working class, its sophisticated mechanisms of
control over both sections of that working class; and
a cordial relationship with the state. The similarities
between the two industries in these and other respects
will emerge in the course of these two chapters.

On the more purely ideological level, mercantilist
Southern Africa was also of relevance to ideologists
of the Rand, and this relevance can be more specifically
placed in the context of the actual process of class
formation as it began to emerge after the mid-1880s.
After gold was discovered in 1886, many of those who
had accumulated capital and acquired an understanding
of the nature of monopoly, labour control and
organisation in Kimberley moved to the Rand, and invested
in the large and potentially profitable gold-mining
industry. Gold was less suited than diamonds to the
development of a substantial digger class, particularly
in the Transvaal where the ore was embedded in rock
deep beneath the ground. Men with capital were the only
ones who could make this non-alluvial gold-mining
profitable, for they could pay for shafts to be sunk
and refineries to be built. The geology of the Transvaal
gold therefore facilitated the transfer of an embryonic
and relatively experienced class of mineowners from
Kimberley to the Rand. Whereas the diamond industry
had taken some twenty years to unite and organise,
within five years of the discovery of gold much of the
industry was in the hands of mining capitalists rather
than petty producers. One of the major mining houses
of the period (Consolidated Gold Fields), and the
Chamber of Mines, had been formed. (18)

And yet capital's media at this time are replete
with discussions, not of the unity of gold-mining
capital, but of its disunity, its inchoateness. In fact,
the industry did not exist as a coherent entity except
on the crudest economic level of the accumulation of
capital in the hands of a small number of people. It
was composed of many mines, often far apart, with varying
types of men as mine managers, different abilities to
obtain labour, whether skilled white or unskilled black,
different rates of profitability, or different owners.

In spite of the fact that the Chamber of Mines had been
formed in 1889 to unite it, the 'SAMJ' of the 1890s
contained frequent references to the disunity of the
industry, and its contrast with the model of Kimberley.
As Rathbone wrote, unlike the Rand, 'the concentration
of the industry, the political power vested by the
Government in the De Beers Company, and the lack of
competition amongst employers of labour, confers upon
Kimberley peculiar facilities.' (19) And of these three,
perhaps the most important indication of the relatively
primitive stage of the Rand's development was the
prevalence of competition between individual mineowners
for labour, capital and privileges dispensed by the
state. The transfer of a rough cohesiveness from
Kimberley was unable to make of this disparate and
competitive industry a workable monopoly, let alone one
able to recognise and tackle the nexus of its revolutionary interests.
    This would seem to explain on a primary level, the
need for the ideological network. For before a class
can even begin to act as a class - before it can even
become aware of its place in the system of production
and power - it must convey to its members a sense of
itself as an entity, of the unity of interests across
its divisions. And in the performance of this task,
the medium, it would seem, is indeed the message. By
its very existence, an organ such as the 'SAMJ'
facilitated the organic intellectual's task of creating
a mining identity. This weekly forum, in which members
of the industry's upper and lower strata took part,
provided a centralised place for discussion by all
mineowners, managers and others, of the issues which they
had in common. Annual reports were published, speeches
made by eminent mineowners and compound managers
reported; minutes of Chamber of Mines, and Association
of Mine Managers, meetings were reproduced, as was
evidence given by the mining industry and other groups,
to important Commissions of Enquiry. Parliamentary
debates of relevance to mining, whether they took place
in the Transvaal, the remainder of Southern Africa, or
Britain, were discussed, and articles on a variety of
matters were written for the journal by ideologists and
intellectuals concerned with general gold-mining matters.
Most importantly, editorials were written with the aims
of communicating both a sense of unity and purpose to
members of the industry, and its 'viewpoint' to outsiders.
As a whole, the journal provides evidence of the complexity of the structure of mining and the extent to which
the great magnates were but one element in a complex of

relationships, in which, for example, the Association of
Mine Managers or the Compound Managers' Association
played an important part in debates on policy and
ideology and in some cases led the debate themselves. It
was here that ideologists developed a coherent conception
of the mining industry itself as an interest, a whole,
a concrete entity, capable of having external relationships on the basis of its own solidarity and unity. The
'SAMJ' articulated the idea of 'the mining industry'
which transcended vertical divisions - such as those
between competing individual mines, between deep-level
and outcrop mines, (20) between the Chamber of Mines and
the Association of Mines, (21) or the pro-Chinese and
anti-Chinese labour factions; and also some of the
horizontal divisions, such as those between mineowners
and mine managers; or shareholders and compound managers.
'The view of the Chamber', 'that friendly feeling of
co-operation which is essential to the welfare of this
large industry', 'we must induce our companies to continue
and work together', and other such phrases were common
to the journal. Much of the unifying effort of the 'SAMJ'
was directed towards improving the ineffectual Chamber's
ability to force employers to act together. Rathbone
often wrote of the 'evil' of the temptation to raise
wages amongst competing employers. (22)
    In the earlier years, this unity was very much an
ideal. We shall see below how long it took before
monopoly over all aspects of the industry's operation
was established, for example. But it was an ideal
first stated and constantly reiterated, by ideologists,
whose practical suggestions as to how it could be
achieved were taken seriously by leading capitalists.
The ideal's realisation was facilitated, moreover, by
the very nature of the circumstances in which the
industry found itself. For it soon was able to make
itself felt as a political, economic and social 'entity'
within the Transvaal economy and polity, where by 1891,
to the outsider at least, the characterisation of the
mining 'interest' had already attained the status of
an axiomatic truth. Its immense size and rapid
growth, its ability to dominate the regional economy,
was perceived as an awesome, fundamental fact. The
forms of social and technical organisation within the
new, brash, and, in the Transvaal, foreign, industry, were
seen as deeply alien to the societies of the region. (23)
This perception of an alien intruder was expressed
primarily at the level of distaste for the social and
cultural trappings of mining, and existed in spite of
the perception by mining people themselves that certain

local forms and structures were of use to them. While
the industry may be shown to have been deeply divided,
it was its imposing solidity which was first
observable: (24)

> The rise of gold-mining in South Africa was like the
> rise of the same industry amongst the original Mexican
> settlers of California. It brought confusion to an
> unprogressive rural society ... this frontier of money
> and machinery leapt into the Boer midst, bringing with
> it an aggressive and incompatible population. A
> country-side that was more sympathetic to tradition
> and uniformity than to innovations and initiative
> could not suffer gladly the newcomers who wanted to
> build, to organise, and to exploit. These newcomers
> put forward their demands vigorously. They demanded
> high returns and security for their investments. They
> demanded freedom to carry out their schemes. Often
> they were careless of the slow pride of the Dutch
> population and indifferent to the social and
> spiritual values of Dutch society.

Perhaps it was as a result of both the conscious
activities of its ideologists, concerned as they were
with ensuring that their audience became a self-
conscious class, and the forces arising out of the
historical conditions under which it was developed, that
this apparently well-knit entity came to possess a
character of its own. Although the full significance
of this character for mining's hegemony cannot be
understood until the class structure within the industry
and the battles outside of it have been more fully
analysed, it would seem appropriate to point to its
existence and main features now, so that its links with
the primary process of class formation may be established.

In spite of the presence of workers and employers of
many different national origins, or races, (25) of the
presence of German and French as well as British capital,
and the fact that the majority of workers in the industry
were black Southern Africans, the character of gold-
mining was British. It was as a British enterprise that
it was perceived and responded to by many of its members,
and indeed by local people. (26) This was the ideological
relevance of mercantile imperialism in Southern Africa,
to its successor industrial imperialism. The mining
industry's ideologists made a conscious bid to incorporate
their constituency of mineowners, managers, and even
workers, into the existing category of 'South African
British'. By the late 1890s, 'South African British' had
been irreversibly influenced as a result: (27)

The term 'South African British' included Cape families
boasting two or three generations of South African born
ancestors as well as Transvaal bachelor artisans who
had recently arrived and intended soon to depart.
Some, like the descendants of Scottish presbyterian
ministers in the Orange Free State, spoke little
English; others, like the descendants of missionaries
in the eastern Cape, placed a high value on the British
cultural connection, and often completed their higher
education in British universities. More than any
other South African community they were involved in
commerce and industry, and were therefore extremely
vulnerable to divisions based upon economic function
and social status. Employers, employees, trades union
organisers, producers, consumers and suppliers were all
subsumed in the blanket description 'South African
British'.

The sense of unity so necessary to the mining industry was
facilitated through the use of English as its language,
through the encouragement of cultural and social links
which their linguistic and historical background implied
between mining people and those English speakers, British
imperialists, settlers and newcomers, in other colonies,
and through a constant focus on Britain as the point of
cultural, as well as economic and political reference for
all white mining groups. This cultural feature of
imperialism, so often taken for granted as an inevitable
concomitant of its economic forces, must be seen, therefore, in terms of its relationship to the needs of
capital, and its mercantile and industrial forms must be
distinguished from one another.

Thus in the Transvaal milieu, the South African
British idea was different in form and function from
that in other colonies, not only because of the form
of capital to which it was allied, but also because of
its particular class basis, and its hostile environment.
From the point of view of hegemony it was highly
significant that because of its particular characteristics
the white working class of the early mining period was
able to be incorporated into the British cultural
character of mining.

British workers, most of whom were skilled artisans
from Cornwall or Wales, were encouraged to ally themselves, on the basis of Britishness, with mineowners and
managers in opposition to 'non-British' unskilled, black
and later, Afrikaner, workers with whom they might otherwise form alliances. The idea of 'Britain as home' was
encouraged too - workers were often migrants on the
international labour market whose wives and families

remained in Britain, while capitalists had more material
ties with the 'mother country'. Patriotism was
encouraged and exploited, and a sense of identification
nurtured between South African 'British' and those
in other dominions - reinforced, no doubt, by the fact
that workers and managers alike moved from mining
industries in one country to those in another, attempting
to accumulate capital or find a mining town hospitable
enough for settlement.

The idea of being British South African in the
Transvaal had local, class-based connotations and
international significance, both based on the experiences
and social positions of those being required to believe
in it. In the hostile Transvaal, and particularly in
relation to its white 'Boer' population, to be South
African British came to acquire a particular external
connotation as well. The alien 'external' world was
defined as that area in which there existed people who
were neither British nor in mining. Non-British people
in mining were sometimes incorporated into the category
of 'British', while non-mining people were incorporated
if they indeed were English-speaking. But neither 'Boers'
nor, more naturally, given the white-dominated nature of
all South African colonies, blacks were incorporated into
this category of 'Uitlander'. (28) While the 'frontier'
between blacks and whites implied by this is discussed
later, here we are concerned with the fact that 'Boers'
formed a kind of 'frontier' of mining ideology of their
own, which coincided with three other aspects of the
position of mining in the Transvaal. 'Boers' were in
control of the state, which was perceived as a major
obstacle to the realisation of mining interests; they
were farmers, who competed with mining for labour and
represented a mode of production not always compatible
with that represented by mining; and the Afrikaner
dispossessed came to form a substantial section of the
white working class during and after the Anglo-Boer War.
The frontier of mining ideology was thus defined by the
class and historical position of those outside of it.
Unlike British workers, therefore, Afrikaner workers
became an 'enemy within' the mining 'camp' when they
were proletarianised, and the frontiers of the unity of
mining were accordingly contracted. The more substantial
and fundamental differences of class and interest between
mining and Afrikaners in their various roles, reinforced
and justified the depiction of the industry as a
nationally, and in the terminology of the time 'racially'
defined entity. (29)

The apparent paradox of the defined identity of the

mining industry was that it was both 'British' and 'South
African' at the same time. While mining capital was the
vanguard of British imperial capital in Southern Africa
in the late nineteenth century, its 'Britishness' should
not be simply (and perhaps mechanistically) attributed to
this fact. There was never a blanket acceptance of
British bureaucratic imperialists by the mining industry,
and indeed they were often regarded as too 'liberal' in
the field of 'native policy' and too concerned with
interests besides those of mining. (30) British South
Africans and British bureaucratic imperialists were
distinct in the eyes of the ideologists, and their
alliances on such issues as that of the Anglo-Boer War and
its aftermath were not regarded as more than
alliances. (31) Being British was thus a device used by
ideologists of mining for certain essential purposes. It
was defined by the interests of capital in South Africa,
and its enemy there. Being 'British' united the industry,
and was as much to do with not being 'Boer', and, of
course, not being black, as it was to do with depending
upon British economic and political structures.

It was under the over-arching idea of British South
Africanness that the ideologists of mining worked to
discover, articulate, further, develop and legitimate
the complex set of interests which they discerned
mining to have. Britishness was not a matter of
consensus; great divisions were permitted, and indeed
in some cases, encouraged to exist within it. It was
not an idea designed to obscure divisions between workers
and capitalists, for example, but rather to encapsulate
them. 'Unity in hierarchy' or 'unity in diversity' was
the spirit in which British South African ideology was
developed.

These, then were some of the complexities of both
ideology and class formation which mining capital was
experiencing in the context of the existing system of
British mercantile hegemony. And to the extent that it
relied on existing social forms and ideologies, gold-
mining's dominance may be regarded as the continuation
of certain aspects of British imperial rule in Southern
Africa; as an English, or British, entity, it seems to
the observer, to have had its roots or foundations
in the earlier parts of the nineteenth century. And
yet how different was mining capital's dominance from
that of mercantile capital! While the latter transformed
its societal victims in a relatively subtle, piecemeal
and insidious manner, its ways of 'underdeveloping'
the many and varied social systems in nineteenth century
Southern Africa being as many and as varied as those

systems themselves, mining capital demanded a revolution
which was nasty, brutish and short, and it had the power
to bludgeon all into conformity with the crude class
structure it wished to erect. There was no attempt to
deal with Southern Africa's existing social forms in all
their complexity and variety - they were to be destroyed
or partially destroyed, depending on their strength and
usefulness. In terms of these criteria, the important
distinction to the budding capitalist class in Southern
Africa was that between Transvaal 'Boer' society, and
subsistence-based black societies, rather than the many
more refined distinctions which mercantile imperial
ideologists might have made, within black social systems,
for example.

Mining's assault on the 'Boer' semi-feudal mode of
production, and its political manifestations, took
precedence over its proletarianising assault on 'black'
modes of production, an interesting illustration of the
complex ways in which capital orders its interests. It
seems likely that one of the functions of 'Britishness'
was to facilitate the expression of this interest, for
it enabled ideologists to define the Transvaal state as
hostile, 'external' to the interests of mining and
'non-British'.

The assault on the 'Boer mode of production' was
primarily articulated and perceived by capital as an
assault upon the 'Boer' state, as a political problem
above all. In the Transvaal system of government were
seen to be embodied many of the problems which confronted
the industry and thwarted its revolution - including
its proletarianising revolution of black social
formations. Not only was the state in the Transvaal
identified as the primary enemy, but in criticising it
ideologists created a skeletal ideal alternative
state form, in which were embodied the aspirations of
capital. Thus the state is the focus of this analysis,
not because economic and class conflicts are not seen
to be fundamental, but because capital itself chooses
to participate in those conflicts in ways that suit
its interests. Revolutionary interests require
revolutionary tactics, and the assault on the state must
be seen as such.

The chief areas of the inadequacy of the Transvaal
state apparatus were defined as those of labour, law,
costs and tariffs. The state's repressive and
administrative apparatuses took priority in capital's
eyes, over all other aspects of its structure - as indeed
they might in the eyes of any revolutionary class. But
in considering the relentless and domineering assertion

of mining's desire for a subordinate and servile state
apparatus, however, we are made continually aware of the
clashing of modes of production which lay beneath the
revolutionary demand.

As far as black labour was concerned, the workings of
the 'ideological network' are at their clearest. It
was the 'SAMJ' and the Mine Managers' Association (MMA)
that began a systematic campaign in the early 1890s to
pinpoint both the inadequacies of the Transvaal state,
and areas in which it could be improved. One of the
first actions of the MMA after its formation in 1892 (32)
was to set up a 'Committee on the Native Labour Question'
which acted as a pressure group from below on the then
ineffectual Chamber of Mines. The Chamber, according to
the Committee's first report issued in 1893, should make
a broad range of demands of the Transvaal government with
a view to satisfying the labour needs of the industry
on a systematic basis. It was suggested that: (33)

The Government be approached with a view
A)   to increase (sic) the Hut Tax
B)   to affording protection to natives passing through
     the country
C)   to forming depots along the lines of the road for
     the accommodation of natives
D)   to enforcing and amending Article 84 of the Gold
     Law
E)   to giving assistance to the Labour Commissioner
     to be appointed by the Chamber of Mines
F)   to calling upon the Government of Swazieland (sic)
     to put a stop to the plundering of natives passing
     through that country.

The document also suggested that 'the Government be
petitioned to enforce, and if necessary amend, the Pass
and Vagrancy law so as to prevent an accumulation of
idle Kafirs in the neighbourhood of the towns'. (34) This
is the first clear indication we have that the ideological
network was not simply concerned with ideas, but also
with 'policy'. The MMA articulated three crucial areas
of interest which it considered capital should demand the
state to attend to. In the first place, the state was
expected to carry out the proletarianisation of labour
through the increase of Hut Tax: (35)

It is suggested to raise the Hut Tax to such an amount
that more natives will be induced to seek work, and
especially by making this tax payable in coin only;
each native who can clearly show that he has worked
for six months in the year shall be allowed a rebate
on the Hut Tax equivalent to the increase that may be
determined by the state.

Second, the state was expected to carry out the
mobilisation and acquisition of the labour once it had
been forced to seek cash earnings, and its transportation
to the mines, and third, it was expected to see to the
question of the regulation and retention of the labour
once it had arrived at the mines through the pass laws.

These matters were indeed crucial areas of interest
for the industry. Not only had the Managers' spokesmen
correctly defined them, but they had also placed the
onus for them squarely on the state and made it clear
that it was to this end that they considered the
Chamber of Mines' effort should be directed. On these
aspects of the issue of 'native labour' the Chamber
followed reluctantly the proposals of Mine Managers
and also those of the 'SAMJ' but even after a series
of meetings between the MMA and the Chamber during
1893-4 very little progress was made, and in 1894 the
Council of the MMA reported that it 'regrets that the
results of the Association's efforts to come to an
arrangement with the Chamber of Mines in reference to
the Native Labour question have so far proved futile.' (36)
Throughout the 1890s the MMA played a vanguard role in
pressuring the Chamber into a more aggressive attitude
towards the state.

The legal system of the state was another area of
conflict. As we have seen, the absence, or inefficient
implementation, of laws designed to proletarianise and
procure black workers was a significant bone of
contention between mining and state. In a more general
sense, the entire legislative spirit of the Transvaal
was regarded as undesirable and in need of reform, almost
certainly because of the fact that the Transvaal state
form was that which was needed by a semi-feudal mode of
production. Farmers not only competed with the mines
for black labour, but through their dominance in the
state were able to shift the balance of the competition
in their favour. Ideologists reacted to this either
peevishly, by complaining of: 'the one sided attempts
of the legislature to save the burghers from the
necessity of work - attempts ... which ... will only
the more certainly ensure their decadence into a poor
white class,' (37) or with direct hostility, such as to the
Transvaal Act No. 21 of 1895 which, according to the
journal, under the disguise of being legislation against
contagious diseases, was designed to ensure that
farmers would have five families of 'free' labourers
each. (38) The administration of the law aroused great
resentment. Acts Nos. 22, 23 and 24 of 1895, ostensibly
designed to provide labour for those who needed it, being

pass laws and Hut Tax laws, were in fact, according to
the 'SAMJ' designed to force blacks to work for burghers
and de facto 'will not be administered to help mining'.
(39)   A more indirect reflection of the state's
incompatibility with mining is seen in refusals by its
functionaries to support some of the more crudely
repressive aspects of mining in their legal judgments.
When, in 1894, a magistrate refused to support the
Worcester Mining Company's prosecution of 100 'deserters',
he drew severe criticism from the 'SAMJ': (40)

> the immediate and expressed conclusion of the
> magistrate that the Company was arrogating to itself
> a petty judicial power and ignoring the authority
> of the courts [was] in our opinion, entirely
> uncalled for. But the discharge of the entire batch,
> without any official direction that they must return
> to their employment, was a course illogical and
> mischievous in the extreme. It amounts to a tacit
> incitement to native labour all along the Rand to
> desert, at the extremely inopportune moment when the
> rigours of winter are upon us, when the native is
> always eager to escape if he can.

Besides what it reveals about the nature of a labour
system from which workers could be described as 'eager
to escape', this comment was provoked by only one of
many similar occasions - court appearances of
compound managers and companies were described as
'frequent'. In 1895, a judge condemned a compound
manager for 'lashing a Kaffir' and thereby taking the
law into his own hands. Once again the journal pleaded
for the necessity of 'some legislation' in order to
'place the question of compound management on a more
satisfactory footing' so that 'some latitude' was
allowed to the manager, and 'some authority' delegated
to him. Instead, lamented the journal, 'he is severely
punished for doing what everyone acquainted with the
circumstances expects him to do.' (41)   Gold mining might
well have looked to other British colonies (such as
Rhodesia) for examples of state legislation that
consistently supported industrial coercion of this nature.

However, it was not only its semi-feudal nature which
bred a Transvaal state inimical to the mining capitalists'
interests. Interestingly and importantly a local class
of capitalists was being nurtured in the Transvaal under
the Presidency of Kruger. High tariffs to stimulate
local industries, and a concessions policy under which
certain industries, that of dynamite being of particular
relevance to mining, were permitted state-protected
monopolies, (42) were two important stimuli to the

development of a national bourgeoisie.   H.J. and
R.E. Simons say: (43)

> Few agrarian societies were so richly endowed or well
> equipped as the Transvaal for an industrial
> revolution.... Left to itself, it would have developed
> an efficient administration, a network of railways
> and roads, and adequate supplies of water and power.
> Far from being intractable, the burghers expanded
> production to provide foodstuffs for the Rand, built
> railways linking it to the ports, enacted an excellent
> mining code, kept order over unruly, rebellious
> fortune-hunters, repelled an armed imperialist
> invasion, and held the world's greatest military
> power at bay for two years.... A war was neither
> inevitable nor necessary to modernize the republic.

Now, whatever the precise nature of the South African
system envisaged by mining, it was not at this stage one
of local capitalism confined to the Transvaal state.
National industrial development was as far from the
interests of mining in the 1890s as was the perpetuation
of quasi-feudalism.   Just as imperial capital in India
and elsewhere had destroyed nascent or existing national
bourgeoisies, so mining capital in the Transvaal made
clear its intention to do the same here.   This intention
was partly expressed through mining's virulent campaign
on the question of costs.   High tariffs and concessions
forced mining to pay more for its own supplies, and
pushed up prices of foodstuffs and other commodities,
thus raising the necessary level of subsistence of the
working class.   The 'high rate of living', due to
protective duties, must be dropped, urged the 'SAMJ'. (44)
The 1897 commission report recommended a 28 per cent cut
in tariffs to this end, causing the journal to comment
that 'it advocates free trade in foodstuffs in a manner
that will astonish the Boers of the Cape Colony.' (45)
The mining industry's opposition to the monopolies is
well known.   Walker talks of 'the official concessions
policy, which bred hangers-on, who bled the Uitlanders
and swindled the state, notably in the case of the
monopoly of the dynamite which was so vital to the mining
industry'. (46) Such attitudes towards the Transvaal's
industrialising policies were commonplace in the 1890s.

Other modifications to the state, some of which, it is
true, extended beyond its repressive and administrative
apparatuses into wider realms, were also proposed.   For
example, the state was too small a political and economic
entity to suit mining; thus in several editorials and
comments, the journal argued that even if every black
man in the entire Transvaal were proletarianised, there

would still be a 'labour shortage'. (47) Not only should
labour be sought beyond the borders of the Transvaal, but
the 'SAMJ' pressed as early as June 1894 for the uniting
of the 'native policies' for all four colonies in
addition to the internal revisions of the Transvaal's
own policies. (48) The Transvaal state was also incapable
of representing mining's interests in relation to white
labour. When new Government mining regulations were
proposed at the end of 1894, the MMA issued a petition
criticising every amendment, with the support of the
'SAMJ': 'does the Government realise that these
regulations encourage the employment of white labour in
preference to black because they are so complex?' (49)
wrote the editor, and during 1895 and the following years
in particular the issue of the state's over-sympathetic
view towards white labour was emphasised. (50) Not only
was white labour rather too well-regarded by the state,
according to the 'SAMJ', but the state's educational and
cultural organs did not breed the right kind of person
for a capitalist system. The Council of Education, a
body formed in 1895 to promote private education in the
Transvaal, received approval from the journal because
the existing state education was 'myopic, deplorable,
feeble and inert'. (51) The schools proposed by the
Council would prevent the morale of the community from
sinking, and would tend to make European workers
'permanent and contented residents' on the mines. Once
more, the ideologist found himself in advance of the
Chamber, which in 1895 refused to support the Council
of Education, and was chastised by the journal, for
failing to recognise that the Council had been advancing
the 'subsidiary interests of the mining community.' (52)
     These specific criticisms made of the Transvaal
state, when taken together, constituted a total, all-
embracing critique. Because of the inherent divergence
of interest between the modes of production underlying
the conflict, the attempts made by the state to appease
mining, although they appeared in some cases to be
substantial, (53) were bound to be piecemeal and partial.
The nature of the state was such that even the early pass
laws (which had been drafted by the Chamber of Mines
itself, and accepted by the Volksraad in December 1894)
were regarded as neither sufficient to satisfy the need
of mining, nor an indication of the Transvaal's conversion
to the industry's viewpoint. (54) Thus in nearly all
respects, a considerable and coherent grass-roots
hostility to the state was being articulated within the
industry's structure of ownership and management, from
the early 1890s. It was, of course, at the 'upper' level

of the structure of the industry that the various issues
were taken up and acted upon. The story of the
negotiations, the attempted coup d'état, the 1897
Commission of Enquiry, and finally the Anglo-Boer War
itself, through which mineowners or their imperial
protectors attempted to convert the state entirely or to
overthrow it is not told here. (55) But even when the
basic issues had been defined and articulated, ideologists
continued to play an important role within the industry
during these accelerating and dramatic events. Not only
did they continue to insist upon their basic arguments,
providing evidence and mobilising support, but they
articulated them with greater and greater confidence
and a growing degree of ideological fervour, against the
background of, in support of, and sometimes in advance
of, the vivid and more direct activities of mineowners
and directors. As the mining revolution got under way,
so its organic intellectuals took on the roles of
strategists and ideological vanguard.

The Jameson Raid itself excited little comment from
the journal, other than complaints of the disruption it
had caused. (56) Moreover, when the Chamber of Mines
split into two after the Raid on the precise issue of
the relationship of mining to the state, (57) the journal
maintained a strict neutrality, playing the role of
discovering the interests which mining companies had in
common, rather than provoking or emphasising differences
within the industry. Within a year of the Raid, it was
provided with an issue on which it could play this role.

Rinderpest, which swept Southern Africa in 1896-7, (58)
destroyed most of the cattle of the region, and mine
employers assumed that it would mean an immediate and
lasting increase in the supply of black workers. On
1 September 1896, in accordance with this belief and with
their apparently convoluted view of the forces of supply
and demand, (59) they dropped African wages by 20 per
cent. (60) The vigorous response of workers to this, and
the onset of a depression during the following few months,
combined to bring into sharp relief the structural
inadequacies of the state system of mobilising labour
once more. Not only were there three strikes, further
threatened strikes, and written protests against wage
reductions, (61) but workers began to 'desert' on an
organised basis, (62) so that within six weeks of the
wage reduction, the journal reported 'a steady efflux
of natives from the whole industrial area', said to be
affecting gold and coal mines, railways and every field
of employment except building. To the surprise of the
journal, during those times of starvation, destitution

and wage reduction, men did not desert their farms, but
stayed behind to give what assistance they could. (63)
They were also said to be leaving the mines because of
'a deep seated fear of speedy and bitter hostilities
between Boer and British', because of resentment against
the harsh administration of the pass laws, and because
they were 'under orders from their chiefs'. (64)   A
'spirit of restlessness' was said to have pervaded the
'natives' and the exodus continued into the depression
year of 1897.

This situation immediately provoked further, greater
and more frequent complaints of the inadequacy of the
state.   The pass laws, despite amendments, were said to
be inefficiently administered, (65) and unable to prevent
'desertions'. (66)   All levels of ownership and
management within the industry articulated the same
views - the MMA, the newly formed Compound Managers'
Association, and both Chambers of Mines.   In April, a
conference was held between principal representatives of
mining groups, traders, professionals, and merchants, and
a petition drawn up in which the entire case against the
state was set out.   The original range of criticism
articulated by mining ideologists was restated - railway
rates, the dynamite concession and the administration of
the pass laws were all condemned.   The liquor law was
added to the list, (67) while there were said to be too
few officials, police issue offices or judicial
commissioners.   Unemployed and landless Africans were
said to have been ineffectively dealt with too, while
the entire situation was said to have affected
investment. (68)

The state set up a commission of enquiry to which
representatives of the industry reiterated this critique
in a variety of different contexts. (69)   In his evidence,
Albu put forward his ideal view of the role of the
state: (70)

> it is my desire to see the strength of the state and
> the strength of the mining industry renovated, as it
> were.   I can only compare these two, the state and the
> mining industry, as twins - twins not in the ordinary
> sense, but which, by some freak of nature, have grown
> together at one point.

The almost complete demise of the pass laws, and their
almost total failure to prevent 'desertions' were the
outstanding issues of the evidence given by eminent
mining magnates and managers.   Desertions in thousands
were reported and many claimed that none of the deserters
at all had returned. (71)   The commission's evidence was
a landmark in the mining industry's statement of its own

position in relation to the state. When it reported in
1897, the commission supported the industry, but both
Kruger and the Volksraad refused to accept its
recommendations. (72) It had advocated so total and
uncompromising a change in the Transvaal state system
that it precluded any accommodation by those in power
of mining demands. This only added to the clamour for a
completely different state and heralded a new, more
polemical, era of ideological activity.

By 1898, ideologists of mining were resorting to more
powerful rhetoric. On paper, it had continually to be
admitted, the Transvaal government was indeed becoming
more acceptable and appeared to be making greater
concessions to mining. But the fact of the matter was
that it 'does not govern'. In one vitriolic editorial,
Rathbone drew together all the ideological resources at
his disposal to make a racist and aristocratic plea for
the mining claim on the state. It began with the old
complaint of maladministration: (73)

> The industry on which the country's prosperity
> depends is cramped because of the insufficient supply
> of native labour, because of the drink traffic which
> diminishes the usefulness of that already inadequate
> supply, because the amalgam thief and the receiver
> snap their fingers under the law's very nose, because
> the police arrangements are such that New York would
> blush to own even when the reign of Tammany is most
> rampant, because, in a word, the Government cannot
> and does not fulfil its primary function.... A state
> in which the hewers of wood and drawers of water
> are either openly rebellious.... or sullen and
> discontented and disobedient when they are sufficiently
> sober to feel actively any sensation, cannot be
> described as a well-ruled state.

It continued with a more generalised view of the ideal
state and the Transvaal's inability to fulfil that
ideal:

> What we desire is that the Government should realise
> its own incompetence and call in the assistance of
> men, whose success in organising the most gigantic
> mining industry the world has seen is a guarantee that
> if they turned their attention to the Government of
> the country, they could materially assist the well-
> meaning but untrained gentlemen who are responsible
> for the state's well-being. Aristotle ... remarks
> that 'that some should govern and others be governed
> is not only necessary but useful, and from the hour
> of their birth some are marked but for these purposes
> and others for the other, and there are many spheres

of both sorts'. Well we are ruled here by one
particular species of one sort. Curiously enough,
that species answers closely and worthily to
Aristotle's description of the people who should
not constitute the ruling class. But they do
constitute the ruling class and they walk by the
light that is within them, at the same time being
curiously indifferent in the matter of assuring
themselves that their light is not darkness....
Why cannot they persuade themselves to ensure the
efficiency of the state organisation by taking
the advice of the men who understand organisation
and the principles of civil government?

In this, an explicit plea for the replacement of the
inferior and inept rulers who were supposedly not fit
to be members of the 'ruling class' by the efficient,
knowledgeable, educated mining Britons who were, mining
ideology reached a peak not without its own kind of
passion. The relatively calm, self-assured tone of
previous claims about the state had suited the
predominantly constitutional methods of approach made
by the industry to the government; now the shrill note
which entered the ideology was deemed by its articulators
to be suitable for the new methods they advocated -
direct takeover. Whereas at the time of the Jameson Raid
the journal had been non-committal about the wisdom
of attempts to alter the state by violent means (which,
incidentally, suggests that the Raid was premature and
uncalled for from the point of view of the grass-roots),
by the beginning of 1899 it had become more enthusiastic
about what had come to seem the only hope of installing
imperial capital as hegemonic. On the eve of the Anglo-
Boer War the 'SAMJ' condemned George Albu for criticising
the South African League. Albu had disapproved of the
League's desire to 'take over the government'. The
journal defended the League, saying that Albu did not
recognise the extent of maladministration and the
necessity for a takeover. (74)

The state in all of these aspects of the pre-war
ideology was depicted as an administrative body in the
'hands' of those defined (both by their 'externality'
to mining, and by the fact that they represented
undesirable economic forms) as the 'wrong' people.
The state embodied Boerness, backwardness, ineptitude
and non-Britishness. Mining, by contrast, embodied the
Britishness, which would by its inherent nature be able
to transform these things. In the absence of such
transformation being possible, mining was seen as having
to remove the 'wrong' people from the apparatus

which they occupied and controlled, and to replace them
with those representing Britishness. This conception
of the state as a separate and mainly administrative
body which was able to be 'in the hands' of particular
groups, suited this particular stage of the 'mining
revolution', concerned as it was with capturing the
skeletal apparatuses of repression and administration.

The victory of the British defenders of mining over
the 'Boers' in the war did not end this ideology, but
altered its orientation. After the war, Sir Percy
FitzPatrick was able to say with relief that it had
solved the 'political uncertainty' of the 1890s: 'we are
able now to deal with our mines and other enterprises
in this country as one would naturally deal with
undertakings which are likely to last over a whole
lifetime.' (75) The issue became what the new state should
do on behalf of mining, in accordance with its duty,
rather than whether it would do it or not. With the
new pass regulations, (76) the building boom, (77) the
increased trade and dividends, (78) the lower average
wage, (79) the increase in productivity, (80) and the
greater administrative efficiency, (81) in the immediate
post-war period, it was as though the new administration
had indeed removed the major obstacles to mining's
development which had first been seen to be intolerable
in the early 1890s: 'The industry has expanded greatly
since the Vereeniging pact. Lower grade areas have
assumed more profitable aspects under a more ambitious
and exacting rule.' (82)

The state was not only amenable to the industry, it
was positively for it. (83) Mining ideologists nevertheless sustained their aggressive and imperious tone
towards the state apparatuses. The idea of state 'duty'
to industry persisted too, while the total unity
provided by the over-arching British South African idea
continued to be used to depict the ideal to which the
state was supposed to, and in some cases did, conform.
Immediately after the war the state came to be under the
control of British imperial bureaucrats themselves who
were subject to political pressures emanating from
Britain. When these pressures encroached upon the state,
and thereby on mining, it was the 'South African' aspect
of British South Africanism that was brought in use, (84)
rather than the Britishness of the anti-Kruger era. Then
again, in the period leading up to the first post-war
election in the Transvaal, however, the South African
aspects of the ideology were put aside once more in
favour of the British aspects, in the face of the
increased strength of Het Volk, the pro-white labour,

'Boer'-dominated party which the journal saw as a potential
threat to mining hegemony. (85)   Thus the definition of
a world 'external' to that of the British South Africans
did not end with the destruction of the South African
Republic, but was put to new uses to maintain the unity
of the mining fraction and its supportive structures in
the more agreeable post-war situation.

In summary, the state was treated in this ideology
as a separate, distinct body, which should be
subordinate to mining. This idea was used to plan and
legitimate the overthrow of the Kruger republic and the
instalment of a state over which mining exercised
political and economic influence, which did not oppose
the interests of mining in any fundamental sense, but
promoted them. However, this was the state in its
narrowest conception - necessarily so, for it is only
the central seats of power and government that may be
physically captured in war or revolution. The question
of what form the state should take under the new order
was one which had to take second place to the prior
question of who should control it. However, while
mining's revolution may have been centrally focused on
state power, it would be more than misleading to equate
that revolution with mining's confrontation with the
Transvaal and its economic forms. In fact, the very
motive force of the new mode of production lay in its
primary opposition, not to quasi-feudalism, mercantilism,
or even nascent 'Boer' capitalism, but to the black
societies whose destruction would produce a proletariat.
In this opposition lay everything that was important to
mining capital. Indeed, a revolution may not have been
necessary had it not been for mining's need for vast
numbers of cheap workers; while certain central aspects
of the state form that emerged during that revolution -
and that have prevailed in South Africa ever since its
completion - had their structural origins here. The
nature of the state which capital required can only be
understood by referring to the proper relationship
of capital to the 'periphery' of society in Southern
Africa.

In the 1890s no capitalist or mine manager was unaware
of the fact that the mines 'needed labour'. Complaints
of labour shortages were part of the average mining man's
everyday vocabulary, and much to the chagrin of the
intellectuals of that class, competition for labour
between the various mines was sharp, and resulted in
wages being pushed far beyond the ultra-low levels the
industry needed. And yet how was the gap to be bridged
between the realisation by the average mine manager (who

in those days had the virtual independence of a small
businessman himself) that there were insufficient
workers, and the wider class interest of capital as a
whole in securing a permanent labour force through
concerted action? Capital, even less than labour, is
not automatically conscious of itself as a class, but
is inhibited by the individual way in which its crises
and problems are experienced.

The ideologists of the 1890s grappled with this
problem on a primary level. Unconcerned with the
refinements of proletarianisation, they were anxious
to convey to their audience the need for it to be
undertaken at all. They searched for broad social
images in which the problem that the individual
experienced as 'too few workers' could be portrayed,
and within which solutions to it could be found, not
on an individual, but on a class basis. They
developed a revolutionary vocabulary, and created an
ideological climate in which 'anything was possible'.
Readers of capital's media of the times are always
surprised, (while those who have not read any of these
absorbing documents may express disbelief) at the
crude, honest and radical manner in which class
relationships and problems were perceived and expressed
in those times of social upheaval. Capital needed, in
its own best interests, to be told the truth about
its relationship to labour and there was no place for
heavily disguised and obscured depictions of the social
order.

As had been the case with those aspects of capital's
ideology already discussed, mining imperialism drew
first upon mercantile imperialism for ideas and
policies suited to its proletarianising mission. The
'frontier' had been one of the important nineteenth-
century conceptualisations of relationships between
imperialists and indigenous peoples, and in some ways,
mining ideology was an extension, though not a replica,
of this view. H.A.C. Cairns, in his work on the
attitudes and ideologies of missionaries, explorers and
other forerunners of full imperialism in Central Africa
describes the ideology of the 'frontier' in these
terms: (86)

> Africa was often discussed as if it lacked any human
> inhabitants. Implicit in many of the statements was
> the assumption that to be the first white man was
> equivalent to being the first man. The African was
> part of the background in which Europeans carried
> out their activities ... the reader of early travel and
> other African literature has to make a deliberate

effort not to see Central Africa as an area where
all the important activities were carried on by a
growing handful of Europeans in the midst of an
environment in which Africans, elephants, and natural
obstacles are lumped together as background landscape.
In both the Central and Southern African cases, the
frontier implied the existence of an 'imperial outpost',
while at the same time referred to the contact between
local and colonising groups: 'The early British pioneer
lived and moved and had his being in the midst of
peoples dominated by tribal values. He was inevitably
compelled to respond to their presence, to enter into
relationships with them', (87) writes Cairns. The idea
of the 'nothingness' of Africa had, therefore, to be
reconciled with that of groups with whom colonists had
contact. The ideological forms emerging from the frontier
situation were correspondingly complex. The 'savage' of
Central Africa could also be 'noble'. (88) In Southern
Africa the variety of economic forms in the various
colonies produced a variety of perceptions of the nature
of the 'frontier', (89) amongst colonists and those
they were colonising. By the late nineteenth century,
the ideologists of capital were able to draw upon an ongoing and living concept of 'frontier' in the Central and
Southern African imperial context in which they worked;
and yet, like all other aspects of mercantile
imperialism, had to turn the frontier ideology to their
own purposes.

The original frontier was both 'the imperial outpost
in darkest Africa', and 'meeting point of black and
white cultures, peoples and societies'. (90) But
mining needed no meeting point. Drawing upon the
former, negative aspect of the frontier ideology, and
rejecting the latter, mining ideologists developed
their own particular version of darkest Africa, a
version which seems best described as that of 'centre-
periphery'. On the periphery were not the varied
groups and societies with which the frontiersman
interacted, but vast numbers of people, frequently
undifferentiated, and usually perceived en masse. It
was the remote void in which the 'centre' was seen
to exist as though it were the solid earth in the void
of space. Differentiation between groups originating
in the periphery did not occur except in relation to
their actual behaviour as workers after their
proletarianisation had been carried out. One ideologist
thus spoke of the 'danger' which: 'besets a small and
scattered white community surrounded and hemmed in by
an aboriginal race outnumbering them by about seven to

one.' (91)   The geography of the periphery was not
realistic but ideological - for it could be physically
as close to the mining centre as the Zoutpansberg, or as
far removed from it as China.   The entire colonised
world, and beyond, was considered as part of the periphery
when proletarianisation was being considered.   In Africa
alone, after the Anglo-Boer War, the industry considered
Madagascar, German East Africa, Egypt, French Senegambia,
Morocco, British West Africa, Congo Free State, Angola,
and German South West Africa as potential sources of
labour; while it actually obtained labour from China,
Italy, Russia, Mozambique, Rhodesia, and many other
places. (92)

The void, the space, of the periphery had no
characteristics except those existing in relation to the
needs of mining.   Mercantile conquerors had had to come
to terms with the realities and subtleties of the
systems they subordinated.   But here in discussions
surrounding the problems of proletarianisation,
ideologists depicted the periphery as a wholly and
uniformly inferior social region.   At worst, it was
unalleviated savagery and barbarism; at best, 'primitive'
laziness and peasant stupidity.   The 'native' - itself
a term which facilitates generalisations - lived in
'natural indolence' (93) and indulgence: 'as soon as the
native has accumulated in as short a time as possible
a certain amount of money, he at once returns to
idleness and lives on what he has saved.' (94)

Primitive laziness and stupidity were the notions
particularly designed to apply to the subsistence
economy which many African pre-capitalist societies
rested upon.   The polygamous character of such an
economy was seen as its greatest flaw.   The men, it was
said, had enslaved the women, who worked hard in the
fields while the men sat under the trees smoking their
pipes.   Polygamy, therefore, was identified as the
structure which provided the man with 'cheap labour' and
'maintains him in idleness'. (95)   Whether or not it was
true (96) this view of African societies was used by
ideologists to condemn them.   In addition subsistence
farmers were supposedly 'little more than raw savages' (97)
at an 'unsophisticated stage of development'. (98)   The
periphery was an 'immoral' place.

Of great significance to the nature of hegemony was
the fact that the periphery was a place where the objects
of state power existed, and was not portrayed as part
of the state-as-community, or of the political state
itself.   The 'centre' was the legitimate state and
community.   Here too, capital was drawing on older

imperial forms. For the exclusion of colonised peoples
from access to the political institutions set up by the
imperial power is a characteristic and significant
political fact. Southern African societies were
exceptional in that this exclusion had taken place in
varying degrees of complexity because of the existence,
sequentially and simultaneously, of more than one
colonising power, the existence of white settlers themselves colonised by others, the particular class
structures of the black societies being colonised and the
changing and varied nature of the various economies in the
region. But whatever the various differences between and
within the regional economic systems in Southern Africa,
its successive imperial and settler rulers had ensured
that by the time the mining ideology was being forged, the
pattern of participation in the state was based on the
almost complete exclusion of blacks in all four colonies.
(99) It was the exclusion of blacks, and hence black
workers, and the inclusion of whites and hence white
workers, which was of greatest import to mining, particularly in the forms it had taken in the British colonies
preceding it.

While there were times during which ideologists
questioned whether these lines of exclusion and inclusion
were correct for their purposes, by the 1890s most of them
had come to accept without question the colonial 'heritage'
and to use its basic premises for their own purposes. The
'excluded' Africans of Southern Africa were seen as the
objects of policy incapable of political response.

Because the periphery was defined as a place upon
which the state acted, and not one which had any
inherent dynamic of its own, those African economic
forms which did not conform to the peripheral norm
of polygamous subsistence were entirely blamed upon
the 'incorrect' actions of previous or existing states.
Most important of these was the growth of an African
peasantry which was taking place in some regions, (100)
which ran counter to the uniformly proletarianising
ambitions of capital. In a typically crude and
unmystified fashion, the ideologists condemned 'the
practice of private owners of leasing their ground to
native farmers' because it 'prevents the competition
which should be the corollary of the overcrowding of
the locations and relieves the natural pressure on
the means of subsistence which otherwise would
result'. (101) British (mercantile) imperial policies,
and the policies of the 'Boer' Republics, were
considered incapable of acting 'correctly' upon the
periphery to improve it. British policy had, by its

'weak humanitarianism' created 'happy preserves of
barbarism', (102) in the 'locations'. (103)   It was
British ineffectualness that had left the periphery
alone and 'free to develop', (104) resulting in the
creation of the peasantry: 'the native has been
left, in effect, in undisturbed ownership of the
land, and is rapidly becoming the small farmer of
the community - able to live, prosper and preserve
his independence by the sale of the products obtained
from the soil by the industry of his wives.' (105)
But when Republican policies were being discussed it
was not that they had 'left the native in undisturbed
ownership of the land' but that they had been
'overzealous' in removing him from it. (106)   The
rebellion in the Zoutpansberg in the 1890s was
allegedly a result of the harshness of methods used
to collect taxes. (107)   Mining had not yet developed
a sure idea of the extent and limitations of the
process of proletarianisation it was demanding.

This ideological structure was significant not
simply because it was an appalling form of racism,
and an illustration of the conceptual lengths to
which imperialists will go to legitimate their
interests. It also provided capital with a framework within which the actual process of
proletarianisation could be undertaken. It was
the intellectual's scheme, not simply for outlining
how justifiable it would be to destroy black
societies, but for informing capital of the nature
of its primary interest in this destruction, and
of the political and social terms in which this
interest should and could be realised.

Thus it followed that the 'improvement' of
the immoral periphery should be undertaken through
the agency of one vital factor - 'work'. The
native must and should work. Advocacy of 'work'
as a solution to the backwardness of the periphery
ranged from broad overviews of the entire black
class structure and its relation to mining, to
specific admonitions.

In the first place 'work' was actually defined
to mean work on mines or in other parts of the
'centre', while on the periphery, whatever was done
there to keep people alive was not work. (108)   The
development of this view was facilitated by the
prevailing idea that African men did not 'work' at
all on the periphery in any case, but were served
by their wives. But exhortations to Africans to

'work' were not merely the converse of the assertion
that in the rural society they were 'lazy'. They
were also an affirmation of the moral and civilising
effects of the 'centre'. Work was to the mineowner,
therefore, what education and Christianity had been
to the missionary - not merely a matter of self-
justification, but the symbol and apex of a social
order. Work was depicted, as in many other systems
where capitalism was achieving or attempting to
achieve dominance, as having purifying and dignifying
aspects to it. The recruitment laws were seen as
being a means of impressing upon the 'native' the
'dignity of labour': (109) 'a course of six or
twelve months labour on the Rand was the easiest
and most profound education that can be afforded to
the native. Here he learns the value of discipline,
regularity and the ways of the white man.' (110)

   The first and most direct policy which accompanied
these assertions was the simple one of force. 'I as
an employer of labour', said Albu in his evidence to
the 1897 Commission of Enquiry, 'say it would be a
good thing to have forced labour.' (111) In this
view he was supported by ideologists and other mining
magnates, (112) in word, and, more importantly, in
deed. (113) It is probably true that throughout the
period of primitive accumulation Africans were
forced, in a direct sense, to leave their farms and
work on the mines for a spell, (114) whether through
physical force (kidnapping or capturing of workers),
or through the system of debt-inducement which the
mining companies encouraged through traders in rural
areas. (115) But this forced labour, while it was
the spontaneous first resort of capitalists
desperately short of labour, did not imply the
proletarianisation of the people concerned. They
were compelled to work for mineowners precisely
because they had *not* been proletarianised.
Ideologists had to curb the spontaneous actions of
individual capitalists and direct them towards
more systematic class action. To this end they
articulated the more truly revolutionary idea of
'indirect' coercion, consisting of nothing less
than changing the social structures already
condemned. This explains the hostility towards
polygamy: 'Polygamy is not an institution which
will find many defenders even among negrophilists,
and it may be effectively destroyed by legislation
without exciting extraordinary opposition'. (116)

Polygamy symbolised the pre-capitalist mode of
production which failed to produce a proletariat for
mining and the far-reaching significance of the attack
on it is spelled out here: (117)

It is practically the basis upon which the present
native social system rests, for in it are combined
in a most ingenious combination, the two recognised
great factors of evolution, namely, the struggle
for food and the instinct of sex. The sexual tie
is connected with the family, which, again, is
essentially bound up with the forms of ownership,
inheritance, and indeed, the whole social structure ...
he institution of polygamy is so interwoven with
his habits, laws and customs, that its destruction
would leave his social fabric a wreck. It would,
in the first place, raise the status of women, and
would also deprive the man of the cheap labour which
now maintains him in idleness; it would seriously
affect the high rate of reproductivity, and would
tend to create wants and assist in breaking up the
communal system by enlisting the woman on the side
of a higher standard of living and individual
ownership of property. But its chief result would
be to force the native man to work, and thus
habituate him to labour. The effect of the change ...
would not, of course, be immediately apparent, but
it is a change which must come at some time, and the
sooner the better for the gold industry.

This kind of argument was made throughout the 1890s and
1900s. (118) To obtain workers for the industry, they
needed to be detached from the land, and to do this,
the economy and the entire social structure which
supported them needed to be destroyed. Thus the language
of violence was used. As has already been suggested,
the new peasantry needed to be eliminated: (119)

Thorough and general eviction of natives from private
property through the country would effectually dispose
of labour troubles as it would force upon the market
the excess population which the existing native lands
are inadequate to maintain, and thus create a floating
population of native labourers dependent upon toil
for its support.

It was not only the social basis of African economies
that should be destroyed, but their material basis too.
The causes of the 'labour shortage' were thus said to lie
in such factors as 'abundance of food' (120) and one
ideologist advocated the 'destruction of crops'. (121)
Every disaster, disease and drought (and there were many)
that hit black economies was greeted with macabre

eagerness. When there was a crop failure in Natal, the
'SAMJ' opposed the sending of relief food to the rural
areas so that Africans were forced to come to the mines.
(122) As we have seen, the rinderpest epidemic was
welcomed by mineowners and managers, for it meant, they
thought, increased supplies of labour. (123) While they
were, in the short run, wrong in this assumption, the
long-term effects of the destruction of cattle by
rinderpest and other such natural epidemics in nineteenth-
century South Africa were to assist the process of
proletarianisation being advocated and promoted by
mining ideologists.

Although the revolutionary intentions of mining were
made explicit by its intellectuals, the question of
what precisely should replace these destroyed societies
was not. The simple statement by ideologists of the need
for a proletariat, and their willingness to advocate
total destruction to obtain it, tended to be supplemented
by contradictory and often negative statements of what
the new mode of production would entail for blacks. The
'floating population of native labourers dependent upon
toil for its support' mentioned above, implied a desire
for a fully proletarianised labour force; and yet, as we
saw in the discussion of the state, capital wanted
effective pass laws to cope with the 'accumulation of
idle Kafirs in the neighbourhood of the towns'. Some
ideologists supported the preservation of certain rural
economic forms, along lines promoted by the Glen Grey
Act in the Cape; (124) the class structure implied by
the persistence of the peasantry however, was also
likely to: 'result in making South Africa a second
Ireland with a peasantry of native tenant farmers and an
aristocracy of absentee landowners,' (125) and this was
not to be encouraged. In spite of this uncertainty and
even vagueness, ideologists seemed to be satisfied, for
the time being, with their depictions of the need for
directly or indirectly forced work on the one hand, and
the maintenance of some form of agricultural production
on the other, as the essentials of their future system.
Whatever the ultimate forms which the mining
revolutionaries decided the subordinate modes in
Southern Africa should take, in the early years it was
their subordination that was at stake, and the creation
by the establishment of mining hegemony of a situation
in which that subordination could be used to transform
or destroy. All of the efforts of ideologists were
directed towards this kind of change and ensuring that
the need for its radical nature was grasped. As the
'SAMJ' editor wrote: (126)

The problem is not solved by tinkering at the means of
communication or the safety of the roads ... it is the
manufacture of these one hundred and one explanations
as to why labour is scarce which has served to obscure
the real reason, which is simply that the native is
under no necessity to labour and therefore does not
seek work.

In developing what I have called the concept of
'centre-periphery', ideologists of capital made three
advances upon the existing mercantile system of racism.
First, they mapped out clearly that capital's relationship
to the pre-capitalist black modes of production was to
be one in which only their subordination was important.
There was to be no interaction, as there had been under
mercantilism. Second, they defined for capital the nature
of this subordination - proletarianisation was to be its
central element; while third, they equated subordination
with exclusion from the legitimate state, from the
'centre'. They gave to the incipient capitalist class
a vision of its future relationship with its black
proletariat and the economic systems from which it arose,
a vision which was at once all-encompassing, honest, and
revolutionary, which was both ideological and a basis
for practical action, and which represented the embryo
of a new form of racism, under a new form of capitalism.

CONCLUSION

The media of capital in the 1890s flourished. We need
to recognise that this ideological creativity took place
for reasons which other attempts to depict the events
of this era have often not been able to portray or
explain. Historians who have tended to examine mainly
the actions and ideas of a few 'great' individuals
dominating the mining industry are forced by their
methodological framework to resort to psychological
or personality explanations of ideologies and their
functions. We have seen clearly that the ideology
emerging in the 1890s was not the arbitrary fancy of
certain idiosyncratic individuals, and was not simply
the conceptual 'heritage' of earlier times, but was
formed by a social process in which a certain category
of persons emerged as ideologists or intellectuals. On
the other hand, those (who may be Marxists) who eschew
the 'great man' theory and tend to attribute the mining
industry's aims and achievements to the more or less
automatic operation of forces produced by a social
determinism, also tend to miss the point. While their

interpretations may be correct in essence, they ignore
the dialectical structure of the historical processes
revealed in this analysis. How are these processes to
be summarised?

It would seem that a picture is beginning to emerge
of the ideologist of capital operating in the gap that
exists between the objective abstract 'interests' of
the class concerned, and the realisation of those
interests in a real historical social formation, on a
class basis. While the ideologists of gold-mining did
not preside over the early accumulation of capital in the
hands of key mineowners (at Kimberley), it seems that
their role was concerned with other aspects of class
formation than the purely economic. Against the
background of the revolutionary interests of mining,
their task was concerned with the revision of the
mercantile inheritance; the discovery and depiction of
the objective interests of mining; the consolidation
of the class through the forging of a unifying ideology;
the detection of the crucial barriers to the achievement
of its first major, revolutionary imperatives - in
particular, the barriers constituted by the 'Boer' and
black social systems - and the discovery of possible
avenues along which these barriers could be overcome.
In all these aspects, ideologists played a complex
double role.

It would be inaccurate to say that there existed a pure
ideology. British South Africanism - a radical, racist,
British, imperialist, and yet South African ideology -
was not explicable in terms of its conceptual content
alone. It was a strikingly programmatic world view
and the ideologists who created it moved with ease
from details of state policy to the overall condemnation
of 'Boer ineptitude', from racist assertions about
black societies, to the provision of a framework in
which the exclusion of blacks from the state by earlier
imperialists could be continued in the new, capitalist
milieu, and from confident assertions of the superiority
of the British, to more down-to-earth suggestions as to
how class unity within the mining industry could be
achieved.

This double role of the organic intellectual will be
seen again and again in this study - for it is suggested
that this may be a crucial element in our search for the
'roots of hegemony'. In outlining for his class audience
where its interests lie, how on a class basis they should
be realised, and in terms of what world view or ideology
they should be conceptualised, legitimated and presented
to the outside world, it seems that the intellectual is

creating for the aspirant dominant class, in the form of
its representative and leading fraction, a blueprint
for its future hegemony. Hegemony too, it will be
remembered, was defined in both ideological and
structural terms - it was at once a way of perceiving
the world, and a set of structures in which actions
were encapsulated. The organic intellectual in
vigorous periods of class formation such as this one
can be clearly seen to be not merely an ideologist,
but a strategist and sometimes a policy-maker.

The individualised and competitive consciousness of
the individual mineowner and his manager presents a
crucial barrier to the process of class formation, and
it is this barrier which ideologists must overcome. To
each mine the 'problems' of the 1890s were perceived as
being maladministration, a labour shortage, high costs,
or any of a number of other matters experienced on an
individual basis. How is it, it must be asked, that
these 'problems' came to be solved through united,
violent and far-reaching class-based action on the part
of the mining industry and its imperial supporters?
Marxist analysis may be accused of being somewhat far-
fetched when it resorts to deterministic explanations
of the relationship between capitalists, and capital.
Hopefully the interpretation of the organic intellectual
put forward here indicates that such determination as
does exist is embodied in a real social process, and is
not mechanical or automatic. The intellectual, the
audience, the ideology, and the historical milieu in
which all are embedded, have been concepts which have
opened up a field of investigation hitherto relatively
unexplored, and one which hopefully through the remainder
of this analysis will prove increasingly fruitful.

2   The hierarchy of exploitation

The 1890s saw the clashing of modes of production and
the Anglo-Boer War could be said to have brought about the
dominance of industrial imperial capital over all other
forms of capital and over existing pre-capitalist systems.
Such dominance took widely different forms, depending on
the strength of the old systems and their potential
usefulness to mining's requirements. In the complex
play of power and weakness in the succeeding years,
white agriculture became an ally of mining's; black
agriculture an economic prop to its migrant proletariat;
while imperial merchant capital and Transvaal national
capital were either destroyed or put to new purposes
under the economic sway of mining capital and its
international allies.

And yet it was not chiefly with these matters that
the post-war ideological network was concerned. Perhaps
this is not surprising, when it is considered that the
new post-war state set up formal political mechanisms
within which the dominant class could manage to form
alliances, and draft and implement legislation. Capital's
strategy of destroying, capturing and re-moulding the
political state structures and their administrative
counterparts before anything else placed it in a
position to forge and consolidate its superiority in the
region as a whole. But what did capital need the grass-
roots ideological network for if it had already managed
to institutionalise mechanisms of a more public, and
legitimate, nature able to cope with its needs? Why did
the network persist after the war, and how were its
functions to be explained in terms of class formation and
hegemony?

Perhaps it would not be crudifying it too much to say
that capital was now concerned with clashes between
classes rather than between modes of production.

Ideologists had played their part in the process whereby
capital had come to realise and act upon its revolutionary
interests *vis à vis* other economic forms. It now had to
be guided in what was ultimately a more basic matter - its
ability to extract surplus from its working class in a
sustained and stable manner *within* the dominant mode of
production.

This was not simply an economic question, although its
basis in the economic imperatives of mining is perhaps
clearer than in any other of its interests, but also a
political and ideological one. For to maximise profitability is to go beyond the technical organisation of
production (a matter with which ideologists were concerned
mainly in so far as it affected the nature of the working
class) into the sphere of class conflict, where labour
resists, sabotages and confronts capital; where its
productivity has to be sustained or increased; and where
it unites to realise its interests in opposition to those
of capital, perhaps also under the guidance of *its*
intellectuals. Objectively, therefore, capital's economic
interests in profitability would seem to imply the existence of political and ideological interests in developing
a system of exploitation within which two essential
functions could be performed - namely, that on the one
hand, the extraction of surplus could be maximised; and
on the other that the inherent conflict between capital
and labour could be minimised. It is these twin interests
that will recur again and again in this chapter, forming
as they do the foundations for capital's overall political
and ideological strategy towards labour.

And yet it again seems clear that the individual
capitalist is not able to conceive of his own interests
in class terms unaided. He will usually act according
to his understanding of the problems of his mine or
company. If a strike occurs, he will crush it with
little thought to the wider implications it may have had;
if the working class is divided into black and white,
he will either accept or complain about this, but make
no particular effort either to challenge or consolidate
that given division; while if white productivity is low,
he may simply employ cheaper blacks, without perhaps
recognising the long-term problems implied by such an
action. He will thus find himself the victim of
unforeseen crises which at best will impair his ability
to continue the operation of his enterprise, and at worst
will destroy him. He may fail to see the path along
which working-class organisation is travelling; he may
fail to prevent black and white workers from uniting in
opposition to him; or he may suffer a severe and crippling

productivity crisis. He needs, but alone cannot create,
a system of social organisation within which he, together
with other members of his class, can sustain production,
and control and channel developing class conflicts on an
ongoing basis.

Like all other features of capital's overall social
strategy, this need can only be understood and
interpreted in historical terms. Every society
presents capital with different configurations of
classes, sub-classes, fractions of classes, and
ideologies, while capital too varies in an infinite
number of ways, depending on the circumstances of its
growth and development as well as on its economic
constitution. Of course there are certain common ground-
rules which every capitalist follows – divide the working
class if you can; create mystifying ideologies whenever
possible, or manipulate whatever cultural and social
factors the working class holds dear. But there is
always a gap between what capital would like to do and
what it is able to achieve, a gap determined mainly by
the strength and pattern of working-class power, unity,
ideology and culture.

Thus the ideological network of the 1900s cannot be
understood without first explaining the historical forms
of class formation and interaction which preceded and
underpinned it. We need to ask what the given structure
of class relationships in South Africa was *before* the
1900s, how it had come into being and whether this
structure suited capital's interests. We must explore
the ways in which capital sought to shape, exaggerate,
mute or change the form taken by the relationships between
capital and labour and within the working class; and ask
what the role of ideologists was in challenging or
perpetuating historically determined class relationships,
in assessing their implications for productivity,
profitability and permanence, and in legitimating them.
Only then can we examine the nature of the system which
post-war intellectuals decided to sustain, and its
relationship to pre-war 'British South Africanism' on
the one hand, and to the central problems with which
this study as a whole is grappling on the other.

The central fact about the relation between capital
and labour at the beginning of the era of gold-mining was
the rough division of the working class into 'black'
and 'white'. It could be said that this distinction was
based upon differences in the milieux from which workers
were initially recruited and was reinforced by the black
exclusion from and white inclusion within the polity,
which the mining industry itself strengthened. But the

reproduction by capital of this system of division between
workers was not inevitable. The fact that it was
reproduced was the result of long years of deliberation
and debate by ideologists, and the decision to preserve
it must be understood to be the result of assessments by
them that such a system was compatible with capital's
twin interests in maximisation of surplus extraction
and minimisation of class conflict. To illustrate this
we need first to examine the position of each section
of the working class in the 1890s and 1900s in historical
terms, and then to explore the creative responses of
capitalists to it.
    We have already seen that the destruction of black
pre-capitalist modes of production to the end of producing
large numbers of labourers had been part of the initial,
revolutionary, strategy of the 1890s. This process of
proletarianisation, once it had got under way, depended
upon the already-initiated processes of underdevelopment
that mercantile imperialism had inflicted upon black
social systems, but extended and deepened them. The
weakness of black social systems placed them in what
Johnstone has called an 'ultra-exploitable' position.
    But if we are to seek links between the deep divide
between black and white in South Africa and the
requirements of capital, we cannot simply allude to the
process of proletarianisation, even if it did take a
somewhat violent and racist form. All capitalist
systems have needed to proletarianise, but not all have
given rise to a proletariat which possesses the
exceptional characteristics of the South African black
one. We need to examine, therefore, how capital sought
to control its black working class immediately after it
had left the land, and what its place was in the system
of production itself.
    Blacks were 'ultra-exploitable', but this might not
have been significant had not mining capital possessed
a central interest in 'ultra-exploitation'. The large
and precarious industry, with its uniquely low profitability and high cost structure, found itself driven
towards placing its main cost-cutting burdens on the
working class, and the black working class at that. It
was the ideologists of capital who first recognised that
this interest should and could be realised through
concerted class action and who first put forward the
remarkable proposals that formed the basis for one of
the characteristically South African mechanisms of
capitalist exploitation. Capital, they surmised, should
take advantage of its great strength and experience,
and the black proletariat's great weakness and

inexperience, to go beyond the normal capitalist
relations of production. 'Normal' capitalism, it would
seem, relies on the fact of proletarianisation to
subordinate its labour force. Once driven off the land
(by economic and 'extra-economic' means), labour is forced
to work for a wage by the very fact of its divorce from
the means of subsistence and production. Nevertheless,
the labourer is 'free' to choose his employer, bargain
for higher wages, acquire skills, resign his post, take
part in social activities, and do a number of other things
which may result in his cost being pushed up and his unity
with other workers being promoted. These 'freedoms' of
the workers go against the interests of capital, but
capital does not normally counter them in terms of the
relations of production themselves - it uses extraneous
political and ideological mechanisms.

But the intellectuals of mining capital in South Africa,
driven as they were to find methods of making the workforce ultra-cheap, and existing as they did in a colonial
situation where that workforce was indeed able to be made
ultra-cheap, sought to introduce into an essentially
capitalist class relationship, essentially pre-capitalist
mechanisms which did in fact enter the realms of the
relations of production themselves. The 'freedoms' of
labour were to be eliminated in this case *a priori*. (1)

The first proposal they put forward was that already
proletarianised labour should not confront capital on a
'free' wage market, but should be supplied, under strict
controls, by a monopolistic labour supplier. (2) Capital's
colonial heritage (particularly the heritage of Kimberley)
had placed it in a position to bring into being an
unusual system. But this, like all of the other interests
of capital, needed to be recognised and articulated on a
class basis before it could be realised, and ideologists
were as advanced here as they had been in other fields.
In its earliest report, the MMA had pressed the Chamber
of Mines into: 'forming a native labour bureau, to be
supported by the mining companies, for the purpose of
sending accredited agents to countries outside the
Transvaal to arrange for a regular and constant supply
of labourers', and a number of other methods for
rationalising the system of labour recruitment, (3) and
had suggested that mining companies combine to carry
out these measures. Establishing a monopoly would make
it possible for companies to lower wages as much as
possible and thwart the relative independence of workers.

That mere proletarianisation was not sufficient to
preserve the ultra-cheapness of black labour is evidenced
by the fact that during the 1890s competition between

companies, the ineffectiveness of the pass laws, and
the limited area of jurisdiction of the Transvaal, all
made it possible for black workers to command higher
wages than companies thought desirable, (4) to desert
on a systematic basis, and thereby bargain for a higher
wage and express protest against injustices on any
mine, (5) and to evade or be ignored by those who were
supposed to prevent these things. As we have argued
earlier, the tightening of the pass system was one of
capital's priorities - but that had to be done through
the state itself. In the meantime, 'The native
labourer is at present master of the situation, and
no-one is more alive to this fact than himself', (6) said
the MMA President in the early 1890s, and in an explicit
statement of the need for a united onslaught by capital,
he continued that this could only be stopped 'if we can
induce our companies to continue and work together in
this matter instead of against one another, and in their
own interests'.

The 1890s saw consistent and regular pleas for unity
and co-operation between separate mining companies and
houses, and for the establishment of a monopolistic
labour bureau instead of competitive methods of obtaining
workers. Evidence of the part played by the ideological
network lies in the fact that in these early years the
Chamber of Mines itself either opposed combination or
only half-heartedly supported it, (7) while ideologists
recognised that a true and workable monopoly necessarily
implied a fully centralised and bureaucratised system,
to replace the Native Commissioner, the tout, the
dependence of some mines on the reputation amongst
workers of their managerial staff, and all the other
entrepreneurial and individualistic systems that prevailed.

Proletarianisation was the primary process under way
in these times, and the ability of intellectuals to lead
capital was partly dictated by its pace and vicissitudes.
Thus in times of labour abundance the ideologists' pleas
for formalised monopoly tended to fall on deaf ears.
When, in April 1895, the journal could report that as a
result of crop failures, 'for the first time for years
past the supply has exceeded the demand', (8) most members
of the industry reduced black wages by informal but
'concerted action'. But on this and other occasions the
'SAMJ' pleaded for a realisation that wage reductions
would not last if labour supplies fell again and
competition between companies was restored. Managers
would find it difficult to adhere to agreements to keep
wages down unless they were made binding. (9)

When this claim was vindicated, when a 'shortage' of

labour rapidly followed this 'abundance', and when the
same pattern began to repeat itself a year later at the
time of the rinderpest epidemic, the call for monopoly
was taken more seriously. The ideologists' perceptions
had, as it were, been confirmed to their audience by
reality. In each case, reductions in black wages,
based, as we have said, on capitalists' perceptions of the
convoluted processes of 'supply' and 'demand' in those
times had provoked workers into leaving the industry in
substantial numbers and at a time of rinderpest resulted
in three strikes and organised desertions.

It was only in response to this second piece of
evidence that competitive companies were not going to be
able to sustain a consistently cheap labour supply that
the various organisations of importance in the mining
industry acted upon their ideologists' recommendations.
In 1896, the Chamber of Mines, the Association of Mines,
(significantly, these two associations were at one on
this issue) and the Association of Mine Managers, met
and together decided to form the 'Native Labour Supply
Association Limited'. (10) This became the Rand Native
Labour Association, (RNLA) and in its ultimate, and more
perfect form, the infamous Witwatersrand Native Labour
Association (Wenela, or WNLA), formed during the Anglo-
Boer War. Just as the increased numbers of workers
resulting from rinderpest began to become a shortage, as
Africans streamed from the goldfields because of fears of
war, famine and rinderpest at home, and wage reductions on
the mines, the general control of the industry over its
workers was tightened.

Labour monopoly was regarded by capital's intellectuals
as the central element, after proletarianisation itself,
in its relations with the black proletariat. Its
ideological implications are therefore important. It
provided a concrete basis upon which the already outlined
concepts of racism could be developed and extended.
The reality of the institution of the labour bureau –
a central body which co-ordinated control over workers
coming from all over Southern Africa, by arranging
contracts, settling wages, and distributing workers to
predetermined mines, and which thus considerably curtailed
the bargaining power of blacks - provided the guide for
the ideology that accompanied it. The first ideological
form which arose was the notion that the operations of
the labour bureau were those of 'dealing with a commodity'.
Labour could be supplied and demanded, its 'excess' supply
could and should be kept 'in hand'. (11) Labour was
conceived of in arithmetical and not human terms. It could
be 'increased' or 'decreased'. To monopolise labour was
to commoditise it.

But the labour bureau was not simply a marketing body;
it was also the mechanism whereby the 'native' of pre-
proletarianised times was transformed into 'labour' - the
peasant into the worker. This transformation was
interesting in that it involved the process whereby the
individual, coming as he may have for a variety of
reasons to work on the mines, was transformed into one
unit among tens of thousands; or the 'periphery' came
to the 'centre'. The labour, defined as inhuman by
virtue of its quality of being a 'commodity' was simply
our earlier 'savage native' transmuted in the mine
context. Fitzpatrick spoke of how the use of black
labour on the mines would have the advantage of 'solving
two questions, viz. the native question as well as the
labour question'. (12) The concept of 'native' gave
rise to that of 'labour', just as the concept of
'commodities' depended upon that of 'savagery'. By the
development of these links the periphery-as-nothingness
was transferred from its identification with the savage,
black, polygamous subsistence farmer, to the anonymous
unit of labour. A clear link was postulated between the
way in which the periphery was depicted during
proletarianisation (when it was an object of state
policy) and during labour recruitment (when it was the
actual place where tens of thousands of workers were
'obtained' at low prices and brought to the mine). In
effect, therefore, the 'native' did not cease to be on
the 'periphery' when he was physically transported to
the mines, the 'centre'.
     But the periphery did change. Instead of being
regarded as the object of moral uplift, as it had been
when proletarianisation was being planned, it now became
the source of what were merely defined as 'units of
production', the 'labour' which was divested of any moral
qualities. Whether or not black workers actually
behaved as mere objects the ideologists and their
audience behaved as if that was what they were. Moreover,
they had power enough to ensure that the reality matched
their ideals. Still the fact that this 'commodity'
consisted of individual human beings had somehow to be
taken into account, and be understood, particularly
because this affected its behaviour as a 'commodity'.
This necessity explains the need to 'understand the
native', a developing preoccupation of the period,
particularly with reference to the desire or ability to
work or not to work on the mines.
     'Understanding the native' was the name given to a
serious attempt by ideologists to define variables by
which the commodity of labour may be usefully judged and

characterised. In this period, the need to understand
was rooted in a simple need for obtaining labour and
keeping it. (This may perhaps be contrasted with the
ideas of later periods, when the concern may have been
more to prevent workers from organising and striking).
Thus, in the 1890s, understanding the native was
epitomised in the already quoted claim that 'the native
is always willing to run away if he can'; his likes and
dislikes, social and geographical origins, capabilities
and behaviour, were all seized upon by the ideologist
and interpolated into the overall idea of a commodity,
its obtaining and retention.

   Liquor, for example, was seen as fulfilling a
characteristic 'need' of black workers, one useful for
the capitalist short of labour. (13) Then, the whole of
the periphery was at times subject to sweeping waves
of restlessness. 'A spirit of restlessness has fallen
upon the natives throughout the whole of South Africa'
it would be said. (14)

   On a more specific plane, different 'kinds of natives'
were said to have particular characteristics. The 'East
Coast Native' was said to be a better buy than any other
kind of native because 'he stays longer, returns often,
and managers experience no difficulty with him' underground. (15) In one article the 'SAMJ' editor asserted
that: 'a native race will make the better labourers
the further their instincts and habits are removed from
the pastoral and vice versa.' (16) He too concluded
from this 'axiom' that the 'East Coast Native' (17)
should be preferred. Thus was the 'periphery' brought
to the centre and conceptualised ideologically without
disturbing its status as an inhuman place.

   The active responses of workers to their own
historical position were transformed into the
'characteristics' of labour, through the operation of
'knowing the native'. A second layer to the structure
and ideology of racism was added by the development of
the labour bureau and its conceptual apparatus.

   Effective as the labour bureau was in curbing certain
of their more expensive 'freedoms' black workers remained
relatively free on the individual mine itself to behave
'as they pleased'. They stole amalgam, drank, 'loafed',
and organised themselves into striking and deserting
'gangs' without much control by managers. At Kimberley
these problems had been lessened by the creation of
entirely closed compounds in which the worker lived for
the duration of his contract under the total control of
managers. In the 1890s it became clear that ideologists
of gold capital were concerned that compounds should be

introduced on the Rand too. The third phase in the
subjugation of black labour originated here.

In 1892, for example, the 'SAMJ' advocated the
introduction of compounds, and referred to the
'magnificent De Beers' compounds'. This plea was placed
in the context of 'the native' as 'child'. Children's
lives are regulated, it ran, and: 'the position of Kaffirs
is in many respects analogous to that of the latter,
and both in their own and in the general interest require
special control and supervision when exposed to
temptations to which, in their natural condition, they
are unaccustomed.' (18) The housing of black workers at
that time was open. (19) It allowed 'the kaffir' to:
'roam, unrestricted, and not improbably inebriated, at
his own sweet will, without consideration of the danger
and inconvenience to which the general community is
thereby subjected.' (20)

The use of the compound system required and bred an
idea of the black man as a child, irresponsible and
uncontrollable. The 'savage' at home, the commodity *en
route*, he was now to become the most humble member of a
hierarchical organisation, in need of protection on the
one hand, harsh repression on the other. This was not
mere ideology. The tendency for the 'total institution'
to divest people of adulthood has been brilliantly
portrayed by Goffman, and pursued in a Southern African
context by several writers. (21) What is significant
about compounds, as van Onselen has shown (and as
Goffman's conceptual framework cannot reveal), was that
they became class instruments of total control, whose
implications are thus far more serious than those of
even the most total of Goffman's institutions.

Compounds bred their own ideology of authority which
played no small part in what van Onselen calls the
'perpetual colonisation' of their black inhabitants: (22)

Placed as he is, in charge of a number of grown-up
children, it is obvious that if the duties of the
compound manager are to be properly and effectively
carried out, some latitude must be allowed him, and
some authority must be delegated to him.... With a
good manager in charge of the compound the work of
the mine will always run smoothly and satisfactorily.
A white man accustomed to the habits, usages and
languages of natives will exercise that quiet authority
which long command of inferiors gives, being firm
without being harsh, and just without being
unnecessarily severe. At the same time he must be
granted sufficient authority to punish for minor
offences, for with natives the punishment must follow

swift on the commission of the offence; otherwise all
discipline is soon lost, and the labourers become
quarrelsome and discontented.

This preoccupation with the 'art of management', in
which the 'characteristics of the natives' are referred
to as a basis from which the white manager must develop
his abilities, was typical. In this example, the analogy
may appear to be with a disciplinarian school. But he
continues to make a more pertinent comparison:

> a good illustration of his position is to be seen in
> the autocratic world of the army regiment, where men
> are dealt with by their own officers, the law specially
> delegating certain limited powers to the officer in
> command. In many respects, the compound resembles
> the barracks, and it becomes a simple impossibility
> to maintain order and discipline unless the compound
> manager is recognised as having considerable power.

The total institution of the army is perhaps the better
comparison, its hierarchy being more rigid and its overall
purpose more inexorable than that of a school. The
ideology of authority depended upon utilising the workers'
own ideologies, such as by: (23)

> establishing the relations of chief and subject between
> each labourer engaged and the mine manager.... It is
> essential to utilise the native habit of looking to
> his recognised head and of implicit obedience to it,
> and that the manager should be constituted in the
> native mind as a tribunal for ultimate appeal under
> any grave sense of injustice.

Black inferiority came to be seen as natural. The MMA
President spoke of 'our rightful position of masters'; (24)
while it was commonly believed that Africans regarded
the kind of treatment they received on mines as no less
than their due: (25)

> in their own kraals natives in general live in a more
> or less backward state of civilisation, and there is
> in my opinion a danger that we may be going too far
> in our endeavours to make them comfortable ... left
> to themselves to seek work, the natives by far prefer
> those compounds which are not too well-ventilated and
> airy ... we should not over pamper him and thus weaken
> his naturally strong constitution.

The proposals that compounds should be introduced to curb
the freedoms of workers again reinforced and extended the
racist construct of the 'periphery'. Because black
workers, once they had been placed at the actual point of
production, had to interact with other members of the
industry in certain important ways, to the concept of the
periphery was added that of 'lowliness'. The periphery,

now occupied by workers and not peasants, became not
simply 'nothingness', not only the source of non-human
'commodities', but the region occupying the lowest
position in a hierarchical system of authority
relationships.

These three phases of subordination - proletarianisation itself, the monopolisation of labour, and the
compound system - created a remarkable proletariat. To
them must be added a fourth construction, the pass
system, also a vital and central concern of ideologists,
but one which they, significantly, considered should be
dealt with through the state as we saw in chapter 1. This
would seem to suggest that the pass system was treated
by capital as an extraneous political mechanism of
control over the working class rather than a 'pre-
capitalist' form of intervention into the relations of
production. Whatever the interpretation, however, it is
clear that this complex four-fold system of ultra-
exploitation, once it had been actually implemented by
capital following the lead given it by its intellectuals,
placed the working-class black in a uniquely subordinate
position. His lowliness was indeed 'overdetermined'.

This unique subordination was, it is suggested, the
support for the ongoing exclusion of blacks from the
legitimate state. The ideology of 'peripherality' was
sustained throughout all the phases of black subordination
because each phase represented further confirmation of
the differences between this working class and most
others. It was not simply because blacks were weak and
unable to resist these onerous restrictions on their
'freedom' that they were still conceptualised in
'colonial' ideological terms, when capitalism had become
dominant. It seems possible that the ability of capital
to subordinate labour in these extreme ways had eliminated
one of the very reasons for the more normal inclusion
of the working class within the legitimate state
apparatuses - the fact that capital needs to exert
political contol over its 'freedoms'. If 'normal'
working classes can strike, organise and bargain for
higher wages, then these things need to be controlled
through the state apparatuses, in which the nominal
participation of that working class is essential. If the
South African working class could not exercise these
'freedoms', then no a *priori* reason existed for it to be
incorporated into the state.

There remains one final matter to be discussed in the
context of whether or not South Africa's proletariat was
unique. This is the all-important fact that the process
of proletarianisation remained incomplete in this region

for a significant period of time. By encouraging the
survival of the remnants of what were once pre-capitalist
modes of production in the rural areas, (26) mining
employers could maintain black wages below subsistence
level, exempting the black worker from paying for his
family's subsistence out of his wages. Not only could
this system be legitimised by the already developed
concept of 'centre-periphery', but it was a concrete
reinforcement of it, since the 'periphery' was not in
fact totally destroyed by capital, but destroyed and
then reconstructed by it, and permitted to survive in a
stunted and rapidly declining form. (27) The 'nothingness'
of the periphery and the 'inferiority' of the blacks who
came from it and returned to it, were both sustained
by the ongoing structure of migrancy. Thus the
integration of the Southern African economy into one
system, dominated by the capitalist mode of production,
was disguised. (28) However, the ideological network of
the 1890s and 1900s did not concern itself with the
partial proletarianisation of blacks to nearly the same
extent as with the systems of labour monopoly, compounds
and even passes. Very little reference is made in
capital's own media to the rural social and economic
systems from which black migrants were drawn and to
which they returned. Perhaps this too is an indication
of the fact that 'incomplete proletarianisation' is an
extraneous, political and ideological mechanism of
control over the working class; or perhaps it suggests
that capital uses other intellectuals than its own to
solve the problem of the reproduction of the labour
force.

Until now, black workers have been regarded as the
only working class, and their relationship to capital
explored in isolation. This was important, not only
because the imperatives driving capital's relationships
to black workers were unique and complex enough on their
own, but perhaps also because they were the determinant
ones. We hope to have shown that these imperatives
were all mutually reinforcing, in the direction of
entrenching the subordination of black workers in an
extreme form. The opposition between capital and black
labour was almost total. But while in a society such as
Rhodesia this antagonistic and extreme opposition takes
an almost pure form, in South Africa the existence of a
strong and growing white working class forced
modifications. Few writers other than Johnstone have
fully conveyed the ultimate inseparability of capital's
relationships with both sections of the working class,
and the complex interplay of forces involved in its

simultaneous juggling with both. And yet it is to work
within capital's own definition of hegemony to treat the
two working classes separately. Here the interdependence
is stressed, and shown to have been a vital variable in
capital's developing strategy.

It was as a result of forces outside of the direct
control of the mining industry that the early white
working class came to occupy a particular place in the
initial hierarchy of exploitation, and to limit the
choices available to mining capital in the later creation
of the production system. (29) In the early years of the
mining industry four factors distinguished white workers
from others and made them relatively powerful, both over
black workers and in relation to capital. In the 1890s
probably the most important of these was the fact that
they were the skilled workers of the mining industry,
the artisans and overseers. They could not be treated
lightly, dismissed readily, or paid below the prevailing
average. Then, the increasingly important fact of their
full proletarianisation, of their having wives and
families dependent upon them for survival, meant that
their wages had to be far higher than those of the black
workers with their surviving agricultural forms. Third,
the fact of their being British in the 1890s meant that
they had brought to South Africa certain powerful, if
often conservative, forms of consciousness and
organisation of their own; while finally, the political
legitimacy it possessed meant that the white working
class unlike the black, had a call on the state itself
and could confront capital in an overtly political
context.

All of these factors confronted ideologists with
entirely different problems of control from those posed
by black workers. In fact, it began to emerge in
mining and in the economic system as a whole that one
of the objective limits to capitalist development at
this time lay in the potential and actual power of the
white workers. Unless they could be prevented from
using this power, capital accumulation could and would
be seriously curtailed and the mining industry's
precarious profitability would be threatened and
possibly destroyed. It was urgent, therefore, that in
the period when mining hegemony was in the crucible,
white workers should be permanently and structurally
placed in as disadvantaged a position as possible in
relation to capital, if they could not be eliminated
altogether. As we shall see, the various ideological
and structural onslaughts made by capitalists on white
working-class power were a result of capital's

compromise between its own interests and the configuration of historical forces at the time.

During their years of debate around these matters an important concern of intellectuals was that the ever-changing consciousness of white workers, instead of being relegated to the sphere of 'understanding the native', had to be taken into account in moulding capitalist strategy. We have already seen how the very earliest uses of British South Africanism included the creation of an ideological bridge across the gap between white labour and capital, and we now explore this feature further.

British workers considered themselves to be exploited. Although in 1897 they received eight to ten times as much as black workers, and four times as much as European workers, the frame of reference of this international migrant workforce was the other goldfields of the world, particularly the Australian ones, where a far lower cost of living more than made up for slightly lower wages. (30) Moreover, the mine managers and other 'British' members of the mine hierarchy, with whom they were supposed to ally themselves, were resented for their high salaries and dividends, (31) and to this was added the continual awareness of the insecure place of the white worker, with his high necessary means of subsistence, in the face of cheap black worker competition. None of these factors contributed towards altering the restless, migrant, rootless nature of the early white working class, and its tendency, like the early black workers, to move from mine to mine, often in what in other circumstances would be called 'gangs'. (32) 'Most miners, like many others amongst us - only look upon this section of the Empire as a place to make money in and then clear out as quickly as possible'. (33)

In coping with white working-class power and consciousness, intellectuals found that once again pure colonial forms were inappropriate. Just as the existence of a powerful white ruling class in the Transvaal had forced the 'imperial' ideology of the mineowners to take a unique South African form, so the presence of a large and strong white working class forced simple racism to be modified into the more complex notion which we have called here 'caste'. The white worker was neither forced down to the level of the black, nor encouraged to identify totally with capital; instead he remained on an intermediate plane. Thus the intellectuals of capital made an early decision to accept initially at least, the given structure of class relationships, and to create ideological interpretations on that basis.

While the black worker's place in the initial
conception had been that of a child, the white worker
was conceived of as a particular kind of ally. He was
not 'part' of capital, however, (as would be the case
in a more truly bourgeois ideology) and thus it was not
an ideology of simple white supremacy. The alliance
was instead between 'breeds', a reproduction, probably,
of the similar prevailing ideologies in Britain at the
time. A structured, formal relationship was postulated
between employer and employee. And yet this was not a
'class' ideology, because British workers here were only
one part of a wider working class, and each of the
various kinds of workers was characterised in a
distinctive racial way. Hence the term 'caste'.

The British worker, in his caste, remained first and
foremost a worker. The economic basis for this will be
discussed below. The 'alliance' with capital was not
an attempt to hide or blur the proletarian condition
of white workers - indeed this would have been impossible,
given the level of their consciousness. Instead, a
worker was a different kind of person from an employer.
To call someone a miner was to endow him with particular
qualities and characteristics, to place expectations
upon his behaviour and beliefs and to typify him as a
member of a social, economic and cultural category. When
the British white working class was being discussed, it
was referred to as 'labour'. But this was not 'labour'
in the sense of a 'commodity' or 'child', as was the
black working class. It defined labour in terms of its
relation to capital. 'Labour', ran one 1895 editorial,
was unhappy about 'capital' taking up the political
crusade. (34) Two years later, the Randfontein strike
was described as a 'symptom of unsound relations between
Capital and Labour - of a fissure between them'. (35)
Such concepts were never used for black workers.

This was one basis upon which ideologists sought to
curb the potential power of workers. To be of 'good
British mining stock' (36) was to be a moderate trade
unionist. When Bain, one of South Africa's most
eminent early trade unionists, held a meeting of workers
in 1899 to start an 'independent labour organisation',
the 'SAMJ' was jubilant because it: (37)

> proved to be a dismal failure. The genuine working
> men of the Rand appeared in opposition to Mr. Bain's
> project and such stormy scenes occurred that the
> Chairman left the chair ... respectable working men
> repudiate the leadership of Mr. Bain, whose chief
> object appears to be to sow dissension between
> employers and employees.

'Genuine' and 'respectable' working men were the core of
the idea of the white worker in these times, particularly
when it came to the question of a 'fissure' between
'capital' and 'labour'. They were supposed to exhibit
good behaviour: 'I cannot pass over the good feeling
that exists between managers and employees which is
general throughout the Rand. So long as this continues,
we will be able to avoid those disastrous strikes that
have ruined prosperous countries'. (38)
     The earliest workers were, in fact, relatively
'respectable'; they had brought to South Africa a
conservative, compliant trade unionism. When in 1898
the Society of Mill and Cyanide Men was formed, its
proclaimed objects were: (39)

     to promote the interests of all mill and cyanide
     employees and assist the Chamber of Mines in stamping
     out and detecting gold thieving. To keep up and in
     some instances improve the status of employees in
     positions of trust in above workings. Keep cordial
     the relations between manager and men.

But, as the example of Bain indicates, this type of
unionism was under siege. During the 1890s, its
supporters diminished in numbers, and it tended to be
increasingly confined to surface workers. (40) Once
'respectability' ceased to exist, capital set out to
re-create it.
     The liberal managerialism put forward by ideologists
and generally accepted by ownership and management as
time went on aimed to encourage the asset of skilled
white labour to remain on one mine, and to develop
loyalties and ties to it, thus reducing its bargaining
power and eliminating the costs of repeated hiring and
firing. Housing, just as it had been with black workers,
was the means whereby this control was to be exerted.
At Kimberley the policy had been tried of housing
workers in a suburban estate - Kenilworth - thus tying
them to the mine. This was one possible solution for
the Rand too, for it could promote stability,
co-operation, and even lower wages. It could be
supplemented by other mechanisms, such as medical and
insurance funds, and generally 'making employees
comfortable': (41)

     some of our larger Companies ... have lately seen
     the advantage of making their employees comfortable
     by the erection of capacious and nicely fitted
     boarding houses where decent meals can be obtained
     at remarkably reasonable rates. The advantages of
     keeping employees contented and comfortable cannot
     be well overestimated.

This sort of plea persisted throughout the 1890s. In
1895, an article appeared deploring the 'disgraceful'
conditions of workmen's housing. A workman's home was:
(42)

> too often a dirty hovel.... A man who is well cared-
> for and has comfortable quarters is far less inclined
> to change, and is far more anxious to keep his berth
> than one who is expected to live in a pigsty.... The
> continual changing from place to place is one of the
> worst features of labour here.

Schools, hospitals and a 'married men's village' were
all proposed by the SAMJ and others, (43) and were
considered to have the potential of making possible
'great reductions in wages' by offering permanency. (44)

Miners were, however, well aware of the nature of
these policies, and of the extent to which they failed
to compensate for the basic unattractiveness of mining
work, to the chagrin of ideologists: (45)

> the tentative expression of the wholly proper desire
> to foster better relations between employer and
> employed on the fields, by making every possible
> provision for their comfort, by granting land for
> the creation of comfortable homes, with all the
> benefits of a civilised environment, has been
> instantly construed as indicating a subtle attempt
> to introduce the close supervision to their
> employment which exist or are supposed to exist for
> the artisan and mining classes at Kimberley.

A 'vague but rooted dislike to Kimberley conditions' ran
deep amongst workers: 'it is enough for the expert
orator to barely mention the name Kenilworth in order
to be perfectly certain of creating distrust and
suspicion.' (46) Despite promises of a 'happy and
settled life', in the pre-war era white workers
remained unsettled and unhappy, many of them migrants, (47)
dissatisfied with their contracts and wages, (48) and
with the Rand itself. (49) Moreover, towards the end
of the 1890s, they began to demonstrate their ability
to organise to greater effect than before, and to
become more radical in their outlook, thereby making
greater use of their potentially substantial power. (50)

Although capital did not succeed in controlling white
workers in these early years, the foundations for its
future hegemony were laid. While black workers were to
be ultra-exploited, white workers were not. 'Caste'
represented an attempt to link these separate strata of
the working class to each other and to capital, through
a conceptualisation of 'hierarchy', which posited
something common to each group. The idea of 'unity in

hierarchy', of divisions within an entity united under an
'umbrella' ideology, characterised the early mining era.
Its political functions have already been hinted at; for
example, the idea of a caste of white workers was useful
in obtaining and maintaining white collaboration and
stability, in justifying the exclusion of whites from
unskilled work, and in coping with the double role of
whites as workers and as allies. However, a second,
and perhaps even more important function lay in the
economic sphere, in aiding capital to define the optimal
structure of relationships between white and black
workers in the workplace itself. Compounds, as we saw,
had a distinctive structure of authority, comparable
with that of an army. But compounds were simply
institutions of direct repression over powerless workers.
The authority structure must enter the working
environment itself, where the fundamental rationale of
any industry is situated - the sphere of production.
Here ideologists turned the caste system into a
distinctive and extremely significant ideology of
authority.
       The cornerstone of production in a deep level mine
was what is known as the 'gang'. Groups of workers,
each member of the group with a more or less specialised
task, worked as units, often at long distances from other
groups. Each group, or gang, had a structure of
authority and skill. Some members of it performed the
skilled tasks of drilling or blasting; others the menial
tasks of sweeping up debris. Each gang was supervised
by an individual miner who himself was subject to the
supervision of a hierarchy of superior miners who visited
the gang from time to time. It was the white miner who
headed the gang. These white workers could not in the
1890s and 1900s be simply seen as a generalised 'stratum'
of workers 'above' black workers. Each individual white
worker in the production process supervised or was
overseer to, and was responsible for, a 'gang': 'white
miners are usually only required to act as shift bosses
to gangs of natives, teaching green hands, pointing drill
holes, firing shots, and getting the most work generally
out of the natives' (51) ran one description; according to
another: 'in this country, the white miner is more a
shift boss than a miner proper, being required to take
charge of gangs of natives, superintend their work, and
get as much out of them as possible'. (52) To be skilled
in the underground situation certainly involved some
training, but was also a matter of experience and general
knowledge about the way a mining operation worked, and
a matter of being able to transmit knowledge, supervise,

and co-ordinate the variety of jobs that required doing,
in an authoritative manner. This function of the white
miner may not have applied to the highly specialised
white artisans on the mine. However, it was the function
which became ideologically dominant.

What is important about this era was that this
relationship between white miner and black gang was not
simply a managerial one, nor can it accurately be
compared with the foreman-worker relationship. The unit
of productivity was not the individual worker in the gang,
but the gang itself. From the point of view of
productivity, the white miner was at the head of an
organic structure, and to that extent was inseparable
from the black workers he supervised, who in turn were
inseparable from him and from their fellow-workers in the
gang. The production demands of the industry did not
fall upon the individuals, but upon the gang as a unit,
an 'organism of production'.

The organism of production had ideological and political
as well as economic functions. It was used to emphasise
to white workers their dependence upon black workers: the
scarcity of black labour, for example, tended to be
regretted by ideologists because it threw white miners
out of work. (53) In general 'the number of Europeans
employed by the industry will largely depend on the
number of coloured workers available', (54) it was said.
Furthermore, the organism had a total value, measurable
in terms of productivity, which somehow had to be, and
could be, made up of the correct combination of the
'white' and 'black' parts which constituted it. The
organism was a caste-like structure whose function was
predetermined, the positions of its members interrelated,
and whose 'value' was the product of the correct 'race
relations', each part acting as it should.

In the 1890s, workers in the workplace did not in
fact fit into the 'caste' ideas of them, of course, any
more than whites had remained 'respectable'. The
ideologist constantly faced the stark difference between
this ideal, somewhat machine-like concept of the
mechanism of production - in which the right colours and
kinds of labour fitted their predetermined functional
positions in the organism, and in which, given the right
motivations and attitudes, productivity and co-ordination
could be maximised - and the reality of the situation -
the necessity for immense brutality, the inefficiency and
conflict it generated, with arbitrary behaviour, flouting
of rules, and workers deserting, striking and sabotaging.
Ideologists spent time trying to explain and alleviate
these 'problems', in terms of the ideologies they had

developed. On the simple managerial level, the 'organism' was said not to work because white workers failed to fulfil their tasks properly, and communication between the functional strata was rendered arbitrary; the idea of 'knowing the native' came up once more: 'their success in their duties greatly depends on their knowledge of the language and treatment of natives; this naturally requires some experience of the country.' (55) In general, white miners were themselves 'racially' assessed in terms of their abilities to 'assess' other races or groups. Afrikaners, for example, were considered better white miners, because they supposedly possessed the quality of 'knowing the native'. However, simply having by nature the right 'knowledge of the native' was not in the end considered sufficient. All sorts of methods of control whereby the native could be 'handled', codes within which this would be regulated, and axioms by which it could be easily taught were developed as part of what at the time was known as the 'art of management'. (56)

Other 'problems' which the ideologists of caste confronted were the result of the higher wages which whites could command. It was considered utterly unacceptable for a white to step outside the boundaries of his role in the organism, unless there was a generally acknowledged 'temporary crisis'; if whites moved downwards in the organism from their defined role as its head, they would inevitably raise the price of unskilled labour. Except in times of severe black labour shortage and white labour abundance, the mingling of or blurring of roles was considered to be some sort of desecration, and whites were said to be in some way defiled by contact with blacks: 'to what extent, if any, can white labour be mixed with black without doing serious damage to the former.... It can hardly be denied that the admixture of the two is directly demoralising'. (57)

Another crucial 'problem' was that whites tended to relinquish the function of worker, and take on that of management entirely. This, too, was a defilement: (58)

white men in subordinate positions and in daily contact with the natives soon become lazy and inefficient, shirking their share of the manual work at every opportunity, and throwing it more and more upon the shoulder of the black ... the existence of an inferior race appeals to that lust of domination inherent in every man, and places the white in a relatively higher position by the simple expedient of creating a class lower than himself. He accordingly becomes inured with a vivid sense of his own superiority and signalises his elevation to the

aristocracy of blood by the customary distinguishing
characteristic of all aristocracies ... that is, by
refusing manual toil.

The clear import of this was that while the white worker
may head the organism of production, it is of that
organism, the 'collective worker' that he is a part, and
not of 'management'. By being part of the unit of
production he is a worker above all else, and it is as
much a corruption for him to consider moving upwards
as downwards. His role was explicitly that of somehow
activating the organism of collective labour, he was
the prime agent, the catalyst of its operations. Furthermore, if this role was inadequately fulfilled, this
meant he was also subject to defilement and corruption,
and that he corrupted the black workers beneath him by
not catalysing them correctly. (59) The white worker's
role was thus ideologically circumscribed. The rigidity
of the role he was expected to fulfil was his equivalent
of the rigidities of law and sanction placed upon the
black worker. He had to be a worker, and yet a special
kind of worker, according to the needs and interests of
the mining industry.

The burden upon the white worker in the early ideology
of mining culminated logically in the express prohibition
of his identification with other sections of the working
class. Whites were bitterly condemned for 'fomenting
discontent' amongst blacks. (60) Here the ambiguities
of the white role were crystallised by ideologists.
While they were condemned as 'defiled' for adopting a
purely supervisory role and identifying themselves with
the 'aristocracy', their loyalty was nevertheless expected
to be focused on supervision, not their common cause with
other workers: 'To remain an overseer, drawing the higher
wages of an overseer, he must adopt the necessary point
of view. He must forego (sic) the reactionary socialistic
bar-room theories of the labourer who thinks that his
mission in life is to obstruct industry, not to aid
it.' (61)

The significance of the caste ideology of productivity
and authority lies in the fact that through it capital
sought to achieve two things. One was to ensure that,
in spite of the differences in their structural place,
both strata of the working class remained truly
proletarian, in that even the 'supervising' white worker
created surplus value through his rigidly circumscribed
role as activator of the organism of production. Perhaps
it is testimony to the white working class's growing
strength in later years that it was able to resist this
particular strategy to some extent, and that it came to

perform the supervisory function far more. (62) The
other function was to divide and thereby rule the
working class as a whole, and to ensure that unity
across its divisions was precluded. Thus can the
organism of production be seen to be contributing to
the fulfilment of the twin needs of capital for the
maximisation of surplus extraction and the minimisation
of class conflict.

It has already begun to emerge from this analysis
that capital found the problem of the white worker more
difficult to solve than that of the black. The 'caste'
system did not solve all of these problems. But it was
only one of several alternative conceptualisations of
the whole producing structure, and was the most
conservative, in that it attempted to conserve the given.
A great deal of light is thrown on both the caste system
and the revolutionary position of mining when we
recognise that other more radical alternatives were put
forward and seriously considered, to improve the less-
than-perfect class structure. What is significant about
these proposals, besides their importance for our
understanding of the nature of capital's eventual
hegemony, was their scope. Only a revolutionary class
would have the ability and audacity to conceive of itself
as able to manipulate, not just its own employees, but
whole classes of people. Vast numbers of workers were to
be imported, exported, employed or left unemployed, to
the end of creating a coherent, profitable and
controllable class structure. That capital could
conceptualise and carry out these things in this era is
remarkable evidence of precisely the issues we are
concerned with - the existence of a crucible in which
capital's hegemony over labour was being forged, in
which different blends, mixtures and moulds were tried
before the revolutionary impetus waned, and the system
crystallised.

The first 'great alternative' to the existing structure
of a hierarchically divided working class and the ideal
one from capital's point of view, was the suggestion that
white workers be replaced by black. At the same time as
workers were being brutally, if only partially
proletarianised, systematically recruited, and the
compound and 'caste' systems of living and production
were evolving, a significant debate was taking place in
mining circles about whether the undifferentiated,
unskilled, 'peripheral' black worker should not perhaps
be replaced by a more differentiated and less 'peripheral'
one. The black working class, because of its cheapness
and the repression which could be exercised over it

legitimately, would be an ideal substitute for the
powerful and expensive white working class, while
although the actual use of black workers might perhaps
be curtailed by white worker power, the threat of their
use would inhibit white workers from exercising as much
power as they could.

In 1894, therefore, the 'SAMJ' proposed that the
solution to the problem of labour lay, not in attracting
'a few more raw thousands of boys to the fields', but in:
(63)

> raising the efficiency of the semi-experienced
> labourer we already possess. This can only be done
> by kind and just treatment, and thus encouraging
> the natives to permanently apply themselves to work
> at the mines. Some of our best companies are already
> realising that cheap and raw labour on low wages is
> less economical than that of well-trained and cared-
> for native labour at much higher terms.

Healthy, contented, and more importantly, permanent
workers were now being proposed together with an
appropriate ideological matrix. Now the concept of
'periphery', was less than suitable. One ideologist
spoke with disapproval of the fact that: (64)

> one of the fixed ideas of some mine managers - and
> for every such man there will be twenty subordinates
> who will adopt the same philosophy - is that the
> native is a lump of raw labour material, a body
> without mind or soul, to be kneaded with kicks and
> curses up to a certain rude state of efficiency
> in skilled labour.

These ideas were consciously replaced by more 'liberal'
ones. (65) The development of such ideas was based upon
the fact that some black workers had already been fully
proletarianised, and returned to the mines so frequently
that they could be considered as permanent workers;
moreover, they had acquired the skills of mining. It
was this that could mean the elimination of expensive
white labour altogether, or at least could provide a
continual threat to its power and security: (66)

> The white is threatened with a grave danger from the
> increasing skill and knowledge of the native miners.
> Permanent work on the mines is producing a class of
> skilled boys who know nearly as much about the work
> of placing the holes, loading and firing the shots
> as any European miner; and unless the latter is
> careful to make himself indispensable, employers will
> be tempted to discard him and his high-priced work.

Furthermore, this possibility had already been seized
upon by mine management: (67)

That this is no idle danger is proved by the fact that
one or two mines already employ natives almost
exclusively, and these mines are remarkable for their
low costs of working. The classification of the blacks
into skilled and unskilled is a change which cannot
long be delayed, and this will improve the position
of the skilled boys.

The division of black labour itself into classes would
be an added refinement which would even reduce the
overall costs of black labour itself. Thus the giving
of certificates to skilled blacks would: (68)

break up the present mass of native labour into
classes, a step which must inevitably be followed by
a similar classification in the rate of wages. The
great difficulty experienced in the mines is to
convince the boys that there are differences between
them in respect of their value as labourers. At
present the boy who is worth a few shillings a month
must be paid at the same rate of wages as another
worth three times as much.... Any device which will
tend to break up this system and pay every man
according to the value of the work done by him, must
go far in the direction of solving the difficult
problem of reducing the present ridiculously high
native wage.

Proposals for a permanent class of skilled black labour
reached elaborate proportions: detailed ideas about how
they could be housed and their families catered for
were put forward by mine managers such as Hennen Jennings,
who in his evidence to the 1897 commission described
how a scheme of permanent 'negro' labour had worked in
Venezuela. (69)

In South Africa, he proposed, 'the men of the strongest
physique could go to the mines, but the younger and
older men and some of the women could work on the farms'.
Another proposal was that women could become domestic
servants. (70) In general the influence of having
families with them was said to be beneficial to workers -
it would 'stabilise' them. (71) Moreover, 'locations'
(used in this context to mean worker dormitories) were
deemed desirable: 'so that unemployed natives could be
concentrated within well-known areas and could thus be
under the eye of Government officials, but would be
readily available for mining companies on all occasions
when a shortage occurred in the labour supply'. (72)
Permanent workers were established on some mines, (73)
'locations' were tried on a small scale in some cases. (74)

Throughout the history of capitalism in South Africa
white workers have always been powerful enough to resist

capital's attempts to replace them by blacks. But this
continued to be a policy-choice put forward by ideologists
at frequent intervals particularly in times of crisis.
Thus after the Anglo-Boer War, at the time of the greatest
labour shortage yet experienced by the mines, the idea
was put forward once more by important individuals and
recommended by the South African Native Affairs
Commission itself. (75)   Then at the time of the 1907
white miners' strike, as we shall see, the idea emerged
again, while of course the culminating clash around this
issue was the 1922 white mineworkers' strike. But it
should be recognised that the white working class's
long-term victories in these battles were not victories
of labour over capital but the victory of one form of
capitalist hegemony - hierarchy - over another - a
totally black workforce. The system of hierarchy suited
white workers more than did the system of their
replacement by blacks - but both systems were designed
to preserve the subordination of all labour to capital
and to limit the ability of white workers to use their
power in significant ways.
   A combination of circumstances after the war changed
the place of the hierarchy in the perceptions of
ideologists and in the real elements of its structure,
and threw up other 'great alternatives' to hierarchical
hegemony. Because the 'Boer' Republics had been over-
thrown by the war and British supremacy entrenched, mining
capital perceived its position to be secure, and its
future long and prosperous. From their newly won place
of superiority, mining capitalists began to look at the
farming and industrial sectors of the economy as allies
rather than as the threatening representatives of an
alien mode of production. 'We have practically decided
to go in to a certain extent for Agriculture', said
G. Rouliot, Acting Chairman of Rand Mines Ltd, in 1901,
'We think it highly desirable to improve the rations
supplied to our natives, and particularly to give them
vegetable food.' (76)   Similarly, another eminent mining
director expressed his concern that the mines did not
compete with others for labour since his company 'has
considerable interests in other industries'. (77)   This
did not mean, as we shall explain, that imperial
capital was now supporting national capital. But it
did mean that diversification of investment began to
increase after the war, and interdependence between
the sectors had grown.
   Second, the problem of obtaining labour in sufficient
quantities for the now secure and expanding mining
industry had grown rather than diminished during the

war. Proletarianisation had suffered a setback, black
farmers had flourished and established themselves on the
deserted land, and after the war the mining industry
experienced a grave 'labour crisis'. (78) In April 1903,
the deficiency of workers was said to be 87,880, more than
half the total requirement of 141,250. The mineowners
wanted labour, but did not want to compete destructively
with the other sectors of the economy; while they also
wished to make use of the opportunity presented to them
by their new-found power over the state after the war, to
explore the possibilities of a different system of
production, a different combination of labour forces,
before their revolutionary power weakened. The post-war
labour crisis provided capital with further 'objective
possibilities'.

A third factor forced capitalists to explore these
possibilities. While proletarianisation amongst blacks
had slowed down during the war, white Afrikaners found
themselves driven off the land in ever greater numbers.
through the accumulated pressures of changes in land
tenure and the devastations of the war. (79) Furthermore,
as imperial capital set about destroying Transvaal
national capital, the already proletarianised Afrikaners
who had been employed in that sector were thrust on the
now swollen white labour market. On the other hand, as
soon as the Anglo-Boer War had appeared to be imminent in
the 1890s, the existing unstable and transient white
working class had begun to leave, by 30 September 1899 at
the rate of 300 a day. (80) Both forces led mining
companies to employ the newly unemployed Afrikaners in
their place. 'Burghers are to be employed as much as
possible', said the journal, and if they failed, the
services of Frenchmen, Germans and Italians were to be
used. (81) After the war the tendency for British workers
to be replaced by other whites had vastly increased.

Afrikaners occupied unskilled, and some skilled, jobs
on the mines as did demobilised and immigrant whites of
a variety of nationalities. (82) With its greater
numbers, its poverty and its unemployment, the white
working class came to occupy an altogether different
position from that of before the war, while a number of
men rose to prominence who claimed to represent these
workers and their interests.

The first response of ideologists to the overall
post-war situation was to seek new and radical ways of
solving the labour crisis. In 1903 they put forward
proposals which seemed to cover every possible combination
of systems of labour usage and structure. A commission
was sent to study the De Beers' compound system; (83)

Chinese labour was proposed; (84) white labour should, it
was suggested, be better housed, organised and stabilised;
(85) black residential locations were again suggested; (86)
and the importation of Italian peasants, (87) Russian Jews,
(88) and other foreign labour forces, proposed. But it
was the suggestion put forward by some important
ideologists and men of action that white labour, and only
white labour, be used on the mines, that presented the
most serious challenge.

The proposal that all mineworkers be white was a
complete reversal of all the prevailing concepts of how
the mining industry should be composed. Creswell, then an
eminent mine manager, was its leading proponent and
ran his own mine on that basis; at the 1903 Annual
Meeting of Rand Mines, FitzPatrick reported that during
the previous 6 months more than a quarter of the mining
staff had consisted of unskilled whites; and a
substantial lobby within the industry developed favouring
the use of white labour. The Transvaal Labour Commission
of 1903 issued two reports - a minority, white-labour,
report side by side with the majority, anti-white-labour,
report.

To the mainstream ideologists of mining, the white
labour proposal was always regarded as impossible,
contradicting the needs of mining in several ways.
The 'SAMJ', the organ which attempted to represent the
true interests of capital in the ways we have described,
opposed the white labour experiment unequivocally from
the beginning. In so doing, it reiterated the foundations
of the basic interests of capital in relation to white
labour in Southern Africa. As Davies has shown, the
primary objection to the use of white labour was that
it was necessarily relatively expensive, because it was
completely proletarianised whereas the black working
class was not. The wage needed to keep a white worker
and his family alive was higher because no surviving
forms of agricultural production existed for them to
supplement their income in any way. (89) The cost of
reproduction had to be borne by the capitalist mode
and, in fact, a great deal of capital's strategy must
be seen as an attempt to lower the necessary means of
subsistence of this stratum of workers. Housing schemes,
productivity drives, tariff changes, investments in
agriculture and a variety of other proposals were put
forward by ideologists of an industry which did not
produce consumer goods whose sale could justify the
paying of higher wages to its employees, and which had
constantly to balance its interest in maintaining the
'underdevelopment' of Southern Africa against its need

to obtain cheap, locally produced foodstuffs and consumer
goods. In these early times whites, said FitzPatrick,
were four and a half times more expensive than blacks,
but only one and three-quarter times as efficient. (90)
The editor of the 'SA Mines' wrote a scathing attack on
Creswell's experiment, pointing out that it had
increased costs by 23 per cent, decreased ore grade by
42.9 per cent, so that profits had been brought down to
33.1 per cent of what they were in 1899. (91) To counter
this unacceptable system, ideologists referred with
approval to the system of division between skilled and
unskilled workers which had prevailed before the war: (92)

> As a mere muscular machine, the best developed native,
> when he has remained long enough at the mines to be
> thoroughly trained, is the equal of the white man.
> The brain and the industrial training are the white
> man's only superiority. In classes of work in which
> brain-power does not enter, or enters only to a
> limited extent, it is hopeless to seriously consider,
> from an economic standpoint, the substitution of a
> mere muscular machine costing 20s or even 10s a day
> for one costing up to 2s or even 3s per day, and
> capable of developing the same energy.

The protagonists of white labour made their
proposals on two fronts: not only were they concerned
that local white workers should occupy unskilled jobs,
but that the shortage of unskilled workers on the mines
should be filled by the importation of large numbers
of unskilled whites from elsewhere. If over 100,000
workers were needed the rapid proletarianisation of
Afrikaners would not fulfil this need while the
importation of Russian Jews or Italian peasants, would.
It was in response to this aspect of the white labour
proposal that ideologists voiced an argument which
Davies dismisses too readily - the fact that white workers
were undesirable because they, unlike black or other
'coloured' miners, were politically 'free', a fact which
ran directly against capital's interest in
of class conflict. In a memorandum to the Transvaal
Labour Commission, Rudd referred to this and to the
'respectability' of existing white workers: (93)

> As regards trade unionism in South Africa, I say,
> encourage married men and co-operation in interests -
> but could Mr. Kidd replace the 200,000 native workers
> by 100,000 unskilled whites, they would simply hold
> the government of the country in the hollow of their
> hand, and without any disparagement to the British
> labourer, I prefer to see the more intellectual
> section of the community at the helm.

Another submission argued that: (94)

> the feeling seems to be one of fear that if a large
> number of white men are employed on the Rand in the
> position of labourers, the same troubles will arise
> as are now prevalent in the Australian colonies, i.e.
> that the combination of the labouring classes will
> become so strong as to more or less dictate, not
> only on questions of wages, but also on political
> questions by the power of the votes when a
> Representative Council is established.

When they were attempting to persuade white miners
themselves of the necessity to curb white labour,
ideologists tended to refer to the caste system itself,
and the privileges white workers would lose if it were
abolished. Thus Farrar, in a speech to 'working men'
said that: (95)

> Supposing for instance unskilled white labour were to
> be largely used; it means that the price of your
> unskilled white labour is regulated by the price of
> your unskilled coloured labour therefore it means
> that we should have to find the cheapest class of
> unskilled white labour that would be prepared to
> compete. That means subsidising labour, in other
> words, bringing it into this country from all the
> sources of Europe. What would be the inevitable
> result? Why, that this unskilled labour would very
> soon become skilled labour, and compete against you.
> For my part I am absolutely against indentured cheap
> white labour.

The sole use of cheap white labour was rejected by the
large majority of ideologists. (96)

Accordingly, ideologists tended increasingly to
support labour schemes which did not disturb the
relationships between classes and castes. The solution
supported by most was one which replaced the absent
black workers by another 'caste' of workers with the
same fundamental characteristics: ultra-exploitability,
and political powerlessness. Within the Southern African
system of legitimacy, these two characteristics were
most likely to occur in workers who were not classifiable
as white. However 'ultra-exploitable' imported white
workers may have been initially, their political power
in the Southern African system would soon render them
useless as substitutes for black workers, as we have seen.
In the early months of 1903, several ideologists proposed
that Chinese labour be imported to solve this problem
while as the year progressed those who had previously
been lukewarm or even hostile to the idea became more
sympathetic. By August the 'SAMJ' said that although

it had been against the idea earlier because
'recruitment procedures' were not adequate, it now
supported it. (97) In September the journal listed all
the people who in the preceding months had 'given in' on
the question of Chinese labour, including FitzPatrick.
(98) 'No honest man can any longer oppose the plea for
imported labour', said the journal, (99) since it had by
now become clear that although the mines were due to
expand rapidly under the new sympathetic state, black
labour was simply 'not forthcoming'.

At the same time as they were developing their ideas
against the use of cheap white labour, therefore,
ideologists went through the various arguments for the
use of Chinese labour, often in terms which indicated
that Chinese labour would not disturb the given hierarchy.
Capitalists would rather leave thousands of whites
unemployed, than risk such a disturbance: (100)

> I can quite understand the opposition to the
> indiscriminate importation of Chinese labour for
> social and sentimental reasons.... I do not deny that
> a great deal is being done to help those who find
> themselves in distress and in need of food and
> shelter ... but this is charity, and no amount of
> the most generous charity can be considered as the
> best or as permanent help to those who are willing
> and anxious to work. The unskilled work which we
> need will not support our unemployed white population,
> and, until we can secure a largely increased supply
> of unskilled labour, I must confess that I do not see
> a satisfactory outlook.

Support for the idea extended to the Chamber of Mines
itself, (101) the Chamber of Trade, (102) and many other
important bodies. In December 1903, the journal could
write, 'it is something, after all, for three of the
central of the representative organisations of this
community to unanimously memoralise the Government on
behalf of imported labour.' (103) On 9 January 1904, the
Importation of Labour Ordinance was promulgated.

The reinforcement of the hierarchy which Chinese
labour entailed was evident from the labour ordinance
itself. They were to perform unskilled labour, i.e.,
'such labour as is usually performed in this Colony by
persons belonging to the aboriginal races or tribes of
Africa South of the Equator'. (104) It was declared
illegal to employ them as skilled workers; to sell land
to them; lease land to them for trading; or harbour or
conceal deserters. Indentured for three years, the
workers were not permitted to 'desert', or to have any
interest in any trade or business. As the journal

wrote, optimistically: (105)

> It is difficult to see how the Asiatic can ever become
> a menace, commercially, socially or otherwise, for he
> becomes merely a labourer without opportunity to
> exercise any personal preference, or being in any
> manner able to change his condition. The length of
> his stay is predetermined. His occupation is fixed.
> He has no rights or privileges except to return to
> his native land.

A list was drawn up of categories of employment from
which Chinese were to be debarred. (106) Despite
objections by spokesmen for the 'poor whites' and those
whose place in the hierarchy would be threatened by
Chinese workers, (107) and protests, riots, and
desertions by black workers on the mines when the
Chinese began arriving, (108) the system of importation
of non-white indentured labour was established. By
January 1905, 27,222 Chinese workers had begun work on
the mines. (109)

Once the Chinese were on the mines, their place in
the already existing hierarchy proved relatively easy
to establish. Although they were extremely cheap, they
were slightly more expensive than black workers, (110)
while the conditions of the compounds occupied by them
were better than those of blacks, because the British
government required it. Chinese labour tended to
occupy a position between black and white workers, an
additional caste in a stratified system of production
and authority. The 'organism of production' was
accordingly improved. The numbers of white workers
were said to have gone up, not down, with the
introduction of the Chinese, since each element of the
organism depended upon the others. (111) One ideologist
said that, 'The Chinaman, in intellect and ability to
learn, is far above the African Negro. They are as a
whole quiet and willing workers, and when better known
and understood it will be easier to get more and good
work out of them.' (112) The intermediate status of
the Chinese was frequently alluded to: (113)

> we should like to remind the skilled miners that a
> Kaffir and a Chinaman cannot be treated in the same
> manner. The one is a raw savage, the other a docile
> creature evolved from centuries of servility, but at
> the same time possessing acute intelligence and
> sensibility.... Once established good feeling between
> the Coolie and his white superior and there will be
> little need for the 'protection' which the white man
> never solicited against hordes of Kaffirs.

The death rates of the Chinese and other workers were

a reflection (perhaps slightly distorted) of the
hierarchy in conditions of employment: in December 1905,
the 'Transvaal Government Gazette' reported that mortality
rates for whites were 23.6 per 1,000 per annum; for
blacks they were almost double: 45.6; while for
Chinese they were 'only' 17.3. (114) Relatively
carefully looked after, but ultra-exploited in terms of
wages, mobility and political and economic freedom, the
Chinese represented a different 'kind' of worker again
from those already existing on the mines. As was the
case with all the other workers, the Chinese failed to
conform to their assigned place. Far from being 'docile',
they struck, sabotaged, rioted and, above all, deserted.
(115) Some became traders. 'They are holding effectively
for the trade of their compatriots employed on the mines
and the prospect is that if many more stores are
secured by the Easterns, white traders on the reef will
soon become almost, if not quite, extinct', wrote the
journal in 1905. (116) Once more ideologists were forced
to devote much of their time to 'understanding the
Chinese' so that these 'problems' could be coped with
without the hierarchical caste system being disturbed.
The 'art of managing the Chinese' became a frequent
subject of discussions by men who mixed their racist
humour with candid authoritarianism. At the time of a
serious riot at the Witwatersrand Deep Mine, a superbly
revealing report appeared on The Management of the
Chinese: (117)

> Much of the trouble has been due to the fact that
> our men do not yet properly understand the Chinaman.
> The Chinaman, during his whole life, has been
> accustomed to quaint, obsolete ceremony, and if he
> is given a casual blow he resents it, but if he is
> ceremoniously ordered to receive a dozen blows he
> submits without protest, even if the punishment is
> unmerited. You can even execute him without arousing
> his resentment provided you give him enough ceremony
> over it.

It continued: (118)

> You cannot use the whip on the Chinaman, and this is
> what Rand managers and miners are now finding out.
> Properly handled, the Chinaman is as docile as a
> child, and what is more you can get him to work
> sixteen hours a day for seven days a week.
> How?
> You must let him know where he comes in - where he
> benefits. And you must put the right kind of boss
> Chinaman in charge. If you get the right kind of
> boss Chinaman, his authority is supreme.... The laws

which govern the Chinese no white man properly
understands. But it ought to be better understood
here how little it is possible to intimidate a
Chinaman - how little he can be punished when he
runs amok. Death has no terrors for him.

Although the Chinese workers were repatriated only a
few years after they had been brought to South Africa,
their ideological significance in this period of mining
experimentation with different systems of labour
relationships was substantial. Once they had left,
however, the mines were once more confronted with the
two problems of an unskilled labour shortage and the
ongoing power of the white workers. These problems,
as has already been implied, were solved through the
preservation of the existing hierarchy, and indeed its
reinforcement. For black workers this meant the
acceleration of the various processes of subordination
and proletarianisation already initiated in earlier
times, and the affirmation of their place at the very
base of the hierarchy. It is interesting that the
ideological network did not make this previously central
matter its chief subject of concern, perhaps because its
function of political and ideological creativity had
already been performed *vis à vis* the black proletariat.
Instead, ideologists turned to deal with problems that
they considered were as yet unsolved - the precise
structures within which white workers were to be
controlled. Ideologists persisted in their advocacy
of a system within which whites could be kept as a
'respectable caste' of workers above all others; for
example, during the war this had been supported by the
Chamber of Mines itself, and as soon as the mines were
re-opened after the war, a number of eminent mineowners
announced that they had at last decided to affirm the
motif of 'respectability'. FitzPatrick announced the
Rand Mines scheme as follows: (119)

> We recognise that until men can settle in their
> homes with their families under reasonable conditions
> as to comfort and cost, a stable and contented mining
> population is not to be expected. We are therefore
> providing on a liberal scale accommodation for our
> white employees.

Even these proposals were conceived of in terms of a
hierarchy within the white caste: 'On all the
subsidiaries, houses of three classes have been or are
about to be built - some detached, some semi-detached,
and some in terraces, the difference being to provide a
little more room, or a little more comfort, according to
the position of the men.' Such schemes were seen as

serving the twin functions of lowering the all-too-high
necessary means of subsistence of white workers, and of
encouraging 'respectability':

> The rent ... certainly does not exceed one third of
> what the men would have to pay for the same
> accommodation in far less favourable neighbourhoods
> and conditions.... Each house has a garden plot,
> water laid on. [The white population] will be able
> to live in comfort and contentment, attracted to
> this place as a home and not as a make-shift,
> permanently settled here to the advantage of
> themselves and the industry and the whole country.

During the following three or four years these housing
programmes were implemented on many mines. (120)

With the importation of Chinese labour, the 'white
labour' school had not disappeared, but simply withdrew,
and when Chinese labour was about to be stopped, when
Afrikaners began to be more rapidly proletarianised than
ever before, and when the first post-war election in the
Transvaal was imminent, it came to the fore once more.
This time it presented itself as the representative of
the interests of white labour in general; of Afrikaners
and Afrikaner labour in particular; and of all those
electors who opposed the 'cheap labour' policies of the
mining industry which had left thousands of 'poor
whites' unemployed and often destitute. (121) Mining
ideologists were forced to debate the issue within a
wider sphere of legitimacy - that bounded by the
electoral politics of the time - and in doing so they
made clear their affirmation of the conception of the
white 'caste' of workers. (122) For example, the journal,
in an article on The Danger of 'Cheap Whites', reiterated
and re-emphasised some of its earlier fears about white
unskilled labour: crime would rise because the whites
would be no more than the 'dregs of European peoples',
while: (123)

> The aristocracy of white labour which since the days
> of earliest settlement has flourished in South Africa
> would be turned into a democracy of the meanest and
> most hungry kind; the colour line ... would be very
> largely wiped out, and the white workman would in
> many respects step down to the level of the Kaffir.

Most virulent of all was an editorial against Solomon,
a recent convert to the Creswell-Wybergh group of pro-
white labour 'socialists': (124)

> In time - and with appalling rapidity - the planes of
> white and black will meet. The result would be
> terrible to contemplate. No-one who has seen the work
> of native tradesmen, the houses they have built, the

joinery they have turned out, the iron work they have
wrought, the books they have printed, can doubt what
the end would be. Today at the Cape the black and
the half-caste are ousting the white tradesman from
the field, and the process must inevitably extend to
the Transvaal unless the white skilled workman
recognises in time that he is artificially protected
against such competition and supports the far-seeing
captains of industry in this Colony to maintain that
artificial protection.... The aristocracy of white
skilled labour must be maintained at all costs, even
at that of Chinese labour.

The concept of a 'labour aristocracy' was thus an integral
part of the ideology of capital.

While preserving and developing the worker aristocracy,
ideologists never ceased working to alleviate its hold
over capital in the two central spheres of maximisation
of surplus extraction and minimisation of class conflict.
In 1905-7 both of these concerns held the attention of
ideologists. Although by that time they had definitely
settled for 'caste', events showed that they needed to
improve upon it. The sudden concern with 'efficiency'
on the mines which erupted in the 'SAMJ' in late 1905
and was pursued with increasing fervour through the
following months, was the most outstanding indication
of this. It was as if the journal had suddenly switched
its tactics from concern with the fundamental
ingredients of the hierarchical system, to a concern with
its overall cost. In this field like so many others, the
journal led the way. In its campaign to 'increase
efficiency' on the mines it was far ahead of the
thinking of the owners of the industry, and indeed it
was only after a few months that mineowners responded.
(125) One of the earlier editorials on the matter
maintained that: (126)

Those who are today applying themselves to the task
of reducing working costs will have to scrutinise
labour changes with the utmost care. Herein they
may find scope for economy – and economy does not
necessarily mean reduced wages. Increased efficiency
is the best economy, and it is well recognised by
mine managers that in this connection, especially
in respect of white labour, there is room for
improvement.

It soon became clear that the call for 'efficiency'
was directed at the unskilled white workers now
occupying a large number of posts on the mines. They had
'good' miners, said one writer; but 'on the other hand,
we have, unfortunately, a considerable number of inferior

men (you might safely call them wasters), men who place
their holes badly, and have been known not to place them
at all, but to leave it to the bossboy to run their
stopes'. (127) This problem was blamed, in accordance
with the nature of the organism of collective labour, on
the fact that 'South Africa's experience goes to show
that as soon as you put white and black in a mine, the
tendency is for the white man to slack off and leave
the native to do the work. (128)

The 'efficiency' campaign constituted a re-affirmation
of hierarchy even amongst the unskilled, for it was an
attempt to install them firmly at the 'head' of the
collective organism of production and to make sure that
they were capable of carrying out the tasks involved in
this position. One writer called them an 'army of
incompetents' - the 'unprogressive miners' who had got
their blasting certificates at the 'time of trouble'. (129)
These men, the campaigners argued, must be given the
knowledge and responsibility which would increase their
'efficiency'. The idea of increasing efficiency
constituted both a challenge to white miners, and a
contrived opportunity for this challenge to be
encapsulated within the newly-affirmed hierarchical
structure. White miners responded on both fronts. In
the first place their representatives expressed great
dissatisfaction with the idea of increased inefficiency,
threatening that if mining work and responsibility were
increased, miners would leave. (130) Conditions were bad
enough on the mines, they said, without more work being
added to the uncomfortable load they already bore.
Ideologists were quick to utilise this objection to the
ends of the caste ideology. Rathbone, for example,
pointed out that this only increased the need for the
making of white miners a more 'respectable' and
'contented' group: 'If the surroundings of the miner
in his leisure hours were more comfortable, and if his
work were healthier, he might be induced to modify his
attitude for the good of himself, of the industry, and
of the colony', (131) a sentiment which he expanded upon
later in a letter to the journal: (132)

It is sincerely to be hoped that when Responsible
Government is finally given to this country, that our
future legislators will insist on absolute competence
of mine inspectors, and the introduction of such
laws as will tend to preserve the health and
encourage colonisation by a good, steady, and
permanent resident class of miner.

However, 'respectable' workers did not constitute the
membership of the mining unions, and this level of

response was hardly sufficient to counter the strike
actions of workers taken against the introduction of the
'three-drills system'.

The 'three-drills system' was the 'solution' to the
problem of productivity which mine ideologists proposed.
Instead of supervising two 'drills' each, miners should
supervise three. Since each 'drill' in fact involved
some fifteen or twenty black workers, this proposal
involved a great deal more work and responsibility for
white miners, both of which were defined in terms of the
'organic' structure of production. The overall result
of the introduction of this system would be that each
'organism' would be enlarged by 50 per cent and that the
numbers of expensive white workers per black worker
would be reduced. (133) This was taken by white miners
to mean that the overall numbers of white workers would
be reduced. (134) Mineowners began, by late 1906, to
attempt to implement this idea of three drill supervision.
In October of that year, the management of Crown Deep
Mine made an attempt to introduce it, but it was resisted
successfully by white workers. (135) Other attempts in
the following weeks also failed. (136) After the election,
in May 1907, when it may be assumed that mineowners were
less concerned about white votes, the industry united
in a concerted attempt to introduce three drill
supervision throughout the goldfields. They provoked
the first major confrontation between white labour and
capital, bringing 4,000 white workers out on strike.

This was a confrontation whose dimensions and content
were determined by the hierarchical structure and
'organic' system of production. White miners found
themselves confronting mineowners not on the issue of
their place in the mining industry, but on the issue of
how hard they should work in that place, already
defined as being beneath that of the owners, and above
that of the black workers. Moreover, the hardness with
which they should work was defined in terms of the
numbers of blacks they should supervise – the organism of
production. The course taken by the strike and its
ideological aftermath were also indications of the
victory of hierarchy. The white workers lost the
struggle, after the state had intervened to 'quell a
riot' on one mine, and many workers had been discharged.
They were replaced, in most cases, by local, unskilled
Afrikaners, while the overall number of whites was
reduced and the three-drills system introduced. (137) The
first major occurrence of open class struggle had been
effectively contained within the class structure set up
by capital – an example, surely of 'hegemony' in operation.

In spite of the victory of capital, ideologists took
seriously the display of white worker power involved in
the strike. While the strength of mining had been
revealed by the acceptance by workers of capitalists'
definition of the 'terms in which the struggle raged',
it remained an important task for capital to make clear
to white workers the other facet of the class structure -
their in-built vulnerability to replacement from below -
what Johnstone calls their 'structural insecurity'.
Most explicit of the attempts to indicate this was of
course the replacement of strikers by un-unionised and
less expensive Afrikaners. In addition, during and
after the strike, articles on the vulnerability of white
workers appeared everywhere. The Salvation of the Rand:
Afrikaner Overseers and Semiskilled Natives, was the
title of one, (138) which epitomised the debate of the
time. For the first time since the time of the
Intercolonial Customs Conference in 1903, the journal
concerned itself seriously with the possibility of
'permanent' native labour, (139) while it consistently
advocated the replacement of politicised workers by
more 'suitable' Afrikaners. (140)

By June 1907 the journal claimed that the view had
become widespread that 'the native' could become more
than a mere unskilled labourer: (141)

> The Kaffir is subject to various mental and moral
> disadvantages in accordance with the laws of heredity
> and the influence of special surroundings, but it is
> absurd to conclude that he is incapable of overcoming
> many of these disadvantages under a course of
> intelligent training.

That month it was reported that 'the richest mines
employ only natives'. (142) Accompanying these
suggestions were ideas about black labour 'permanency'
which had last been seriously and consistently advocated
in the journal in the 1890s, and taken up by some in the
1903-5 period. Blacks should be allowed to become a
permanent proletariat, ran the argument. Locations,
with proper homes and gardens for workers' families
should be built on, nearby, or even within commuting
distance from, mines. (143) The advocacy of permanent
and skilled black labour thus seems to represent the
reserve power to which ideologists resort when white
workers display and use the powers they possess in ways
inimical to the interest of mining.

Thus it would seem that the 1907 strike symbolised
the confirmation of hierarchy amongst the owners of the
industry and their ideologists, and even its acceptance
by white workers themselves. The main elements of the

structure within which class struggles were to take
place in the mining industry for the following years, had
been established. Both class conflict and production
in the industry were in future to be regulated by this
hierarchy, although by no means eliminated by it.
Ideologists were aware that the matter 'was not yet over'.
But it was clear that the working class had been
successfully divided and white working class power
diluted by this division, while profitability had been
maximised within the constraints of the class structure.
The tasks of ideologists in the succeeding years were to
be almost entirely concerned with the lowering of the
costs of labour in the industry; while their considerations
were almost always within the structure of hierarchy
already established.

CONCLUSION

In 'Class, Race and Gold', Johnstone describes the class
structure of South African gold-mining in the era leading
up to the 1922 strike in the following terms: (144)
    It comprised two classes differentially related to the
    means of production: a class of owners of the means
    of production ... and a class of workers who, not
    owning means of production, were thereby compelled
    to subsist through selling their labour power to the
    owners in exchange for wages.... Politically, the
    industry was further characterised by a divided
    working class with a small group of politically free
    workers and a large group of politically unfree
    workers, all working in the same industry but subject
    to fundamentally different and unequal political
    relations with the capitalist class employing them.
    ... The industry was made up of members not just of
    two classes but also of two different pigmentation or
    'racial' groups ... related together in a dominational
    system of racial differentiation, operated by the
    'whites' over the 'non-whites'. The 'whites'
    comprised the employees and one group of workers, the
    politically free workers, and the rest of the
    workers, the politically unfree workers, were
    'non-white'.
What we hope to have done here is to have shown
capital's part in forging this structure, on the economic,
political and ideological levels, in the revolutionary
decades 1890-1910. Two forces determined capital's
strategy. On the one hand, there were its twin and
basic interests in the maximisation of surplus extraction

and the minimisation of class conflict. On the other, there were the 'given' historical forces and factors within whose framework capital had to operate. The hierarchy of exploitation was the synthesis of these two dialectically interacting forces; it was initially conceptualised by intellectuals, and forged by capital itself.

In the revolutionary crucible of the class structure, capital's ideologists set out to ensure that the large majority of the labour force was ultra-cheap, and was prevented from realising some of its primary class interests through the insertion of 'pre-capitalist' forms of control into the relations of production themselves. Racism was the ideological expression of the 'overdetermined' subordination of blacks; while on the political level, it was suggested, capital had no need to introduce extraneous controls over blacks because of their subjection to the said 'pre-capitalist' controls; one of the primary incentives to capital to incorporate its working class into the state was removed.

However, capital's relationship to this black proletariat was complicated by the existence of a white and powerful workforce whose potential ability to confront capital had at all costs to be curbed and whose tendency to move out of the sphere of production of surplus value into that of pure supervision ran against capital's interests in maximising its profits. These workers were too powerful to be eliminated and had to be coped with in other ways. Ideologists set out to create an economic and ideological set of structures to this end. Basing their strategy on the nature of the consciousness of the early British craft workers, ideologists created the construct of the 'good', 'respectable', and above all British worker, who did not ally himself with black workers, but who also 'knew his place' to be beneath that of his employers and their managers. He belonged to a 'caste' of his own. That capital was as much the creator as the recipient of this kind of worker was evidenced by the fact that when the nature and consciousness of the white working class began to change, ideologists sought to set up structural means whereby the 'intermediateness' of whites would be maintained.

The functions of the hierarchy which capital thereby created and sustained were most clearly displayed in the labour process itself, where the ultra-exploited black and the intermediate white were put to work together in the 'gang system'. Here productivity was maximised

and class conflict minimised through the ideological
and structural circumscribing of the role of the white
worker - who was forced to remain a producer of surplus
value; and yet was prevented from allying himself with
black workers performing the same function.

The revolutionary nature of these decades was
evidenced by the fact that capital continually considered
possible alterations to the class structure contained
by the hierarchy, particularly when it was confronted
by crisis. It never succeeded in eliminating white
workers, but this did not mean it did not continually
attempt to threaten them with replacement by cheaper
blacks. These threats were not quite the same as
those made after 1910, for they included visions of a
settled, fully proletarianised black labour force, a
black labour aristocracy perhaps, and implied the
stratification of the black working class along a number
of lines. After the Anglo-Boer War, when large numbers of
unemployed, newly proletarianised whites flooded the
Reef, and the industry experienced a labour shortage in
the tens of thousands because black proletarianisation
had been slowed down, a second major alteration to the
class structure was considered - that all workers on
the mines become white. Although some capitalists
considered this seriously, the ideological network was
quick to point out that their higher necessary means of
subsistence and their political call on the state both
rendered white workers undesirable. Whatever the
disadvantages of hierarchy, a shortage of whites was
not one of them. The need for an 'ultra-exploited'
workforce continued to be capital's central concern,
determining all its other class relationships.

The other major alteration in the class structure
proposed at this time was a confirmation of the form, if
not the content, of the hierarchy of exploitation.
Chinese labour, non-white and ultra-cheap, was imported,
and a place was found for it in the stratified working
class. After the Chinese labour left, capital sought
to alleviate its ongoing labour shortage through
productivity drives. The terms in which these were
conducted indicate that capital had not only decided
that the hierarchy must stay, but that it had begun to
make it work in its interests. The 1907 strike may be
interpreted as proof of the effectiveness of the
'organism of production' in containing class conflict
and predetermining the rules within which it took place.

More than one aspect of what we initially defined as
'hegemony' seems to have emerged here. Determining the
rules of class struggle is one clear and perhaps the most

important one. But there is also the fact that capital
seems to have been busy creating ideologies within which
its subordinate classes were to see themselves and the
system of which they were a part. Not only were white
workers part of a hierarchy, but many believed in it as
a just and correct form of social organisation; not only
were black workers ultra-subordinated, but not a few
came to think of themselves as 'only natives'; not only
was capital British in origin, but a great number of
people came to value 'Britishness' as a superior
cultural attribute, while a great number of others,
Afrikaners in particular, came to feel their subordination
to capital in terms of 'national' oppression for this
reason. If any one ideological pattern was common to all
of these aspects of imperial hegemony, then perhaps it
was that of what may slightly inaccurately be called
racism. Cultural, political and racial categories
abounded, and were the chief means by which people of
that time conceived of one another. Workers in the
process of being proletarianised and subordinated to the
demands of capital were all treated as members of one or
another 'race', depending on their place of origin, the
method of their proletarianisation, or other factors.
'Knowing the native', 'understanding the Chinese',
describing the 'characteristics' of Russian Jews,
'assessing' the Afrikaner, and evaluating the British
worker, were typical ideological activities of the time,
and were woven into the overall ideology. Management
practices, productivity demands and a variety of other
problems confronting capital were all contemplated in
terms of the 'races' concerned. We have seen how these
'races' or 'castes' were ordered in specific ways.
Perhaps the mining hierarchy was capital's concession to
the social Darwinism of the time, for the different
races were arranged in descending order from the
ownership of the mine downwards. The hierarchy was
potentially infinite in that it could incorporate any
new category, and could expand within itself,
proliferating its own categories. Self-reproducing and
self-expanding, it constituted a flexible system which
could be used against workers, since the power to
change, expand or contract it lay with the owners of the
means of production
    This chapter has thus explored the second stage in the
mining revolution. In the first stage, capital set out
to capture the state and to assert its dominance over
other modes of production. It would seem that in the
second stage it was concerned not with the skeletal state
apparatuses as much as with the overall state form. It

was now concerned with the ideological state
apparatuses, with the scope of legitimacy, and with the
nature of hegemony, in the captured state.   It sought
to determine the political, ideological and economic
nature of the class structure; the lines of inclusion
and exclusion of workers from the state along racial
lines; the forms in which the legitimation of the
participation of the included workers should be carried
out; and the overall nature and even the detailed
content, of the complex hegemonic ideology.

Thus it would seem that to examine class formation
amongst a class seeking hegemony is to examine more
than simply those factors which determine its relationship
to other classes in the system of production.   Class
formation in an aspirant hegemonic class seems to have
a great deal to do with state formation in the social
formation as a whole.   If to realise its class interests
capital must attain dominance, then its intellectuals
must assess the wider factors affecting it as a class,
and these include the very nature and form of the state
itself.

3 The seeds of a national bourgeoisie

In spite of its revolutionary nature, what mining
capital brought to Southern Africa was not development,
but a continuation and deepening of the underdevelopment
that its mercantile predecessors had initiated. The
crushing of the Transvaal national bourgeoisie and the
subordination of pre-capitalist modes of production to
the capitalist one were two of the features of mining
underdevelopment examined earlier. A third feature,
which was not explored because it was of only marginal
importance to the tasks of mining ideologists, was the
ongoing and central role of merchant capital. Mining
may have become the foundation for the imperial network
of economic relationships, but import-export commerce
was its central pivot, forming the indispensable link
between the South African and the imperial economies.
It was merchant capital whose business it was to see
to what many regard as the most important feature of
underdevelopment - the prevention of the rise of a
national bourgeoisie - through its monopoly of the
import-export trade. 'Free trade' - defined as the
unrestricted entry of foreign, mainly British, goods
into the South African colonies - was the means whereby
local manufacturers were prevented from entering the
competitive market. Even during the 1890s, before
capital's hegemony was entrenched, the workings of this
system of imperial trade can be seen in the example of
mining machinery, potentially one of the most profitable
arenas for the growth of national capital. As early as
1893, the 'Standard and Diggers' News' described how
makers of mining machinery complained that: (1)
    many Boards are little better than unacknowledged
    agents for certain machinery makers, and that 'no
    others need apply'.... Sufficient proof has been
    given us that the grievance is not unfounded, and

to suggest very strongly that the ordering of
machinery in certain quarters has come to be a cut
and dried perquisite; that in many cases the
shareholder pays through the nose for it; and that
a trade that might be a benefit to the land generally,
were justice done to the local man, is being taken
away from him and placed with a high hand in certain
restricted channels that benefit the few and deprive
the many.

In 1894, the journal 'The Critic' undertook to expose
the monopoly in mining machinery which was indeed run
by mining magnates and their connections with British
firms, whether producers or commercial traders. (2)   In
fact, in most of the major sectors of the new market,
small local manufacturers were completely excluded by
mining and commerce from participation in the system
being imposed upon South Africa as a whole.   One irate
manufacturer wrote to the 'Standard and Diggers' News'
in 1894 complaining of this: (3)

It is in vain that manufacturers here endeavour to
do business with the large importers, probably
because most of the import houses are supported
by larger foreign ones, where they have long and
almost unlimited credit, and for other reasons
known to themselves. The welfare of colonial
affairs and trade does not disturb them, for they
are guided by a short-sighted, money-seeking policy.

After the Anglo-Boer War, these structures of underdevelopment were consolidated.   In December 1903, the
'SA Mines' reported that between 1893 and 1903 South
Africa had moved from being sixth of Britain's
customers to being second (to India).   Imports from
Britain had risen from £9m to £26m. (4)   A new tariff
policy was introduced, and a Bluebook on South African
Trade issued in that year outlined the great potential
fields for the expansion of British exports - mining
equipment, mine stores, railway expansion, construction
and public works were the chief of these - while it
outlined a system of advice for British manufacturing
firms on how to improve their competitiveness in South
Africa. (5)   Thus it seems clear that there was no logical
and necessary path from the establishment of mining
to the full industrialisation of South Africa.   The
interests of mining and commerce together lay in the
preservation of the structures of imperial trade, and
of the underdevelopment implied thereby.

However, Southern Africa's political economy was a
peculiar hybrid, a cross between the 'white dominions'
of Canada, New Zealand, Australia and earlier the United

States; the Latin American systems with their surviving
'feudal' forms; and the more typical contemporary African
underdeveloped systems. As was remarked upon earlier,
Southern Africa's capitalist revolution involved, not
two, not even three, but no less than four distinct
social and economic systems: the nineteenth century was
dominated by pre-capitalist subsistence agriculture
(as in many African countries); semi-feudal agricultural
and political forms (as in Latin America), and merchant
capital (as in the 'dominions'). Into these three
varied systems entered the fourth remarkable force - the
particularly large, and particularly devouring, imperial
mining industry. The four-dimensional revolution that
resulted has already been shown to have had quite
exceptionally complex consequences in the formation of
class, state and ideology. Further complexities emerge
when it comes to the ability of the resulting system
to sustain itself. Great contradictions arose within
it, partly as a result of its inability to destroy
completely the preceding systems, and it is with one of
those contradictions that this chapter is concerned.
    This contradiction consisted of the fact that in
spite of its interest and short-term successes in doing
so, imperial capital was, in the long term, unable to
prevent the rise of a national bourgeoisie in South
Africa. In the Cape, Natal and the Transvaal precisely
at the time when imperial hegemony was being consolidated,
small manufacturers were struggling to establish
themselves as a class with interests opposed to those
of imperial capital, while farmers, traders and even
white workers supported them. South Africa's first
national bourgeoisie was not, as popular belief would
have it, an Afrikaner-led one, based on the 'Boer', semi-
feudal modes of production, however. These small
producers and their trading counterparts, were quite
clearly English-speakers and preceded the Afrikaner
bourgeoisie by several decades. Like the national
capitalists of Australia, New Zealand, Canada and the
USA, these petty-bourgeois industrialists arose out of,
and in spite of, the mercantile British imperialism that
had preceded and now accompanied the hegemony of mining
capital. Here we ask how this class came into being,
and what its central interests were, once again entering
the field of class formation; what the ideological
and political implications were thereof; how the
contradiction between this class of national capitalists,
and the imperial capital that it opposed, came to be
expressed on all three levels of class formation and in
the social formation as a whole; and what form of

'hegemony' over subordinate classes and in relation
to the state South African national capital would require
it to oust imperial capital. In this chapter these
questions are confined to the period before any
fundamental changes took place in the system of imperial
domination, for the period during which national capital
underwent the processes of class formation was a period
of opposition and struggle on its part, and must be
interpreted as such, if the nature and significance
of its ideology is to be understood.

In conventional views of the history of local capital,
its development has been depicted as the result of the
protection introduced by the Labour-Nationalist Pact
Government in 1925. When they have been examined at all,
local capitalists have been seen as the passive recipients
of a change in policy brought about through the removal of
the anti-protectionist mining party from political
power. (6) However, an embryonic local bourgeoisie
existed long before 1925, and fought actively and hard
for the protection it required to expand and become
stable. In 1904 manufacturing capital possessed a
surprisingly substantial and widespread economic basis.
There were 4,778 factories in the four colonies of South
Africa, which together produced goods valued at the high,
and probably inflated, figure of £19.3m. (7) Local
industries, which processed local agricultural products
or imported raw or semi-processed materials, had multiplied under the stimulus of the natural protection
afforded by the Anglo-Boer War. Based largely in the Cape
and Transvaal, (8) most of the industries were small and
relatively under-capitalised, (9) with certain notable
exceptions such as those of brewing, distilling, tobacco
and sugar. In spite of the fact that many of them had to
spend much of their time trying to keep their economic
heads above water, (10) the owners of these industries did
not lack ideological vigour and articulateness, from the
earliest years of their existence. (11) But the stimula-
tion they had received by the Anglo-Boer War was greater
than at any previous time, and the fear of bankruptcy
through vulnerability to overseas competition correspondingly more widespread particularly when the post-war
depression loomed; while the British victory, and the
subsequent hopes for a united, stable and above all,
capitalist, South Afirca raised the hopes of manufacturers
for their own future.

For a combination of reasons, therefore, it was after the
Anglo-Boer War that manufacturers began to identify with
one another between colonies, to make their point of view
more widely known, forming the nucleus of an embryonic

national, as opposed to regional or imperial,
bourgeoisie. The first decade of the century saw a
flurry of ideological and organisational activity amongst
manufacturers and those who supported them. A widespread
and complex class-based ideological network - with, as we
shall see, the same dual ideological and strategic
functions as the mining one had performed - was being
created. In the Cape, the South African Manufacturers'
Association, formed during the 1890s, underwent a
revival in 1904; and in 1906 the 'Cape Times' ran a
series of articles on Colonial Industries. (12)   In 1907
the Transvaal Manufacturers' Association was formed
and said to have 53 members, (13) while the Cape
Association launched its official journal, 'South African
Commerce and Manufacturers' Record', whose stated aim
was 'to advocate and support a legitimate and reasonable
policy of Industrial Development in South Africa'. (14)
Other organisations were formed in that year whose base
was somewhat broader and extended beyond manufacturing:
the South African National Union, for example, was
promoted by eminent and wealthy farmers who saw in
manufacturing a potential market for their products, (15)
while the South African National Alliance was formed
by a combination of farmers, politicians, manufacturers
and commercial men with one of its stated objects that
of promoting 'the spirit of national patriotism with a
view to eradicating the existing prejudice against South
African products and manufacturers'. (16)   The Colonial
Industries Protectionist League was also formed in
1907, (17) while in London Sir Pieter Bam, who had been
instrumental in an exhibition to promote South African
products, formed the South African Organisation Union,
to encourage British-South African trade.
      Furthermore, the South African Native Affairs
Commission, the coming elections in the various colonies
and the Bloemfontein Intercolonial Customs Conference
had all encouraged manufacturers to express their
viewpoint. As the 'SAC' editorial commented: (18)
      A feeling in favour of supporting Colonial industries
      is now manifesting itself all over the country, and
      proposals are being made to establish organisations
      which will pledge their members to use only colonial
      products and manufactures as far as possible. This
      feeling is so spontaneous, widespread and strong,
      that we begin to think we are on the eve of important
      developments which when complete, will be found to
      have altered the fiscal policy of the whole
      sub-continent.
Even the mining industry joined the industrialisation

bandwagon, admittedly less because it wished to create
a national bourgeoisie than because it needed urgently
to reduce the cost of living, and its ideologists went
through a brief spell during which they thought
incorrectly, (as they were soon to discover) that
protective tariffs would do so. (19)

Ideologists identified the primary economic need
of their national bourgeois 'audience' as being
protective tariffs for their goods, such as other white
settler areas such as Canada, Australia and New Zealand,
had already obtained. Protected from cheap overseas
competition, local industries could develop a market of
their own. In South Africa, what little protection
there was had been instituted by farming interests, or
as a means of raising revenue, and was perceived by
manufacturers as being irrational and insufficient for
their purposes; John Rothes pointed out that South
African industries were 'backward' because of: (20)

> the hesitating and uncertain policy pursued in
> regard to protection by public opinion and by
> successive Governments. The want of a firm,
> settled policy is one of the principle causes of
> the backward state of most of our industries.
> Up-to-date and progressive manufacturing requires
> large outlays of capital in plant, and manufacturers
> could scarcely be expected to sink thousands of
> pounds in machinery which might be at any moment
> rendered useless, through the withdrawal of the
> little protection which had only justified its
> purchase and installation. But let the country
> commit itself definitely to this policy, and our
> industries will at once make large strides in
> development.

From the point of view of the ultimate establishment and
entrenchment of South Africa as a truly bourgeois state,
protection was an infrastructural component which
imperial capital could not, in its own interests,
institute. It became the central concern and rallying
call of manufacturing and other 'national-bourgeois'
ideologists, particularly in the 1900s.

Just as had been the case with mining, manufacturing
capital needed to be informed of its own best interests
and how to act upon them, being unable to reach a
spontaneous understanding thereof alone. As Rothes said,
the problem of many manufacturers was that they did not
fully understand the economics of their cause and the
nature and incidence of protection they required. It was
for the ideologist to inform them of these matters and
place them in a suitable ideological matrix. W.J. Laite

was the dominant figure amongst the two dozen or so
important manufacturing ideologists of the early part of
the century. He arrived in South Africa in 1901,
providing the sector with an organiser and ideologist
precisely when it needed one. He started the 'SAC',
and the local Eastern Cape Manufacturers Association,
encouraged the Transvaal Association, and in 1908
became secretary of the Cape Association. (21) As a
journalist and paid official, he could devote most of his
time to the cause of manufacturing, and as a result
attained a high degree of ideological sophistication.

Although there were several other ideologists of
manufacturing, they were usually less committed to the
role. The group was as yet too small to afford to
sustain many full-time thinkers and organisers. Large
and wealthy manufacturers tended to articulate
manufacturing interests in their roles as public figures.
But it was the small man whose horizons were most
limited, because of the absence of the protective tariff,
and whose ideas were least tainted by those of the already
existing British South African ideology. The ideologists,
of whom Laite was an example, who sought their audience
amongst the petty-bourgeoisie first and the large
manufacturers second, were not well-known outside
manufacturing circles. But their ideas were original
and their activities creative. Thus not only was the
national bourgeoisie to be led by the manufacturers
within it, but manufacturers themselves were to be led
by the petty-bourgeoisie within their ranks.

During these early years of embryonic consciousness,
ideologists tried first to communicate to their
audience a clear self-definition. This process is
particularly interesting to us, since mining ideologists
had not needed to carry it out on this rudimentary
level, the process of class formation amongst mineowners
having been initiated at Kimberley. By outlining life
histories, discussing the origins of, and analysing
the present position of, individual manufacturers
whenever they were able, ideologists conveyed to their
audience an impression of who their fellow-protectionists
and allies were. These biographies provide a valuable
source for us as well as a foundation for a sense of
class unity. From them it emerges that the small
manufacturer was a petty-bourgeois, whose capital had
been acquired from small trading or savings from a
skilled artisanship. James Sanderson's life story
provided a model for his fellows of good, pioneering
behaviour. It seems he acquired his initial capital
in the mercantile milieu of the diamond fields, then in

about 1887 he: 'left the Diamond Fields and moved to Cape
Town where he started in business as a harness and saddle
manufacturer in a small way'. He was close to his
employees: 'Both in Kimberley and in Cape Town,
Mr. Sanderson, in the early days of his business, worked
side by side with his men and no doubt the knowledge thus
gained gave him that sympathetic understanding which so
endeared him to his employees.' He was quick to
mechanise, being 'one of the first to instal steam and
electric power, and he never hesitated to scrap
existing machinery to make room for the latest types
placed on the market and proved.' He was vulnerable
to wars and depressions; during the war he supplied the
British army with saddles and other leather goods and
his business expanded rapidly. But his firm was one of
those that suffered after the Anglo-Boer War 'when the
slump set in (and) it was found necessary to close down
many of the branches'. Four hundred men were thrown out
of employment, and most of them left South Africa. He
survived because his firm did have some measure of
protection.

   The business expanded and underwent a boom during
the First World War, and the South West African campaign,
when Sanderson's again supplied saddles for the army.
At the time of his death in 1917, Sanderson was planning
expansion throughout Southern Africa and had even opened
a factory in Walsall. Sanderson had a 'great interest',
a 'belief', in 'industrialism in general', and was a
founding member of the Cape Manufacturers Association.
Furthermore, his early closeness to his white employees
meant that: 'As an employer he was held in the highest
esteem, and the relations between the management and
the employees were always of the most cordial,
Mr. Sanderson exercising an almost patriarchal control
in his establishment of something like 600 employees.'
Sanderson was a 'fine example of a self-made man'. (22)

   Some were from smaller beginnings than Sanderson, (23)
while others were far wealthier. But Sanderson's firm
epitomises the vulnerability of these small industries
to 'outside forces', in spite of which many firms
survived; the consequent image of the manufacturer as a
hardy pioneer; the 'family firm' as a typical pioneering
structure, with the father as the patriarchal innovator
and his sons as the inheritors of both the firm and its
'tradition'; and the petty bourgeois blurring of class
divisions between owners and non-owners of the means of
production. These characteristics of manufacturers
formed the basis for their ideology. Their attitude
towards each other, towards 'outside forces', towards

their employees, the state, the future and the past were
all rooted in their own historical and social situations.
Ideologists built upon manufacturers' own experiences
and lives, their own ambitions, hopes, and, of course,
fears. Although both groups were able, at different
times, to embody the 'spirit of capitalism' in South
Africa, it is difficult to imagine two more different
kinds of capitalists and employers than mineowners and
manufacturers in these early years.

Ideologists attached great importance to the petty-
bourgeois nature of their audience. Using the existing
consciousness of the members of the class as a basis for
its ideology writers of potted biographies in journals
would lay emphasis on the artisan origins of what they
called 'Pioneers of Industry' and would describe how
they had 'risen' through 'perseverance', to become
'self-made men'. The concept of 'pioneer' transcended
the economic and social limits which were placed on
the manufacturer and was a means whereby his vulnerability
to outside forces could be expressed and his 'valiant'
attempts to overcome them encapsulated. It also
included both the past, his origins, and the future, for
the sake of which the 'pioneering' was performed - so
that the two might be linked through 'progress'. The
pioneer moved forward always, from a lowly past to a
future in which all obstacles were overcome and the
outside world was conquered and converted to a
realisation of the worth of his cause.

The 'best' and most successful manufacturers were
therefore naturally those with 'qualities' such as
perseverance, business aptitude, determination and
purposefulness. (24) This was altogether a different
kind of pioneer from the mining pioneer, whose success
had depended upon his subordination to the larger
structure of 'the industry' as a whole, united organic
and of course, monopolistic, entity. The manufacturing
pioneer was an individual and his struggle, while it
might be waged together with other fellow-pioneers, was
an essentially lonely one, requiring proportionately
greater fortitude and self-reliance. This is probably
a typical characteristic of petty-bourgeois ideologies,
being, as they are, based upon a competitive economic
system, and in South Africa as elsewhere forms a
fundamental basis for the later development of a
bourgeois ideology. (25)

The next task of the ideologists was to assist in the
process of consolidating and uniting industrialists as
a leading 'sub-class'. This was an activity which we
were able to observe in early mining. After the initial

post-Anglo-Boer War depression, the groups which had
formed to defend manufacturers' interests persisted and
extended their activities beyond those of protection into
fields such as advocating political Union in South Africa,
or the formation of a specifically manufacturing political
party. They tried unsuccessfully to unite local
manufacturers' associations, (26) but found at first that
conflicts of interest between the colonies on the issues
of labour costs and railway rates were greater than the
common interest upon which unity could be built. (27)
In spite of these and other differences of interest
between manufacturers, they did succeed in meeting to
discuss common problems in 1909, 1911 and 1912, in
what came to be known as the 'Industrial Parliament',
and were seen to constitute a united and increasingly
powerful pressure group. Laite wanted them to be even
more united and moreover to act together politically, in
spite of regional differences: 'The ideal action of the
manufacturing interests would be to form a definite
political organisation with its own propaganda and its
own candidates.' (28)

Soon after the first Union election the Botha
government responded to manufacturing pressure by
appointing a Commission of Enquiry into industries. (29)
In response to its 'halfhearted' support for protection,
(30) in 1913 Laite published an important statement of
the manufacturers' case, (31) and later in the year a
'Great Producers Congress' was held, where manufacturers
and agriculturalists met to discuss their common
interests. State response remained ambiguous.
Manufacturers were to be appeased, not accommodated;
while consistent support was obtained from the old
Het Volk stalwarts of Botha and F.S. Malan, men like
Smuts tended to waver on the issue of protection. (32)

The nature of this situation shaped the response
of ideologists to it. While manufacturers were more
or less united, they had no clear base from which to
work. No political party, economic organisation or
trade union was united on protection, and hence on the
issue of the growth of a national bourgeoisie, and the
wavering of public figures was but a symptom of the
status of the issue in general. Ideologists actively
tried to promote and emphasise the unity of manufacturers
in the face of this hostility and ambiguity. At the
same time as they emphasised the individualism of the
pioneer, they made sure of pointing to and encouraging
the willingness of manufacturers to act together in
their own collective interests. Once an organisation
was formed, its annual reports and minutes became 'our'

property and matters for 'our' interest. If the structure
and limits of the category 'manufacturers' were in doubt
for any reason, the ideologist tended to smooth over
cracks and emphasise cohesion by identifying 'friends' or
'enemies' of the group. (33)
    At the same time, ideologists, working from the
somewhat precarious but developing basis of unity within
the manufacturing sector, attempted to develop specific
strategies towards each hostile, wavering 'outside'
group. Whereas in the case of mining, the 'outside
forces' had been tackled in the form of one overwhelming
evil (the Transvaal state) in the case of manufacturing,
they surrounded the group as individual, structured
obstacles, each of which could and must be overcome.
Here, the activities of ideologists must be divided
into three distinct spheres; the first is the sphere
of class formation itself. Ideologists of the leading
section of the budding national bourgeoisie (manufacturing)
set out to lead and forge class unity across those other
sectors of capital (commerce, agriculture and mining)
that were potentially able to switch from their alliances
with imperial capital. The second sphere was that of the
forging of links across the class barrier with those
sections of labour that capital hoped to use in a
'supportive' role. The third sphere, possibly the
most important, was that in which the national
bourgeoisie's ideologists set out to attack and pose an
alternative to the state form developed under mining's
hegemony.
    An attitude of evangelistic proselytising developed
in each of these spheres. It was maintained that the
'true' interests of each group (i.e. national interests)
were being suppressed by the forces of reaction and
conservatism (i.e. imperial interests). Natural
justice was on the side of protectionists, invariably
the minority, who, given time, would eventually prevail。
Manufacturing ideologists made a correct analysis
of the nature of imperial power, because the first of
the groups to whom this protectionist evangelism was
directed was that of commerce. Not only was commerce
the chief economic and political obstacle to the
development of national capital, but a major ideological
obstacle too. But merchant capital, the oldest
imperial fraction, was divided between the large
importing houses of the Cape, who depended upon imports
of foreign goods into South Africa for their profits,
and the smaller inland traders who, if they had not been
directly controlled by the importing houses, would have
benefited from the development of local industries. (34)

As early as 1909, the Association of Chambers of
Commerce passed a resolution supporting the appointment
of a Commission of Enquiry into local industries, and
into 'the steps which should be taken to encourage the
trade and present industries of this country and the
establishment of new industries'. (35) This protectionist
group was supported by the many manufacturers who
themselves had begun in commerce. (36)

However, in these early years they were overshadowed
by the dominant importing houses of the Cape, which
were owned by eminent and wealthy members of a social
and political elite. The 'merchant princes', such as
Jagger, Cowie and Martin, frequented the exclusive
social clubs of the large cities, and had social, and of
course, economic, imperial ties of great strength. As
a result they were proportionately resented by
manufacturers: (37)

> The majority of men have been educated and trained
> in Great Britain, and in whatever community they
> may be, we find them taking the lead in public affairs.
> In some cases these merchants are looked up to as
> oracles on every question under the sun and their
> influence is almost absolute.

This group, which provided the basis for the social
superiority of the Cape which persists in South Africa
to the present day, opposed protection economically by
preventing store-keepers from trading in locally
produced goods, (38) and by establishing a system of
'tied' retailing; and politically, through the
parliamentary platform they had obtained and entrenched,
and the use of their socially and politically eminent
position. They objected to protection on the grounds
that it would raise the cost of living, (39) by
'pampering' 'bastard industries'. Jagger epitomised the
'Free Trader': (40)

> In his economy, there is only room for three
> communities - the agricultural, the mining and the
> mercantile. Mr. Jagger believes in the 'wisely
> directed assistance of the farmers by the state'
> plus brains and enterprise, and the co-operation of
> the mercantile community in organisation and
> distribution, and in finding new markets for the
> products of the country. But apparently in his
> economy there is no room for the manufacturer, who
> must sink or swim according to circumstances....
> Mr. Jagger's statesmanship is the narrow and
> utilitarian scheme of taking as much as possible
> out of the soil by agriculture and mining and exporting
> the produce to foreign markets.

This basic economic conflict was expressed on the
ideological level - importers used the ideology of
'Free Trade' for their purposes, and manufacturers
countered with expressions of resentment at the
elitism, parasitism, and dogmatism of Free Trade, as
compared to the patriotic, pioneering protectionism
and production of the manufacturer: (41)

> The majority of these men were trained in the free
> trade school, and are still free traders. But they
> show a strange lack of adaptability, and they fail to
> see that their cast-iron principles are unsuited to
> this country. Too often, the manufacturers have
> been flouted, jeered at, and neglected by them, and
> have had to go directly to the retailers for their
> market. They do not seem to recognise the fact
> that if South Africa supplied her own wants from
> her agriculture and industries, their own working
> expenses would be less, their elaborate business
> organisation greatly simplified, and their
> financing easier. But the point to note now, is
> that all their influence has hitherto been directed
> against a policy of protection.

Free Traders are depicted as having 'cast iron principles',
while manufacturers are by implication more flexible
and practical, simply performing their patriotic tasks.
Free Traders are ideological, manufacturers are not.
This ideology of non-ideology, a major theme in later
times, is already strong in manufacturing: 'Free Trade
or Protection is not a moral question at all ... it is
simply a matter of business policy - of national
business policy.' (42)   Free Trade was called a 'worn
out creed'. (43)   Such concepts were appealing to the
audience of worker-producers, who liked to think of
themselves as 'down-to-earth' anti-elitists. Laite
used to provoke his upper-class acquaintances by wearing
evil-smelling South African *velskoene* to meetings. (44)
Manufacturers were considered to be of a lower class
than the rest of employing, English-speaking society,
and their ideology did not attempt to refute this. (45)

Mining capital was included with commercial capital
by manufacturing ideologists. Laite wrote: (46)

> The crux of all opposition to the fostering and
> encouragement of manufacturing industries, and the
> helping of agriculture by the imposition of Protective
> duties, centres in Johannesburg. The Chamber of
> Mines has stated its case most explicitly, and it is
> evident that the opinion holds that every interest
> in the country must be sacrificed to the stated needs
> of the mining community.

Some mining men, such as Samuel Evans, were ardent Free
Traders, (47) but generally the opposition to protection
within the mining industry was not expressed as
frequently or as coherently as it was by commercial
ideologists, although it seems certain that most
mineowners saw protection as an expensive fantasy,
themselves primarily as consumers, and the industrialisation of South Africa as impossible without an
unacceptable increase in their costs: (48)

> The life of the gold mining industry is limited by
> the cost of production. That is to say, if anything
> is done by the manufacturing community to induce
> Government, by means of protective tariffs or
> preferential railway rates, to increase the cost of
> production, owing to the higher cost of mining plant
> and the higher cost of living, then you create a
> condition of affairs by which your gold production
> is limited to a fixed number of dwts. per ton....
> If there is any tendency to increase the cost of
> production, then you are cutting off the life of a
> big industry, and you are limiting that life to a
> basis of 6 dwt. to the ton propositions, which would
> have a very serious effect on the industry and the
> country, generally.

The contradiction between mining and manufacturing
interests was not as fundamental as that between commerce
and manufacturing - for while it was the very existence
of importing houses that depended upon the imperial
connection it was simply the greater profitability of
mining that would be affected by protection. The 'SA
Mines', the voice of local mining, could even admit the
desirability of South African industrialisation, as we
have seen. To the protectionists, therefore, commerce
represented imperialism in South Africa, although
mining underpinned it.

The combined opposition of mining and commerce to
manufacturing, based as it was upon imperial economic
structures and reinforced by political, social and
ideological factors gave manufacturing ideologists
cause to cast their ideology in nationalist, popular
and anti-imperialist tones. We have already seen how
the patriotic production of manufacturers was compared
favourably with the parasitism of commerce. This
patriotic tone was used in relation to mining as well:
'The aim of the Mining Houses is capitalistic control
and the truth of this is being realised at last in all
its nakedness', (49) wrote an ideologist. Laite himself
wrote: (50)

> For years this country has been the plaything of a few

alien mineowners, and they have never shown, as the
late Mr. Rhodes did, that they have in any measure
the interests of the country at heart. The increase
of dividends and the manipulation of the share
market have been the only objects of their solicitude,
and all their acts - public and private - are for the
furtherance of these ends. But one thing is certain,
and that is, that the whole country cannot afford
to be kept in perpetual turmoil by this gold
industry - important though it may be - and that
unless those responsible are content to adopt a
policy of common sense, and remember that the
interests of ,the whole people take precedence of (sic)
the interests of the few, we fear that drastic
measures will have to be taken and all control of the
industry taken out of the hands of those who are
presently responsible.

Rhodes in the Cape, and Botha and Smuts in the Transvaal,
were preferred to the 'capitalistic' mineowners: (51)

It is better to keep our own capital and our own
labour employed than to keep the capital and labour
of other countries employed.... It is better to
keep our money in use and circulation among ourselves
than to send it abroad in exchange for commodities
which we can make as well at home.

It was the interests of South Africa that manufacturing
ideology claimed to uphold, in contrast to the commercial
and mining concern with their own or with imperial
interests. Thus here we find the first major component
of the ideology called here South Africanism - its
anti-imperial and anti-elitist origins in the early
protectionism of the small businessman.

Nascent capitalist agriculture was distinguished by
manufacturers from imperial commerce and mining; it was
here that a greater potential for an alliance existed
than in any other capitalist sector at the time. However,
agriculture too was divided between pro- and anti-
protectionists, and it too was treated in an evangelical
manner by South African ideologists. Not only did
farmers possess a considerable amount of political and
economic power in a still predominantly agricultural
region, hence making them important allies, but they
also had interests in protection which objectively
coincided with those of manufacturers.

However, agriculture was divided in manufacturers'
eyes between landowners, and agriculturalists proper. The
interests of 'landowning monopolists', as H.P. Gordon
wrote in one article, lay in 'locking up' large areas
of land; while objectively those of the 'industry of

agriculture' lay, or should lie, in developing a local
market, and the enlargement of the white population. The
forces with greatest control over the farming interest
did not acknowledge or realise this and consistently
opposed protection: (52)

> At intervals, and usually when the country was passing
> through a period of depression, the manufacturers would
> manage to obtain a hearing, and occasionally secured
> a little mitigation of their lot. But as soon as
> the depression passed away, the farmers and the
> commercial representatives combined gaily in
> revising the tariff and managed to deprive the
> unfortunate manufacturers of what they had so hardly
> gained.... If the farming classes would only pause
> to consider the question, they would at once see
> that a policy of protection for South African
> industries, while being just and equal treatment
> to the industrial population would also materially
> benefit themselves.

Time and again this failure of agriculture to recognise
'its own interests' was attributed to the hold over the
sector of the 'landed aristocracy', or monopolists.
Laite wrote of how: 'the aristocracy of the land is
very old, very conservative, and very insistent upon its
rights', (53) while in 1913, at the time of the miners'
strike, he declared that in South Africa, it is 'not
democracy which rules, but the landed aristocracy,
which would defend its interests with a strong hand if
it were threatened'. (54)

More than was the case with mining or commerce,
manufacturers wished to emphasise the potential for an
alliance between farming and manufacturing. In fact,
representatives of the 'landed interest', such as Botha,
F.S. Malan and other eminent farming men, as we have
seen, had actively promoted industries and contributed
in their own way to the new ideology particularly through
the formation of the South African National Union. In
1908, for example, F.S. Malan had actually used the
phrase 'South Africanism' in the 'Yearbook' of SANU: (55)

> The South African National Union embodies a young
> and vigorous South Africanism, a South Africanism
> which is animated by the highest patriotic sentiments
> as well as by a practical spirit; South Africa cannot
> be the home of a happy and prosperous people unless
> all animosities are buried and South Africans become
> more self-supporting, and consequently more self-
> respecting.

This, indeed, was a potential power-base for
manufacturing. Farmers, in a fully industrialised system,

would have a bigger market than ever before for their
products, in the form of industries processing fruit,
animal products and grains, and, of course, by
encouraging the development of a consumer population. (56)

This had far-reaching ideological implications. Since
most farmers were Afrikaners, any alliance between
farming and manufacturing would have to involve an
alliance across the barriers of the divisions between
English-speaker and Afrikaner in the region. As is
evident from the F.S. Malan statement, South Africanism
could not conceive of this alliance in terms other than
those of 'consensus'. There thus developed a strong
'anti-racialist' tone to the ideology, race being
defined at the time in terms of these sorts of
divisions: (57)

> racial quarrels must be avoided like the plague if the
> Act of Union is to spell peace, progress and
> prosperity, and if the declarations of the Opposition
> leaders are sincere they will join hands with the
> government in thwarting any attempt to revive the
> dying feud between Dutch and British members of
> the new South African brotherhood

wrote Laite in 1910. This South Africanist idea was
reinforced by the attitude, discussed below, of
manufacturing capitalists towards the white working
class. It could not have contrasted more vividly with
the anti-'Boer' racism of the mining ideology, and yet
it could not be said to be an 'Afrikaner' ideology in
any sense of the term, but remained the ideology of a
class led and dominated by English-speakers, as the
more radical of Afrikaner nationalists were later to
point out.

Just as mining hegemony had been the result of a
compromise with the existing social formations, so
national capital had to forge its ideology and strategy
in terms partly dictated for it by imperial hegemony
itself. Ideologists of manufacturing worked in the
shadow of British South Africanism and had to counteract
it on every level. Because of the similarities of
interest between the two classes as employers and
capitalists, their spheres of activity coincided, although
their ambitions for South Africa diverged. Both
employed white and black workers while both were
anxious to establish their hegemony over the state.
But mining's system of class relationships and its
overall state form possessed features which the national
bourgeoisie could not tolerate.

Manufacturing ideologists argued that mining's system
of white worker control was caste-like, manipulative and

confrontationalist, for example, whereas the petty-
bourgeois manufacturer who might himself have started
as a skilled artisan, or working and living very close
to his white employees, had a basic sympathy for white
workers: 'out of our present situation it has come
about that there has been begotten a sullen class hatred
which is quite as acute here in democratic South Africa
as under the most despotic forms of government in
Europe', (58) ran one 'SAC' editorial. Instead of being
a place for conflict and confrontation, industry should
be:

> a true meeting place of labour and capital, in which
> they become the most potent factors in ensuring
> the progress and stability of every great nation'. (59)

The manufacturer's approval of the 'dignity of labour'
was of a different sort from that of the mineowner - it
sprang from his own experiences. (60) This was not
simply a result of the artisan origins of manufacturers,
but had roots in the basic need for manufacturing as a
fraction to woo, not antagonise, its white employees.
White workers were also consumers, voters and potential
political allies. Whereas imperial capital resisted
and even feared a large, white working class, national
capital could not afford to entertain such fears. After
the 1913 miners' strike, Laite wrote of Smuts: (61)

> the recent industrial upheaval has got on the
> Minister's nerves. He knows that the introduction
> of an adequate protective tariff would mean the
> advent of new industries which would necessitate
> the importation of skilled artisans and their
> families from overseas, and apparently he fears
> that such a step would ultimately strengthen the
> Labour Party - a contingency he is not prepared
> to face.

But white labour too was split on the issue of
protection. In 1907, H.W. Sampson, of the Typographical
Union, spoke at a meeting of the Transvaal Manufacturers'
Association in favour of protection for industries
which meant the employment of more whites; in 1912,
the Labour Party was divided, in the words of the 'SAC',
between a 'militant Free Trade section' and
protectionists. White labour was therefore yet another
object of manufacturing ideologists' evangelising
attentions: 'How the Labour Party proposes to harmonise
its advocacy of a minimum wage with a policy of
unrestricted competition with low-wage proletariats
of other countries is inconceivable.' (62) An increased
white population was something to be striven for: 'The
establishment of industries is the only perfect solution

of the question of how to find employment for all who are
willing to work - the only true means of securing the
residence in a new country of a desirable permanent
population.' (63)   A further reason for their professed
support for white workers lay in the fact that the
flourishing of local industries required a local
consumer market, while imperial capital, particularly
gold-mining, did not.   The ideological horizons of the
employer expanded to include his workers as consumers
of his products, while another social group hitherto
almost entirely ignored by ideologists of capitalism in
its various forms - women - came to be embraced within
the concept of 'consumers' or the 'general public'. (64)

Working from the sympathy that the petty-bourgeois
manufacturer felt for white workers, ideologists
developed a fully rounded ideology of conciliation.   The
existence of a class difference between worker and
employer was acknowledged; but ideologists denied that
it was based on conflict: (65)

> the average fair-dealing manufacturer is too often
> misled into believing that the archfoes of his progress
> are they of his own household.... The mechanic and
> factory hands of today are sufficiently educated to
> realise that to so hamper a good master as to
> eventually effect his ruin, and the closing up of
> his business, would be also disastrous to their
> immediate interests, but that by doing their best to
> help on and increase the business, they are also
> improving their own prospects of advancement.

The manufacturing enterprise did not place barriers
between employers and workers, but encouraged an
identity of interest between them, in which it was
important for workers to believe. (66)   Ideologists
extended the pioneering ideas of social mobility and
identity of interest between capital and labour.
Confrontationalism must be rejected whatever the
temptations: (67)

> The master in nearly every case makes the man.   Display
> to your servant selfishness, want of consideration
> and disregard for his comfort and general welfare,
> and he pays you back in your own coin.   To get
> consideration, you must give consideration.... Working
> men and women nowadays are not the vassals working for
> the right to live they once were.   With education
> spreading, the workers of today are thinkers, with
> hopes and ambitions in life such as the workers of a
> century ago were incapable of.   The turner at your
> lathe might be the Prime Minister of your country
> in a few years.

In 1915 an article in the 'SAC' argued that 'Loyalty in Business' was important: (68)

> even though its sole function were to secure united
> action on the part of the officers and men. Where
> no two men or groups of men are working to counter
> purposes, but all are united in a common purpose,
> the gain would be enormous.... Such loyalty is always
> reciprocal. The feeling which workmen entertain of
> their employer is usually a reflection of his own
> attitude towards them. Fair wages, reasonable hours,
> working quarters and conditions of average comfort
> and healthfulness, and a measure of protection against
> accident are no more than primary requirements in a
> factory or store.

While in mining the kind of loyalty ideologists wished to exact had been that of well-treated inferiors, in manufacturing it was that of men 'united in a common purpose' with their employers. Workers were not destined to remain inferior but were supposed to be able to redeem their inferiority through a recognition of the avenues for 'advancement' opened to them when and if they identified with their employers. Ideologists also rejected the 'double-bind' which mining had placed upon white workers. There white workers were themselves restricted from upward movement, and were in turn threatened from below by the potential upward movement of cheaper black workers; but manufacturing ideologists acknowledged that true 'loyalty' from white workers would not be possible unless the continual threat to them from black workers was lessened. As early as 1911, Laite advocated a minimum wage for coloured workers: 'The white worker has his wages maintained at a certain level, and the fear of being undercut is eliminated.' (69) Ideologists predisposed employers to accept such measures as part of the price they would have to pay for the more general support of white workers in future years.

In the early years, white workers in manufacturing did not approach the degree of organisation of white mineworkers, and tended not to confront their employers. Manufacturing ideologists' experiences of worker organisation tended to be vicarious - most pre-First-World-War comments on strikes, with some notable exceptions, were on miners' strikes. This, of course, made it possible for them to articulate the ideology of tolerance relatively unrestrainedly. In the white miners' strike of 1907, the 'SAC' supported the white workers and opposed the mineowners' plans for reducing the numbers of whites, describing the workers as 'miserable, misled men, hopelessly beaten' who had

fallen 'into the pit that had been dug for them' by
mineowners. (70) By the time of the 1913 miners' strike,
however, their attitude had changed. It had become clear
that white worker organisation was not to be confined
to mining forever; the strikers had tried to encourage
a general strike. The ideology of conciliation was
forced into a more repressive mould than that in which
it had originated: (71)

> Most of the leaders are miners; they are acquainted
> with the conditions of mining, but they are ignorant
> of the economic conditions governing other branches
> of national enterprise, and they attempt to apply
> to all enterprises in South Africa the same
> truculent defiance they have adopted to the mining
> houses.

Instead of this 'truculent defiance' in the form of a
direct and unregulated confrontation with employers and
even the state, ideologists were quick to suggest the
development of regulated and state-controlled and
legitimated channels of grievance. White workers'
'ignorance of economic conditions governing other
branches of national enterprise' referred to the absence
of these channels and the consequent increased likelihood
of direct confrontation. Not only did workers show an
undesirable 'truculent defiance' but they stepped
outside the bounds which imperial hegemony had set for
them:

> They go further, and it is on record that they have
> been guilty of making overtures to native labour
> to join with them, while at the same time denouncing
> the right of citizens to protect their lives and
> property through a revolutionary principle of
> treating special constables as 'scabs'. Here are
> two examples of dangerous and criminal teaching
> utterly in conflict with the traditional policy
> of the people of South Africa; in themselves quite
> sufficient to stamp the labour leaders as worthless
> guides. In a country where the natives outnumber
> the whites by six to one, the policy has been to keep
> the natives outside the relations existing between
> the different sections of the white population, racial
> or industrial, but the labour leaders not only broke
> that salutary rule, but they attempted at the same
> time to terrorise the whites by a presumptuous
> declaration against special constables.

It is clear that ideologists were already concerned
with developing a structure for the regulation of white
worker power and resistance. As in mining's hegemonic
system, white and black workers were to be prevented

from developing class unity; beyond that, national
capital was concerned with matters which imperial
capital had only marginally considered.

Thus one of the first recommendations of the 'SAC'
in relation to the 1913 strike was: 'we strongly urge
that employers should organise quite as thoroughly
as labour with a view to defend their interests in case
labour attempts to dragoon the public.' More often,
manufacturing ideologists turned to the state. Under
imperial hegemony the state's role in labour conflicts
tended to be entirely coercive, as for example in the
1913, 1922 and other strikes. National capital
considered that the state should create apparatuses
to regulate the relationship between capital and labour
in an ideological and legal manner as well as the
existing coercive one. This would indeed be an
alteration to the existing state form. As the 'SAC'
wrote in 1914: (72)

> Coercive or drastically repressive legislation is no
> panacea. The solution ... will be found in an
> elimination of political fraud from the conduct
> of government, and the introduction of curative and
> conciliatory legislation which shall provide the
> necessary machine for removing real grievances and
> adjusting differences where such are found to exist.
> The purpose of the state is to develop social unity
> and whilst safeguarding the rights of all, there
> must be a due recognition of the duties and
> responsibilities pertaining to citizenship.

As early as 1908, the journal had recommended the
establishment of a Ministry for Labour, (73) while in
1909, apropos of the recent Natal railway strike, one
ideologist had pointed out the need for arbitration and
conciliation legislation, since in none of the colonies
was there any act to deal with strikes and lockouts. (74)
In 1911, H.P. Gordon advocated the establishment of
Wages Boards, which, as he pointed out, had in Australia
'proved a most effective means for the prevention of
strikes'. (75)

In pre-war years these remained only suggestions, but
their future importance was to be substantial. Workers
must submit to the legitimacy which was developed and
approved for them by ideologists of their employers. The
1913 miners' strike once more provoked the ideologist
into an explicit statement of this: (76)

> The labour leaders posed as dictators. They
> endeavoured to set up a new authority which would
> intervene between the state and the Peoples'
> Parliament and issued ultimatums demanding that

Government should surrender its functions. There
could be only one answer to such an imperious demand,
and the paramount political interest made the answer
by at once calling upon the strength of organised
society to repel the assault of organised
syndicalism. [The leaders] ... were provoking an
irresistible force. They, a comparatively small
body in a pastoral country drawing its labour from
native supplies, deliberately provoked a trial of
strength with the dominant class; provoked the
trial in such a way that the challenge had to be
taken up, and as a result they were crushed by the
first stirring of huge forces.

Perhaps it is unnecessary to point out that in this
sphere no less than in the sphere of mining, white
workers did not always, or even usually conform to the
pattern set for them - or not yet.

In two crucial respects manufacturing ideologists
initially accepted the structures, if not the spirit,
of mining hegemony. They were the basic issues of the
exclusion of blacks from the legitimate state and of
the unacceptability of any unity between the black
working class and the white working class. Blacks were
objects of policy to manufacturing ideologists as they
had been to mining. 'The native question' was a frequent
issue for discussion in manufacturing journals whose
concern was whether or not blacks were a 'menace' or
could be prevented from becoming one. In 1908, for
example, the 'SAC' ran an article on Natal: 'The people
of Natal have been living for years upon a volcano which
might be expected to burst into eruption at any moment,
and spread desolation and death throughout the whole
colony. We refer, of course, to the Native question.' (77)
In a series on 'The Commercial Aspect of Closer Union'
in the same year, the journal wrote of how: (78)

the only serious stumbling block to Closer Union,
lies in the difficulty of evolving a policy which shall
be satisfactory to all regarding the political status
to be accorded to the native races and Asiatics,
and the lines upon which their future development
is to proceed.

However, in this as in other examples, it was clear that
manufacturing rightly considered itself too small and
powerless to have much influence over so crucial an issue.
Hence it was discussed more as an external than an
internal problem - with none of the commitment, vitality
and ideological creativity which pervaded mining journals
on the subject.

The issue of the undesirability of white-black working-

class unity was treated with more passion and invective.
Whereas in the mining system it had been coped with
through 'caste', here it needed to be made compatible
with the system of collaboration between white workers
and capital which ideologists were developing. This
led to an ideological structure which was more classically
'racist' than the mining one had been - for blacks were
separated from white employers and workers virtually
entirely on grounds of their race. Appeals to the ideas
of 'purity' and hierarchy were virtually absent from
manufacturing ideology: '[the natives are] as a rule
of splendid physique and vitality. They are the
country's hewers of wood and drawers of water, and for
them work must be found', ran one article. White
mobility and unity, rather than the maintenance of pure
hierarchical forms, was seen as the means of preserving
this: 'the most we can hope for today is to develop
the best side of the white race and keep the natives
under control, and to this end industries should be
encouraged to apprentice white labour and train boys
in the high arts of industry so as to maintain
supremacy.' (79) However, here too blacks involved a
major contradiction which was compounded by the
existence of a white working class. While as workers
and the unenfranchised, blacks could be coped with in
racist terms, for manufacturing they were also consumers,
and this presented a problem. Blacks in the early years,
and in the absence of the 'large and contented' white
population manufacturers advocated, were major
private consumers of the region. The epithet 'kaffir
goods' or 'truck' was frequently applied to South
African-made products for this reason. Thus in 1911,
the 'SAC' virulently opposed Creswell's all-white
labour policy not only because 'South Africa can never,
in the full sense of the word, become a white man's
country such as New Zealand undoubtedly is' (80) because
of the existence of 6 million 'natives', but because:
'storekeepers throughout would suffer, and hundreds
dependent upon the sale of 'Kaffir truck' to the
natives would be swept out of existence commercially.' (81)
Manufacturers' relationships with the 'periphery'
were real and substantial and could not be conceived of
in an ideological void. An interconnected network of
suppliers and stores covered the country and the region,
(82) while producers were themselves scattered amongst
their black consumers. Everywhere that blacks earned
or were in possession of cash was a potential market
for manufacturers: 'who earn the bulk of the millions
of wages in South Africa? Ask Kimberley, ask

Johannesburg, ask every farmer ... and he will tell you
his workman is the native.' (83) In South Africa, as
elsewhere, manufacturing possessed the two contradictory
imperatives of requiring a cheap labour force, while at
the same time requiring an ever-expanding market, which
may be obtained through exports, the payment of higher
wages, or the alteration of values in its own workforce.
     Their social, geographical and economic proximity
to blacks, and their dependence on them for a consumer
market, led manufacturing ideologists to modify the
'centre-periphery' ideas about black rural worthlessness
and urban ultra-exploitability. On the one hand, this
led to a reinforcement of the kind of racism described
above - for if black repression was to be less harsh,
then white superiority would have to rely on 'natural
superiority'. On the other hand, it led to a more
consistent and thorough advocacy of the kinds of
'tolerant' policies towards blacks which mining
ideologists only advocated rarely: (84)

> The skilled white worker will remain supreme in
> his own fields of industry, but that does not mean
> that the coloured worker is to be excluded. A
> prosperous, self-respecting and industrious
> coloured or black man is a good citizen, and the
> only sane solution of the coloured problem is that
> policy or system which advances the coloured man
> to the status of a good citizen whether he be
> engaged in the industrial, agricultural or mining
> field.

In spite of their exclusion from participation in the
state apparatuses themselves, blacks should be
encouraged to develop loyalty, become 'good citizens': (85)

> First, the native should be justly treated, and his
> interests properly looked after by Government. At
> present he lives under laws he does not thoroughly
> understand, and when he looks to the laws to protect
> him he finds both they and himself helpless against
> some Peruvian swindler, cute enough to evade any law,
> or to invoke its aid for his own acts of oppression.
> In Cape Colony little of this fleecing of Natives
> occurs, because it is not tolerated by Government.
> Secondly, some modification of the present policy
> of dealing with the Native Territories must be
> sought. At present the tribes have little or no
> sense of the power of the Government or of their
> responsibility towards it.... Today they have less
> respect for Government than they had twenty years ago.

This sort of paternalism, later to be a hallmark of the
fully-fledged South Africanist ideology, must be

distinguished from mining repression.

The sphere of the state represents the area of
greatest significance of national capital's budding
ideology. Manufacturing ideologists needed to work
towards the creation of a form of state suited to the
needs of the fully-industrialised capitalist economy
that their interests demanded, with all the problems
of class conflict that this implied. The state ideology
is examined last because not only was it built upon the
various economic and ideological interests which have
already been analysed, but its overall purpose was to
capture and transcend them so that the 'state' became
synonymous with 'the nation' and 'society' and both
with capitalism itself. The state was no longer to be
confined to its apparatuses, repressive and ideological,
as it had been under imperial hegemony, but was now
to expand to become identified with what some have
called 'civil society'. The basic class structure of
the future capitalism, as perceived and depicted by the
ideologists of its manufacturing vanguard, would have
to be three-fold: first it would have to unite all the
different forms of capital in a recognition of their
common class interests. Farmers, mineowners and commerce
would have to join manufacturers in the realisation that
national capital must replace imperial capital. Second,
it would have to incorporate the white working class
as a 'supportive class', which would have to give up
its consciousness of itself as deprived or underprivileged
in relation to capital for a recognition of their
common interest in national capitalism. Third, it
would have to balance the non-incorporation of the black
working class in the actual political institutions
which the future state would possess, with the need
for their compliance with the overall production and
consumption mechanisms of the economy and the legitimacy
of the governmental system which it set up. It was
this three-fold class structure that the new capitalist
state would have to defend, were national capital to
oust imperial capital and its state form.

The co-existence of these three structural requirements
was reflected in the ideological constructions which were
developed by manufacturing ideologists in relation to the
state, both as a system of 'apparatuses' and as 'civil
society'. First, the very purpose, or 'duty' of states
was: 'to develop their various countries by encouraging
immigration, settling people on the land, and fostering
developing industries. There the end in view is the
building up of well-organised, self-supporting and
prosperous nations.' (86)

thought-out ambition, almost a vision, legitimised
by comparisons with other capitalist countries, (87) but
more usually with the 'dominions' - Canada, New Zealand
and Australia: (88) 'we are passing through successive
stages of growth through which our sister colonies ...
have passed before, and we shall probably continue to be
guided by the same conditions which influenced them. (89)
This was not a 'British' ideology in the sense that
mining's had been, but could be called 'dominionism' -
loyalty to the Empire and strong national patriotism
being united in that ideological combination peculiar
to English-speaking communities settled in British
colonies: (90)

> The Manufacturer, the Farmer, the Merchant and the
> Miner, must work in close and cordial harmony,
> producing for one another, helping one another ...
> giving and receiving, offering and accepting, always
> in the spirit that everything we do, we do for
> South Africa and the Empire.

The hostility of this peculiar breed of nationalism
to the imperial domination of the mining and commercial
sectors of the economy has already been emphasised: (91)

> The fact is the system of Protection ... is not a
> class policy, but a national policy. It is for
> national reasons that we urge its adoption and it
> is for national reasons that we seek a method of
> administration which will ensure continuity of
> policy.... It is a plain question of the duty of a
> nation to encourage the industry of its own people
> in preference to the industry of overseas people.

National patriotism did not preclude a strong sense of
patriotism and loyalty to the empire, but it was
nevertheless the more powerful mobiliser. It was
essential, if people within South Africa were to change
their minds about wishing to become industrialised,
that they should believe that they were engaged in a
task so worthy that it justified the changes, even
hardships, which they would be required to experience,
even on the level of acceptance of inferior expensive
local products rather than better quality, or cheaper
imported goods. (92)

The vision of the society which was to be attained
through the patriotic adaptation to South Africa of
policies developed in other Dominions or countries, was
Utopian: (93)

> Governments that assist industries are progressive
> governments; nations that are not industrial become
> decadent, th r brains atrophy, and they devote their
> energies to war, revolution, etc., as for instance,

Portugal, Spain, Greece, Turkey and Mexico. Industrial nations increase in numbers, strength and power, as witness Great Britain, America, Germany, Canada and Japan. These are the countries from which inventions for the benefit of mankind emanate; these are the countries which control the destinies of the world.

In a race-conscious and imperially dominated settler society it was not surprising that this concept of capitalism as something powerful and creative, in which brains did not 'atrophy' and wars and revolutions were not endemic (the very opposite of decadence) should be related to the concepts of white civilisation, racial superiority, progress, and the other attributes of imperialism. Protection was seen as: 'the policy of patriotism, of progress, of civilisation - a policy that defends the weak against the strong, and stands resolutely for one's own against all assailants', (94) while the toast at the first national meeting of industrialists in 1911 was 'Protection, Production and a White Population'. (95)

Ideologists also developed the more specific concept of the 'nation' whose loyalty and patriotism were being evoked. It was not particularistic, but consisted of 'everybody': 'The problem of Colonial Industries [is] one which affects not only the manufacturers but the whole people', (96) wrote Laite, while another author spoke of the tariff being 'moulded by the will of the people'. (97) Because it was the people as a whole who were involved in the nation, their ideas could be equated with the notion of 'public opinion'. This notion, although it was only fully developed during the 1930s, when a process of 'externalisation' of the ideology took place, appeared as early as 1910 in manufacturing ideology, in an article on What South African Newspapers can do for South Africa's Prosperity: 'The proper function of the South African Press is the formation of sound public opinion on South African affairs.' (98) By this was meant: (99)

The Press is best cognisant of the importance of industry to the country. Its first duty then is to encourage trade and industry, and this is a work which has been neglected in the past.... What the newspapers can do is to make an intelligent and painstaking study of the experience of the past, and the best that has been done, or is being done for industrial progress everywhere - here and abroad, and inform the people of the facts.... The newspapers can teach more effectively than they have yet done, that the production of honest business and industrial

prosperity is one of the greatest moral works in
which right-minded men can engage.

This concept of the 'nation' as being the whole people
legitimated the need for imposing upon the society the
one, uniform goal of capitalist development. It thus
placed considerable emphasis on social unity, and
deplored anything divisive in the society. This
applied particularly to the divisions between Afrikaner
and English-speaking whites. As we have observed, under
British imperial hegemony these divisions had been
encouraged, but manufacturing ideologists sought to
obscure or, they claimed, obliterate them: (100)

> The Union of South Africa, being a nation in the
> making, cannot afford the luxury of perpetuating the
> race feud, with all its sordid insincerities, its
> internecine quarrels and its resulting blight ...
> racial quarrels must be avoided like the plague if the
> Act of Union is to spell peace, progress and
> prosperity, and if the declarations of the Opposition
> leaders are sincere they will join hands with the
> Government in thwarting any attempt to revive the
> dying feud between Dutch and British members of the
> new South African brotherhood.

The rejection of 'racialism' was accompanied by an
emphasis on the indivisibility of politics. The nation
was one, and should not be divided; hence its political
activities should reflect this. Politics, as an
activity, should not be rejected, but should be harnessed
to the common goals of the society - industrialisation
and capitalist development. Thus the ideology, while it
accepted the legitimacy of party politics, attempted to
divest it of its overtly political content: 'Judging
from the Press reports of the debates in the Cape House
of Assembly, the present political factions appear to
be dominated by one desire - to make their opponents
angry. This may be amusing to the gallery but it is
not business.' (101) What was 'business' was the
elimination of division and of a party system compatible
only with imperial hegemony: (102)

> the time is ripe for the shaking up of the dry bones -
> for the founding of a New Party, a National Party, with
> aims and objects totally different to that of the
> factions now controlling the destinies of this great
> country. The electorate is tired of the cry 'Pro-
> gressive versus Bond', which, being broadly interpre-
> ted, means little else than 'Town versus Country' or
> 'British versus Dutch'. We are one people, under
> one flag.

This was the foundation of the idea of politics somehow

being 'non-political' which, when South Africanists
eventually did dominate a 'national party' in the 1930s,
was a powerful force in South African legitimacy.   But
until then no single political party could represent the
interests of national capital and manufacturers sought
political allies where they could find them. (103)

One contradiction needed to be solved if the idea of
'one nation' was to be integrated into the particular
ideas about the various groups in South Africa and their
attitudes towards protection - that between the division
of the society into its various clear-cut interests by
the ideologist, for purposes of identifying enemies and
friends of manufacturing, and the overall assertion that
division was to be eliminated.   This was resolved by the
concept of 'mutual interdependence', a concept of
'pluralism' (in the sense in which it is used by political
scientists), where separate and sometimes contradictory
interests are, or should be, united by their common
purpose.

Some examples of the idea of 'mutual interdependence'
have already been used - the idea of the farmer, manufacturer, mineowner and commercial man working together
for the common good, for example, quoted above.   But it
was an idea which not only included employers, but *all*
white members of the 'nation' - consumers, workers,
producers, and ultimately, 'the common weal': (104)

> It is a question of diversified employments and
> unbounded possibilities for a country capable of
> great achievements, rather than a limitation of its
> powers to such occupations as will prevent it from
> becoming independent and its people from going
> forward.   This is our protective policy.   It is ...
> the foe of all monopolies, domestic and foreign. ...
> It is not the instrument by which one class of the
> community is to be benefited at the expense of
> another class, for it seeks the common weal by
> affording employment to all classes.   It is not a tax
> upon one industry for the benefit of another industry,
> for its design is to impose taxes upon foreign
> producers, that domestic consumers may obtain cheaper
> commodities. ... It is not a hindrance to commerce
> but a help to it.

This idea of the mutual interdependence of all sectors was
a mobilising force in the manufacturing ideology.   It
sought to capture the support of the wavering protectionists within each sector and transcend the narrower
interests of each, by offering, in tandem with the
nationalist appeal of the ideology, a common aim and
goal.   The good, popular and progressive policies of

industrial development could and must rise above the
divisions between the white 'races', and between the
white classes.

CONCLUSION

A national bourgeoisie was in the making in South Africa.
On the economic level a petty-bourgeois section of
manufacturing capital, combined with odd fragments of
commercial and agricultural capital, formed its
precarious and disunited foundation.   But, as we have
argued, economic ownership of the means of production
does not constitute class.   And here, as in mining, we
find that the political and ideological translation of
the interests of this fragmented class, undertaken by
the ideologists of its central and leading section,
constituted the real meat of the process of class
formation.
     In these first years in a hostile imperial state the
national bourgeoisie had very little real experience of
power, class struggle and hegemony.   Operating in the
unreal context of Utopian visions and what they surmised
were pertinent comparisons, ideologists nevertheless
managed to map out for their audience how the interests
of an industrialising capitalist class could be translated into the South African environment, with its
peculiar imperial hegemony, its divided working class,
and its complex market.   We shall see that most of these
translations were proved accurate, if immature and
unformed, when tested under more stringent conditions.
But for the moment, the point is that an understanding
of its roots in the early years of the formation of this
class is essential to any explanation of the kind of
hegemony South Africa's national bourgeoisie sought.
     To begin at the end, we found that the culmination of
the work of the ideologists examined here lay in their
articulation of the inseparability of the 'nation' from
the 'state' and both from the capitalist system itself.
It is interesting that only national capital is thus seen
to be expressing its desire for this kind of state form -
for certainly imperial capital did not wish its hegemony
to be sustained through the identification of its
interests with the interests of the nation as a whole;
rather it sought to imbue each of the 'castes' in its
hierarchy with the sense of the rightness of its place,
and to institutionalise the stratified system through
law, politics and ideology.   By contrast, national
capital found it imperative to oppose hierarchy and rigid

stratification - for if local capital's interests were to
become the 'national' interests then class and ideological
distinctions between social groups must at all costs be
minimised and blurred.   Perhaps this is a common interest
of all national bourgeoisies - certainly the work of
Poulantzas would seem to imply this.   Here manufacturing
ideologists in the early period seemed concerned to translate this interest into South African terms, through a
series of interpretations of the class structure and the
balance of class forces.

The 'nation' must be identified with capital, but the
'nation' was only a small portion of South Africa's
population - the whites.   National capital accepted
imperial capital's exclusion of blacks from the legitimate
state.   However, this might have been as much because of
inertia - the black working class was as yet a small part
of the sector's employees, and was therefore not in a
position to make demands upon capital - as because it was
central to capital's interests.   Certainly the idea of
the black 'good citizen' implied some sort of limited and
paternalistically controlled incorporation into 'civil
society', while the consumption function of the black
population precluded any adoption by national capital of
imperial capital's 'periphery' for blacks.   In fact the
early manufacturing ideology towards blacks is a good
illustration of the immaturity and ambiguity of South
Africanism at this stage, for as we shall see later, it
was subsequently forced into a more systematic and
consistent mould.

Part of the reason for this immaturity was that the
black working class was not the most important of local
capital's problems at this early stage.   It is thus not
surprising that ideologists were far more advanced when
it came to building the 'nation' itself, and to making its
identification with capital possible.   'The nation' was
a white one; and yet the ideologists of capital were
aware (more than many of today's social scientists are)
that the function of its whiteness and unity was to mask
important and deep-seated class and ideological divisions,
which mining capital had exalted.   What is interesting is
not simply that the concept of 'white civilisation' under
the banner of capitalism attempted to mask the objective
division of whites into workers and employers, imperial
and local capitalists, English and Afrikaners, merchants
and manufacturers - for this is perhaps a crude and simple
point which most Marxists might make - but the precise
economic and political foundations for the incorporation
of each of the many and varied interests that ideologists
were concerned with, and the necessary ideological structures each implied.

Manufacturing capital's own petty-bourgeois nature, and
the ideological features displayed by its opposition,
formed the bases from which it attempted to mobilise other
sections of capital, such as merchant, mining and
agricultural capital.   It made the economic interest of
'protection' a rallying call, which it articulated in
terms of notions such as 'progress', 'struggle',
'pioneering' and 'self-improvement', concepts which
ideologists had used during the primary processes of the
formation of manufacturing itself.   The fact that most
other forms of capital at the time had strong roots in
the imperial system meant that protectionism had to be
linked with popular anti-imperial nationalism, and that a
patriotic sort of evangelism was evolved to 'convert' the
unconverted.   This nationalistic form of the ideology
took the form of 'dominionism' rather than a more radical
form of nationalism, perhaps because of the mercantile
origins of much of this part of the manufacturing sector.
    The 'South Africanism' that resulted had another
feature which contrasts with mining ideology, and which is
rooted in its need to mobilise other forms of capital.
This was that it sought to mobilise Afrikaner agricultural
capital on the ideological level, through a rejection of
'racialism', and the positing of the existence of a
united, white, South African nation.   But the
mobilisation of Afrikaner capital was and remained under
the dominance of primarily English-speaking
industrialists.   South Africanism was not an 'Afrikaner'
ideology, but one designed to manoeuvre this class of
Afrikaners into a co-operative stance - like all
colonising and hegemonic ideologies it operated to retain
the superiority of the dominant group in this case through
the incorporation of a group whose subordination had
already taken place under imperial hegemony.
    The white working class too was already subordinated;
it now had to be mobilised on the side of national capital
and incorporated into the 'nation' as a whole.   This
supportive class had to be conciliated rather than
repressed and manipulated, as it had been under mining.
Ideologists recognised early on that one of the prices
capital would have to pay for the support of this sub-
class would be to accept white labour's demands for
protection from the encorachments of black labour - an
illustration of how even the most commonly acknowledged
'victories' of a working class may be foreseen by capital
and thus ultimately controlled by it.   In addition
national capital would have to reject rigid hierarchy by
opening up the possibilities for white worker mobility
into the middle class.   This was articulated in terms of

South Africa's version of the American Dream so well
dissected by Chinoy (105) - the petty-bourgeois
manufacturer's artisan origins were used to place the
burden for its own improvement upon the working class, and
to develop the myth of the possibility of substantial
mobility from the working class into the middle class.
The final element in the structure of appeasement was the
advocacy by ideologists of the development of state
apparatuses within which white working-class organisation
and resistance could be regulated, and kept under capital's
control.   The links between this proposed system and the
development of the 'white nation' are best illustrated by
the firm stance of capital on the issue of white-black
working-class co-ordination.   On no account was white
labour to collaborate with black, and this would be
institutionalised through the confinement of conciliatory
machinery to the white working class.   A latent ambiguity
lay here - for both the white and the black working classes
were to constitute the consuming population of locally-
produced goods, a fact which could potentially break down
the rigid divisions between them;   this too was an as yet
unformulated aspect of capital's strategy, one which
reached maturity in later years, after its primary aim of
protection had been realised.

In these early times it seemed that the embryonic
national bourgeoisie had mapped out the crude outlines of
the kind of social formation that it would bring into
being in South Africa were it to replace the imperial
ruling class.   Ideologists had in this sphere, as in the
others we have examined, worked as policy-makers and
ideology-creators.   Capital had not needed to subordinate
the working class or other modes of production since that
had already been done by imperial capital.   Ideologists
could thus confine themselves to assisting in the
formation of the class of local capitalists itself, in
the development of the kinds of structures through which
its various interests could best be realised, and in the
creation of a popular ideology through which those
interests could be made synonymous with the 'general'
interest.   They had not fully developed strategies for
capital to adopt in the fields of black labour and the
consuming public, however, while their placing of
'protectionism' at the centre of capital's interests
would remain correct only as long as protection was
absent.   But in the significant and central sphere of the
state, they had made great innovations in their expression
of opposition to the prevailing hegemony of imperial
capital.   New state apparatuses were envisaged, a new
political system was proposed, while the hierarchical

state form was to be replaced by a consensual one, in
which the area of consensus was identified as 'the
nation', the nature of the consensus as 'mutual
interdependence', and its aims and content as the ideals
of progress, development and industrialisation in the
spirit of national patriotism.   The state would be, not
simply its apparatuses, but the all-pervading, benevolent,
non-ideological and even non-political presence, the
embodiment of public opinion and of the objective good of
the 'nation', in which ideals could be realised and
common aims pursued.   In summary, the embryonic
bourgeoisie was already envisaging the creation of a
South African, white, version, of a bourgeois state.

4 The emerging contender

The problem of the explanation of large-scale economic,
social, political and ideological changes in social
systems is not made any easier when the particular system
concerned is as complex and under-researched as is the
South African one.   And yet this analysis demands that
such an explanation be undertaken.   The First World War
finds us with an imperial system, dominated by mining
capital, and dependent upon and defended by merchant
capital, that had, in spite of itself, spawned a
challenging national bourgeoisie, the realisation of
whose interests implied the destruction of many facets of
imperial hegemony.   By the Second World War, by contrast,
it seems that most would agree that many of the interests
of the national bourgeoisie had indeed come to be
realised, and that by implication, therefore, imperial
hegemony had ended, or at least been severely undermined.
If this latter assumption is true (and it should be one of
our tasks to discover the extent to which it is) then we
are bound to ask how such a change took place, and whether
the kind of analysis of capital and its interests being
put forward here is a sure foundation for undertaking an
explanation of it.
    It has been a consistent weakness in Marxist
explanations of the South African state that 'hegemony'
has been simplified and often reduced to its barest
economic and in some cases political bones;   while the
resulting conceptual and explanatory shortcomings have
often been obscured by the use of language which at times
seems unnecessarily esoteric. (1)   Here we embark upon an
explanation which will hopefully go some of the way
towards illustrating the complexities of this matter - for
not only is a change in hegemony something which cannot be
viewed other than as the result of contradictory and
opposing forces acting against one another over a period

142

of time, until some resolution is reached; but it, of all
the problems in Marxism, is something which must be
explained on more than simply the economic level.
Political and ideological forces and contradictions must
be combined with economic factors in an interpretation
which must be as multi-faceted as hegemony itself. Thus,
of course, the first task is to discover what were the
economic interests of the various forms of capital and how
they changed over time. But we cannot stop there. We
must know what the changing balance of power was in the
contradictions that were implied by these economic
interests; whether the state apparatuses had the capacity
to reflect and perhaps assist in the resolution of these
contradictions; what the place was of the struggle
between capital and labour in affecting their resolution;
and finally, what the role of ideologists was in the
struggle, and whether they were able to make ideological
and political prescriptions on behalf of capital that
affected its outcome. These are not simple matters, and
answering these and related questions takes up much of the
remainder of this work - for the rise to power of national
capital in South Africa was not as short and swift as had
been that of imperial capital, while the changes it
attempted to bring about were every bit as complex, and
always beset by the problems of its own relative weakness.
     The first task would seem to lie in demonstrating the
relationship between the early petty-bourgeois
manufacturing section of capital, and the wider class
which it hoped to lead. In the early years, as was
demonstrated in chapter 3, there *was* no wider class to
speak of, manufacturing's allies consisting of minority
groups within all sections of capital and some of labour.
Manufacturing capital was all set to lead the national
bourgeoisie in the fight against imperial capital, but
had nothing other than the mythical forces of 'evolution'
and ideological conversion to rely on for the creation of
more substantial class allies and supporters. The
aspiring bourgeoisies of today's underdeveloped countries
would be wrong to rely on such forces for the widening and
consolidation of support for their interests - for it was
neither the automatic evolution of the anti-protectionists
within each interest group nor the conversion of all to a
belief in protectionism that eventually led to the
creation of a large, complex and comparatively powerful
national bourgeoisie in South Africa; instead, it was a
process attributable to no single cause, but a combination
of historical forces and circumstances.
     Prime amongst these was the First World War. Wars
always stimulate the growth of local industries,

particularly in peripheral countries usually dependent
upon imports which may be halted in wartime.   Often (as
had been the case in the Anglo-Boer War) these local
industries collapse or are crippled when the war is over
and colonial economic relationships are once more restored.
But if, as was the case in South Africa, the war is long,
the existing local industries are fairly widespread, well-
organised and large in number, the cessation of imports is
severe, the local network of commercial capital is
potentially effective, the market is large, and, moreover,
the very imperial power upon which the existing dependent
system is based, is itself irreparably damaged by the war,
then it would seem the conditions exist for the wartime
expansion of industries to be more than simply an
epiphenomenon.   Add to this the existence in South Africa
of a powerful working class, which after the war presented
substantial challenges to mining capital, and it may be
seen that the First World War and its aftermath were
capable of providing the conditions for the rise of a
strong contender for hegemony in South Africa.

Manufacturers in all countries flourished during the
war, and South Africa was no exception.   Local producers
were ready to seize the opportunities offered them by the
severely restricted imports of British and other foreign
goods into the country for expanding production and
capturing markets previously closed to them.   Laite wrote
in 1914: 'With war in the air in Europe, South African
manufacturers have the opportunity of making war upon the
market which naturally belongs to them. ... Manufacturers,
the opportunity is yours.   Rise and take it.' (2)   Under
this, their third major stimulus in three decades (early
Cape protection and the Anglo-Boer War providing the other
two), manufacturers were in an excellent position to make
the most of this 'natural' protection.   Industrial growth
was remarkable.   From 1915-16 to 1917-18, 1700 new
factories were opened, while in 1919-20 the gross value of
manufacturing output had doubled, rising from £35m (in
1915-16) to £76.8m.   Existing factories expanded, new
factories were opened, more workers were employed, and
more local raw materials consumed by manufacturing. (3)
As if in recognition of their new strength, manufacturers
were able at last to overcome their regional differences
in 1917 when they formed the Federated Chamber of
Industries, the body whose future role as the vehicle for
the expression of industrial interests was to be
vital. (4)   Industries had indeed been transformed, and
an ideologist such as Laite made the most of this: (5)

What a change has come o'er the scene!   The European
conflagration resulting in the upheaval of the world's

economic fabric has completely changed the outlook of
both merchant and consumer.   No longer does the
producer exist by virtue of the grace of the merchant!
Both he and the consumer are now prepared to humble
themselves before the all-necessary producer,
he wrote.   Elsewhere he elaborated on the changes as
perceived by manufacturers: (6)

A few years ago a manufacturer had almost to apologise
for his existence.   He was treated with contempt by
the importing and distributing community; and the
Government completely failed to realise his value as
an economic asset.   Not only was assistance withheld,
but obstacles were deliberately placed in the way of
progress, the idea being that this country could never
become a manufacturing centre, and reliance could only
be placed upon mineral production and, to a limited
extent, upon agriculture.   The folly of this benighted
policy has at last been recognised.

The 'South African Commerce and Manufacturers' Record'
became the more strident 'Industrial South Africa',
because of 'the enormous development of our manufacturing
industries and the federating of industrial organisations'
which had: 'resulted from an economic awakening throughout the Union. ... As the pioneer mouthpiece of South
African Industrialism, we have long felt that our old
title was not sufficiently indicative of our ideals and
policy.' (7)

When the war was followed by a severe depression,
manufacturers were forced to close their ranks and fight
to preserve the progress they had made.   But now they
were no longer alone in their protectionist battle, and
the new post-war period was greeted as the 'dawn of
protection'. (8)   Through the immediate post-war
depression, until the introduction of protection itself,
manufacturers continued to press for protection, to seek
allies, and to propagate their ideology, in this changed
economic and political environment; for the first time
they were able to plan realistically for their own secure
future.

It was merchant capital whose increasing support for
protection and growing local strength and vociferousness
represented the most significant change in those years.
Merchant capital is always a dependent form of capital.
In South Africa, however, its dependence was of two kinds.
It was unevenly divided between its original structured
dependence upon the imperial economy, which had made of
it manufacturing's most outspoken and implacable enemy,
and the emerging structures of dependence upon local
trade.   It was during the war that the original imperial

structure of relationships was damaged irreparably, and
that the decline of the Free Trade domination over the
sector began.   Commerce was more badly affected than any
other sector by the almost complete cessation of imports
during the war, since importing was its business.   At the
same time, the boom in manufacturing during the war meant
greatly increased trade for non-importing commerce.   That
the balance of power between the two halves had shifted by
1916 was indicated by the fact that in that year the
Association of Chambers of Commerce (Assocom) passed a
resolution advocating local industries. (9)   By 1918, not
only had Laite been able to write about merchants being
prepared to 'humble themselves' before the 'all necessary
producer', but Sir Meiring Beck, Minister of Posts and
Telegraphs, could say that 'hitherto unsympathetic bodies'
such as Chambers of Commerce, had changed their views
about protection.

The primarily economic changes brought about by the
war, and continuing after it, led to a series of complex
political and ideological changes in the nature of
merchant capital, changes in its organisation;   its
representation and interest-articulation;   its relations
with manufacturing and other groups;   and its ideology.
Commercial capital's interests were now closely enough
allied to those of manufacturing for the two to form a
solid partnership and for a number of important processes
to flow from that partnership.   Thus commercial men were
anxious to show their new protectionism, and to de-
emphasise the hold over their sector of the residual
importing and wholesaling free traders. (10)

One writer records the new attitude amongst the
'stalwarts of commerce' who, in the 'changed economic
conditions' of 1925: (11)

became advocates of a policy to protect legitimate
secondary industries at least moderately through the
tariff. ... The policy of moderate protection has been
largely due to the influence of some of those very
stalwarts of free trade who, in the face of the
experience of those other countries, were strong
enough to sink their personal prejudices.   Not for
some years now has the policy of protecting the Union's
secondary industries been seriously challenged.   The
voice of the 'whole-hog' free trader is no longer heard.

Commerce and industry began to meet officially and
unofficially, (12) and to express sentiments of mutual
support, co-operation and defence against other more-or-
less hostile interests in the society. (13)

During the 1920s, commercial supporters of industries
became more and more outspoken, while the merging of the

sectors was consolidated on the economic level.   One
industrialist spoke of how 'it is no uncommon thing to
find merchants becoming interested in manufacturing
enterprises', (14) while in 1917, the President of the FCI
remarked on how it was 'an encouraging sign that a number
of large mercantile concerns are entering the ranks of
industry'. (15)   Thus although importing Free Traders
still existed, (16) and commerce and manufacturing were
always to be divided over the issue of the precise degree
of protection which was desirable, (17) a powerful
alliance had been formed between two highly interdependent
forms of capital, and on most issues they were able
to act as one.

In addition, in later years a more generalised change
began to take place in the relationship between the two
sectors, and those outside of them.   By the 1930s
'commerce' began to be a term used to represent a far
wider spectrum of economic actors than previously.   To
the merchants, wholesalers and retailers came to be added
a number of other kinds of people.   First among these was
the industrial, manufacturing community itself, which
began to seek representation through the Chamber of
Commerce movement in addition to its own Chambers of
Industries.   The journal, 'Commercial Bulletin', started
in 1921, of which much more will be said later in this
study, reflected this new audience.   Its proclaimed
function was: (18)

> to provide a link, not only between our widely
> scattered Chambers of Commerce, but also between
> Commerce and Industry, regarded in the widest sense of
> these terms.   That it has succeeded to a very
> considerable extent in this aim there can be no doubt
> whatever.   There is no longer that sharp dividing line
> between the interests of the wholesale distributor,
> the merchant and the manufacturer which existed some
> years ago.

In 1932, it could be claimed that 'prominent
manufacturers' had been elected to the Presidency of 'all
the leading Chambers of Commerce and of the Association of
Chambers of Commerce'. (19)   In the following year the
'Bulletin' claimed that: 'the Chamber of Commerce
movement has in recent years extended the scope of its
activities to such an extent that the term "commerce" has
failed to be an adequate designation.' (20)

Not only did the alliance between commerce and
manufacturing become institutionalised through the
Chambers of Commerce and 'Commercial Bulletin' but
'commerce' now began to be able to claim to represent a
whole spectrum of interests: (21)

> Merchants and importers form only a minor proportion of
> the membership of the organisation, in the ranks of
> which are to be found all the leading manufacturers,
> bankers, financial houses, insurance companies,
> shipping firms, and several prominent legal and other
> professional men,

wrote the 'Bulletin' of Assocom.   A network of financial,
commercial and industrial, as well as professional,
interests had developed around the solid commerce-industry
alliance; in 1929, a manufacturer pointed to the
functionality of this new interdependence; he noted: (22)

> the closer association of finance with industry all
> over the country.   I notice that the individual owner,
> the family company, and the partnership are being
> superseded by public and private companies.   Where,
> formerly, the proprietor was in control, in many cases
> the financier now directs, with the aid of expert
> technical advice.   This country, in common with
> others, is seeing the rise of the man who brings
> capital and labour into co-operative action.

Around the developing industrial sector, and the pro-
industrialisation commercial sector, was growing a new
class of people, a disparate group, composed of those
whose functions were necessary in the context of
industrial expansion, diversification, and the growing
complexity of the new system.   They included those
directly related to the operation of the emerging
structures of capital - the financiers and shipping firms,
the commercial and industrial men themselves.   But they
also included the subsidiary functionaries - the
insurance men, the lawyers, the 'other professional men',
such as scientists (23) - and what could perhaps be called
the 'non-organic' intellectuals of capital, the
academics whose support for the idea of industrialisation
had already been remarked upon in manufacturing
circles. (24)   A number of subsidiary educational,
scientific and other institutions grew up in the late
1920s and early 1930s.

A real transformation of local capital had taken place.
What we have observed here has been the continuation of
the process of class formation which had begun at the turn
of the century.   Whereas in the 1900s, manufacturers had
been a minority of apparent fanatics, with no societal
support and no legitimacy at all, in the 1920s and 1930s
they began to become the leaders, together with commerce,
of a new and maturing bourgeoisie, a class which had
begun to make itself felt in economic and political terms.
With commerce, which had a legacy of respectability, they
were able to seek and find powerful allies, to appeal to

'public opinion' and to envisage a future where their
supremacy was certain.   We shall see below that these
economic and political aspects of class formation had
their ideological counterpart, and that their
repercussions in the existing state apparatuses were
important.

Agriculture continued to be divided on the issue of
protection, but during and after the First World War the
protectionists in this sector too began to predominate.
Manufacturers, with their increased size, growing wage
labour force and general acceptance were now able to
offer to some farmers a sound market which would not be as
subject to violent price fluctuations as was the world
market.   Manufacturers frequently pointed this out to
farmers.   For example one ideologist said in 1922 in a
major speech: (25)

> the country does not yet realise the full extent of the
> interdependence of the primary producers (or farmers)
> and the secondary producers (or manufacturers).   When
> the artisan population is out of work, the spending
> capacity of the country becomes lessened, and the
> demand for the food products of the farmer is
> restricted.   When the market of the manufacturer is
> severely cut down he is unable to buy freely from the
> farmer those raw materials necessary for production
> purposes.   When to this is added a falling overseas
> export market, the position of the farmer must become
> acute.   It is surely most in the interests of the
> farmer, and the country at large, for the Government to
> do everything to maintain our manufacturing activities
> at the highest possible pitch ... it is better for the
> farmer to rely upon a properly organised industrial
> activity for his chief market than to be at the mercy
> of every wind that blows overseas.

In the Transvaal in 1917 a Farmers' Congress passed a
resolution including the proposal that: 'the Government
should be urged to take immediate steps to ascertain in
what steps the export trade of South Africa may be
developed with profit, and by what means local industries
may be encouraged.' (26)   This support was reaffirmed at
subsequent national congresses. (27)   In addition, the
South African National Union grew in strength in these
years, continuing as the chief agricultural protectionist
pressure group. (28)   In April 1923, the South African
Agricultural Union brought these developing processes to a
climax when it entered into what was called a 'working
arrangement' with industries. (29)   Finally, the rise of
the rurally based, protectionist Nationalist Party
provided the strongest political reinforcement the
movement had so far received.

However, agriculture's economic ties had been forged in
imperial times, and these were difficult to break.   The
old farming-commerce-mining alliance which had been the
bugbear of manufacturing protectionists in pre-war South
Africa persisted, and was made evident as some sections of
agriculture increased their support for protection.   Not
only did agriculture's own anti-protectionist mouthpiece,
the 'Farmers' Weekly', express continuing disapproval at
the protectionist statements of other farmers, (30) but
commerce's outspoken Free Trader, W.A. Martin, expressed
his outrage at the South African Agricultural Union's
alliance with manufacturing, (31) while in the sphere of
mining, Frankel's book on Railway Policy in 1929 was seen
by manufacturers as containing statements designed to
drive a wedge between themselves and farmers. (32)   The
structural basis for this ongoing opposition was clear.
Important as the manufacturing market was, even as late as
1936, many manufacturing firms were processing mainly
foreign raw or semi-processed materials, and by-passing
local agricultural products, (33) and it was only because
the proportion of local goods used was rising rapidly
during the wartime and post-war years that agriculture
became protectionist at all.

Thus, although agriculturalists were increasingly
useful to manufacturers as allies in their battle for
protection, they were far from being ideal.   They would
be with the bourgeoisie but not of it.   The interdependence which industrialists insisted upon between themselves and their rural collaborators was there, and it was
growing, but it had not reached the level which
ideologists depicted.   Moreover, although farmers were
employers, protectionists and owners of the means of
production, they were neither industrial capitalists nor,
like commerce, the handmaiden of industrial capital.
Indeed, as far as the issues of labour and taxation,
subsidies and marketing, and many others were concerned,
the interests of manufacturing, commerce and mining on the
one hand, and farming on the other, diverged.   From the
point of view of the formation of a bourgeoisie capable of
realising and expressing the point of view of the
interests of capitalism itself, farmers were unsuited as
partners for other capitalists.   Overall, protectionist
agriculture was no more than a useful tactical ally.

Capital's other useful ally was not only not a potential
part of the bourgeoisie - it did not even own the means of
production.   But white workers, as is well known, came to
be second only to manufacturers in their protectionism
during and after the war.   The protectionist faction
within the Labour Party rose to dominate white labour

151 Chapter 4

policy in general, and the party in particular. That a
party claiming to represent workers should support
policies which would primarily serve the interests of
their capitalist employers, is as much a reflection of
the structural and ideological hegemony of capital as of
particular historical circumstances. But the
proletarianisation of whites, whether Afrikaners from
the local rural areas, or Englishmen and women from
overseas, had occurred as a result of the dominance of
forms of capital external to and preceding the
manufacturing sector. Whites were separated from access
to any means of production in Britain and in South Africa
because of the respective rural revolutions in those
countries, which had transformed both. So to those
claiming to represent white workers, the *new* form of
capital - manufacturing - appeared chiefly as the sector
able to provide employment for those who, because of the
effects of *older* forms of capital would otherwise have
been unemployed during and after the war. In 1915-16,
the number of manufacturing employees totalled 101,178;
this rose to 155,008 in 1919-20. (34) In the post-war
depression, the employed became unemployed once more,
and their numbers were swelled by the increasing numbers
of Afrikaners leaving the land. At the same time, it
seemed that the mining industry was based upon a rapidly
wasting asset, (35) while, given the hierarchical form of
imperial hegemony, mineowners were anxious, as ever, to
replace expensive white workers with cheap black ones
during these years of class conflict. The combination of
these factors led the Labour Party to adopt a
protectionist policy with conviction and to pursue it with
vigour. More industries would mean more jobs, while
unlike mining, industrial development would, it was
argued, be unending.
    However, the Labour Party, realising its value to the
industrialisers, was in a good bargaining position. It
could offer its support for protection in exchange for
concessions by employers to white workers. Its
'socialism', therefore, extended to the support it gave
for improved working conditions, the legitimation and
regulation of worker organisations, and the guarantees to
white workers of jobs in manufacturing industries in
preference to black workers. Grudgingly, the
manufacturers accepted the bargain which, as we have
shown, their ideologists had predicted and approved.
They supported the argument that industries would solve
unemployment amongst whites, and sometimes even went
further. In 1918, E.G. Saunders wrote: (36)
    it is of vital importance that the protection shall be

afforded in a manner which will prevent the
exploitation of workers, especially the semi-skilled
and the unskilled, who are not combined in powerful
unions.   Labour, indeed, must have the first
consideration of any scheme of protection for
industries.

In 1922, Frank Gibaud said that: (37)

In my opinion, the solution of unemployment in South
Africa lies in production.   It is only in production
that we can find work for the unemployed, and that
production can only be attained when our manufacturing
industries are put upon a fair basis of competition.

Implicit was the idea that white workers' demands for
improved working conditions constituted the price
manufacturers would have to pay for protection.   As
early as 1917, Laite commented on the proposed new
Factory Act, designed to reduce sweating and improve
general factory conditions, saying that: (38)

It is urgent that steps be taken during the war period
to produce such a tariff as will level up the basis of
competition after the War, and put manufacturers in a
position to compete effectively, whilst allowing to
labour, those conditions which are essential to its
well-being.

In spite of the tremendous growth in local industries,
the changed nature of the British empire after the war,
and the growth of a strong and well-supported bourgeoisie
the most powerful interest in South Africa - the gold-
mining industry - did not change its attitude to
protection in particular and to industrialisation in
general.   Indeed, if anything, circumstances after the
war caused the mining industry to become even less
sympathetic to protectionism.   In the post-war
depression mining costs spiralled, causing mineowners to
search harder than ever for ways of reducing costs, while
a severe shortage of cheap black labour in this
depression was blamed by many on the competing and
better-paying industries which had grown so rapidly and
attracted so many workers. (39)   While the voice of local
mining, the 'SA Mines', continued periodically to put
forward its view that industrialisation would be 'good'
for South Africa, the cost structure of the industry was
so delicately balanced that its own self-interest could
not be reconciled with the degree and breadth of
protection which such industrialisation required.   As one
prominent manufacturer wrote as late as 1924: (40)

Their business makes them ardent supporters of Free
Trade, their policy being to buy everything in the
cheapest possible market, regardless of the interests

of the country.   Large numbers of shareholders have
never seen South Africa and have no direct interest in
the advancement of the country, and so long as
dividends are paid, it is all that concerns them.
In the same year the Gold Producers' Committee of the
Chamber of Mines issued a pamphlet: 'Party Programmes and
the Mines: A Business Statement', in which the post-war
position of the industry was made clear.   It had not
changed much from its position in 1911: (41)

The danger of protection is that, in order to assist
mushroom industries the system is extended bit by bit,
every movement bringing about a rise in the cost of
living, and in the cost of production of commodities.
Gold mining, farming, and other exporting industries
are thus placed at a serious disadvantage for their
expenses are determined by the high costs prevailing
in a protected country, while the selling value of
their products is determined by world prices. (42)

It seems clear from this that it continued to be
impossible for gold-mining to change its attitude to
protection mainly because its structure was determined in
the days of investment imperialism.   Any short-term
change in the cost of living would undoubtedly have
decreased profits; any further development of industries
would have forced mining to compete for labour; while the
network of commercial and industrial trade, upon which
some British firms depended, would have been disturbed.
Instead of supporting protection, mining chose to pursue
short-term profitability by confronting the white working
class, and persisting with the ultra-exploitation of black
workers, and to maintain the crucial engineering industry,
for example, at the level of repair shops and petty
production, by opposing protective tariffs particularly
effectively in that region. (43)

The old hostility between mining and manufacturing,
therefore, persisted and even grew during the 1920s.   The
growing constituency of the manufacturers' journal, for
example, did not include mining men; while mining
ideologists continued to hold public sway, and to condemn
protectionism outright. (44)   Even so, mining did begin
to show signs of changes.   In 1921, one observer claimed
that 50 per cent of mining personnel were now South
African born; (45) it was clearly a time of localisation
in the industry.   In addition, the idea grew that the
mines were to be short-lived, and in the 1920s it was a
common claim that because of this industries were
necessary to provide alternative employment and revenue
for the country. (46)   But a more significant change in
the nature of the mining industry lay in the rise to a

position of influence of the Anglo-American Corporation,
directed by Ernest Oppenheimer, in the 1920s and 1930s.
For this mining house, with its roots in the mercantile
diamond industry rather than in the later gold industry,
was not tied to the system of underdevelopment and non-
industrialisation, but was rather able to support and even
guide the national bourgeoisie in its industrialising
ambitions.   Thus in these years the split between
'imperial' and 'national' capital ceased to be clearly
expressed as a split between 'mining' and 'manufacturing'
and became far more complex.

However, as late as 1934, when the Customs Tariff
Commission sought to establish the views of all major
interests in South Africa on the best uses of protection,
the evidence of the Gold Producers' Committee remained
deeply hostile to the use of protection at all, and called
for the government to concentrate on the expansion of
gold-mining. (47)   It was only then that the first signs
of a more friendly alliance between mining and
manufacturing began to appear; as one ideologist of
manufacturing said in November 1937: (48)

> It has been held in the past that the interests of the
> gold-mining industry and secondary industry in this
> country conflict insofar as costs and the effect of
> tariffs may be said to conflict.   There is, however,
> today, I believe, fuller recognition on all sides of
> the very great part, yes even fundamentally so, to the
> economic and social well-being of the people of this
> country, now taken by secondary industry in its
> employment of white or civilised labour.   Industry, as
> represented by our organisation, can only add its voice
> to those who have pleaded so strongly that the state
> temper the direct contribution by the mining industry
> to the Treasury, in the form of taxation, in keeping
> with a policy of the fullest development of that
> industry.

This was part of a generally growing recognition of a new,
more tolerant mining-manufacturing relationship.   For
our present purposes, its significance is that this
merging took place at the very end of the period under
discussion.

While the interests of the mining industry remained
overwhelmingly in the system of underdevelopment it had
established earlier, its ability to sustain this system
was weakened by two major alterations in the balance of
power.   The first was the fact that the evidence seems to
suggest that mining's interests began to diverge from
those of the imperial power which had spawned it.   Far
from attempting to crush the South African bourgeoisie,

British capital was quick to come to terms with its own
weakness after the devastation of the First World War,
and with the strength of local capital.   To British
investors the industrialisation of South Africa was now
not only a distinct possibility, but given the right
circumstances, it was bound to be highly profitable.
Thus the 'British Trade Review' pointed out in 1917: (49)

South Africa possesses practically all the elements
essential to the development of manufacturing
industries.   Coal is very cheap, and is carried long
distances by the Government railways at low cost;
other raw materials abound, labour is plentiful, and,
what is enormously important, the Captains of Industry
are distinguished for their zeal and initiative.   The
task that lies before the Federated Chamber of
Industries is that of utilising all these resources
by means which will benefit both the manufacturers and
the community.

Mining capital was also shaken by two major strikes.
In 1920, 71,000 African mineworkers in twenty-one mines
struck and 'paralysed the industry' over the issue of
wages.   Their short-term defeat was complete and
devastating.   But it has been suggested that the
challenge put forward by black mineworkers in this strike
was far-reaching, and that it represented the first
concerted action by a labour force which by now had been
almost fully proletarianised, and which was thus in a
position to challenge the hegemony of mining, based as it
was upon the partial proletarianisation of the majority of
its labour force. (50)   Then, in 1922, the far better
known white mineworkers' strike, the Rand Revolt, took
place over the old issue of the white job colour bar, the
mining companies having yet again attempted to solve a
profitability crisis through undermining the white
workers' protected position in the hierarchy.   Although
the white workers were crushed in the strike and its
aftermath, they then turned their now considerable
strength 'to more conventional forms of political action',
throwing their weight behind the Labour Party.   The
forces that were undermining mining hegemony during this
period were thus considerably strengthened, not, it is
true, by a revolutionary workers' movement, but by a
bourgeois and petty-bourgeois alliance with interests
opposed to those of mining.

In spite of this, the state remained anchored in the
imperial structures forged under mining hegemony.   Still,
the local bourgeoisie's new-found strength could not but
be reflected within the state apparatuses.   Indeed the
manufacturing-commerce alliance sought first to work

within these apparatuses in their attempts to achieve
their primary aim of protection, and it was only after
protection had come about that they came to realise that
the very state form itself was unsuited to their
requirements.   The existing, imperially-forged state
operated on three levels, and in all of these the new
bourgeoisie made itself felt after the war in ways which
provide an interesting example of the workings of the
capitalist state in circumstances of challenge from
within the ruling class itself.   The first level was that
of the party system, of what Poulantzas calls 'political
practices'.   The South African Party was forced to take
account of the new capitalists, while at the same time
manufacturing had covered itself by planning and forging
a co-operative stance towards the interests represented
by the two remaining parties - Labour, and the
Nationalists, the latter representing sections of
agricultural capital.   The second level was that of the
permanent state apparatuses - in particular the civil
service.   Not only was it impossible to ignore the post-
war protectionist surge at this level, but a realistic
awareness emerged within the bureaucracy that it was
advisable and necessary for it to be prepared to initiate
or at least direct, the physical planning of South
Africa's industrialisation.   Indeed several new
apparatuses were created to this end.   But these two
levels of state response are not discussed at length here,
for they fall more naturally into our later discussion of
the processes whereby national capital sought to change
the form of state itself.
     The third level of response is, however, relevant to
the processes of class and ideology-formation being
analysed here.   This was the level of public ideology
and legitimacy - that arena in which the more intangible
aspects of hegemony are expressed.   The 'problems' of
South African society of the wartime and post-war period
came to involve industries in two regions, whose overall
importance made it necessary for state ideologists to
incorporate the concept of 'industries' into their
language and rhetoric.   The first was the fact that the
wartime expansion of industries provided many with their
first opportunity for even noticing that South African
goods existed in the variety and quantity that they did.
In a short space of time the war removed from
manufacturing ideologists the burden of having to
establish their own legitimacy at the primary level.
Reinforcing this was the fact that local industries had
actually visibly made the South African and British
imperial war effort in South West Africa more effective.

The state therefore found itself in the position of having
to be 'grateful' to the industries which had previously
meant nothing in South Africa's political culture.
Industrial ideologists pointed this out: (51)

It is inconceivable to me, after the experience of the
war, that there should be any question of the value of
industrial development.   Where would South Africa have
been were it not for our industries during the years
1914-18?   Where would we have found the equipment for
the South West Campaign?   Would it have been fought in
mufti and with inadequate supplies?   I venture to
think so, had it not been for our industries.
Remember the German East Campaign and how our
industries prepared for that and maintained our troops
while still catering for the ordinary needs of the
country.   I say that in face of this record no man
dare suggest that the development of industries is not
in the best interests of the country.   The country was
glad of its industries then, and today any man, be he
statesman or not, who refuses to help forward the
policy of development is guilty of a crime against the
country and its people, and the greater the man, the
more scathing will be the judgement of future
generations on his lack of foresight and action.

This new legitimacy was further reinforced at the
second level - that of the rising unemployment in the
country, (52) and the visible 'contribution' which
industries had made towards 'alleviating' it.   The new
political culture provoked by the war and by the enormous
increase in the white working class's size and militancy,
made the solution of white unemployment a political
problem for any government in power, including the South
African Party.   Support for protection at state level
therefore was orientated towards this.   Smuts in
particular, but all supporters of industries at every
level of the state, therefore placed their speeches
firmly in the context of the solution of unemployment;   it
was almost as if the governing party was taking over the
rhetoric of the Labour Party. (53)   As the world
depression of the late 1920s began to loom, and
unemployment threatened to grow, protectionism as a
solution became more entrenched as part of the South
African political culture. (54)

In the end it was the local bourgeoisie's two least
amenable allies - agricultural capital, and white labour -
who were the instruments of the entrenchment of its first
requirement: protection.   When, in 1924, the Labour-
Nationalist Pact government came to power, local capital
was now in a position to make the exchange for which it

had prepared itself - protection was introduced through
the Tariff Act of 1925, while industry complainingly
accepted the Wage Act which accompanied it.   But this
exchange did not mean that national capital had
achieved hegemony.   No changes of a fundamental nature
had taken place in the state form, while national
capital was soon to discover that protection was only
the beginning of the realisation of its interests,
not the end, and that the existing state form
presented substantial obstacles.   Nevertheless, it
was the Tariff Act which made it possible for the
industrialisation of South Africa to get under way, and
for the full interests of the new bourgeoisie to begin
to be realised.

It was incumbent upon us to demonstrate the relationship between manufacturers and the growing bourgeoisie
they were to lead.   But what of ideology and ideologists?
In this study of capital's intellectuals and their role in
the forging of hegemony, it is essential that we discover
the nature of the relationship between manufacturing
ideology and bourgeois ideology.   This question, like
others raised in this chapter, is discussed throughout the
remainder of this work.   Here, however, the foundations
of our answer to it are laid.

They are laid through an examination, not only of the
ideology, but also of the 'ideological network' of the
emerging bourgeoisie.   We have already seen how
manufacturing capital created early on a set of media for
the systematic creation and dissemination of conceptual
and practical data for its own use.   What we now explore
is the manner in which new media and new intellectuals
were brought into being to serve similar functions for the
larger and growing bourgeoisie.   On the one hand these
media are unlike any we have encountered so far;   on the
other their message is readily recognisable as a 'South
Africanist' one.   Here we see early manufacturing
ideology's basic suitability for use by the new
bourgeoisie.   It is only later that its shortcomings
are revealed.

Manufacturing's own ideological network was greatly
strengthened during and after the war.   Laite continued
as a central intellectual.   In 1917 some of the early
pioneering ideas were repeated in a minor masterpiece of
ideological craftsmanship: (55)

May I, in view of the changed and improved Industrial
Outlook in South Africa, urge the wisdom of striving
for Higher Business Ideals, Better living conditions
and a Nobler Manhood.   In these Modern Times, what
better life is there than that of the Honourable,

Successful Manufacturer and Producer?   To have endured
Early Hardships with Fortitude, and overcome
difficulties with Perseverance; to have founded a
business, useful in itself, and giving Employment to
many; to have achieved Position, Influence and perhaps
Independence; to have given of Money to Charity, and
of Time to Citizenship; to have established a
Character above reproach; to have accumulated the
Confidence, Admiration and Friendship of one's
fellows; and to have gained all this of the World
without losing the Soul by Avarice, or Starving the
Heart by Hardness of Conduct.   He who has so lived has
Nobly lived, and he should find Peace as the Shadows
begin to lengthen, and the Evening of Life draws on.
Men of this Character are indeed a blessing to the
State, and the State has need of many such today.

Patriotism had been evoked by the war, and reinforced by
manufacturing's growing need for the state to assist it;
in 1918, one article on The Great National Duty linked the
patriotic and economic aspects of the state: (56)

To Contribute to War Funds does not liquidate our duty
to those who are fighting the battle of Liberty.
We must extend our duty to seeing that the Factories,
Farms and Mines of this fair country are so organised
that the returning boys will be welcomed to a
Prosperous and Happy South Africa.   South Africa, with
South African Capital and Labour, can produce,
manufacture and distribute products sufficient to keep
the Wheels of Industry turning.
'Development' and 'Efficiency' must be our watchwords.
Producers must set up the Standard of 'Quality'. ...
Let the Standard of every South African producer be:
'The Hall Mark of Quality is "Made in South Africa"'.
The Nation is one.   Industrial Prosperity tends to
the happiness of all - on Farm, in Factory, Warehouse,
Store and Home, the effect of prosperity is cumulative.
South Africa needs saner, better and bigger business.
She needs internal development; for her Fighting Sons,
for the Empire, for Herself.

The protectionist political culture which emerged during
the post-war depression was a justification for
reiterating the ideology even more frequently and
strongly; if manufacturing was not allowed to survive in
this period all would suffer. (57)

The glimpse of a potentially fully capitalist South
Africa obtained during the war encouraged ideologists to
explore the possible future on a more realistic basis than
before, and there was a growing realisation of the
complexity of industrialisation.   In 1922 Frank Gibaud,

President of the FCI, toured the whole of South Africa,
investigating its industries, and his comments reveal both
the state of industries themselves at that time, and of
manufacturing thinking.   'Do you think the country has
lost much of the development which took place during the
war?' he was asked.   'It is in suspense,' he replied, but

> that development was greater and more widespread than
> is generally imagined.   In fact I doubt whether many
> people realise what it really meant to the country.
> We are too apt to take things for granted, and it
> would astonish anybody who took the trouble to enquire
> into the position to see just what has been done.   I
> wonder how many people have ever visited any of our
> factories and seen for themselves the manifold and
> complicated processes carried on, the large investments
> of capital in machinery and buildings and sales
> organisation, the large amount of raw materials used,
> and the many skilled, semi-skilled and unskilled, but
> industrious workers employed?

Gibaud was undaunted by the decline of these developing
industries, and saw in their resurrection the solution to
the depression itself.   'Instead of saying that we are
suffering from depression, it would be more to the point
if our leaders would tell us how the trouble can be
mitigated,' he said.   'The opportunity for development is
here, at the least to the extent of our present import of
competitive products.   We have the capital, plant and
labour to meet that demand.   Why, therefore, should we
not do so, and mitigate the depression to that
extent?' (58)   His interview and subsequent speech were
able to offer industrial policies, specific solutions to
specific problems, within the South Africanist idea of
mutual support and progress.   The depression,
unemployment and the plight of farmers in a world
recession were all to be solved by industries, he
argued. (59)

In 1926, a new ideological forum was created for
industrialists: the 'Transvaal Chamber of Industries
Journal', which in 1927 became the 'Transvaal
Industrialist'.   The ideological leadership of
manufacturing, which until then had centred on the Cape,
was greatly strengthened by this addition.   Not only was
the Transvaal the home of some of the largest and most
powerful industries, but the journal was the specific
forum for the greatest victim of mining hegemony - the
unprotected engineering industry, whose ideologists used
the South Africanist ideology to great effect in
attempting to get themselves included in the new tariff.
The journal was filled with South Africanism.   Its

editorials urged industrial development, its advertisements pleaded for the purchase of South African-made
goods, while it performed the same functions as had
earlier journals of discovering and articulating the
interest of Transvaal industries by the use of biography
and historical sketches of the development of the
Transvaal.   The Chairman of the Engineers and Founders
Association, L.E. Lintott, made a speech in 1927 which
typified the approach of the journal: 'at times our
legislators appear to be anxious to hasten too quickly.
South Africa is in danger of being overgoverned,' he
argued, reflecting the growing apprehension amongst
industrialists about the new role of the state.   In
addition he made a strong plea for pragmatism - an
integral part of South Africanism: (60)

It is quite easy to talk about our political problems
and to suggest remedies, but I believe that common-
sense is the panacea of most of our troubles, allied to
the right spirit and, above all, tolerance.   The
Native Problem is bristling with difficulties, but even
this question if taken in hand carefully and fairly
will no doubt be solved.

Many other elements of the South Africanist ideology
appeared in his speech:

Industry, in spite of the great difficulties that
beset it, will take its rightful place.   We are at
the beginning of the voyage.   The Ship Industry will
make good passage once she gets into the open sea.
There are signs of rapid development.   In the past too
much reliance has been placed on others.   Let us
decide to rely upon ourselves, and if the necessary
encouragement is given by those who rule our destinies
we need have no fear. ...
Our greatest needs are Patience, Perseverance and
Population.   Our people have energy and a great
capacity for getting things done, and with our wealth,
actual and potential, and with an earnest desire for
progress, South Africa will be a truly great country
second to none in everything that goes to make a great
nation.

To the nationalism and patriotism expressed here were
added expressions of the 'non-racialism' of the early
ideology.   One speechmaker said that: (61)

A satisfactory solution of the Flag Question comes as a
happy augury precedenting this Annual Meeting, and it
is the fervent wish of all present, I am sure, that all
racial questions shall be studiously avoided in the
common interest of the industrial resources of our
great country.

Its individualism too reappeared: 'the human factors of
energy, initiative and personal service are greater
creative forces than any Government assistance', (62) as
did its developmentalism: 'Development is the gospel
which it is the purpose of the Journal to preach', (63)
and the idea of interdependence, albeit in a slightly
different context;   one article talked of: (64)

> the inseparable connection between the three great
> partners in industry - Capital, Labour and Management.
> ... Capital, unless it is put to use, has no value;
> Labour can do nothing without material and machines.
> Combine Capital and Labour and still you produce
> nothing.   You must introduce the third partner,
> Management.

By the time of the 'Great Depression' of the 1930s both
this journal and the original manufacturing journal,
together with the ideological forum provided by FCI
meetings and other occasions, were established media for
the reproduction of the basic tenets of South Africanism,
and for the minor and major innovations in the ideology
which circumstances required.

Other innovations were made in the structures and
orientation of the media in which ideology was created and
through which it was disseminated.   One of the most
significant of these lay in the development of an
ideological network within the existing state apparatuses
themselves.   Key politicians and civil servants began to
emerge who articulated and contributed towards South
Africanist ideology and policy, directing their statements
towards both protectionist public opinion and the
bourgeoisie itself.   Using the concepts of 'citizenship'
and 'duty', state functionaries began to exact a tribute
from the industrialists who were becoming their clients,
by linking the individual manufacturer to the
'nation': (65)

> there is a growing consciousness today that the man who
> has brains, education or skill, owes something of the
> product of what he has acquired and developed under the
> aegis of the state to the service of the state which
> protects him. ... The great employer is no longer a
> private person building up a private fortune, but is a
> trustee holding his privileges in trust for the nation
> and for others than himself.

Manufacturing ideologists responded positively to this
new emphasis on 'responsibilities' and 'duties', even
though they contradicted the old pioneering
individualism: (66)

> Every man, no matter what his calling, who assumes a
> position of authority in any undertaking in which a

number of human beings are employed, assumes also ...
moral responsibilities the range of which is increasing
with the science of citizenship.   That science ...
emphasises ... a steadily increasing dependence of
individual upon individual and it recognises the
necessity in certain cases of the subordination of
individual interests to the interest of the community
... the individual in a civilised community has growing
responsibilities towards his fellow-beings ... if he is
an employer of labour, his responsibilities are so much
the heavier.

More specifically, state ideologists adopted central
South Africanist ideas such as 'mutual interdependence'.
Warington Smyth, stalwart of the state bureaucracy's
industrially-oriented civil servants, spoke in terms of
mutual interdependence when he said that industries
were: (67)

unquestionably as essential in the growth of the modern
state as the steel reinforcement is essential to
reinforced concrete.   Without the binding qualities of
commerce, industry and manufacture, the concrete fabric
of the state cannot carry the heavy burdens or stand
the rending stresses to which it will be subjected.

Smuts alluded to the 'curative' qualities of industries
for all the problems of the modern state, when he made
several emphatically protectionist speeches after the
war: (68)

[industrialisation would] solve most of the difficult
problems now facing South Africa, the Government and
the people of South Africa.   The Native problem, the
racial issue, industrial unrest, and all the
accompanying ills directly traceable to these factors
in our social and economic life, would vanish if the
scope of employment was widened and plenty of good work
at good wages was offering on every hand.

Politicians such as F.S. Malan and Smuts were
ideologically at home in the South Africanist context and
placed all their protectionist speeches in its
language. (69)

The state-created structures of the Advisory Board of
Industries and Science, and the Department of Industries,
also reproduced South Africanism in their protectionist
and industrialising statements.   Men such as H.S.
Caldecott, H.E.S. Fremantle, H.J. van de Bijl, and Bernard
Price were nurtured in the world of scientists,
engineers and planners created after the war, and in their
milieu a 'scientific' brand of South Africanism came to be
developed which depicted the process of industrialisation
as a matter of 'policy', not 'politics', of 'science' and

not 'ideology'.   In this they were simply emphasising the
pragmatic and secular aspects of the South Africanist
ideology. (70)   The journal of the Department of
Industries, 'The South African Journal of Industries',
started in 1917, under the Ministership of F.S. Malan,
was the chief medium for the expression of this developing
branch of the ideology.   It was a journal with a
distinctly more professional and authoritative tone than
any of the manufacturers' own journals, in which
industrialisation was treated as a problem of expertise,
although it reproduced the same, more ideological,
speeches and writings of manufacturing and state-employed
speakers and writers, as other manufacturing journals.
It was in this journal that the somewhat isolated
activities of the South African National Union, the
original voice of agricultural protectionists, and those
of the mainstream of industrial life were brought
together, and a number of important articles on SANU's
concepts of development, the state's role therein, and the
relationship of agriculture thereto, appeared in the
'SAJI'.   Here too, a developmental, scientific, and
planning-orientated ideology was expressed: (71)

> The South African National Union holds that there is no
> driving force to compel the initiation and the carrying
> out of a definite policy in the scheme of development.
> It is contended that there is an urgent necessity for a
> force compelling action to be taken on approved lines
> for the common good.   It is a continuity of the work
> of development that is so essential and that, it is
> considered, can hardly be attained under the present
> system.

Other ideologists were given the opportunity of
expressing South Africanist ideas, if they held them, in
the 'SAJI'.   It thus became the forum for the expression
not only of scientific South Africanism, but of the South
Africanism of the disparate interests in the society who
were not, supposedly, members of the bourgeoisie itself.
The President of the Chamber of Mines, for example, was
quoted when he made the South Africanist claim that
relationships between white workers and management should
be run along conciliatory lines; (72)   A. Crawford, trade
unionist, was quoted avidly, when he made a statement
recommending the formation of a 'Triple Alliance' between
agriculture, workers and manufacturers 'to work for the
benefit of industry and the community as a whole'; (73)
while the academics and scientists whose protectionism
Laite had remarked upon earlier were given a forum for the
expression of their views here too. (74)   The journal,
taking on an explicitly 'educational' and 'propagandist'

role, (75) had created a new, non-manufacturing audience,
to whom it propagated older, manufacturing ideas.   It was
in the 'SAJI' that the speech Warington-Smyth made to the
Conference of Employers and Employees in 1919 was
reprinted, in which the spreading spirit of South
Africanism was expressed: (76)

> Development of our resources and growth in production
> is the only watchword in a country such as South
> Africa, if it is not to go back into a mere pastoral
> community and to fail as the home of a white race worth
> talking about.   For the sake, therefore, of white
> civilisation, of ourselves - of employers and employees
> - for the sake of our children, it is up to us to push
> ahead with the development of this great country of
> mineral and agricultural resources.   A courageous and
> constructive conception of industrial statesmanship is
> needed, which shall call forth, in place of the old
> divided councils and bitter contests, the co-operation
> of all who are engaged in industry, whether as
> managers, employers or employees, in one common object
> - that of increase of industrial activity and
> efficiency, which is the only true road to real self-
> betterment.   This is our true self-interest, if you
> will look at it so, and is the only way to real
> betterment of each man's own trade, or industry, and
> betterment thereby of the living conditions ultimately
> of the whole population of the country which we serve.

The mining industry, in spite of its hostility to
protection, was not immune to the changed climate.   Thus
its 1924 anti-protectionist pamphlet, 'Party Programmes
and the Mines', is sub-titled A Business Statement, and
the pamphlet is at pains to emphasise the importance to
South Africa of the mines, in the new, patriotic currency;
while it tries to perform the South Africanist separation
of 'ideology' from 'business', and of 'politics' from
'policy': (77)

> The Industry's importance to South Africa is so great
> that the Gold Producers' Committee feels it to be its
> duty to the community to set out, in a plain, unbiased,
> business statement, the effect on the Mines of the
> adoption of the various projects affecting them
> proposed by the opposing political parties.   The
> following statement contains nothing political, and it
> is hoped that the facts set out in it will be pondered
> by the public of the Union, whose economic welfare
> depends in so large a degree on the prosperity of the
> Mining Industry.

Sir Ernest Oppenheimer was well-placed to link the mining
industry with the new South Africanist structures.   His

biographer described Oppenheimer in entirely different
terms from those which are usually used to describe the
older mining magnates.   His 'charm', for example, (78)
> was not in the least calculated, but reflected an
> essential simplicity and goodness of heart, which won
> affection and devotion from those with whom he came in
> contact, whatever their status in society, or the race
> to which they belonged.

More explicitly: 'He was a passionate South African, who
felt that he had a duty towards his country to build up
its industries and to further its economic progress.' (79)

By 1927, according to Gregory, De Beers' had
transferred the bulk of its resources to South Africa, so
that the industry over whose final centralisation and
organisation Oppenheimer presided was a fully localised
one at the time of his greatest eminence as a Member of
Parliament for the South African Party. (80)   In
Gregory's eyes, Oppenheimer was ideally fitted for the
'new' kind of leadership which the developing society
required: (81)
> he must possess the ability to judge, in the light of
> his own interests and those of his workers and share-
> holders, the import on his affairs (including the
> supply of capital) of the vast forces now at work.
> He must deal and negotiate with government, and with
> the departments of government; he must consider
> public opinion and even if he cannot bend it to his
> will, he must at least attempt to influence and
> persuade.   The ability to maintain a business
> organisation and to expand it calls, therefore, for a
> very wide range of qualities.

If, as Gregory claims, a man such as Oppenheimer was able
to perform these duties and functions, then he did indeed
epitomise the South Africanist revolution.   All the
elements he mentions - the state, capital, public opinion,
and the evolution of the 'business organisation' - were
the problems which concerned the new, consolidating
bourgeoisie itself at the time.

Naturally it was commerce which adopted the South
Africanist ideology most completely.   In spite of the
power of the free trade ideology in the early years, the
existence of full-time, creative ideologists, and of
media for the dissemination of ideology was something new
in commerce, an interesting indication of the relationship
between organic intellectuals and class disadvantage.
Early annual reports of Chambers of Commerce are
strikingly devoid of a social ideology of the range and
complexity of those found in the equivalent mining and
manufacturing sources, while no commercial journal of any

ideological significance existed until the 'Bulletin'
began. (82)   In 1933 the editor of the 'Commercial
Bulletin' pointed to the relative recency of full-scale
ideologising at Assocom Congresses too: (83)

> Presidential addresses at Congresses of the Associated
> Chambers of Commerce have in recent years departed from
> stereotyped lines, and the old tradition of avoiding
> controversial subjects and suppressing the personal
> view is no longer adhered to.   Presidents like the
> clergy, are in the privileged position on these
> occasions, of being able to express their opinions
> without fear of challenge or interruptions, which from
> many points of view is all to the good.   The common-
> place and platitudes, the easy refuge of those who do
> little thinking for themselves, will never succeed in
> provoking thought in others.

The 'Bulletin' and the speeches of Assocom presidents
became the most well-known and controversial platforms for
the South Africanist ideology in its most highly
politicised form after protection.   Not only did they
become the arena in which South Africanism was
consistently expressed, but they were used consciously by
ideologists for purposes of making far-reaching
innovations in the ideology of the interwar years:

> These annual meetings of the Parliament of Commerce
> have proved of immense value not only to trade but to
> the country generally.   Bringing together as they do
> all the leading business men from all parts of the
> Union, they serve to focus attention on every important
> phase of the country's economic development.   They
> afford an opportunity for considering impartially and
> in a non-political spirit, the work and enactments of
> Parliament during the preceding session.   The value of
> this is greatly enhanced by the presence at these
> annual meetings of the heads of all the principal
> Departments of state and not infrequently by one or
> more Cabinet ministers.   But probably of still greater
> value than the debates and resolutions is the
> opportunity afforded for personal contacts and
> conversation between the leading business men of the
> four provinces.

It is clear from this that commercial ideological
events were of a different nature from those we have
examined in both the mining and the manufacturing
contexts.   The public, generalised ideological functions
are added to the specific, intrasectoral functions which
the other ideologists performed.   The state and 'the
public' are part of the audience, although the commercial
men themselves still form its core.   This too is made
explicit: (84)

The primary function of Congress is the creation of
public opinion without which no reforms can be brought
about.   Looking back over the history of the
Association, now in its fortieth year, there is ample
evidence of the invaluable work it has done in this
respect.   Changes and reforms which it has
persistently advanced have come about unobtrusively and
almost unnoticed.   Again and again public opinion has
been created and influenced for which the Association
has claimed no credit.   Its views, if not always
adopted, are at least listened to, and are frequently
quoted during debates in Parliament.   The very fact
that these views are the considered opinion of not one
Province or section, but of the whole of the Union,
and every branch of trade and industry, lend weight,
which demands attention.   If it were not so, it would
be impossible, year after year, to bring together a
hundred or more of the busiest men of affairs in the
country to discuss matters, many of which do not
concern them personally.

This long quotation contains a number of illuminating
statements.   First, it should be said that the claim that
the 'invaluable work' of the Congress has been performed
'over the last forty years' does not contradict the
assertion made above that commercial ideology, in a
coherent and systematic form, was a post-protection
development.   In fact, the 'invaluable work' which
Congresses are supposed to have done lay in the field of
the bringing about of 'changes and reforms' which may not
necessarily have involved organic intellectuals.   Second,
it reveals that commercial congresses and ideological
media contained, and had been developed to contain, the
very ingredients which ideologists of the 'new
bourgeoisie' were to need - the ability and facilities for
the spreading, as well as the creating, of views and
opinions.   In addition, in the case of the post-
protection period, this ability could easily be adapted to
the function of spreading the ideology which commerce had
adopted - South Africanism.   The quotation is an
illustration of the tendency of commerce to externalise
its ideological events; and of its ability to be
concerned with matters which do not concern business men
personally.   The 'Bulletin', too, did this: (85)

One of the primary functions of this journal is to
reflect as accurately as possible commercial opinion on
all subjects directly or indirectly connected not only
with trade, but also with all that concerns the
economic progress and development of the country
generally. ... This is not always an easy task.

Public opinion is notoriously difficult to judge with
any degree of confidence.

The external orientation of the 'Bulletin' was made
even more explicit when, in 1932 the editor employed a
columnist who was self-consciously not a 'business man',
and yet whose task it was to inform commerce, as an
interest, how it 'looked' from the outside.   This was
something which neither the manufacturing nor the mining
journal editor would have done.   'Quandell', as he was
called, explained that his column was to be called 'From
an Onlookers' Armchair': (86)

It is not always true that 'the onlooker sees most of
the game'. ... But it is true that in commerce, as in
many other things, the onlooker may see aspects of the
game which are not obvious to the man who has his head
down in the scrum.   I am not engaged in the practice
of commerce in the ordinary sense of the term;   nor am
I much concerned with academic theories of economics.
But it is my business as a journalist to keep a finger
on the pulse of the world;   and the world goes its own
way with as little respect for the theories of the
academicians as for the struggles of the practical man.
The newspaper man who takes the whole wide world for
his province, as he watches each today grow out of its
yesterday and stretch out to its tomorrow, gets a
general impression of the trend of events which sometimes shows things in different proportions from those
in which they appear to other people.

The nature of the ideological activities of commercial
'intellectuals' made them particularly suited to the new
ideological needs of the emerging, non-imperial
bourgeoisie.   The reasons for this are explained in more
detail in chapters 5 and 6.   For the moment, it should
suffice to say that not only did commerce adopt South
Africanism, but that it adapted it and was well-placed to
redirect it in the directions required by the bourgeoisie
itself.   While manufacturing, state and other ideologists
simply used South Africanism, commerce took over the
creative role itself.   Ideology was created and modified
in commercial circles, and commerce claimed to be the
ideological centre of South Africanist activity for the
whole bourgeois audience.

The listing of specific examples of the adoption by
commerce of the South Africanist ideology might tend to be
overwhelmingly repetitious, since the ideology has been
exhaustively examined in chapter 3, and has already been
repeatedly quoted in this chapter.   Moreover, so much of
the analysis of the remainder of this study is based upon
the commercial innovations *within* the South Africanist

ideology, that it should become clear the extent to which
it dominated commercial culture.

Thus it seems that accompanying the process of class
formation in the case of South Africa's national
bourgeoisie after the First World War were two other
processes.   On the one hand, there was the adoption of
'South Africanism' in one form or another by groups other
than manufacturers.   On the other, there was the creation
of new media through which intellectuals could perform
the functions not only of reproducing South Africanism,
but of modifying it.   These processes seem to have taken
place in three spheres.   In manufacturing itself the
ideological network grew and was consolidated.   In
commerce, the other half of the new bourgeoisie, new media
were set up whose most interesting function was to create
a link between the bourgeoisie and the wider society, the
'public'.   The third sphere was perhaps the most
remarkable.   For here we find intellectuals of capital
emerging in the state apparatuses.   And yet these were
not mere propagandists, but seem to have been mandated to
produce a practical blueprint for the bourgeoisie - a
function performed by more clearly 'organic' intellectuals
in the case of mining capital.   The existence of these
planners and ideologists is not evidence of national
capital's early hegemony.   As we shall see, the
industrial planning bodies were largely ineffectual.   But
they should also not be dismissed as a mere cardboard
concession to a growing pressure group - for this would be
bourgeois political science at its worst.   What such an
explanation would miss would be the fact that these media
served a creative intellectual function for national
capital.   Furthermore they undertook to perform a
function which perhaps is classically performed under the
aegis of the state - the co-ordination of data from the
various sectors now coming together to form the
bourgeoisie, and their allies.   In these state media, it
seems probable that national capital had thus laid the
ground for working out and developing its future relationship with the state apparatuses, and for changing the
state from its old imperial form to one more suited to its
needs.

CONCLUSION

In this pivotal chapter we have tried to portray a massive
change in the nature of capital in South Africa.   In
order to capture the essence and significance of this
change we need to move away from the endless and

multiplying 'sectors', 'sections' and 'fractions' of
capital, its allies and its enemies, that have littered
this and the previous chapter, and to consider capital on
a more general plane.

One's first inclination in seeking to rise above the
various sectors of capital is to consider it as a single,
if complex, class.   Is what we have examined here best
viewed as a process of economic, political and ideological
change in the capitalist class in South Africa?   It would
be simpler if it were so.   However, what would be gained
in simplicity would be lost in validity, for large and
central portions of this account would be left unexplained
by such an interpretation.   Unfortunately for the
historian of capital, it seems that there is a good case
for arguing that we have not one, but two distinct classes
of capital here, and that *both* have been shown to have
undergone far-reaching and simultaneous changes in this
period. (87)

If 'class' is used in more than simply an economic
sense, then it would seem valid to argue that we have in
this South African example a class of 'imperial capital',
and a class of 'national capital'.   These classes existed
side by side, and each was composed of several distinct
sections.   Imperial capital, at the *beginning* of our
period, consisted mainly of mining capital, merchant
capital, British-based manufacturing capital, and
agricultural capital.   What distinguished these various
groups as members of a class was their economic place in a
distinct system of imperial exploitation of South Africa;
their political representation through a state forged to
serve those imperial interests; *and* the expression of
these interests through a clear-cut and distinctive
imperial ideology.   Of these several sections of imperial
capital it was mining that was the leading one.   As well
as constituting a class, imperial capital was the
hegemonic, ruling class in South Africa.

National capital, by the *end* of the period under
discussion, was also a class of great complexity, made up
of industrialists, traders, certain mining companies, and
farmers.   But it was led by one of its sections -
manufacturing.   Just as mining capital had led and forged
imperial hegemony, so did manufacturing capital seek to
lead the process whereby the national bourgeoisie could
replace the imperial one.   Manufacturing ideologists, it
seemed, were best placed to articulate the interests of
national capital as a whole.   The most likely reason for
this is that it is only local manufacturing capital that
has a necessary and unambiguous interest in local
industrialisation.   The constituent parts of the national

bourgeoisie too were distinguishable as members of a class
through their economic place in a system of local
capitalism;   their actual or attempted realisation of
their common interests through the polity;   and their own,
different, clearly bourgeois ideology.

The change we have documented here has thus not been a
change *within* a single capitalist class;   it has not been
a change, say from 'mining' to 'manufacturing' dominance
within capital, as some have seen it.   Nor has it been a
change *from* imperial capital *to* national capital, a uni-
linear progression, as perhaps others might see it.
Instead there has been a simultaneous change in both.
While imperial capital's influence declined, that of
national capital rose;   while the elements that
constituted imperial capital were shaken by war, those of
national capital seized the opportunity to grow and become
firmer;   while the constituent elements of imperial
capital shifted in one direction, those of national
capital shifted in another.   To some extent the changes
in the one class were a function of the changes in the
other - although there is no functionalist assumption that
this would be automatic.   The forces that made this so
were complex enough to have provided the material for much
of this long discussion.   Not only have we seen these two
classes form on more than one level, over a period of
time, but we have seen parts of one dissolve into the
other, under the catalysts of war, unemployment, labour
resistance and industrial boom.

Out of these large-scale changes in the nature of
capital in South Africa there emerged a challenging
contender for the hegemony held by imperial capital since
the turn of the century.   A national bourgeoisie was
consolidating itself around the core sectors of
manufacturing and commerce, and was creating for itself a
network of subsidiary functionaries, as well as a widespread ideological network for the articulation of its
changing interests;   while its two allies, agriculture and
white workers, had fulfilled its first and indispensable
requirement through the 1925 Tariff Act.   However, these
events were not the culmination of a change in hegemony in
South Africa, but only the beginning.   It remains to be
seen whether and how this bourgeoisie set about
transforming the South African polity according to its
needs.

5   The foundations of the white state

Imperial capital usually creates states whose area of
legitimacy and incorporation is confined to a small ruling
group.   That this group was exclusively and rigidly
defined as a white one, and that it included workers as
well as capital, may have been an unusual feature of the
imperial state form in South Africa, but it represented a
variation on a common theme.   National capital, on the
other hand, seems very rarely to create state forms of
this exclusive and minority nature;   while surely no
national bourgeoisie has attained hegemony and brought
into being a minority state circumscribed by race, outside
of South Africa.   One of the central questions that must
concern us, therefore, is that of the relationship between
the national bourgeoisie in South Africa, and the
persistence of the racist, imperially-forged state form.

In attempting to discover this relationship in this and
the subsequent chapter, we must explore two major issues.
The first is that of the actual structure and ordering of
capital's interests in the new situation we analysed
above.   Now that imperial capital was on the decline, and
national capital on the ascent, how did the latter define
its economic and political interests?   Were they the same
as they had been in the days when South Africanism was
forged, or did the fact that the industrialisation of
South Africa had now become a real possibility change
capital's interests and its ideologists' translations of
them into political and ideological prescriptions?   Foremost in our discussion of these questions must surely be a
concern to discover whether South African national capital
possessed interests roughly the same as those of other
industrialising bourgeoisies.

If we find that the fundamental economic imperatives
driving national capital in South Africa are not
strikingly different from those operating in capitalist

systems elsewhere, then we must raise the second major
issue: what was it about the *realisation* of those
interests that rendered the South African state form
unique?   Clearly all of capital's economic interests are
also political interests, for their realisation involves
the acquiescence or co-operation of other groups and
classes of people.   We must thus look at the historical
roots of the various classes and sub-classes with which
capital had to interact; at their necessary place in the
structure of capital's interests; and at the implications
of this for the formation of the state.

Our analysis of these issues falls into two parts.   In
this chapter we examine capital's interests *vis-à-vis* the
class structure; in the next we explore the implications
of these interests for the state apparatuses.   But it
should be remembered that the state itself comprises both
of these aspects, according to our understanding of it -
for the ways in which capital controls subordinate and
collaborating classes are not confined to the visible and
tangible state apparatuses, but include the intangible
forces of ideology and its structural manifestations.
Thus we are talking about the state in both of these
chapters - about capital's need for a particular class
structure, a particular definition of 'civil society', a
particular formula for legitimacy, a particular set of
state apparatuses, and a particular political system.   In
sum, we are examining capital's own conception of the kind
of hegemony it needed.

It should first be made clear that on a general and
primarily economic plane, the interests of South Africa's
new bourgeoisie were comparable with those of any other
capitalist class seeking to reproduce and expand itself.
It has been said that the best capitalists are also
Marxists, and it is remarkable the extent to which the
ideologists of industry in South Africa in the late 1920s
echoed Marx's own analysis of the complex structure of the
forces which drive the capitalist economy.   J.E. Borain,
in his presidential address to the FCI in 1929 spelled
them out one by one: (1)

> Nearly all of us live very close to our businesses, and
> are so absorbed in details that we do not realise,
> perhaps, the great changes in production, distribution
> and consumption, which are taking place so rapidly.
> ... All over the world, mass production is becoming the
> normal method of industrial operation.   More and more
> machinery is being used to perform operations
> previously undertaken by hand labour.   Work, which
> formerly required weeks and months is being done in as
> many days.

This, the first of the new needs of South African
capital - the need to compete with mass production systems
throughout the world by producing low-priced goods - was
complicated by the second: 'side by side with this has
gone a revolution in social and labour conditions', said
Borain, who meant by this that throughout the world,
wages, hours and conditions of work were improving partly
as a result of vastly increased worker militancy, and thus
the prices of goods were raised.   Added to this was a
third problem, not universal to all capitalist systems,
but common to those whose industrial revolution was
relatively late:

> We are told that our manufacturers should use more and
> more machinery so as to produce in large quantities and
> bring the cost of production down to that of competing
> countries.   This is not so easy as it sounds.   We are
> doing all we can, but it is a question of markets and
> clearly we cannot produce as cheaply as other countries
> can, owing to the limitation of our available market.

The cheapness of industrial goods was thus determined by a
third force;   this problem was solved in many countries by
the intervention of an independent force, he said: 'For
that reason, it is necessary to ask the Government to
assist us by endeavouring to bring the competitive factors
upon a more level basis.'   But this too, in countries
with a weak bourgeoisie, such as South Africa, had a
price: labour demands for better conditions and wages in
a situation of low profitability:

> We as a community have never opposed these demands in
> principle, but the time is coming when it will be
> impossible to concede more because the available
> resources of industry, within our limited market, will
> not permit of further additions to the cost of
> production. ... Competition today is very keen, not
> only among domestic producers, but also from imported
> goods.   Business is done on small margins of profit,
> and he is fortunate who is engaged in an industry
> which has a sufficiently large volume of turnover to
> enable him to accumulate substantial profits.

In the words of a prominent manufacturing ideologist
himself, whose audience, as he correctly points out, may
be too concerned with their own businesses to see the
overall needs of the class to which they belonged, the
nature of the complex nexus of restraints and imperatives
which drive the capitalist economy, is sketched here.
And as ideologists were aware, they are imperatives which
are filled with contradictions and over-lapping and cross-
cutting demands.   The basic drive for profitability, the
resulting competitive rationalisation, mechanisation and

mass production, and the need for state regulation of both
of these, through protectionism and the regulation of
competition, are threatened by the growing power of
workers to raise their own cost to capital, the access of
some of them to the very state which is essential for
capital's purposes, and the smallness of the market.   The
class struggle and the prevailing economic structures, the
state apparatuses and the state form itself, are all
directly involved in capital's interests.   The way in
which ideologists directed their audience towards
realising this nexus of interests was dictated by the
particular conditions of South African society.   It
provoked some important changes in the content and
orientation of South Africanism.   Just as the new
interests of the 'new bourgeoisie' formed a complex nexus
of overlapping and cross-cutting forces, so did the
ideologists' responses to them.   In the spheres of the
white working class, the black working class, the 'general
public' and the state apparatuses ideologists worked to
transform petty-bourgeois South Africanist ideas into a
corporate class consciousness for the entire bourgeoisie
and to develop a practical blueprint for the
transformation of the class structure and state form to
accord with the bourgeoisie's interests.

It will be remembered that a conciliatory system of
white worker control had been advocated by early
manufacturing ideologists in the days when the petty-
bourgeois nature of production, the need of capital for
allies, and the white worker interest in protection had
combined to make it both feasible and desirable.   With
the expansion of industry, the beginnings of mass
production and the growth of white working-class
consciousness in the industrial sphere (as opposed to
mining), ideologists considered their older stance in a
new light.   During and after the war, employers faced
greatly increased white worker organisation and
militancy.   Whereas in 1915, there were 10,500
unionists, by 1920, the depths of the post-war depression,
this had risen to 132,000 members of ninety recorded
unions. (2)   In October 1917, a tailors' strike provoked
intense ideological response from manufacturers, as one of
the most outstanding indications of a 'good deal of unrest
in labour circles, having as its foundations the rising
cost of living due to War conditions'. (3)   By 1919,
building workers had held a twelve-week strike, the
longest in South Africa's industrial history, (4) which
was accompanied by the simultaneous development of what
the manufacturing journal called 'unconstitutional
movements' amongst the employees of the Johannesburg Town

Council. (5)   By that date, the journal could say that
the 'whole country is seething with unrest', and, moreover, that 'there are aspects of the industrial situation
which, to say the least, are extremely grave and call for
urgent action, unless the country is to be forced into
revolution and perhaps internecine war.' (6)   Strikes
were so frequent that one journal ran a column on 'strikes
of the month', and it was clear to many that, as one
writer put it, 'The whole labour situation is proceeding
by well-defined steps to a certain end - a general
strike.' (7)   Certainly white workers were challenging
not only the share of the industrial cake they were
getting, but the system of hegemony itself, both by their
establishment of 'Soviets' in Johannesburg, and, later,
Durban, and by the failure of some of them to accept the
illegitimacy of black worker 'imitations' of their
militancy. (8)   To manufacturing ideologists, this sphere
of 'unrest' was of far greater significance than the
dispute between white mineworkers and their employers,
which was, naturally, part of the general increase in
labour organisation and militancy, but which was
essentially the culmination of a long-standing conflict
within the mining industry and was, moreover, controlled
within the existing hegemonic order.   Industrial
unionisation and unrest was something new, and ideologists
were forced to re-think their somewhat naive ideas about
conciliation.

   A distinction needs to be made between two levels - the
ideological and the practical - on which the entire period
of confrontation between white labour and capital was
conducted.   On the practical level, the individual
employer or group of employers responded to strikes and
confrontation with the aim of preserving their position
and the overall legitimacy of the system within which
they existed and operated.   Strikes were condemned and
attempts made to crush them, while wages were lowered. (9)
The ideologists of capital, however, were, from the very
beginning of the post-war 'troubles', actively considering
and even designing means whereby such confrontation could
be redirected, and avoided, along the very lines which
manufacturing ideologists had been proposing since their
ideology was first developed.   Their deliberations were
now altogether more serious and their designs geared ever
more to real possibilities.   Dozens of lengthy and well-
considered articles appeared in the manufacturing journal
in particular, in which the issue of 'Industrial Unrest'
was foremost.   Ideological creativity was at its greatest
in this sphere - in the journals of the 'new bourgeoisie',
which provide a vivid contrast to the 'South African

Mining Journal' of the time, where ideology was not being
created around the 1922 strike, but simply
reproduced. (10)

In December 1917, Edmund Hastings wrote of the
'lessons' which could be learned from the tailors' strike:
'Conciliation Boards are a proved necessity, since they
may be the means of preventing strikes', and later:
'There is every indication that the Tailors' dispute has
hastened the introduction of Wages Boards. The system
has worked admirably elsewhere, and there is not the
slightest objection to it on the part of employers.' (11)
In an analysis of existing industrial legislation, Patrick
Duncan pointed out to manufacturers that only two Acts of
Parliament claimed to deal with the problem of 'providing
machinery for the fixing of wages, for the settlement of
disputes etc.' - the Industrial Disputes Act of the
Transvaal, and the recently-passed Regulation of Wages
Act. While the former failed to prevent strikes, the
latter was criticised for its narrowness. (12)

Manufacturers were agreed that both were inadequate,
and all sorts of conciliatory proposals were put forward.
Higher protection, it was argued by some, would obviate
the need for legislative conciliatory measures since
higher wages should become possible; (13) the
establishment of communications between employers and
employees - through conferences, for example - it was
argued by others, would alleviate the problems of
industrial unrest, leading to: 'that complete fusion of
interests which will allow the country to march to its
destined end under the most enlightened conditions
possible.' (14) But the weight and thrust of the debate
centred on one thing - the perceived necessity for the
government to deal with, and establish structures for the
solution of, industrial unrest. 'The labour situation
... has developed with practically no check on the part of
the authorities', according to one ideologist: (15)

> What Acts of Parliament there are in existence are
> practically inoperative, and, in any case, they only
> affect the Transvaal. It is surely not too much to
> ask that our legislators shall bend their efforts
> towards endeavouring to find a solution to this
> problem.

He referred to the long series of discussions held in
recent years on how to deal with 'industrial unrest', and
urged that:

> Labour and Capital must arrive at an understanding, and
> that without delay.
> Some method of achieving it has to be found, and it is
> useless either to try to crush labour movements or to

talk the platitudes of the classical economists of the
Victorian era.   Labour must be satisfied, and unless
we start with a recognition of this fact, plus a desire
to deal with the situation adequately and
sympathetically, the only outcome will be chaos.

The need for government action was desperate:

The Government must realise this fact, and must also
understand that every week delayed in endeavouring to
secure a means of settlement is retarding the progress
of the country as a whole: trade will be restricted,
and industrial ruin will stare us in the face, while
the country is in the throes of internal labour
revolt. ... If nothing is done, the blame for whatever
happens must rest with the Government.   The sinister
shadow of Bolshevism already spreading in the Transvaal
simply serves to confound further an already confused
position.   The growth of labour unrest is spreading,
and as it spreads it becomes more difficult to realise
actually what is involved in it.   The various demands
of different sections of labour put forward as they are
under conditions of stress and excitement only
complicate the issue, and it is the duty of the most
authoritative body in the land to adopt some means
which will clear away the verbal trappings, and lay
bare the actual underlying basis of the whole movement,
with a view to presenting some satisfactory and
concrete method which will result in settled
conditions.

This long extract is a good indication of the anxiety
amongst employers, of their relative weakness and
consequent reliance on the state, and of the
perceptiveness of the ideologist, who attempts to
summarise for his audience the range of alternative
solutions open to them, and to assess their potential.
Other conciliatory policies, some of which resembled
early mining, as well as manufacturing ideas, were put
forward; many of them also required the intervention and
co-operation of the government.   Unemployment
insurance, (16) worker education, (17) 'giving labour a
voice in industry', (18) reviving white 'respect for
work', (19) and making labour realise that its interests
were identical with capital's (20) were all suggested as
possible strike-prevention methods.   Workers were to be
encouraged to participate in the creation of the
institutions which channeled their grievances.
'Participation in conciliation' may have been the motto of
the 'organic intellectuals'.

In the 1920s, the intrusion of the Labour Party into
what ideologists considered to be matters which

exclusively concerned them and 'their' party - by then,
the South African Party (21) - complicated and confused
the issue.   Ideologists' pleas for conciliatory
legislation were directed at the government in power at
the time, and they were beginning to obtain some hearing
in the form of the abovementioned Wages Regulation Act
of 1918, a further Wages Board Bill of 1921, an abortive
Industrial Conciliation Bill of the same year, and,
finally, the Industrial Conciliation Act of 1924 itself.
When the Pact Government introduced the Wages Act of
1926, however, capital's desire for conciliation now
found an echo in the Labour Party's moderate trade
unionist approach to the question of the regulation of
relationships, and at least as far as English-speaking
labour was concerned, policies of conciliation,
arbitration and institutionalised, ritualised labour-
capital relationships, won the day over the more radical
and uncompromising designs of the non-Labour Party
members of the labour movement.   In the words of a
South African government publication of the 1960s: (22)

> The [1924] government was sympathetic towards trade
> unions, being of the opinion that they were instruments
> which could be usefully employed for regulating
> management-labour relations.   This was a courageous
> policy considering the militant attitude of trade
> unionism in many countries.   By various measures ...
> the Government enhanced the status of trade unions and
> made them equal partners with employers' organisations.
> Later events have fully justified the trust placed by
> the authorities in the common sense and moderation of
> South African labour.

The earlier Industrial Conciliation Act of 1924 had
been a deeply conservative measure which realised
capital's interests more than labour's.   Designed to
place obstacles before potential strikers, it made the
procedures for regulating wage and other negotiations
complex and multi-faceted, and, moreover, compulsory.
Employers' Associations, Trade Unions, and Industrial
Councils were all to be registered in the various
industries, and it was through these that the initial
negotiations had to take place.   If these failed,
conciliation boards could be appointed; and if these
failed, arbitration could be used.   The essential
industries of water, light, transport, sanitation and
fire, were excluded from even these provisions.   Beyond
that, any agreement could, with the approval of the
Minister of Labour, be declared binding by him upon the
employers and employees concerned whereupon it became a
criminal offence to break the agreement.

The conciliatory view had won a substantial victory by
the mid-1920s, while conciliation had the desired effect
of channelling and preventing worker grievances.   As one
ideologist said in 1927: (23)

> the position was getting desperately serious prior to
> the passing of the Conciliation Act in 1924.   Not only
> was there the great mining strike, which ended in
> bloodshed, but from 1920-1924 there were one hundred
> and twelve strikes in South Africa, and we are only a
> small community.   One hundred and forty five thousand
> were involved and two million one hundred thousand
> pounds were lost in wages.   In 1924, the Industrial
> Conciliation Act was passed by the late Government.
> It has been energetically administered by the present
> Government, and I think the Act is well in advance of
> similar legislation in any other country ...
> 1925 - No strikes whatever.
> 1926 - Three only, involving sixty six Europeans and a
> few hundred natives.
> 1927 - Promises to be equally peaceful.

The writer saw the system of industrial relations
established at this time the beginning of the way to a
'permanent industrial peace', which suggests that in one
central respect the realisation of capital's interests had
been successfully negotiated and the first stone had been
laid in the foundations of the new state.

Black industrial worker militancy and power had also
grown in South Africa after the war.   Not only had blacks
in factories begun to strike and organise, but increasing
numbers of them had become fully proletarianised and hence
represented a force in the towns which had to be
confronted and coped with by capital in different terms
from those used to manage migrant workers separated from
their rural families.   Black worker militancy occurred on
two levels.   Workers confronted their employers directly,
by organising and striking either alone, or in combination
with white workers;   and they joined the mass organisation
of blacks which dominated the era - the Industrial and
Commercial Workers' Union (ICU) - to confront white power
in South Africa as a totality.   Both were regarded with
grave concern by ideologists of capital who recognised,
just as they had done in the case of white workers, the
need for a long-term strategy.   The fact of the increased
proletarianisation of blacks contributed substantially to
this perception;   the decline of black subsistence
agriculture had proceeded so rapidly that some have argued
that as early as 1920 manufacturing and commerce did not
employ migrant males, but whole families of workers, who
had little or no ties with the land, and no means of

subsistence other than the selling of their labour
power. (24)   Apart from the fact that this raised their
costs, this meant that, unlike mining, industrial capital
had to devise methods of control which did not depend on
the peripherality of blacks.   The complex and broadly-
based ideology of liberalism, which rose to prominence in
South Africa between the world wars, was the bourgeoisie's
response to this situation.   Following on the paternalism
of the early years, liberalism towards the black working
class was almost certainly a bourgeois ideology, centred
on manufacturing and needed by commercial and other
sections of the employing class for their own purposes.

The first notable aspect of liberalism was that it was
intimately related to, and in some respects a function of,
the policy of conciliation towards white workers.   It was
the relationship *between the sections of the working class*
that capitalist ideologists dealt with first.   Indeed, it
is a common mistake for capital's strategies towards
different sections of the working class to be taken by
scholars entirely separately, as though the 'two working
classes' were the given reality and not a creation of the
dominant class.   The explanation of the development of
liberalism has been particularly restricted by this
approach.   As black worker militancy grew it began to
become clear that one of the reasons for conciliating
white workers was to prevent black workers being provided
with an example of how working classes would challenge,
and in some cases defeat, capital.   This was itself the
confirmation of mining's tenet that white and black
workers must at all costs be kept separate.   During 1920
the ICU began to gain massive support amongst black
workers and peasants and to confront employers directly.
'If any of the Native strikers believe they have won a
victory by using white man's methods, it is pretty certain
they will spread the gospel, and in the end the natives
will move like an avalanche of destruction', wrote the
'ISA' after a strike in early 1920: black workers would
inevitably resent those who 'gave way to the white man,
but coerce the Native'.   As a result: 'The Native will
get out of hand, and the man-child will act like a child
but with a man's strength.' (25)

Blacks, being 'children', were considered to be incapable
of dissenting without the actions of the 'agitator', be he
a white worker or an 'educated native'.   The greatest
folly of the white worker would be to perform this
'agitating' function, for given their privileged and
collaborating position, they, like employers, would
ultimately be the losers.   Blacks would descend like an
'avalanche of destruction' and 'get out of hand'.   The

answer, therefore, was for whites to conform to the
patterns of industrial conciliation set up for them by
state and employer and to leave the black working class
well alone.   Methods applicable in a 'white man's
country' were not to be used in South Africa;   while the
divided working class must be recognised as such.   It was
along these lines that 'ISA' treated subsequent black
militancy: (26)

> The labour situation is becoming daily more
> threatening, and the action of the Lovedale natives in
> donning the red tie and setting out on a campaign of
> destruction of property, should give pause to those who
> essay to be the leaders of Labour in South Africa.   We
> have before pointed out that whilst agreeing that
> Labour has every right to a larger proportion of the
> wealth it creates than it has had in the past, and
> whilst it may be necessary on occasions for action to
> be taken to enforce legitimate demands, yet the policy
> which may be perfectly permissible in a white man's
> country, must be discarded absolutely and finally in a
> country where a handful of white men is surrounded by
> 6,000,000 child-like natives.   The Lovedale outbreak
> is a straw which shows which way the wind is blowing,
> and unless the Labour leaders of this country are
> prepared to think before they act, the ultimate end is
> terrifying to the imagination.

The journal referred explicitly to the 'International
Socialists' who had been pleading 'Equality, Fraternity
and Brotherhood' and who had not distinguished white from
black workers sufficiently to satisfy capital:

> Why these gentlemen should feel themselves called upon
> to interfere with the native, it is difficult to
> imagine, but having done so, they now have the
> satisfaction of knowing that, thanks to this insidious
> propaganda, the country is in the position of a man who
> has been playing with a detonator - it is badly hurt.
> There can be no doubt, too, that the ordinary leaders
> of labour cannot hold themselves entirely blameless for
> the present state of native unrest.   Without thought
> of the consequences, they have urged the white worker
> to go all out in achieving a settlement of his demands
> - reasonable or unreasonable.   Strikes and threats of
> strikes have been common.   The value of labour
> organisation has been shouted from every platform, and
> whenever an employer has ventured, with all deference,
> to hint that there is also his view which might be
> taken into consideration, he has been met with an
> immediate stoppage of work, and threats as to
> consequences to follow.   The native has seen all this,

and, turning it over in his childlike mind, has come to
the conclusion that it would be no bad thing for the
black man to follow the lead of the white.   He is
hardly to be blamed for this;   and so, with both
precept and example before him, he has taken action.
The result has been that perfectly innocent parties
have been killed and injured, and there has been laid
up for the country a store of troubles of which the
end is not yet.

Yet another long extract gives a good indication of
capital's perceptions of the links between
proletarianisation, labour 'unrest', white-black
working-class unity, and the need for a structural remedy
for these problems: (27)

Perhaps the outstanding feature of the labour situation
during recent months is the growth of the Industrial
and Commercial Workers' Union of South Africa, an
organisation designed for the protection of the
interests of Native and Coloured unskilled workers.
... This development is not altogether unexpected, as
it has been obvious that the Native and Coloured
workers, at some time or other, would take a leaf from
the book of their white confreres.   And so the Native
has been given a new thought, viz. organisation and
direct action!   Already demands have been served on
industrial and commercial bodies, and the Railways, and
it is not to be expected that these demands will cease
in the future.   The fact that this force has arisen in
the industrial life of the country is disquieting.
The dream of the aborigine is a Native Africa, as
witness the recent Conference in America.   This may
sound ludicrous, and given (sic) rise to laughter, but the
thinking man cannot see much humour in the movements
of an educated, organised Native people.   It is
possible that if the Leaders of White Labour had
realised the effect of their actions, South Africa
might have had less unrest in the past, and would
probably have been saved the spectacle of an organised
Native proletariat.   How serious this movement may be
in the future will appeal to all who give a few
moments' consideration to the question, and it is the
duty of all - employers and employees alike - to see
that they so order their affairs that the country is
spared Native uprisings and perhaps years of upheaval.

Ideologists incorporated the 'periphery' into the new,
liberal, concept of the native.   The danger, it was
thought, would come not from the workers alone, but from
the entire black population.   Working-class organisation
was but a catalyst for this potentially destructive and

even lethal force which the 'man-child' was considered
capable of unleashing.   But in this case, the 'danger' of
the periphery, it began to emerge, must not be averted by
repression.   Because in national capital's conception it
was not an inhuman place, nor even an inherently dangerous
place, the periphery could be redeemed, and steps taken to
divert the danger in harmless directions.   Whereas in
the mining hierarchy the two working classes had been
separated rigidly in a violent context, a conciliatory and
incorporationist method was devised to keep them separate
under national capital.   We have seen something of the
system created for whites.   A special kind of
'conciliation' for blacks was also proposed; most
characteristically 'liberal' was the suggestion that the
improvement of the conditions of the working class, would
prevent it from confronting capital.   Its wage was one
channel: (28)

> there must be grave cause for discontent amongst the
> Natives of the country.   It is an old axiom that there
> is no smoke without fire, and it would appear that
> there is every reason for special consideration being
> given to the present Native unrest. ... Too little
> attention seems to be devoted to the needs, and
> aspirations of the Native peoples of the country ... it
> is surely better to settle grievances and remove the
> causes of discontent, than to allow matters to take a
> course which can only lead to disaster,

said the 'ISA'.   For example, the ICU's demand for a
minimum wage had been ignored and: (29)

> it fell to the lot of the natives of Port Elizabeth,
> led by an agitator, to make good their threat of
> creating trouble in the event of their demands not
> being met. ... It behoves every employer of native
> labour - Government or private - to ask in all
> sincerity whether the wages of the natives employed
> have been advanced in ratio to the cost of living
> which the native is called upon to bear ... everything
> should be done to remove possible causes of friction
> from the great body of native population which South
> Africa possesses.

This represents the most vivid possible contrast with
mining cost-minimisation and repression.   So clear was
the distinction to the ideologists themselves that in the
same article, the 'ISA' said that: 'In this connection the
mine native is not indicated, as his conditions vary
considerably from those of others.   It is the town "boy"
who is referred to'.   The hierarchy itself was preserved,
but the black lower orders were to be incorporated by
opening to them a possible channel upwards from their low

status.   In addition, whilst the one was a hierarchy of
'castes', the other was to be one of wages, skills and a
differential necessary level of subsistence: (30)

> In South Africa, the difficulties are aggravated by the
> coloured population who are willing to work for, and
> can live at, a much lower rate of pay than Europeans.
> ... The best method ... to deal with this question is
> on the principle that each trade can, or should,
> employ certain percentages of skilled, semi-skilled,
> and unskilled labour, and that these proportions should
> be decided by Joint Councils of Industry presided over
> by a judge.   Having arrived at above percentages a
> minimum wage should be fixed for each grade
> irrespective of colour.   By this system each class
> would be graded on a practical and equitable system,
> employers would be at liberty to engage any workers
> they chose, and labour would have its protection in the
> standard and minimum wages fixed for each class.

It is of great importance to the process of state
formation that liberalism accepted hierarchy, albeit with
an 'incorporational outlet' for the lower orders.   It is
also important that this was not only different from the
ideas of mining, but from those of white labour itself,
whose 'civilised labour' policies constituted a rejection
of blacks as workers altogether.   White workers must,
according to this policy, be given preference over blacks
in unskilled as well as skilled jobs in spite of their
greater cost to employers.   In a sense white labour was
operating within the hierarchical categories of mining
hegemony, and had failed to recognise the differences
between old and new capital.   Mining hegemony was
successfully dictating the terms of the struggle.   Thus
the new bourgeoisie found itself confronting white labour
and mining together.   Manufacturing and bourgeois
ideologists were active in opposing the 'Colour Bar'
Bills of the Pact government, advocating their hierarchy
of skill and wage rather than of colour;   making explicit
reference to the proletarian condition of blacks;   and
couching their objections in the new liberal language.
The skill-wage hierarchy would conciliate both white
workers who, as long as they had preferential access to
training in skills, would not be threatened by cheap
black labour;   and black workers, who would be allowed to
move upwards.   It was also a policy which would prevent
the potential 'threat' from the 'periphery' from becoming
real due to black grievances;   because a small number of
blacks could move 'upwards' the vast majority could be
maintained at the lowest wages possible, without provoking
them into dissatisfied rebellion.

These ideas form the elements of the liberalism which
was being nurtured under the umbrella of South Africanist
ideology (whose roots, of course, in the economic and other
interests of capital we have already examined).   Centre
and periphery were to be brought together; blacks were to
be somehow incorporated; their lowly status was to be
alleviated by the provision of outlets - a 'ladder' which
they could climb; and suitable ideological forms were to
be created for each.   In the later 1920s and 1930s, the
journals of the new bourgeoisie were filled with debate
and discussion of these themes.   At the same time a substantial group of non-organic liberal intellectuals had
developed out of the old mould of segregationist liberalism
that had characterised early mining hegemony. (31)   The
journals of the bourgeoisie courted and developed links
with these ideologists, using their sophisticated concepts
of black worker control to refine their own developing
liberalism.   An important article by a non-organic intellectual who nevertheless wrote for the bourgeoisie at times
reveals the hiatus between imperial and national ideology.
It was by S.H. Frankel, whose earlier links with the mining
industry on the issues of tariffs and railways had angered
manufacturing ideologists. (32)   Frankel contributed
substantially to the debate in manufacturing circles,
however, making clear and explicit distinctions between
'old' native policies, and the 'new' ones which he thought
that by the late 1920s South Africa needed: (33)

it was a policy which regarded the conquered as existing
solely for the benefit of the conquerors.   Insofar as
one needed him, the native was allowed to remain, otherwise, he has ... pushed back further and further into
areas of his own.   And here attention must be drawn to
the psychology which dominates a policy of this nature.
It is compounded of an instinctive military attitude on
the one hand which fears the native and seeks to keep
him at arm's length from white civilisation, and a cal-
culating, more rational, attitude which recognises that
it is conveniently in the interests of the white man to
have the native's labour - no matter how inefficient it
might be as long as it was plentiful.   This mental
attitude combined with the characteristic ... that the
conquerors legislated at all times in what they thought
to be their own interests, and not in the combined
interests of both the races in South Africa, is
illustrated over and over again in the native
legislation of the past.

What Frankel called the 'military mind' created
structures of black labour control and exploitation which
were suited to that time, but which had lost their

function in the light of recent changes in the economy.
The 'periphery' dominated the 'military mind':
'Economically, the subject races were not to be regarded
as an asset but as a vast threatening danger to be kept
at bay.'   In an interesting indirect reference to the
question of hegemony he claimed that the Bills relating to
blacks which the Pact government was busily drafting at
the time had failed to leave this old 'military' mould:

> The mental attitude towards the subject races and the
> principles at the bottom of the proposed native
> legislation today are the same as those we have just
> outlined.   The only change appears to be that an
> attempt will be made to apply the erroneous beliefs of
> the past more radically in the future.

In discussing industry, Frankel made the liberal ideology
more explicit than ever:

> [in other countries] huge streams of immigrants are
> composed mainly of the poor.   They emigrate to seek
> for better opportunities.   They desire to find in the
> country of their adoption, an economic and social
> ladder, whether in agriculture or in industry.   A
> ladder which beginning as labourers at the bottom they
> can climb to reach the independence it offers at the
> top.   In South Africa there is no such ladder.   There
> is instead a deep gulf between the native workers who
> toil at the bottom and the small number of skilled men
> who hold the citadel of independence at the top.

By 1938, the journal of manufacturers was quoting the
liberal journal 'Forum' on the 'native problem', and was
itself proposing a variety of liberal measures along the
lines described above.   The views of the bourgeoisie
were epitomised in one editorial comment in that
year: (34)

> Somewhere between the extremism of the Left and the
> reaction of the Right lies the path which the native
> must walk.   Organisation among natives cannot be
> prevented, and it only remains for the Government to
> guide it by advice and constructive suggestion, and so
> enable the leaders of the natives to evolve a form of
> organisation suited to the needs of their people and
> the conditions of the country.

The evidence seems to suggest that from capital's point
of view it was its developing struggle with fully
proletarianised black labour, rather than any other
factor, which gave rise to the liberalism of the interwar
period.   While the ICU may not itself have been the
movement of a fully-fledged proletariat, but was rather
one of a class undergoing the process of
proletarianisation itself, (35) it, together with the

increase in black labour organisation and militancy of
later years, forced capital's intellectuals to plan
strategies for channelling, and possibly eliminating,
black challenges to capital's dominance.   One thing was
certain - that these plans should not in any way lead to a
united black and white working class.   This is surely a
crucial confirmation by national capital of mining
capital's initial state form, one which may be obscured by
the rhetoric of liberalism.   It is only within this that
the 'incorporationist' strategy should be understood.   A
working class that was first and foremost separated, cheap
and confined to the lower rungs of the prevailing
hierarchy, was to be controlled through the creation of a
small incorporationist 'outlet' for a tiny minority of its
members, and was to be in a limited and partial manner,
relieved of its 'peripheral' status.

Trivial as these modifications to mining hegemony may
seem in the light of their preservation of the divided
working class, and the persistence of repression, they
provided one of the major issues for debate and conflict
within capital in South Africa between the wars, and in
academic circles since.   It is not easy to decide the
extent to which they were successfully implemented.
While within the immediate state apparatuses very little
in the way of incorporationism was brought into being, and
indeed there is every indication that imperial hierarchy
and segregation continued, capital seems to have been
largely successful in creating para-statal apparatuses for
the realisation of its liberal interest, through its use
of a wide network of 'non-organic' intellectuals and
organisers, both black and white.   The universities, the
Institute of Race Relations, the ICU, the ANC, the Joint
Councils of Europeans and Natives, certain of the black
trade unions, and a variety of other bodies, were either
created by liberals or placed directly under their
influence in these years, and it is almost certain that
the effects of this were those desired by capital.   Black
challenges to capital's hegemony were defused and
redirected, through these concrete apparatuses, while the
ideological hold of liberalism over black organisations
was surely as powerful as the hold any hegemonic ideology
has over subordinate groups.   Whether capital chose to
impose liberalism on blacks through these channels
because it preferred it that way or because it had no
option is not clear.   But what is clear is the fact that
the use of only para-statal apparatuses to control blacks
left the way clear for capital to put its remaining
energies into the creation of a central state that was, to
all intents and purposes, an entirely white one.

As will be recalled, the nexus of capital's new
interests contained the elements of competition,
production, markets, worker demands, and the state.
Policy-makers, when faced with this complex set of
factors, found it difficult to approach them in a
systematic fashion.   While some of the factors were
'given', such as the power of white workers, the
proletarian status of black workers, the militancy of
both, and the relatively weak control of the bourgeoisie
over the state, others were not.   And yet they seemed to
ideologists and others to be so interconnected and interwoven that any one of them could not be removed from the
others, and, moreover, that any action by them on any
single factor might affect the other factors in
undesirable ways.

In general, the solution to the problem which most
ideologists made, was to tackle the nexus of interests
through one interest, itself highly complex, that of the
market.   The 'market' became to some extent the symbol of
all of the interests of the bourgeoisie of the 1920s and
1930s, just as had protection in earlier times.   Through
the market, it was felt, the other problems of realising
capital's interests could be approached relatively
systematically, and political and ideological solutions to
them found.   The market distinguished manufacturing and
commerce from mining, moreover.   But focusing on the
market should not be allowed to obscure the fact that
there remained a nexus of interests, that all of capital's
interests were inseparable.   Ideologists calculated,
perhaps correctly given the stage capitalist development
had reached in South Africa, that the discovery of large
and growing markets would solve all the remaining
contradictions and problems, that it would 'unlock' the
chain of capital's seemingly inseparable needs.

The market was thus one of the most common topics for
discussion in all the journals examined in the 1920s and
1930s.   Some ideologists, such as those of commerce,
which *is* the market in a sense, were more concerned with
it than others.   State ideologists too, with their more
global, planning-oriented view of the economy, were able
to see the future needs for a larger market as being
problematic.   Generally, in so far as there was an
ideological division of labour, manufacturing ideologists
tended to cope with conciliation and 'industrial unrest',
and commercial ideologists with the 'market', (36) while
state ideologists coped with both. (37)   The combined
effort of all, however, was to bring to the fore the issue
of South Africa's market most strikingly and consistently.
The main topic of concern was to find a social region,

either within or outside of South Africa, which would come
to believe of its own accord, or through persuasion, that
goods produced by South African industries were desirable
in ever-increasing quantities.   The market had, therefore, to be both economically and ideologically suited to
capital's needs and it had to have the capacity to grow
steadily and continually.   This apparently economic
interest of capital thus had important political
implications.

H.E.S. Fremantle summed up the problem of the market as
it was perceived at the time: 'As long as the population
remains small, it will not be economical in many
industries to have more than one factory, if they are to
cater for South Africa alone. ... Therefore the first
thing needed by our industrialists is the filling up of
the country with consumers.' (38)   In fact, manufacturers
had long recognised that South Africa's consuming
population was relatively small, and had from the earliest
times orientated themselves towards exporting finished
consumer goods to other African countries. (39)   Exports,
therefore, were the first line of attack for those seeking
markets.   During and after the war this emphasis on
exports persisted in manufacturing circles, and began to
gain reinforcement from protectionists within state
organisations, such as Fremantle himself:

> there is something like a national movement in which
> the Government is taking its share, in regard to the
> establishment of several great key industries.   This
> development must itself drive us to an export trade,
> as there are many things which it is easier to make
> for the world market than for a small market such as
> that of South Africa at the present time.   The home
> demand for finer sorts of leather, for instance, is so
> small that the tanners are seriously handicapped
> compared with tanners overseas working for the markets
> of the whole world and combining the advantages of
> specialisation and mass production. ... In other cases
> the establishment of home manufacturers will quickly
> lead to overproduction. ... Once the young giantess of
> South Africa awakes she will soon consume and will find
> herself invading the markets of the world, with all
> sorts of food and metal and worked-up raw materials in
> her basket.

With the institution of protection, this exporting
approach was even further reinforced, with Laite changing
his journal to cope with the information needed by
potential foreign importers of South African goods, and
the new Pact government instituting Trade Commissioners in
several countries in and out of Africa. (40)   It was the

African, and particularly the Rhodesian, market, which
struck the aspirant exporters as being most suited to
South Africa's requirements.   In 1930, the President of
the FCI visited Rhodesia with this in mind, (41) and the
Minister of Railways, C.H. Malan, emphasised Africa's
buying power, and the need for South African goods to
break into the markets captured by other countries during
times of imperial domination: (42)

> Look beyond the borders of the Union for markets.
> The southern and central portion of the Continent of
> Africa is our natural market, and there lies
> opportunity for our industrialists.   Blue prints and
> other textiles, glass beads, bangle wire etc., are
> today being manufactured in the USA, Germany and Japan
> to supply the demands of the millions of natives at our
> very doors.   Why cannot we produce these and other
> lines?   The market is next to us and the demand great
> enough for us to produce on as large a scale as any
> overseas manufacturer. ... Not only Rhodesia, but also
> the Congo, Nyasaland, Angola, Tanganyika, Kenya and
> countries even further north, should look to South
> Africa much more than they already do for their
> supplies.

The Rhodesian market had been so effectively captured by
South African exports by the mid-1930s that the nascent
Rhodesian manufacturing interest, which resembled that
which had arisen in South Africa in the early 1900s, began
to object to the terms of Rhodesian-South African
trade. (43)

It was commerce that pointed out that this first course
of action contained a contradiction which was at the time
insoluble: (44)

> The production costs of our secondary industries are
> the highest in the world.   This has been deliberately
> brought about by political interference ... meanwhile
> the same political interference is at work trying to
> get markets abroad for the products of primary
> industries.   These products have to compete with
> products of other countries, where costs of the
> products of secondary industries used by them are
> vastly cheaper than ours.

By 'political interference' he meant the high wage
determinations of the Wage Board, and the 'civilised
labour policy', which required the use of white workers in
preference to cheaper black workers wherever
possible: (45)

> The politicians cannot have it both ways.   They cannot
> force our industrialists to use only a certain kind of
> labour, and at prescribed rates of pay, and when the

resulting costs of commodities are increased turn
round, enter into treaties with foreign countries - who
have no such bans, nor such prescribed wages - and who
can therefore easily undersell our own produced
commodities.   Here is a problem that lies at the root
of our national existence.   Its successful solution
will prove the bridgehead to our complete economic
independence.

The price of protection and conciliation - concessions
to the power of white workers - contradicted the need of
industries for cheap production.   But it was not only the
Labour-dominated situation of the time, itself partly a
result of the relative weakness of the bourgeoisie, that
was blamed for this, but protection itself.   Once again
it was commerce that pointed out that while industries
could not develop without protection, it was protectionist
tariffs that kept the cost of production high, by
shielding industries from competition which might otherwise force them to rationalise.   Protection, argued the
editor of the 'Bulletin', should be removed as soon as
possible after an industry had been established, so that
this might be avoided. (46)   Thus the conflict between
the interests of commerce and industry over the desirable
amount of protection, is again not to be seen only as a
struggle between fractions, but as a reflection of a
contradiction within the needs of capital itself,
particularly in a country which is industrialising late.
While exporting as a solution to the problem of the small
market has been a subsidiary policy of South African
capital ever since industries first began, it did not
provide a key to the unlocking of the nexus of capitalist
interests at that particular time.   A combination of
factors made local products prohibitively expensive for
the time being.

The second line of attack of those wishing to solve the
problem of the small market lay within South Africa
itself - amongst the large black, and small white,
population.   Here once more, policy-makers were
immediately confronted by a contradiction.   If products
are to be sold within the country, to workers
particularly, then employers are generally faced with the
dilemma of whether their workers should be seen primarily
as producers, whose price should be low and productivity
high, or as consumers, whose wages should allow them to
purchase commodities in increasing quantities.
Productivity and cheapness on the one hand, contradict
consumerism on the other.   The particular ways in which
capital in various contexts resolves this contradiction
are determined by a variety of factors and forces.   South

African capital operated within a particularly complex
framework, already discussed in this chapter, and its
ongoing solution needs careful analysis. Basically, it
was the solutions to white and black worker militancy
discussed above that formed the framework within which
the internal market was tackled. The class struggle thus
determined the pattern of consumption!

In the early years, the black market had been part of
the imperial structure. Such items as blankets, 'blue-
prints' (a popular peasant cloth), other textiles, glass
beads and bangle wire were all the preserves of British,
American, German or even Japanese producers. Thus the
first blankets were only made in South Africa in 1925,
when imported goods were excluded by the high protective
tariff. (47) It was only after protection in this and
other fields came about that producers were able to plan
realistically their expansion into the black market.
Philip Frame, South Africa's largest textile and woollen
producer, started his factory in 1928, for example, and
was able to capture the market relatively rapidly. (48)

As soon as protection seemed likely, ideologists made
much of the black population's potential consuming
powers, and considered seriously the possibility of
raising its 'standard of living'. This was a
reinforcement for liberalism. H.E. King wrote in 1919 of
the growing demand for boots, blankets, shirts, clothing,
soap, candles, matches and many other goods amongst
'natives', including both local and foreign blacks in his
calculations: 'even a slight increase in the standard of
living of the 42,000,000 natives for whose wants we
should be catering would alone mean an enormous market
for South African products.' (49) In many similar
articles on this theme, the possibility of making a
consumer out of the peasant or subsistence farmer and
worker was explored. (50) The old mining ideology of
centre and periphery, of 'civilised' and 'savage' was
irrevocably modified. Through the spread of consumerism,
the periphery became indistinguishable from the centre,
'civilisation' spreading throughout.

The aim of those who would sell their goods to black
workers and peasants was basically the raising of their
necessary means of subsistence. This could be done
simply by proletarianisation, which forced workers to
purchase things they would otherwise have grown or made
themselves; or through a kind of cultural imperialism.
Usually, of course, the one was the corollary of the
other, while together these two forces constituted the
means whereby the 'savage' was 'civilised', just as
proletarianisation alone had done in the case of mining.

'Quandell' of the 'Commercial Bulletin' makes clear what
this means: (51)

> Tourists visiting the neighbourhood of Native locations
> are often amused at the sight of a stalwart Native
> striding, or ambling, along the high road with bare
> feet, but carrying a pair of shoes slung over his
> shoulder with the rest of his impedimenta.   The road
> may be as hard as a road can be; he prefers to walk
> thus.   To him a pair of boots or shoes is an
> ornamental luxury, not a necessity. ... For the Native,
> a pair of shoes is an unconscious recognition of the
> superiority of customs other than his own. ... If every
> inhabitant of the Union ... wore out at least one pair
> of boots or shoes every year, there would be a great
> deal more work and profit for the manufacturers and
> distributors of footwear.

However, whichever means was used, any substantial
increase in the earning power of blacks beyond the £25m
which they were said to earn in 1923, (52) would have to
come from black wages; (53) and since it was hardly
likely that the hostile and labour-repressive mining
industry or the semi-feudal agricultural sector would
raise wages to this end, the brunt of the necessity of
raising black wages would have to fall on manufacturing
and commerce.

This fact reinforced the interest capital had in
raising workers' wages so as to control militancy. Black
wages in industry were already marginally higher than
those in mining, although this still did not make much of
a consuming force of the black working class. (54)   But
proletarianisation had affected black consumption: 'The
period when beads and a loin cloth and a blanket
constituted the whole wardrobe of an African Native has
largely passed.   Now the Natives look for low-priced
clothing, boots and hats.' (55)

In that year another writer could say that 'the natives
form our principle consuming population'. (56)   This
situation provoked this ideologist and others to
emphasise the need for black consumption to be sustained,
and, if possible increased: 'It is, of course, elementary
economics to point out that if every native worker in this
country was earning his 20s a day, South Africa would be
in a much better condition than it is at present.'   This
policy should, he continued, be associated with the
remainder of the ideas we have defined as 'liberal':   'In
other countries the low-paid workers generally have
opportunities to work up into the higher paid classes, and
the more skilful may eventually enter the more or less
independent class, but such avenues for economic self-

realisation are not open to the South African natives in
our industries.'   He concluded that:

> Big organisations like the mines and many of our
> farmers complain frequently about the shortage of
> labour, but what they really mean is a shortage of
> labour willing to accept the meagre wage paid to
> natives.   Often this is so low that it barely provides
> the essentials of existence to native workers.   If,
> instead of regarding it the duty of the Government to
> maintain a steady supply of such labour, captains of
> industry in the Union organised operations on a more
> scientific basis and demanded a fair standard of
> efficiency from employees, it might never be necessary
> to complain of a shortage of labour.   If Henry Ford
> can pay a man five dollars a day for screwing nuts onto
> bolts, surely native labourers can be paid up to 10s a
> day for working jackhammers or for doing work of
> similar importance in our other industries.   What with
> special and general taxation (the native) is subjected
> to undue economic pressure and thus forced into the
> labour market, contact with a European civilisation has
> increased his needs, and to satisfy these and to
> relieve the congestion in the native reserves, he must
> submit to European exploitation.   The number of South
> African natives in industries is on the increase, but
> there has been no similar increase in their rate of
> payment, especially when considered on the basis of the
> purchasing power of money.

Similarly, in the 'Commercial Bulletin' it was reported
that the Durban Chamber of Commerce had 'stressed the
connection between low wages for natives and white
unemployment'.   It pointed out that: 'in consequence of
its low cost, there was a general absence of incentive to
increase the efficiency of native labour, and that the
native market for commerce and industry was therefore a
comparatively poor one.' (57)

Thus it should not be thought that capital was
concerned with black impoverishment *per se*.   Ideologists
seeking markets were concerned to develop methods whereby
black wages could be raised without impairing industrial
profitability, and 'efficiency' was the means they chose.
As one perceptive writer put it: (58)

> It is a fundamental fact that increased wages and
> improved conditions tend to raise costs of production.
> This is offset by the extent to which consumption
> demand can be enlarged, either through protective
> tariffs, or as a result of greater output due to the
> use of machinery, the extension of scientific
> management, and a higher standard of labour efficiency,

or a combination of all of these factors.   It must be
considered that in a small market, such as that of
South Africa, saturation point can be reached
comparatively quickly, and there is a point at which
diminishing returns set in, making any additional
output uneconomic.   Up to this point the cost, if any,
can be passed on to the public, as the price to be paid
for necessary social legislation.   Thereafter remains
the export market, but as few South African industries
are able to cater for this trade, it has yet to be seen
whether increased efficiency can produce a surplus for
export at low enough prices.

Thus the same liberals who were concerned to provide black
workers with 'ladders' into the higher reaches of
industry; with higher wages; and with better living
conditions, were the chief advocates of the managerial
ideology towards blacks which emerged in the 1940s. (59)
No increase in consumption was to be permitted without an
increase in productivity.

However, because of its relatively lesser political
power, the black population could be treated by capital in
an altogether more repressive manner than white workers.
This meant that the 'saturation' point for black wages was
reached at a far lower level than for white wages - indeed
it could be said that this saturation point must differ
for all distinctive working-class groups whose access to
the institutions of power in society differs from others.
For as the astute ideologist quoted above recognises,
capital regards consumerism as the price to be paid for
what he terms 'necessary social legislation'.   And yet
the relative powerlessness of blacks renders such social
legislation as will raise wages, barely necessary.   The
'saturation point' to which the ideologist refers, is
determined by the long-standing and entrenched political
weakness of the black working class, and so the black
market, like the export market, was incapable of
providing the key to the unlocking of the nexus of
capitalist interests at this early stage.   Blacks were
not yet able to provide an expanding and accumulating
consumer population, for the limits to their wage levels
were set by the profitability demands of capital and their
own weakness.

White workers, by contrast, were, because of their
greater power, by far the wealthiest workers and hence the
most obvious internal market.   Their necessary means of
subsistence was at a higher level too (a fact which was of
great use to the propagandists of racism), and which
encouraged manufacturers to aim ruthlessly at the white
market.

While the white market needed no cultural imperialism
or proletarianisation in the early years, it too was
affected by its structural formation in imperial times.
White consumers did not consider South African-made goods
to be of good quality and preferred, even at higher
prices, foreign-made ones wherever possible.
Protectionism, as we have seen, was partly designed to
overcome this problem while much of the attention of
ideologists of manufacturing and commerce had to be
directed towards simple propaganda - the encouragement to
'Buy South African' - which they incorporated into the
overall patriotism of their ideology.

However, if the white market was to be increased, white
wages needed increasing and this, just as in the case of
black workers, contradicted the profit-imperative of
industries.   But in the case of whites, wages in
manufacturing, commerce and mining were by 1924 beyond the
specific control of the owners of industries.   Because of
their power, English-speaking male white workers in
particular had entrenched means whereby their wages could
be kept above certain minima, while because of their
relative lack of power the new bourgeoisie had reluctantly
acquiesced.   This fact, although it did not alter the
ingredients of the equation, altered its balance.   White
workers became the central target for the market-expanding
efforts of the new bourgeoisie because the result of their
power had been to confront employers with the *fait
accompli* of higher wages.   In a complex spiral of factors
and motives, the ideological and practical choices of the
bourgeoisie seeking a market had been ultimately
determined by the *status quo*.   The historical circumstances of their development had granted power to white
workers, and their power was to determine their position
as ideological and practical targets for consumerist
ideology.   Having been forced by circumstances into
choosing white workers as the chief targets for
consumption, industrialists and their ideologists adopted
a policy of delay in relation to the other two, less
convenient, market alternatives.   High white wages
prevented local South African goods from rapidly becoming
as cheap as those produced in Japan or other competing
countries, so the export market had to wait until mass
production and efficiency lowered the costs of South
African production.   Black purchasing power, as we have
already argued, could not be increased until 'efficiency'
or mass production were introduced on a scale which
would keep profitability margins up.   Both of these
alternatives could wait, as markets, until, with the
assistance of, and indeed on the basis of, white

consumption, industries had expanded sufficiently to make
mass production and efficiency possible; hence to lower
prices and open up possibilities of exports, and sales to
blacks.   The vicious circle which was the problem of the
market could be broken with time and massive white
consumption.

These tendencies towards emphasising the consuming
power of whites and the productive power of blacks were
doubly reinforced by white power which blunted the ability
of capital to make heavy productivity demands upon its
skilled, light-pigmented upper stratum of workers.
Although interest amongst employers in the views of Ford
and Taylor, (60) in the creation of an Efficiency
Institute, (61) and in the prolific writings of the
managerial ideologists of American and British industries
of the 1920s and 1930s, (62) grew parallel to the growth
in the realisation of the need for greater markets, these
were all directed towards blacks and no indigenous South
African productivity creed developed in relation to the
white working class in the interwar years; and what
productivity attempts were made were staunchly resisted
by white unions.

In summary, therefore, while market expansion policies
were pursued in all three fields of black consumerism,
white consumerism, and exports, the white consuming
population became the chief target of these policies in
the interwar years.   At the same time the black
population, despite its significance as a consuming
force, bore the brunt of the productivity demands upon
which industrialists depended for the realisation of the
nexus of their interests.

The ways in which capital had chosen to realise its
interests in the spheres of class struggle and of the
market were of great importance to the process of state-
formation.   For not only did they provide the basis upon
which intellectuals performed the fascinating task of
creating the sphere of 'public opinion', but they found
the structural foundations upon which capital ensued that
this 'public opinion' would be exclusively white.   They
formed, in other words, the primary underpinning of the
white state.

As we have already seen, the earliest form of white
consumerism was in the 'Made in South Africa'
campaign: (63)

Now is the time for all true South Africans to realise
that it is their plain duty to assist the development
of our industrial life by using the products of our
fields and factories.   Every consumer should, as far
as possible, insist on being supplied with goods which

are 'Made in South Africa', and thereby help to
strengthen the social and economic forces of the Union.
This is a form of patriotism which is more dignified
and serviceable than the waving of many flags,
wrote Laite in 1914.   In that year a 'consumers alliance'
was formed, and in 1916, the South African Industrial
League was formed with 'the declared object of developing
a keen public interest in industries'. (64)   Activities
for the promotion of consumerism amongst whites persisted
along these sorts of lines in the years of the rise of
protectionism.   'Buy South African' campaigns were
frequently held, and the government industrial journal was
filled with advertisements urging patriotic purchasing.
After protection, the campaign intensified under the
Labour-Nationalist government, which perceived 'Buying
South African' as a corollary of the higher white wages
they promoted.   In 1927, an Industrial Exhibition was
held in the Transvaal, with the theme of 'getting rid of
prejudice against South African goods'. (65)   But the
campaign continued to be necessary, as the FCI President
pointed out in 1929, when, he claimed, the general public
still only purchased South African goods if they thought
they were made overseas.   'The old prejudice against the
local article has not entirely died out', he said. (66)
But the problem of consumerism lay not simply in the
substitution of foreign goods by South African goods, but
in the increase in the consumption of goods in absolute
terms.   The white population, the chosen target for
consumption, needed to be encouraged to perceive the
values of consumption as good values, and thereby use
their unavoidably higher wages in ways which suited their
employers.   By 1929 this had begun to happen: 'People
have more wants today, and few are interested in the
simple life.   Better houses, clothes, food, more travel,
more entertainment at the cheapest possible rates, are all
indications of this change of outlook.' (67)
It was commerce, with its closer relationship to the
consumer, which claimed to speak for him (or her).   'The
consumer at long last is beginning to come into the
picture', wrote the 'Bulletin' in 1934.   It claimed to
defend consumers against state or industry, or against the
'suffering' which they were said to undergo because of the
incessant demands of industries for increased protection,
which meant higher prices.   When Professor W.H. Hutt
joined the pro-consumer lobby and spoke to the National
Council of Women, it was the 'Bulletin' that supported
him, saying that 'it is high time that the voice of the
housewife, who is now an elector, should be heard on
questions of this kind', and urging 'the woman electors of
the country to organise as a consumers league'. (68)

The progressive embourgeoisement of at least part of
the white working class was reinforced by the ways in
which employers tended to carry out their conciliatory
policies.   By encouraging the suburban nuclear family
system, both mining and manufacturing employers wished to
encourage docility and peace in the white working class;
at the same time, this system provided the basic units for
consumerism as they appear in all Western capitalist
systems - the home, the suburb, the individualised purchase
of major and minor commodities and appliances, the indi-
vidualisation of housework, and the ethic of competitive
consumption.   For example, in the mining industry the
system of nuclear family embourgeoisement on Crown Mines
reached its peak in the 1930s.   There white workers were
separated from black workers both physically and culturally:

> For most of them, it was a very happy life.   Though
> they were only ten minutes from the centre of
> Johannesburg, they had, within the boundaries of the
> mine property, every thing they needed, including a
> magnificent golf course, tennis courts, swimming pool,
> bowling greens, and genuine, home-made entertainment.

Accompanying the physical and cultural situation of a
working class which was being to some extent 'de-proletar-
ianised' were the ideological trappings;   the new manager:
'welded them into a team and built up the *ésprit de corps*
for which Crown Mines was famous in later years.   The
result was that when the boom began in 1933, and the mine's
tonnage rose to 4m tons a year, they set world
records.' (69)

The example originally set by the diamond industry,
which had established Kenilworth as part of its policy of
appeasement was followed not only by the gold-mining
industry, but by other individual industries such as AE
and CI, whose relationship to the mining industry was
close, (70) and Lever Brothers.   But most industries were
too small to be able to carry out the creation of white
worker suburbs on their own.   It is therefore significant
that in the wake of the post-war industrial militancy of
the white working class, the state set about implementing
these ideas of embourgeoisement on a national scale, with
the active encouragement of organised industry.   In 1919,
the FCI urged the establishment of a housing department:
'amongst employers, the feeling was steadily gaining
ground that, in addition to fair wages, good housing was
essential to secure that class of healthy and contented
work people without which no manufacturing concern could
continue to operate successfully.' (71)

Their request was reflected in the statements of the
Inspector of Factories himself in 1923, when he expressed
the opinion that: (72)

factories should be erected out in the country and
homes for the workers provided in the immediate
vicinity. ... In this country of wide open spaces the
... idea appeals strongly ... not only on the score of
health but as an inducement to promote efficiency and
a reasonable standard of contentment.   This opinion is
formed largely on account of the fact that the
'factory-type' of individual, as met with in Europe, is
more or less non-existent in this area. ... The writer
is of the opinion that, apart from hygienic conditions,
the housing of operatives, skilled and unskilled, on
'garden city' lines (separate and distinct for
Europeans and Natives) would tend to develop and evolve
the type of labour necessary to guarantee stability,
progress and industrial efficiency.

It was the upper stratum of the white working class
(which we may assume was largely English-speaking) that
was encouraged to buy homes, built in relatively spacious
and individualised suburbs: (73)

Every manufacturer must necessarily be interested in
the aim of the Government to strengthen the position of
the middle-classes by giving them the opportunities of
home-ownership.   This aim recently received practical
expression in the new building scheme formulated in Mr.
Hofmeyr's Housing Bill.   The object in view is to make
it possible for the better-paid artisan, the black-
coated worker and other members of the middle-class to
purchase their own houses.   In doing so, the
Government is breaking new ground, for hitherto their
efforts have been confined to providing houses for the
poorer classes. ... When the scheme materialises, many
South Africans hitherto denied the security and
satisfaction of home-ownership will be able to afford
it.   Every new home means an extra outlet for South
African products, and every branch of industry must
ultimately benefit from increased home ownership.   A
better standard of living for the middle-classes is a
valuable factor for greater social stability.

One further quotation, a retrospective one made in the
1960 Jubilee Yearbook of South Africa, a government
publication, captures the essence of the conciliatory,
repressive and consumption-orientated nature of the policy
of house-ownership for the white working class: (74)

In the twenties, when industry began to push ahead, a
limited body of planning experts was available whose
advice helped much to avoid the mistakes Europe had
made in its early industrial history.   Industrial
townships were separated from the residential townships
of the workmen and no workmen's slums were allowed to
develop.   Whereas in Europe the majority of workmen

are still housed in multi-storey flat buildings, South
African workmen enjoy the luxury of home ownership in
houses surrounded by gardens.   No proletarian class
consciousness could develop in these surroundings, and
South Africa was spared the scourge of a militant
labour movement.

Another factor entered into the process of partial
embourgeoisement: this was the growth of a genuine
middle and lower-middle class suburban culture in South
Africa, in the interwar years.   Not only did this provide
a model for the white working class to emulate, but it
helped swell the ranks of whites willing to co-operate in
the industrial revolution.   The new middle class (which
again we may assume was English-speaking) provided an
enlarged white consuming population, as well as having
other functions in the system.   As early as 1920, the
existence of a significant number of 'small investors' was
noted by industrialists, and the need for their
incorporation into industrialising South Africa pointed
out: (75)

> there is still ... a prejudice amongst some of the
> small investors against industrials.   Their
> willingness to save or to invest their savings in sound
> South African industrials may be less if they cannot
> obtain the security which they think is guaranteed in
> state and municipal issues.

Since the small investor's usefulness to industries in
need of capital was not doubted, the author of this
article proposed remedies such as the promotion of
industrial shares by banks, the advance of loan funds by
the state to industrialists, and other methods of capital
distribution.   In the following two decades these and
other methods of mobilising the capital of the small
investor were indeed introduced.   Domestic saving, writes
one authority: (76)

> naturally increased considerably while the savings
> pattern changed perceptibly with the rise of
> manufacturing industries and the associated
> diversification of economic activity.   Thus personal
> savings began to assume importance along with the
> savings of companies and noncorporate undertakings ...
> and in this manner promoted the growth of financial
> institutions.

While it is difficult to pin this process down to
specific dates, it was certainly during the 1920s and
1930s that the mobilisation of the capital of the 'white
man in the street' began to assume some significance in
the overall financial structure.   By 1938, building
societies, the institutional expression both of the policy
of white home-ownership, and of the ideology of thrift,

held assets of £52m;   the Post Office Savings Bank (which
'helped promote thrift among poorer people as it accepted
small deposits', (77)) and Union Loan Certificates £25m;
and a combination of other institutions for the individual
investor, £15m.   The total of these was nearly £100m,
which compares favourably with the total assets of £150m
which the Reserve and Commercial Banks held between them
at that time. (78)   The stock exchange, moreover, had
begun to become a popular institution in those years, and
after protection the commercial ideologist could no longer
complain that the small investor was ignoring
'industrials': (79)

> there is more South African capital invested in
> industries than is generally imagined.   Retired
> business and professional men invested much of their
> savings in South African industry.   The income of many
> widows and children depends upon dividends and similar
> investments. ... Most of these investments were
> encouraged by the very definite statements of the
> Government's industrial policy.

The new bourgeoisie wished to defend and incorporate
the 'small investor';   their manipulative intentions were
made as explicit here as they had been in the case of the
proletariat: (80)

> It is stated that [an] organisation ... is to be
> formed, with the special object of protecting the small
> investor. ... There can be no diversity of opinion
> regarding the desirability of giving every possible
> protection to the small investor.   He is the
> community's first line of defence against anti-social
> and anarchistic forces.   In these democratic days, no
> society could survive for long, much less prosper, in
> which a hard and fast, impassable line was drawn
> between the 'haves' and the 'have nots'.   Some of the
> conditions which make for prosperity and more
> particularly for security and stability - conditions
> which are of extreme importance to the commercial
> sector of the community - vary directly according to
> the opportunities given to the 'have nots' to make
> their way into the ranks of the 'haves' and to the
> 'have littles' to advance among the 'have muches' by
> honest methods.

These factors - the incorporation and embourgeoisement
of the white working class, and the growth and new significance of the white middle class - provided the basis for
the consolidation of the white (English-speaking) polity.
Together with a number of corollaries - such as the
ongoing collaboration between (English) industry and
(Afrikaner) agriculture, which had been one of South

Africanism's original cornerstones, the increased female
consuming and wage-earning population, and the adoption by
the state of limited social security measures for whites
such as pension, unemployment and sickness benefit schemes
- made of the late 1920s and particularly the 1930s, a
time of 'coming together' of the interests of capital in
relation to the white population.   To the new
bourgeoisie, all things pointed towards the need for co-
opting, conciliating and accommodating whites of all
classes into the industrial revolution, whether as voters,
trade unionists, consumers, workers, or investors.

South Africanism, in its radical, anti-imperialist
form, was not suited to the more conservative needs of
legitimating the embourgeoisement of the working class,
and guiding the co-optation of other groups into the
industrial revolution.   Whatever its potential, the
ideology as it had been developed by industrialists in the
early years, was originally a petty-bourgeois and radical
ideology, not a bourgeois and conservative one.   The
original conciliation of white workers, to give one
example, had been designed so that the overthrow of the
old caste-like and manipulative ideas of the mining
imperial ideology by the 'people' would be facilitated.
This was not the primary motivation of the new
bourgeoisie.   To overcome this difficulty in the
harnessing of South Africanism to new ends, ideologists
set about the task of emphasising its conciliatory,
consensual, popular and patriotic aspects, and de-
emphasising, even removing, its negative, radical or anti-
imperialist elements.   Even the more explicitly petty-
bourgeois aspects, such as the emphasis upon pioneering,
faded in significance, although English-speaking culture
has never freed itself entirely from its petty-bourgeois
basis.   Furthermore, so that it should become a force for
conserving and assisting the industrial revolution, they
set about popularising and externalising it.   A
systematic campaign for the dissemination and propagation
of the ideology was set under way amongst the groups whose
co-operation was most needed.

Once more we find that commerce, whose ideological
networks already contained an external orientation, took
on the task of relating ideologically to 'the people' most
seriously and consistently.   The first thing commercial
ideologists did was to create the useful and all-embracing
concept of 'public opinion', with its subsidiary concept
of 'the (white) man in the street'.   'Public opinion
wants change', commercial ideologists would say; (81) or
'the man in the street has almost completely lost touch
with and interest in politics, and has learned to submit

to the inevitable and to be governed by regulations'. (82)
It was apparent that 'public opinion' was not, as it might
have been in the earlier days, the opinion of powerful
interests themselves, (83) but that of the mass of the
white population, which ideologists hoped nevertheless
embodied and reflected the opinions and requirements of
the powerful interests which they themselves represented.

Ideologists outside of commerce also recognised the
value of the notion of public opinion.   As early as 1919,
H.E. King of the SANU had written: (84)

> What is it in this glorious country that strikes so
> many of her sons and daughters into sordid apathy?
> We come of the same, even a greater freedom than other
> countries; we come of the same vigorous races; we
> have the same forms of self-government.   Everything is
> the same except the informing spirit.   South Africa
> does not yet possess a sincere articulate public
> opinion on any of its great and obvious needs.

Then, five years later, he wrote on the same theme.   'Why
is South Africa not progressing more rapidly?' he asked;
because 'a national ideal has not yet taken definite
shape': (85)

> [SANU] had not been able to build up a pronounced
> national sentiment such as is found in Canada,
> Australia and the US.   Although, however, the spirit
> is not so obvious as in these countries, it neverthe-
> less exists, and should in the near future show signs
> of greater virility.   The present separation of the
> two white races is being gradually narrowed as each
> realises more fully that their interests in the country
> are in common.
> There have been political reasons for retarding the
> fusion of the national spirit, which at one time
> undoubtedly existed in each Province, into a love for
> South Africa as a whole.   Patriotism is largely
> local, its horizon is not readily enlarged to cover
> new ground.   The bigger outlook and sentiment
> necessary in our case can come, but gradually.   The
> infancy of the 'national spirit' in the Union is
> undoubtedly one potent reason why South Africa has not
> progressed faster.   If all the people were determined
> to make the Union of South Africa a great country, it
> would be bound to go forward.   But as long as we
> continue to be wrapped up in parochialism and
> individualism there cannot be a sustained common
> effort to weld together supposed conflicting
> influences.   More strenuous efforts must be made to
> educate the backward section of the people to the
> advantages to each one of them of a general forward
> policy.

Instead of simply asserting, as the earlier ideology
had done, that South Africanist ideas of industrialisation
embodied the spirit of the people, ideologists were now
proposing the active propagation of this idea, and indeed
of the general 'national spirit' itself throughout the
population.   'Public opinion must be educated', was the
import of the new mood;   'it was essential, therefore,
that the public should be educated rightly on all
questions which directly affected industrial prosperity,
because a country lived and traded by virtue of its
national production.' (86)   While commercial ideological
machinery was suited to this task, most other industrial
ideologists were somewhat inward-looking, and orientated
towards the discovery and articulation of the interests of
their audiences and their audiences alone.   Only
commerce could say that: (87)

> we are convinced that with a fuller measure of co-
> operation from the business community of South Africa
> the *Bulletin* can be made a very valuable medium for
> influencing and educating public opinion in regard to
> many matters of vital importance to the country.

It would seem not to be coincidental, therefore, that it
was in this period of the rising need of the new
bourgeoisie for a 'new' public opinion that great changes
and expansion took place in the field of South African
journalism and other media.

Some idea of the ways in which this took place can be
gauged from the history of the Argus newspaper group.
For one thing, the old identification of newspapers with
individual interests which had in the past characterised
South African journalism came under attack from various
quarters.   In 1926 the Pact government introduced the
first restrictions on the press that had ever existed in
South Africa - the requirement that political articles be
signed.   Arthur Barlow, prominent Labour MP, said
that: (88)

> The English press in South Africa, with one or two
> exceptions, practically belongs to the same people,
> and it is time we clipped their wings. ... We know that
> the editor's 'we' means a lot to the man in the street.
> What we would do is to stop this anonymous 'we', this
> gentle dew that falls from heaven.   If the people of
> Cape Town saw leading articles day by day signed
> B.K. Long ['Cape Times' editor] they would get sick of
> them and say 'It is only his opinion and we know he is
> a strong member of the South African Party'. ... The
> signing of these articles is going to do more harm to
> our friends on the other side than anything else I
> know.   We have got to bind down these great financial
> interests.

The implication of this plea for a more 'neutral' press is
that there was a significant 'popular' English-speaking
readership developing in South Africa (89) - the growing
middle, lower middle and white working classes - and that
it was both in the interests of labour and in the
interests of South Africanism that the old pattern of the
press be changed to suit this fact.

In that year the Argus group itself, without government
prompting, began to observe this fact.   Amongst a list of
recommendations made to its staff, the Argus group
included the ideas that political news be presented without party bias, and that comments be strictly confined to
editorial columns;   that all company reports be issued as
advertisements, and marked as such: 'such reports should
never be connected with the paper, not appear to have been
written in the office.'   Popular readership, in fact, was
to become de-politicised, to be converted to the cause of
'non-ideology' which South Africanism was soon to espouse.
In addition, consumerism and wider reader participation in
the popular ideology were to be encouraged, also as 'non-
ideology':   'the importance of women readers was beginning
to be recognised and special attention was paid to their
interests.   Additional space was given to social items
and descriptions of women's dresses at dances and race
meetings.'   Not only did the 'Star' develop a women's
section, covering cookery, millinery, flowers, embroidery,
and 'Home Economics' but a more general recognition of the
new readership was made:

> The idea of catering for special interests expanded and
> a Features Bureau was established in the Argus papers
> which was ready at any moment to prepare special pages
> on motoring, new buildings, holiday seasons, back to
> school requirements, dancing, suburban shopping.

But the 'Star' could not quite yet divest itself of its
old, mining house image, and 'advertisers themselves
declined to place their announcements on the special
feature pages, which they found were apt to be ignored by
the general reader.' (90)

In the mid-1930s, what Neame calls the 'newspaper war'
took place, and it was here that the conflict between the
old and the new journalism was more satisfactorily
resolved.   I.W. Schlesinger, 'the largest employer of
labour in the sub-continent', was head of business
interests which were intimately linked not only with the
new middle classes, but with consumerism and the media of
popular ideology itself - his empire included insurance,
real estate, theatres, cinemas, amusement parks, catering,
hotels and retail shops.   During and after the gold
standard crisis he felt that 'there was a need for a new

and independent press', and in 1934 became Chairman of
Union Newspapers Limited, which then became African
Associated Press.   He launched Sunday and daily papers,
although the daily field was already virtually monopolised
by the Argus group, set up an independent distributing
organisation and printing works, and consciously
orientated himself towards the consuming, popular
audience.   As a result, 'the group of papers made headway
more rapidly than any other new newspapers had ever done
in South Africa' and forced the Argus group to reconsider
its position.   Finally, in 1939, the Schlesinger group
was absorbed by the other major newspaper groups, its
point having been effectively made.   With a new series of
editors and the death or retirement of many of the old
journalists of the Argus group, a new generation, with a
suitably new approach, was able to emerge.   In the same
period - the 1930s - another journal 'The Outspan' was
launched and was an even more explicit example of the need
for and rise of a new type of journalism.   This, a
'family paper' with a South African name and a South
African orientation, expressed precisely the new spreading
South Africanism, and its circulation rose soon after its
start to a record 40,000. (91)
    The changed situation was reflected in other areas.
In September 1934, for example, the 'Junior Chamber of
Commerce' movement was launched with an explicitly
ideological orientation: 'by the training of their
executives in Chamber of Commerce work employers are
laying the foundation for younger men stepping into their
places, practised in debating matters of vital interest in
the commercial world', (92) said one ideologist.   Another
pointed out that the functions of the Junior Chamber of
Commerce were not only internal to commerce but had an
external orientation too: 'the movement', he said, 'would
undoubtedly have a great influence in the formulating of
public opinion'. (93)   Another similar movement which
arose in the 1920s and 1930s was the international social
and ideological organisation of Rotary.   This middle- and
lower-middle-class movement provided a meeting place for
representative members of many sections of white
society which needed incorporation;   many manufacturers
belonged to it, as did prominent middle-class, almost
entirely English-speaking, men from all occupations.
As early as 1921, the 'SAJI' editor had pointed out the
significance of a movement such as Rotary, which, with its
motto of 'Service not Self', or 'he profits most who
serves best', was the ideal means for disseminating a
conservative and compliant ideology. (94)   In Rotary only
the myth of the original, radical pioneering individualism

of the manufacturers was preserved, and that only
because, as one commercial editorial pointed out, its
removal, for example through the introduction of the
uniformity being propagated by Hitler at the time, would
be bad for business: (95)

> If a quasi-regimental discipline is to be applied to
> the leisure hours of the community, its clothes and its
> meals, there will be a very pronounced acceleration of
> the tendencies, already far advanced as a result of
> mass production and big advertising, in the direction
> of the standardisation of Demand. ... The prospect for
> Commerce would be fraught with disaster, certain and
> complete.

While the myth of individualism was sustained it was more
often the co-operative and compliant ideas of 'service' to
the community that were inculcated.   'Business morality',
as the 'SAJI' wrote, 'is changing from "individualism" to
"co-operation" in our civilisation'. (96)

In these and many other ways the process of
'externalisation' of the ideology was set under way in
white South Africa.   A new network of media, both
organisational - in the form of clubs and societies such
as Rotary - and disseminatory - in the form of popular
newspapers and journals - was set up.   South Africanism
had until this time appeared in the established
ideological arena, had been espoused by public figures,
and reproduced in interest-based journals.   It was now
launched on to an altogether different and broader plane.
Ideologists multiplied, every white man and woman became
a potential consumer and participant in capitalism (as
long as they accepted, even espoused, the new values which
South Africanism represented).   In addition, the stage
was set for the ideology to become a 'non-ideology' and
for the popularisation of South Africanism to be disguised
as the spread of truth and science.

> It is, in fact, in capitalist formations that the
> political category of public opinion, and the related
> category of consent ... first make an appearance. ...
> Political ideology, in the form of public opinion,
> presents itself as a body of practical rules, as
> technical knowledge, as the citizens' 'enlightened
> consciousness' of a specific practice, as the 'Reason'
> of this practice,

writes Poulantzas. (97)   The remarkable thing is the way
in which 'public opinion' and the consensus entailed by
it, had become, by the force of historical circumstance in
South Africa, confined to the white race, and controlled
by its English-speaking section.

CONCLUSION

What has this discussion told us about the reasons for the
preservation and modification of an essentially imperial
state form?   We established that capital's economic
interests were not dissimilar to those possessed by an
emerging bourgeoisie anywhere.   However, their
translation by intellectuals into political and
ideological interests took a path all of its own.   The
first point to be made is the extent to which this path
was historically determined.   The past form of capital's
development in South Africa, and the past choices made by
imperial capital *vis-à-vis* the white and black working
classes imposed a pattern of class relationships in South
Africa with which a new and not particularly powerful
bourgeoisie would have found it difficult to break
completely.   And in any case the fact that the working
class was divided did not run against capital's interests
- far from it.   The high economic and political price of
the white working class was offset by the cheapness and
powerlessness of the black, while the lack of unity
between the two reduced the potential threat which a
united working class could be to capital.
     However, 'history' is not a determining force in its
own right.   As we have tried to stress continually
through this work, mere inheritance of ideological and
political forms is a necessary, but not sufficient,
explanation of their persistence, particularly in times of
radical change in the structure of the ruling class.   We
have to discover how capital came to terms with the
existing structure, and more importantly perhaps, what the
forces were that lay behind its decision to do so.
     When mining first sought hegemony it was the clashing
of modes of production that was the central contradiction
upon which capital's strategies were built.   After the
Anglo-Boer War, it was the contradiction between owners
and non-owners of the means of production.   Later, when
national capital was still embryonic, it was the clashing
of classes of capital.   It would seem that now, with
national capital's growth and new-found importance, it was
once again the clash between capital and labour, the
struggles and contradictions between two opposing classes,
that determined the choices made by intellectuals.
     The primary decisions made by capital were those
concerning its need to control labour's growing
consciousness, organisation and action.   In the case of
the white working class, the decision was made to pursue
the strategy of conciliation.   Elaborate and central
state apparatuses were devised and, mainly under the Pact

government, brought into being.   As a corollary, it was
decided that whatever strategy was used for controlling
the black working class, it would be a separate one.   The
divided working class was to be maintained with whites
holding the superior positions.   Within this basically
divisive strategy an 'incorporationist' liberalism was
conceived for controlling black workers.   It was not to
be developed through the central state apparatuses,
however, but through what were termed 'para-statal'
apparatuses.   Thus while the structure developed under
mining hegemony was indeed preserved, the strategies
devised within it were different.

     While coping with class struggles might have been
capital's primary need, it was not its only one.
Intellectuals set about tackling the nexus of economic
interests which underlie and drive the capitalist economy
in terms dictated by the decision to divide, conciliate
and/or incorporate, the working class.   The term 'nexus'
is hardly adequate to portray the inexorability and
interconnectedness of the forces with which intellectuals
had to cope.   While profitability may have been the
central of these, it would be crude to assume it was the
only one; profitability itself was affected by and in
turn affected, the degree of competition, mechanisation,
the level of labour's challenge to capital, the role of
the state and the size and nature of the market.   While
gold capital's interests were complex, it is true, they
lacked the contrariness of industrial capital's, for they
included neither the driving force of competition, nor the
need for a consumer market and all the intricacies of
social and political organisation that went with it.

     Ideologists recognised that the interests of capital
were inexorable, and that they could not be realised in a
piecemeal or partial manner.   Thus their approach cannot
be understood in terms of 'pressure group' or 'interest
group' theory.   While capital's 'issues' appear to be
single ones, fought for in a purposeful and directed
manner, no sooner is one interest realised than another
arises, while all the time a whole range of subsidiary and
related interests is being catered for in perhaps a less
public manner than the apparently 'single' one.   It seems
that this is the way capital chooses to fight its battles;
in the cases of both mining and manufacturing capital, we
saw ideologists select key 'issues' around which they
gauged the majority of their audience's many and interconnected interests could be mobilised and realised.
Thus while the 'Kruger regime' appeared as the primary
enemy of the 1890s, and 'protection' as the rallying call
of early manufacturing, both of these issue-orientated

strategies were best understood in terms of the nexus of
complex class interests which underlaid them and which
continued to need realisation when the particular 'issue'
had been resolved.

It is in terms such as these that the organic
intellectual's choice of the 'market' as the key issue
around which national capital's interests could be
realised, may be understood.   Given the stage of
capitalist development at the time, the absence of a need
for a market under mining hegemony, and the underdevelopment of Southern African local production in
general, the market was probably objectively the
appropriate economic and political focus for capital.
But it was appropriate only because it was through the
market that the remainder of capital's economic interests
could be untangled, and not because it existed as a
single and separate issue.

How capital tackled the market seems to have been
determined, as we have already suggested, by the pattern
of the clash between capital and labour.   With exporting
out of the question until the forces of production had
developed further, and the black consumer market
dependent upon raising the productivity and low wages of
black workers, it was the already privileged, relatively
well-paid and 'incorporated' part of the white working
class that was to be cultivated as the local consumer
market.   A policy of delay was adopted for black
consumers and exports, while a full-blooded strategy of
consumerism was directed towards whites.   This reinforced
the fact of the perpetuation of the imperial white state,
although it, too, implied certain modifications to it.

Not only did intellectuals develop an ideology of
consumerism for whites and propose structural forms in
which it could be made concrete;   they also sought out
the non-proletarian members of the white population whose
consent and participation in capitalism was required.   An
overall consensus ideology arose on these interlocking
foundations, which resembled that which others have
identified as characteristic of capitalist states.   But
it was a white, English, consensus in a predominantly
black state - a fascinating deformity.

The foundations for capital's overall strategy towards
blacks also seemed to interlock.   While both the class
struggle and the need for markets contributed towards the
creation of a liberal ideology and strategy, neither of
these entailed an urgent call upon the immediate and
central state apparatuses.   Liberalism was relegated to a
secondary and in a sense extraneous place in the new
hegemonic order being forged.   Its status as a weapon of

the ruling class has consequently been difficult to assess
and frequently misunderstood.   While there seems little
doubt that it was a powerful part of the armoury of a
rising bourgeoisie (and not, as some have suggested, the
mere mouthings of a group of free-floating intellectuals,
or the ideology of an insignificant, manufacturing,
fraction of capital) its lack of entrenchment in the
central state apparatuses seems to call into question
either its significance, or the extent to which its
creators had achieved a place of dominance.   But there
seems a good case for arguing that neither of these doubts
is valid.   Both the effectiveness and the
institutionalisation of liberalism are clear and
documented - that it operated outside of the central state
seems to be more a function of the peculiarity of the
South African social formation than any other factor.

Perhaps because it was deformed, the process of the
emergence of this divided state form has already raised
several questions about the nature of the state under
capitalism.   Some of these have been mentioned in the
text in this and earlier chapters, but nowhere have they
been systematically explored.   It remains for us to
examine capital's approach to the state apparatuses themselves, now that we have determined the rough outlines of
the class structure it deemed desirable.

6   A second revolution

Throughout this work we have used the term 'the state' to
mean two different although related things.   On the one
hand it has been used in a 'narrow' sense, to mean the
immediate system of government.   This is perhaps the
conventional, layman's understanding of the term, and
indeed is certainly the sense in which capital's ideologists themselves use it.   In common parlance, 'the state'
refers to structures such as the parliamentary system,
the party system, the civil service, the systems of law
and repression and other recognisable and central
institutions.

And yet we have also used 'the state' in a 'wide' sense.
Either explicitly or implicitly we have used the term to
refer to the entire system through which the ruling class's
dominance is exercised.   This system, it has emerged here,
seems almost certainly not to be confined to the central
state institutions but to include such general and broad
features of the social system as the class structure as
moulded by capital, the ideology propagated by capital, and
its manifestation in a variety of structural forms.   We
have also seen how such things as housing policies, newspaper readership, trade unions, authority in the workplace
and a whole variety of other social forms and forces may be
directly linked to capital's aspirant or actual rule.

In the last three chapters a great deal has been said
about both aspects of the state.   We examined, for
example, capital's early perception of the need for a
changed 'narrow' state;   the changes in the system of
legitimacy brought about by the First World War;   the
nature of the 'wide state' needed by national capital, and
innumerable other matters.   While out of these
discussions a picture may have emerged of what capital
wanted of the wide state, we are left with an incomplete
view of capital's precise relationship to the narrow

state.   The sphere that is most commonly conceived of as
'political' has only entered our discussions sporadically
and indirectly.   This is partly for historical reasons.
As we shall see, capital could only tackle the 'political'
after the other changes we have documented here had taken
place.   This is why it is only now that we explore the
processes whereby national capital sought to bring into
being a new, different form of narrow state;   the underlying forces which dictated why and how it did so;   and
the historical circumstances which made it possible for it
to succeed.   In all of these matters it would almost
certainly be impossible to understand capital's strategy
and the path it took without the background of the
preceding five chapters.   The original, four-dimensional
mining revolution and its implications for the peculiar
form taken by the imperial state;   the creation of the
'hierarchy of exploitation';   the original crucible in
which the national bourgeoisie was forged;   the context in
which it grew and imperial capital declined;   and its
basic compatibility with the imperial division of the
social formation into black and white spheres, are the
historical and structural roots of the hegemony now being
brought into being.

In the previous chapter we saw something of the extent
to which the existing 'wide state' was compatible with the
new interests of capital, while we also pointed to some of
the incompatibilities.   One of the first points to be
made about our analysis of the 'narrow state' is the
extent to which the demands made upon it were confined to
the racial boundaries set by imperial hegemony and now
perpetuated.   There seems to be no evidence that during
this political revolution the new bourgeoisie sought to
alter the fact of the exclusion of blacks from, and the
inclusion of whites within, the state.   While new
apparatuses were created, a new party system brought into
being, a new ideology propagated, and a new role for the
'public' proposed, all of these changes were confined to
the white population, while blacks continued to be coped
with through direct, unmediated repression, and the
operation of 'para-statal' structures and ideology.

Against this background of the wide state we begin our
analysis by examining the role of the narrow state in
interwar South Africa, and asking what was the extent of
its compatibility or incompatibility with national
interests.

While the mining industry had required that the narrow
state merely acquiesce in mining domination, industrial
interests required that it be 'no longer ... satisfied to
be an onlooker', (1) since 'the need for assistance is ...

likely to be greater in countries which are only
beginning their industrial life.' (2)   Around the symbol
of protection, and later of the market, capital's vast
wants were made clear.   Two of them have already been
discussed: the elaborate and sophisticated attempts made
by early manufacturers to persuade, seduce or force the
state to introduce protection in chapter 3;   and the ways
in which the new capitalists attempted to persuade the
state to assist in developing structures of conciliation
for white workers in chapter 5.   On both of these
matters ideologists had placed their faith in the South
African Party and were encouraged by the indications they
received of growing support within the party for
industrialisation (3) and even conciliation.

State aid was also needed in the matter of the planning
and supervision of the industrialising system.   As early
as April 1916, manufacturers sent a deputation to F.S.
Malan, then the Minister of Mines and Industries, to ask
him to establish a full Department of Commerce and
Industries, (4) while after the war 'SANU' complained: (5)

> that there is no driving force to compel the initiation
> and the carrying out of a definite policy in the scheme
> of development.   It is contended that there is an
> urgent necessity for a force compelling action to be
> taken on approved lines for the common good.

Then in 1920-2, interest both within and outside of
manufacturing circles in the establishment of a state-
operated iron and steel industry began to grow.   In this
key industry, which could provide a powerful basis from
which South Africa's full industrialisation could be
launched, state participation, though not state control,
was deemed necessary by manufacturers and their
allies, (6) since only the state could supply sufficient
capital, diverted from mining, for its establishment.
The ability of the state to supply capital for more
general uses was another issue.   During the First World
War, when industries expanded rapidly, the need for
capital was felt severely.   The self-financing mining
industry was no help unless the state would act to divert
resources to industry - an unlikely event at least until
full bourgeois hegemony was achieved.   In 1917, several
institutions combined their resources to form the
Industrial Development Company, which, with its initial
capital of £100,000, aimed to support new undertakings. (7)   But many felt this was the state's role.
In 1918, the FCI pressed the government to establish a
national industrial investment board, (8) while in 1919
the manager of the National Bank proposed that the state
should 'cultivate an atmosphere of industrial investment'

to induce private owners of capital to assist
industries. (9)   As Laite wrote in 1917: (10)

> In the troublous times still ahead of us, this country
> will need all the help she can secure from men of
> enterprise, from men of business capacity who, when
> opportunities present themselves, can quickly secure
> and supply the requisite capital to bring profitable
> industry into operation.   South Africa can best obtain
> that form of help by shaping her fiscal policy so as to
> create such opportunities.   If that is done, capital
> and enterprise will do the rest.

Another area was that of the seeking and establishment
of export markets.   Industrial ideologists had long
urged that the state enlarge the legitimate sphere of
economic activity.   This was often conceived of in terms
of the political incorporation of other states.   In its
earliest form it was expressed as passionate support by
industrialists for Union itself. (11)   Later,
industrialists became interested in the possibility of the
state enlarging its sphere even further.   In 1915, as we
saw earlier, Laite visited Angola, and returned urging
that it should be treated as South Africa's 'natural
market'. (12)   Later, when the possibility of Union
between South Africa and Rhodesia was considered,
manufacturing ideologists were prominent in the pro-
unification lobby, and when, in 1922, Rhodesia turned down
the proposal, the 'SAC' wrote: 'Economically the
interests of the North and the South are identical, and
sooner or later the destinies of both will be found in
unification.' (13)   In the fields of education, (14)
railway policy, (15) and scientific and industrial
research, (16) to mention only a few, the state was
required not only to extend, but also to modify, the
patterns which had initially been established by the
mining revolution.   Finally, the over-arching function of
the narrow state had to be the reconciliation of interests
within the new bourgeoisie itself: the interests of
commerce in a lower tariff needed to be reconciled with
those of industries in a higher one;   the hostility of
mining needed to be neutralised through the diversion of
mining resources elsewhere in the economy;   while the
setting up of institutions such as commissions of enquiry,
committees, or conferences, provided centralised and
relatively neutral territory in which the various
conflicting interests of the different sections of capital
could be reconciled.

Because these needs of capital's constituted a
coherent and interlocking whole, a set of interests, they
added up to the need of the new capitalists for the

establishment of over-arching structures, embodying what
could be called a 'consultative relationship' between
themselves and the narrow state.   By 1921 this need had
become so pressing that the manufacturers' journal could
point to the fact that the state was continually
'inundated' with recommendations from all the most
important bodies in the land: the FCI, the Agricultural
Union, the Chamber of Mines, Assocom, and the South
African Industrial Federation.   It was the ideologists of
the leading section - manufacturing - who proposed that
the problem be solved through the establishment of a co-
ordinating 'Economic Council', (17) the perfect
institutional expression of consultation.

     It may at first glance seem surprising that the party
in command of the narrow state, the SAP, made attempts to
assist industrialists in virtually all of these spheres.
The SAP actually contemplated introducing tariffs to
appease the protectionist lobby.   A Tariff Committee was
set up in 1917, and a tariff law passed in 1923. (18)   In
the sphere of conciliation, the SAP considered Wage
Boards, and passed a Wage Act, (19) set up an 'Employers-
Employees Conference', and eventually passed the
Industrial Conciliation Act of 1924, (20) while its
Unemployment Commission in 1921-2 argued, within the
conciliatory idea, that factories would solve
unemployment. (21)   In the sphere of planning, F.S. Malan
received the 1916 deputation sent by the industrial
community to ask for a Department of Commerce and
Industries, and in his capacity as Minister, announced
only a few months later the establishment of an
'Industrial Advisory Board'. (22)   In 1917, the
Government held the first industrial census, (23) and by
1920 the Advisory Board had not only taken over the
functions of research and scientific development, (24) but
had begun to issue reports urging the planning of South
Africa's industrial future, (25) emphasising 'that the
Government should endeavour to create such conditions as
will stimulate private enterprise to develop the resources
of the Union.' (26)   In the writings of members of the
Board (27) and elsewhere the official support for the
industrialising viewpoint grew.   In particular, it
flourished in the Government journal 'South African
Journal of Industries', established in 1917, which, with
its planning approach and specific policy orientation, was
a great government fillip for industrialisation. (28)

     The iron and steel industry was an issue which could
not be ignored, and in 1922 the Government passed an Iron
and Steel Industry Encouragement Act; (29) and the
establishment of the Reserve Bank in 1921 could be said to

have been an attempt at shaping the financial system of
the economy.   As far as markets were concerned, SAP
support for Union with Rhodesia placated the
protectionists, (30) while the 'SAJI' was filled with
suggestions about the enlargement of South African
markets, and in 1920, it was reported that 'bioscope' was
being used by the Union Government to 'present South
African industries to overseas audiences'. (31)   In 1922
F.S. Malan, the SAP's most vocal protectionist, visited
the Congo in an attempt to set up a market there;   and the
Electricity Act was passed, establishing the Electricity
Supply Commission (Escom) after a three-year
investigation.   Its report included the observation that:
'The importance of developing the provision of electricity
in the Union is dictated by the need to encourage its
existing manufactures and to attract new and permanent
industries as soon as possible.' (32)   It was the SAP
government which had established the 'Scientific and
Technical Committee' in 1915, the purpose of which was to
carry out research into trade and industry in South
Africa, and which was later incorporated into the Advisory
Board. (33)   It also wooed the eminent ideologist and
planner of state corporations, H.J. van der Bijl, from his
American post, to head the Advisory Board in 1920, and
Escom in 1922, (34) while the Board and other state
institutions provided an important forum for the
development and dissemination of the South Africanist
ideology.

Finally, a Committee, headed by Caldecott, was set up
by F.S. Malan to enquire into the 'Economic policy of the
Union'.   It was its report which appeared to be the
confirmation of the acceptance by SAP men of state
participation in and guidance of industrial development.
Its conclusions included the finding that: (35)

> The end in view cannot be achieved except as the result
> of the action of the Government.   In the modern
> industrial state no other course is possible, and no
> other machinery exists by means of which a truly
> national policy can be evolved and made effective.
> Action by the state should, however, be mainly devoted
> to promoting or creating conditions which will induce
> private enterprise to develop the resources of the
> country, and increase its aggregate production.

It proposed action in no less than seventeen fields, and
was the most considerable support manufacturers had yet
had from state officials.   It provoked an optimistic
editorial from the 'SAJI'. (36)

What was the meaning of this state support for local
capital?   Did it mean that imperial capital was no longer

hegemonic?   The evidence seems to indicate that it did
not.   In almost every case, the concessions made to
industrialisers were partial and insufficient.   The
state failed to free itself from the constraints imposed
upon it by its structural origins in imperialism, and was
restricted by the existence of powerful opposition to
industrialisation.   Party decisions were compromises.
Protectionists were treated not as a rising class, but as
a pressure group within a conglomerate political party.
   The 1923 protective tariff went further than any
previous tariffs, but it did not go beyond a certain
limit, since the party did not wish to antagonise the
imperially orientated, import-export commercial firms
within it. (37)   Smuts's several passionate speeches in
favour of protection were not reflected in cabinet
decisions, and manufacturers were quick to point out that
his cabinet were not behind him. (38)   The government
budget too, was criticised by industrialists for being of
no help to them in 1921, by which time protectionism
within the party was supposedly well on the way. (39)   In
general Smuts's ideas were acceptable to industrialists,
but his execution was poor: (40)

> In spite of the sentiments expressed by the Prime
> Minister just 12 months ago, the problem has remained
> untouched in this country.   It is true that the
> Advisory Board of Industry and Science was asked to
> report on the position, but no notice was taken of
> their report, and the matter ended with its
> presentation to the Government.   A further Board,
> known as the Board of Trade and Industries, has been
> appointed. ... It was only after repeated
> representations by the Chamber of Industries that, last
> month, the Board undertook to go into the whole
> question of the Tariff.   In other words, the whole of
> the work accomplished by the Advisory Board of Industry
> and Science has to be done again.   In the meantime,
> and in spite of the urgent views put forward by General
> Smuts, the country is suffering as a result of the
> restriction of its manufacturing industries.

As far as planning was concerned, it seemed to
manufacturers that the 'Advisory' Board would never be
more than that.   Not only did they claim that no notice
was taken of its reports, but they repeatedly urged that
it be given power: (41)   'it is essential that the
constitution, powers and personnel of the Board be
immediately revised.   It is absolutely impossible for a
part-time Board to devote the time and attention necessary
to a study of the intricate and involved problems
associated with tariff adjustment.' (42)   But when this

newly proposed board was actually elected, it was clear to
manufacturers that it, too, represented an attempt to fob
them off.

Even the much-vaunted Conference between employers and
employees which the Government held as part of its
declaration in favour of long-term conciliation, was held
to be a 'dismal failure', (43) by manufacturers and other
employers who had hoped it would herald the beginning of a
new policy on the part of this apparently
confrontationalist government.   In addition the iron and
steel issue was quite clearly treated half-heartedly by
the SAP government.   An 'encouragement' act was no
substitute for the real thing.   The old relationship
between the mining industry and the British engineering
industry prevented the mining-dominated SAP from
developing the iron and steel industry beyond the limited
scope of the time. (44)   The action taken to provide
capital for industries was also half-hearted.   While the
Reserve Bank was formed in 1921, (45) the taxation of the
gold-mining industry was at a lower level that it might
have been under a protectionist government. (46)   In its
fiscal policy the government favoured importers and
snubbed manufacturers, while it was complained that the
SAP had failed to 'broaden the basis of taxation'. (47)
In the area of market-enlargement, the government's
attempts to placate manufacturers were circumscribed by
the complexities of manufacturing interests.   As we have
seen, in the initial absence of a truly conciliatory policy
towards white workers, and of a whole-hearted approach
towards protection and industrialisation, attempts to
establish larger foreign markets, or even local markets,
were of little use to manufacturers, since local goods
tended to be too expensive to compete elsewhere, while the
local population's purchasing power remained low.
Finally, in the report of the Committee investigating the
'Economic Policy of the Union', the imperial attitude
towards industrialisation was revealed to be as powerful
as ever.   A 'minority' report (written by five of the
eight members of the committee!) concluded that: (48)

Whilst there is in the main report much with which
agreement can be expressed, we regret that we feel
ourselves unable to sign it.   The principle
recommendations of the Committee seem to be in the
direction of granting very wide functions and duties to
the Board of Trade and Industries, and as members of
the present Board, we should prefer not to be
associated with any recommendations of the kind.

The idea that somehow South Africa's industrialisation
could be carried out without disturbing imperial mining

hegemony, and without state guidance on a large scale, was at least as powerful as the idea that it could not.

It was because the interests of local capital were interlocking and interdependent, that they could not be realised by partial approaches. By blocking certain central programmes, such as full protection, the iron and steel industry, and the granting of full planning powers to the Advisory Board, anti-industrialists could block other manufacturing interests since they were all inter-twined. The narrow state thus operated to preserve mining hegemony and underdevelopment. National capital was to be accommodated only in so far as its interests did not threaten those of the mining industry and its related commercial and agricultural friends. While the party system seems to have performed the function of absorbing and expressing the interests of whichever sections of capital needed this done, it did so within the structure determined by imperial capital's primary interests in a particular system of underdevelopment. This would seem to provide further evidence of the fundamental class difference between imperial and national capital, and their ultimate irreconcileability, as well as being a good indication of the circumscribing and controlling functions performed by the narrow state irrespective of party policies.

When the SAP government was replaced by the Labour-Nationalist Pact in 1924, some ideologists (like certain of their historians) thought bourgeois hegemony had been achieved. From now on, they assumed, whichever party was in power national capital would remain unchallenged: 'Governments come and go, but the national interests continue unchanged, except by virtue of the natural process of evolution,' (49) wrote the editor of the 'SAJI'. And, in fact, because it was a government with an alternative source of legitimacy from that of the old imperial governments, and because it came to power at a critical time in the tussle between local and imperial capital, it provided a basis for challenging and even overthrowing imperial control of the narrow state. Because of its domination by the protectionist Labour Party the Pact's interests coincided with those of the new bourgeoisie on precisely those three issues on which imperial capital and its allies had been able to block the development of local capital - protection, state planning, and the iron and steel industry. In all three the new government acted quickly and whole-heartedly. Protection was introduced in 1925 on a broad enough basis to satisfy manufacturing leaders; (50) the Iron and Steel Bill was passed in 1928; and a full Department of Industries, and new Board of Trade and Industries, created with 'full-

time, independent, judicious men' whom the government
journal contrasted with the personnel of the old Board,
who had been men 'representing various interests'. (51)

It was under Pact rule that perhaps the most telling
conflict between imperial and national interests took
place, with victory going to the latter.   This was the
conflict over the establishment of the Iron and Steel
Industry, during which the Pact government was bitterly
opposed by older imperial interests: (52)

> The campaign against the Bill was carried through the
> length and breadth of the country.   It found a willing
> ally in the old colonial idea that South Africa's
> contribution to the welfare of Britain and the Common-
> wealth was as a supplier of raw materials and minerals,
> while manufactured goods should be imported from
> overseas.   Supporters of this idea could not imagine
> South Africa becoming an industrial power in its own
> right.   In these days wide sections of the public
> though accepting the new slogan of 'South Africa First'
> were still sceptical about the Union's future as an
> industrial country.   Circumstances seemed to prove
> them right, because the market was small, trained
> workmen and managers were lacking and capital fought
> shy of industrial investments. ... In the battle over
> Iscor the outdated colonial spirit had flared up for
> the last time.   All the forces against
> industrialisation had combined to wreck the scheme, and
> had failed.   The success which Iscor ultimately proved
> to be was the death knell of economic colonialism in
> South Africa.

The political importance of Iscor was perhaps greater than
that of protection - for it was not simply a set of
abstract tariff regulations, but a solid, visible,
producing and employing institution, a ready symbol for
imperialists, industrialisers, and the 'general public'.

However, it soon began to emerge that even these
victories did not constitute bourgeois control of the
narrow state.   This government was forced to make
concessions to mining interests - for example the crucial
engineering industries were not included in the new
protective tariff, while despite its extension and
entrenchment, 'consultation' was still, in the eyes of
the new bourgeoisie, insufficient.   In 1930 one
prominent manufacturer, in complaining that the 'advisory
function' had not improved since 1925, gave a
comprehensive outline of the functions and workings of
capital's ideal and as yet non-existent system of
consultation: (53)

I suggested ... that the Government should establish an

Advisory Council of Industry, Commerce and Agriculture,
which would be in a position to consider all questions
affecting the economic activities of the country, and
to lay its advice before the Government.   Such a body
would be in close touch with the National Economic
Organisations of the country and be able to secure
advice from them from time to time on all subjects of
interest and importance.   The Council would, in my
opinion, strengthen the activities of the Board of
Trade and Industries, which has already done sterling
work for the national development of the country.   It
would prevent controversy due either to a lack of
knowledge or a feeling that the essential interests of
any sections of the community had not received the
consideration which they deserved.   Such a Council
would be composed of representatives nominated by the
communities concerned, and it should be a fundamental
of its organisation that any decisions laid before the
Government should be arrived at unanimously, and so
prevent the necessity for minority reports, individual
representations and lobbying. ... I still wish to
suggest that consideration be given to my proposal for
the formation of an Advisory Council, as I am sure that
not only would it save the Government a great deal of
time and worry, but it would be welcomed by the
producing and trading communities as a piece of
machinery calculated to be of the greatest benefit to
the country, while preventing injury to any one
section.
In fact, at the same time that they were pleading for
an extension of consultation, intellectuals were gradually
coming to realise that even if 'consultation' were
extended into every field this would not in itself
constitute the kind of change in the narrow state that
they needed.   Their position was analogous to that of
mining in the 1890s, when even Kruger's most generous
concessions to what he treated as simply another 'pressure
group' were insufficient for the needs of what was really
an inherently revolutionary class.   Furthermore, another
perhaps even more serious problem began to become apparent
after 1924.   This was the fact that the Pact government
showed every sign of pursuing its own particular policies
without regard for the interests of the new capitalists at
all!   This, too, was a problem which 'consultation' alone
could not solve, and intellectuals began to consider other
means.
The state's potential for autonomy was epitomised by
the Wage Act on the one hand, and by the general increase
in state power and control over spheres of activity which

capitalists considered to be their preserve, on the other.
The initial response of manufacturing and commerce to the
Wage Act was favourable.   It, together with the existing
Industrial Conciliation Act, was thought to be part of the
policy of 'repressive tolerance', of conciliating the
white working class so that its grievances might be
controlled and channelled.   Of the Industrial
Conciliation Act, the 'Commercial Bulletin' said:
    Commerce did not in any way oppose the Industrial
    Conciliation Act the primary aim of which was to give
    both employers and employees a fair deal.   It was
    recognised at once that the machinery set up under that
    Act provided the best possible means not only of
    dealing with the 'sweated' industries but also of
    creating a better atmosphere in the world of labour,
while of the Wage Act it said: 'At the time it was felt
that in practice the Wage Act would be rendered nugatory
by the successful functioning of the Industrial Councils
or Conciliation Boards, and the country was thus lulled
into a false sense of security.'
    However, before long it was realised that the Wage
Boards were not simply empty institutions.   The
'Bulletin' describes the effect of this realisation: (54)
    The first blow fell when the personnel of the newly
    constituted Wage Board was announced, the second when
    the first report of the Board was published.   Then,
    for the first time it was fully realised that we were
    face to face with a situation as startling as it was
    revolutionary.   By a stroke of the pen all that sense
    of security and stability which was gradually being
    restored since the war upheaval, and which was
    inspiring fresh courage for business enterprise in all
    directions, was severely shaken.   Gloomy reports from
    Australia of the disastrous effects of similar
    legislative attempts to establish a millenium for
    workers added to the general feeling of pessimism.
    South Africa, the youngest aspirant in the ranks of
    industrial countries, had set out to achieve by
    legislation the ideals of the theorists in the oldest
    civilised communities of the world.   We were to learn
    to run before we had started crawling.
    The Federated Chamber of Industries criticised the
'revolutionary' decisions of the Wage Board as early as
February 1926, (55) while the 'Transvaal Chamber of
Industries Journal' mounted an elaborate critique, (56)
which was supplemented by frequent and virulent attacks on
it in other industrial and commercial writings and
speeches.   In November 1928, for example, Karl
Gundelfinger, Assocom Chairman, 'vigorously denounced

the trend of wage legislation, initiated by the Union
Ministry of Labour during the last year or two.   It was,
he declared, in downright terms, a serious menace to the
healthy economic development of South Africa.' (57)
Other criticisms, too numerous to catalogue, were made
throughout the late 1920s and early 1930s. (58)

The strengthening of consultation was one proposed
solution to this problem: (59)

> All that is required is for the Government to suspend
> for the time being ... the activities of the Wage
> Board, and to summon a conference between the two
> official bodies, the Board of Trade and Industries, and
> the Wages Board, together with representatives of
> industry, commerce, employers and employees, in order
> to review the whole position and present a considered
> report to the Government.

We find ideologists criticising other things.
Manufacturing, according to Cullinan in 1927, 'is
carrying as heavy a weight of industrial legislation as it
can bear'. (60)   In 1933, 'Commercial Bulletin' described
how: 'One of the chief grievances in Commerce in recent
years has been what is commonly termed Government
"interference" in matters which were formerly regarded as
domestic affairs and which should be controlled by the
trading community itself.' (61)

Specific criticisms were made of state interference in
banking, (62) while even in relation to the Iron and Steel
Act, which had been supported by manufacturers, the extent
to which the state granted itself control was
sobering. (63)   Although evidence of the beginning of a
firm consultative relationship is to be found in the late
1920s, ideologists became increasingly concerned about
capital's ability to limit and control the resulting state
autonomy.   Furthermore, the passage of time only
increased the problem; the more capital developed, the
more dependent it became upon the state, in all of the
ways outlined earlier in this chapter, and in new ways as
well.   By 1930 government speeches seemed to indicate
that the state no longer ignored manufacturing; it sought
to control it.

Ideologists took steps in two spheres in response to
the rise of state autonomy.   Following is an analysis of
them as they operated before the depression; later we
shall discuss the same two spheres during the depression
and the 'gold standard crisis'.

The first action taken by intellectuals was to glorify
what has been called here the 'consultative relationship'.
Here we find that the existence of a consultative
structure of institutions, linking the narrow state with

the new bourgeoisie, was elevated to the status of being
'natural', and was identified with the values of 'harmony'
and 'progress' already present in the ideology.   Its
absence, moreover, was conceived of as unnatural, and the
system depicted as being 'out of balance' and in a state
of 'crisis'.   Furthermore, to be natural was identified
with being non-political, while to be unnatural was
identified with being 'political', or even 'ideological'.
     The old idea of 'interdependence' provided an
historical basis for the newer concept of 'natural
harmony', first used in relation to the Wage Act.   So
interdependent were all social forces, ran the argument,
that any alteration in one factor would inevitably disrupt
the rest.   This would create 'imbalance', 'disorder', or
even 'chaos'.   These calamities would occur particularly
in cases where the alterations in any of the factors were
not in accordance with the interests of manufacturing,
commercial, or even mining, employers, such as, for
example, in the case of the Wage Act.   According to
ideologists of the time, therefore, wages could not, and
should not, be raised 'arbitrarily' or 'high-handedly',
suddenly or steeply, or the overall social balance, the
harmony which grew out of interdependence, would be
disrupted.   An example appeared in 'Commercial
Bulletin': (64)

> If wages are forced artificially beyond an economic
> level, one of two things must happen: either a number
> of industries will close down, creating a new problem
> of unemployment, or they will be enabled to carry on by
> increased protection through the Customs Tariff. ... It
> is a position which heralds a revolutionary change in
> our economic policy and an all round increase in the
> cost of living.

By circumscribing the limits within which choices may be
made - *either* industries will close down, *or* they will
need higher protection - the ideologist makes it
impossible for those adhering to the ideology of natural
harmony to conceive of that harmony outside of those
limits.
     The state of harmony, or balance, in which society is
maintained by natural forces, is accordingly held to be
very precarious.   Any upsetting of the balance is said to
be 'artificial', as in the example given above,
'irresponsible', or the way to beginning the
disintegration of the society: 'We have been brought to
the verge of an economic precipice, and withdrawal from
that position would surely be no sign of weakness.   Let a
halt at least be called before the leap is taken, ' (65)
wrote one ideologist, referring to Wage Determinations.
Another said: (66)

> We know that in industry nothing is to be gained by
> methods which lead towards unsettlement and so,
> ultimately, to chaos. ... If it [the Wage Board]
> persists in trying to force upon industries conditions
> for which they are not yet ready, then its activities
> can only be detrimental to the country.

Conversely, actions taken by employers in their own
interests were always seen as being favourable to the
maintenance of balance and harmony: (67)

> It is not an uncommon remark that manufacturers are
> taking advantage of the state of depression and
> unemployment to force wage reductions. ... The fact is
> that depression and unemployment exist because the
> industrial situation is out of balance, and there is no
> remedy except such readjustments of wages and prices as
> will restore the balance and enable the various
> industries to exchange products on a fair basis. ...
> The depreciation of money which resulted from the war
> was not a natural or permanent development. Nothing
> of that kind has ever happened without a readjustment
> afterwards, and it is always the case that the sooner
> the adjustment is accomplished, so that normal
> relations are restored between the industries, the
> better for everybody.

Harmony was preserved by a 'gradual' approach to changes
in society:

> I believe that the Wage Board has done valuable and
> constructive work, and that in time to come this will
> be recognised more readily, when new and better
> conditions for the worker replace those that were
> sometimes enforced upon manufacturers by unscrupulous
> and uncontrolled competition. In this, however, as
> in all legislation that affects industries, we must
> proceed slowly, and persuasive co-operation is always
> better than harsh compulsion.

The opposite of this 'moderate' approach was the
'extreme', 'political' or 'ideological' approach: (68)

> Unfortunately, this is a country where extreme views
> are common. Possibly it is because there are sharp
> political cleavages. But, whatever the cause,
> extremism is the unnatural mother of opportunism. In
> our economic life, co-operation in all national effort
> is essential. That connotes the moderate view in
> outlook, and in practical affairs, that careful and
> scientific investigation that alone leads to successful
> pre-determined achievement.

The critique by ideologists of the 'extreme' approach
forms a major part of the last section of this chapter.
   Of course the less the state 'interfered' in the

preservation of harmony, the better;   although the purpose
of natural harmony as an ideology was to identify the
state with nature, this identification, like the other
aspects of the concept of harmony, must be confined to
certain limits.   'Limited *laissez-faire*' should
prevail: (69)

> While I realise that in this modern era interference
> is a *sine qua non* of good government, yet I do feel
> that Governments have their own functions to perform,
> and unless unusual conditions require their special
> attention, they should, as far as possible, refrain
> from mixing themselves up with business.   Private
> enterprise is still able to do things economically and
> well, but it is rather much to expect it to continue to
> do things well, while it is burdened by taxation,
> regulated in every direction, and then forced to face
> the competition of Government departments in its actual
> business. ... South Africa is as yet only partially
> developed.   New areas are awaiting to be opened up and
> settled;   vast mining areas need exploitation;   great
> resources of raw materials await development for
> manufacturing purposes.   To do this work we need
> pioneers, men who are willing to take risks, and who
> will back their own judgement.   I plead with the
> Government not to hamper such men but rather to do
> everything possible to encourage them.

The Iron and Steel Bill, setting up as it did, a vast
state corporation, provoked the most passionate statements
of the ideology of (almost) free enterprise: (70)

> This Bill was important because it marked a principle
> entirely new in South Africa, namely, the association
> of the state with an industry hitherto conducted by
> private enterprise - a principle which, as was to be
> expected, gave rise to considerable discussion.   While
> the manufacturing community appreciates the desire of
> the Government to create conditions conducive to the
> building up, and extension of, this basic industry, it
> was felt necessary to make strong representations to
> the Select Committee on the following points: it
> seemed reasonable to the Executive Council that, if the
> Iron and Steel Industry is to develop as it should,
> steps should be taken to develop the market for its
> products. ... It was urged that the power of the
> proposed corporation to undertake the manufacture of
> goods from Iron and Steel be definitely limited.
> Representations were made also against the state
> control of industries normally operated by private
> enterprise.   The Federated Chamber adheres to this
> view, but recognising that there may be times and

seasons when the Government would feel justified in
adopting an advanced policy, it was prepared to accept
arrangements whereby the Government, if sincerely
convinced of the necessity of establishing the industry
beyond its present dimensions, should help to raise
capital for its development.   But it was emphasised
that if the Government considered the time had arrived
to do this, it should make provision in the Act for the
relinquishment, after a period of years, of all
Government financial interest.   This would mean that
while achieving its object of developing the industry,
the Government would not be utilising public money to
inaugurate and support the socialistic principle of
state control of, and managerial interest in, an
industry.

By 1929, the limits of state autonomy had been more
clearly conceptualised in relation to the issue of the
Wage Board too; in that year 'Industrial and Commercial
South Africa' began to concern itself with the issue of
why wage determinations made by the controversial Wage
Board, had been challenged by the courts.   In one of a
series of articles on 'The Wage Act Fiasco', it
commented: (71)

> The fact that Wage Determinations, made by the Minister
> of Labour under the Wage Act, are regularly being
> declared *ultra vires* by the Courts, has caused
> considerable criticism as to the methods of making
> determinations.   The establishment of the Wage Act was
> welcomed by the country in general, and by employers
> and employees in particular, as an instrument which
> would serve to stabilise industry and trade.   These
> successful attempts to upset the Determinations
> nullify the usefulness of the Act.   The decisions and
> recommendations of the Wage Board, which have led to
> the present unsatisfactory state of affairs, have been
> many.   Most of them have been inexplicable, except on
> the assumption that the Board may feel it has a divine
> call to act John the Baptist to the coming Social
> Revolution.

In summary, the view of ideologists of the role of the
state was that 'at times our legislators appear to be
anxious to hasten too quickly.   South Africa is in danger
of being overgoverned.' (72)   What ideologists sought was
the identification of the narrow state with nature *in so
far as it accorded with capital's interests*.   When the
state behaves correctly, harmony ensues; chaos and
unnaturalness when it does not.

Consultation and its ideological glorification
constituted one clear channel through which state autonomy

could be controlled.   However, it was certainly not
sufficient.   For one thing, to whom was the ideology of
'natural harmony' or 'limited *laissez-faire*' directed?
Surely not towards civil servants or MPs?   The control of
state autonomy implied control over the general (white)
populace, the public whose allegiances and ideologies the
state was surely supposed to crystallise and embody.   If
control over the answerability of the state to the public
could be established, if the very legitimacy of the
political system itself could be circumscribed, then
capital's interests within the state would be secured on a
more permanent, stable basis.   Intellectuals began to
propose that capital enter the more overtly 'political'
arena in several ways.

Attempts to mobilise the electorate on issues
specific to manufacturing and commerce had long been made
by capital.   These were, until the First World War,
somewhat unrealistic, since protectionism was not an issue
which fired the imagination of the white electorate;   they
were often made with purely rhetorical intent.   But with
the wartime surge in protectionism, ideologists felt that
electoral mobilisation on their behalf was more likely,
and, moreover, that it was necessary: (73)

> The industrialist alone is voiceless, and will remain
> so unless a determined effort is made to secure
> adequate representation. ... The chance once lost, will
> not recur for many years, during which the fate of
> industrialism will be decided.   In fact, the next five
> years will be the most momentous in our economic
> history, and if the manufacturing community is not
> represented in the deliberations of Parliament and has
> no voice in moulding the legislation which will be
> passed there, there will be no need to worry specially
> about direct representation for the next generation or
> two.   It will be useless for the manufacturer to rebel
> against the economic control of the merchant if he lets
> pass this great opportunity to obtain representation,
> and to maintain it.

They tended to move away from the idea that manufacturers
should stand for parliament as independents, (74) and to
consider the South African Party as the most suitable
basis from which the mobilisation of the electorate on
behalf of industrial hegemony could be carried out.

However, this mobilisation had to be performed in
particular ways according to the interests of local
capital.   Industrial hegemony, as we have seen, needed to
be co-operative and voluntary within the white polity.
Whereas in imperial days parties were clearly linked with
class interests, now their industrial basis needed to be

disguised and their participatory and co-operative aspects
emphasised.   Furthermore, given the disparate nature of
the electorate, and of the SAP itself, electoral
mobilisation had to be under the aegis of a generalised,
embracing ideology, capable of establishing a consensus.
On the one hand many of these requirements were to be
found in the South Africanist ideology.   It was
voluntaristic, co-operative and embracing, emphasising
consensus and harmony.   Moreover, it was spreading
through the white polity during and after the First World
War, and finding a home in the SAP itself.   The first
thing that was needed, therefore, was the consolidation of
South Africanism's place within the SAP.

    But on the other hand, South Africanism was not an
ideology which had disguised its aims and purposes.   At
least until the First World War, if not later, it had
existed in a highly political and overtly ideological
form.   Its industrial roots, far from being concealed,
had been exposed;   its anti-imperial and creed-like
qualities had been displayed;   while its desire to embrace
the white working and middle classes had been explicit.
Ideologists sensed that these qualities of South
Africanism were not suited to its future hegemonic role.
As we saw in our discussion of the process of
externalisation, they were active in the 1920s in laying
the foundations for the disguise of the roots and
intentions of South Africanism.   Here we see this
process carried through to its conclusion.   It has been
called here 'secularisation', since it involved the
removal from the ideology of its explicitly 'creed-like'
qualities.   It became the ideology of 'non-ideology', by
denying that it was anything other than a reflection of
reality, or the ordinary person's perception of that
reality.   This process of secularisation made easier the
identification of party (the voice of the people), with
ideology (the conceptualisation of the world in which the
people lived), with capitalism (the destiny of the
people), with nature, and hence with the state.

    Long before the Pact government, ideologists had been
concerned with the secular side of South Africanism.   At
first, this was because of the ineffectiveness of
industrial politics.   The depiction by Laite of elections
as 'petty and irrelevant' in 1915, (75) must, in the light
of his having been crushingly defeated by Jagger in a Cape
constituency in that year, have contained an element of
sour grapes.   Yet this concept was inherent in the South
Africanist idea.   South Africanism, which supposedly
embodied the true interests of the nation, had been
designed to appear to 'transcend' politics, since it had

been designed to pose an alternative legitimacy.   The old
legitimacy, and hence the old politics, were easily
relegated to the position of being 'petty' or
'irrelevant'.   South Africanism, on the other hand,
contained the seeds of new legitimacy, and hence a new
politics; one which could go above and beyond the old.

   Examples of the ability of South Africanism to envisage
a new politics appeared in the early manufacturing
ideology.   One of Laite's political proposals had been
that: 'Relief will be found in a combination of the
progressive elements of all existing parties, the first
principle of which must be fuller development of the
agricultural and industrial resources of the Union.' (76)
Similarly, his journal had maintained that if
manufacturers failed to make themselves felt in
parliament, then 'The two "isms" so fatal to the country's
progress - "Racialism and Mercantilism" - will continue
to dominate our national life.' (77)   In the 'political'
as well as in the 'consultative' field, therefore, the
concepts of nature and harmony prevailed, against the
hostile forces of outdated ideologies and chaos.

   When the autonomy of the narrow state from capitalist
interests began to make itself felt, and the notion of
recapturing it through the mobilisation of the electorate
began to develop, then these ideas of a secular South
Africanism spread, and began to be used in new ways.   The
fact that the new bourgeoisie had to work within the South
African Party provoked a new interest in the relationship
between the electorate and the ideology.   Dissatisfaction
with the party's old imperial mould was widespread,
particularly in commercial circles.   To some, this
dissatisfaction was so great that they proposed working
outside of the party, in an independent business
movement.   The editor of the 'Commercial Bulletin', for
example, wrote of the Wage Act: 'Had there been as many
business men in the Assembly as there are farmers or
lawyers, there would be a very different story to tell
today.' (78)   This was the old idea that businessmen
should become MPs.   This plea was never successful -
a fact which supports the view that capital's relationship to the state cannot be assessed by examining the
social origins of MPs.   Later he made it clear that
this plea was part of a wider concern.   It was the
'party system' as a whole which was inadequate, and
which had, moreover, developed into a 'dictatorship':
(79)

   [there have been] views expressed from time to time in
   these columns that there should be a commercial and
   industrial party in Parliament.   We have a nucleus of

such a party already, and it will be admitted on all
sides that Parliament would be poorer without them.
They have done work of outstanding importance and value
on Select Committees and their business and
professional training and experience has on many
occasions raised the standard of debate from a very
ordinary to an exceedingly high level.   They have, in
short, demonstrated that a numerically strong
commercial party would be an enormous asset.
This was because, he said, parliament was being diverted
from its natural spheres of activity by the evils of
politics and race.   The real, or true, course of events
would not be concerned with such irrelevancies, but would
be devoted to non-political issues, such as harmony,
development and progress.   The strong commercial group
would therefore 'be a still greater asset if it could be
diverted from political allegiance to any party'.
The President of Assocom extended this proposal even
further.   He made explicit his conception that the
electorate should, in the 'new politics', be mobilised by
industrial and commercial interests, and said that, if
these interests did come to power: (80)
It would only be by the will of the people.   Such a
party, if it materialised, would never maintain its
position on a racial or sectional basis.   It would
undoubtedly cut right across the artificial barrier of
existing political parties, opening its ranks to the
agriculturalist, and the industrialist, employers and
employees, the protagonists of the interests of the
interior, and those of the coastal areas.   Its watch-
word would have to be the reconciliation of all these
divergent interests on business lines.   Admittedly a
tremendous task, but a task calculated at least to
unite rather than divide our people no one section of
which can prosper without co-operation and compromise.
Sound business principles, unity of purpose, and
general readjustment of our ideas regarding our
relative importance in world economic development -
that is all we plead for.   Politicians need not be
alarmed.   They will always have their innings.   But
that political party which grasps the fact that
commerce and industry must have more voice in the
government of the country than is the case today, and
that business principles are of paramount importance in
the government of the country will score heavily. ...
In South Africa ... the different, wider, and more
dangerous gulf of racialism is gradually securing a
stranglehold on everything which would make for
prosperity and development.

Here the desire for industrial and commercial domination
is expressed in the form of 'secularised' South
Africanism.   Businessmen and industrialists are claimed
to be the only people capable of expressing the 'true'
interests of *all* the white people, through their
conception of a new, transcending, political system, which
would make it possible for all to develop and progress in
harmony.   The present party political system - the old
politics - was beset by 'politics' and irrational
racialism which contrasted unfavourably with the non-
political, non-racial character of business interests.
The evils of racialism and party politics would disappear
under the banner of the all-embracing industrial party.

These, then, were national capital's ambitions for
moulding, influencing and controlling the narrow state.
But how were they to be realised, given the absence of any
overriding revolutionary force acting on capital's behalf?
We shall argue here that capital's tactics were to seize
whatever opportunities were offered it by the force of
historical circumstance.   It had already exploited one
opportunity offered to it by the advent of the Pact
government.   A second, more promising, chance presented
itself in the early 1930s, when the combination of the
effects of the depression and the politically inept
behaviour of the Hertzog government over the 'gold
standard crisis', caused an unprecedented politicisation
of the white population, and created a rift between the
old state system and the electorate.

The new bourgeoisie began to comment on the effects of
the depression during 1930.   By October, they were
seriously concerned by the amount of 'dumping' which was
taking place.   Morris Kramer, in his FCI presidential
address for that year, warned that the coming depression
was more serious than any other which industrialists had
experienced. (81)   Amongst the new bourgeoisie and the
population as a whole, a feeling of helplessness in the
face of impersonal and distant forces began to grow.
Kramer himself placed the blame for the depression on the
fact that 'the extraordinary development of science as
applied to methods of production' (i.e. the growth of
efficiency and rationalisation), had led to a 'much
greater volume of goods ... being produced than the
existing consuming markets could absorb'.   All that
commerce could do in the light of falling imports and
revenue was to hope for an improvement: 'Commercial South
Africa is, as I have indicated, maintaining its position
and acting with extreme conservatism, and holding itself
ready to take advantage of any world improvement in trade
conditions.' (82)

'Extreme conservatism' prevailed in a time of ignorance and helplessness. When, in September 1931, Britain went off the gold standard, the South African government had the full support of commerce, industry, and the Chamber of Mines in its decision not to follow suit. (83)   Some sections of industry maintained a consistently pro-gold standard line throughout the following months. (84) However, within commerce and the majority of industry, the opposite view began to prevail in the months after Britain's devaluation. (85)   In a memorandum on the subject submitted by Assocom to the Select Committee of the House of Assembly in June 1932 commerce argued that none of their earlier orthodox predictions had come true, and that South Africa was seen to be suffering material disadvantages by remaining on gold: (86)

it is not denied that the maintenance of a stable currency based on gold is of the greatest importance, and that all sections of the population should be willing to undergo considerable sacrifices to this end. It is, however, submitted that there is a limit to which such sacrifices can be justified, and we are of the opinion that the limit has long since been reached, and for the following reasons: Capital is being withdrawn from the country to such an extent that commercial and industrial enterprise and development are so seriously affected as to necessitate drastic reductions in personnel, and in salaries and wages, throughout the country. These reductions decrease the spending power of the people, which results in an alarming increase in poverty and distress, and still further augments the already grave state of unemployment. This withdrawal of capital will inevitably continue so long as sterling remains at a substantial discount with South African currency.

If the Union left gold, capital would return, primary producers would more easily be able to market their products overseas, the life of the gold mines would be extended and trade would revive generally, according to the memorandum.

However, not only did the government insist on remaining on gold, but Hertzog attempted to mobilise support for this decision from nationalists, on the grounds that South Africa's dependence on British imperialism was symbolised by, and, indeed, grounded in, its dependence on sterling. A stand against sterling was a stand for South African nationalism. (87)   The gold standard controversy proved to be a symbol of the conflict between Afrikaner and English-speaking nationalisms in South Africa, just as Iscor had been between local and

imperial capital.   To the English-speaking manufacturing
and commercial classes the ties of South Africa to the
British economy were acceptable as long as they allowed
local capital to flourish.   To the Afrikaner farmer and
worker they were not acceptable under any conditions.
But the stand of the nationalists proved futile.   South
Africa's dependence on Britain's and the world's economy
was too great to be severed by a single stroke.   The
commercial memorandum summed up this dependence: (88)

> the gold contents of any currency unit cannot, without
> serious complications, be permanently maintained at a
> higher level than the gold prices of the products of
> the agricultural, pastoral, and base metal industries.
> The bulk of the commercial transactions of this country
> have for over a century been settled through British
> sterling.   This channel cannot be suddenly altered ...
> without grave adverse effects on all commercial
> operations, through uncertainty in fixing contracts,
> and the arrest of the flow of funds on normal lines.
> ... Whilst it may be possible to maintain the gold
> standard on the basis of existing currency, it will be
> at such a cost as will shake the economic fabric of the
> Union to its very foundations.

Because of the government's decision to remain on gold,
South African industries suffered unnecessarily from the
depression, from whose effects the gold mines would
normally have protected them.   1932 was described by one
eminent merchant as 'the most difficult year for commerce
that South Africa has ever experienced.' (89)

> Imports had dropped by half, exports by 10 per cent,
the volume of trade had suffered 'very serious shrinkage',
unemployment had risen and spending power had fallen;   and
of course, capital continued to leave the country.   Bank
deposits had dropped by £9m, while every financial
institution, trust company, or building society, had had a
drain on its resources: (90)

> Until capital which has left this country comes back
> again, we can look for no permanent or substantial
> improvement in trade. ... Capital is to commerce as
> blood is to the human body, and a country which is
> suffering from loss of capital and bad circulation has
> no more hope of being healthy and vigorous than has a
> human being suffering from bad circulation and an
> extensive loss of blood.

For a period of several months, therefore, commerce and
industry felt themselves to be in a grave position, for
which the state was to blame and whose effects caused
suffering amongst the entire population.   If evidence was
needed of the new dependence of South Africa's economy

upon its commercial and industrial, and not just its
farming and mining, enterprises, then the gold standard
crisis and the depression provided it.   Moreover, these
events revealed the invisible underpinnings which the
state normally provided for the operation of the new
industrial economy.   As soon as the state ceased to
provide its normal, ongoing services to commerce and
industry, the much-feared 'chaos' ensued.

In spite of the fact that this was a grave crisis for
capital, the events of the early 1930s provided the
bourgeoisie with precisely the opportunity it had been
seeking, to make an assault upon the political apparatuses
of the social formation.   Under the leadership and
guidance of its intellectuals, capital launched a four-
fold attack on the imperial polity.   First, an appeal to
the popular imagination was made and exploited.   Second,
the irrationality of nationalism and all it represented
was asserted, and contrasted with the rationality of South
Africanism and all it represented.   Third, the
'consultative relationship' was extended and consolidated.
Finally, ideologists sought and urged a 'political
solution' which both incorporated and transcended the
'consultative solution', to the problem of hegemony.
The interests of the 'new bourgeoisie' and the pattern of
its past were the basis of these developments.   The
structure of South Africanism in its original form;   the
modifications which were undertaken by ideologists during
and after the First World War, and the particular ways in
which it coped with the interests of manufacturing and
commerce concerning white workers, the middle class, and
the state, must all be kept in mind during the discussion
that follows for the ways in which capital sought to
capture the 'narrow state' were determined by the changes
that had already taken place in the wide state, which in
turn were determined by capital's interests.

The first factors evolved by ideologists were the
interests of capital in, and the actual burgeoning of, a
public consensus - 'public opinion'.   On the ideological
level the crisis had served the important function of
forcing the public into an awareness of the extent to
which all sectors were caught in a web of mutual causes
and effects: (91)

Money is scarce, and business is almost at a stand-
still.   Exports of manufactured goods to Rhodesia have
almost disappeared.   The low prices obtained overseas
for many primary products, and the loss in exchange in
bringing money from overseas has caused a heavy fall in
purchasing power.   Storekeepers find the greatest
difficulty in securing payment for goods sold, and in

consequence are unable to meet their own liabilities.
Importation has, therefore, fallen, and wholesale
merchants are unable to sell anything but the smallest
quantities from hand to mouth.   The position is
exaggerated by the unemployment in the country today
... when people are out of work they are also out of
consumption, and consequently to that extent the market
is still further restricted.   The position of
agriculture is deplorable ... the prices for primary
products have fallen to ridiculously low figures and
farmers are vainly striving to operate on capital
investments based on the price of land and
agricultural plant in the days when prices were high
and the world's market was buying voraciously and
crying for more. ... Manufacturing is at an extremely
low ebb; indeed industries are seriously dislocated.
The fall in consumption ... has meant a fall in
production.   It is impossible to obtain advances from
banks, and manufacturers are unable any longer to grant
the credit necessary to enable storekeepers to purchase
and sell to their customers on terms.
     The mutual interdependence between all classes,
sections of classes, social groups and economic forces,
which intellectuals had so long proclaimed as part of
capital's ideology was revealed by the crisis to have
become nothing less than the truth.   All sections of
society suffered under the state's mismanagement.   It was
against this background, and building upon the interests
of the new bourgeoisie in conciliating and incorporating
the white working and middle classes, that ideologists
pointed to the government's failure to recognise the
popular resentment its gold standard policy had caused.
The government was clearly unable to relate to the demands
of 'the people', they claimed, and had failed to seize the
chance offered to it by the crisis to consolidate white
unity.   Business, on the other hand, was both willing and
able to do these things.   It had an inherent ability to
relate to the people, ran the argument, and had always
advocated, if not embodied, white unity.
     The degree of public interest in the issue was indeed
unprecedented in South Africa.   In January 1932 the
'Bulletin' said that the controversy: 'has completely
eclipsed weather, gossip, and the Springbok football tour.
It is strange at first sight that a subject so highly
technical and remote from the ordinary ken should have
made such an appeal to the popular imagination.' (92)
     It was on the basis of this widespread interest in the
gold standard crisis that commerce based its claim that
the 'voice of the people' should determine its

solution. (93)   The government was utterly unable to
articulate what the voice of the people was;   and, moreover, had failed to acknowledge its responsibility for its
guidance and education.   In this view of public opinion,
it was not a spontaneous thing;   or if it did contain an
element of spontaneity, it usually led it in the wrong
directions.   Public opinion needed to be trained by those
who understood it: (94)

> Public opinion is to a large extent becoming a
> manufactured product.   It is not only swayed, but it
> is created, by politicians, and the press, the process
> varying only in degree in different countries.   The
> average individual rapidly assimilates an idea which is
> hammered into his mind with sufficient persistence.
> There is nothing he likes better, and nothing easier,
> than to persuade himself that it is his own idea, the
> creation of his own brain, and based on the soundest
> reasoning and logic. ... It is safe to assert that not
> one out of a hundred individuals who are daily
> discussing the subject [of the gold standard] in their
> homes, clubs and offices, could commit to writing a
> reasoned statement of their views which would secure a
> third grade matriculation pass. ... It is clear ...
> that the ultimate responsibility in a problem of this
> kind must rest with the Government.

Instead, it was the view of 'commerce and the country
generally' that the government had not accepted this
responsibility.   Instead of taking advantage of the
'heaven sent opportunity' which the depression provided
for 'putting an end to racial strife, for sinking petty
and personal party political differences, and for
demonstrating to the world the value of true national
independence', the government had failed in both statesmanship and leadership:

> In business circles everywhere, it was felt that the
> depression might well prove a blessing in disguise, and
> well worth the cost if it resulted in bringing together
> all the best elements in the political life of the
> country, with a common determination to put South
> Africa before party, race and self.   It was a natural
> aspiration at a time of grave national crisis, and it
> is certain that it was shared by the great bulk of the
> people.

It was hoped that the depression would allow South
Africanism, and not 'imperialism' or 'Afrikaner
nationalism', to prevail.

Not only had the government failed to take advantage of
the opportunities offered by the crisis in relation to the
general public, but it had even alienated its own

supporters.   Farmers in particular found the depression
severe enough, without the additional burdens placed on
them by the gold standard crisis.   They, too, became
highly politicised as a result:

> During the weeks preceding the opening of Parliament,
> an extraordinary wave of agitation had swept the
> countryside against the gold standard policy.
> Strangely enough, it originated, not with the
> politicians, but simultaneously all over the country,
> among farmers, who for the most part support the
> Government through thick and thin.   Politics for once
> were put on one side.   They saw their markets falling
> away, and prices collapsing at a calamitous rate,
> mainly through the exchange.   Nothing else mattered.
> Here, of course was the time and golden opportunity for
> the politicians to step in, and right nobly they
> responded to the call.   Forces were rapidly moved up
> to the disaffected districts, and a battle royal ensued
> between the opposing forces.   Meeting after meeting
> passed resolutions condemning the gold standard, and
> expressing confidence in the anti-gold speakers, and a
> veritable landslide in the government strongholds
> appeared imminent.

The solution of the governing party to this grass-roots
rejection simply reinforced South Africanism, since it
seemed to be artificial and desperate, and did not reach
the hearts of the people:

> Something had to be done, and done quickly to save the
> situation.   Whoever else suffered, it must not be the
> farming community.   Tell the farmer that he will get
> back in hard cash whatever he loses through the
> unfavourable exchange, and all his objections to the
> gold standard would melt into thin air.   And so, of
> course, it proved.   More meetings were held, and the
> same audiences which had a few days previously
> condemned with all vigour the gold standard became its
> most enthusiastic supporters.

To shore up its gold standard policy, the government
pledged subsidies to the farming sector.   This could not
under any circumstances be seen as a policy which aimed to
realise the will of 'the people':   'This sums up the whole
attitude of the Government throughout the crisis;   an
attitude which, rightly or wrongly, gave the impression of
almost complete aloofness from public opinion, and of
self-enforced isolation.' (95)

A further region in which South Africanism was
reinforced, and nationalism and imperialism threatened,
was in that the existing lines of division in South
African political culture were challenged: (96)

Public opinion in regard to the Gold Standard policy of
the Government was so sharply divided that the leaders
of both political parties saw their authority
threatened and party discipline slipping away.
Meetings were held at which previous political feuds
and differences were forgotten, and 'Nats' and 'Saps'
voted shamelessly together.   That, of course, if
allowed to continue, would have been fatal to the
political game.   A united party front had to be
preserved at all costs, and on both sides recantations
and conversions became the order of the day.   The
public, anxious for a lead, in the end did not know who
to believe. ... Both political parties are so intent
on either remaining in power, or getting into power,
that, as at present constituted, they have completely
lost touch with public opinion in regard to many
matters of national importance.

With unemployment high, popular disillusionment rife,
and the level of politicisation growing, commercial,
industrial, and other ideologists were offered an
exceptionally suitable opportunity for the putting forward
of their solutions to South Africa's problems.   This they
did, in several different regions, and political forms.
A number of 'alternative' political and non-political
organisations sprang up around the problems created for
all by the depression, and around the specific issue of
the gold standard.   As the 'Bulletin' said, this
indicated more than simply a desire for new policies: (97)

The devolution movement in Natal, the abortive attempt
to form a central party, and the expressed desire of
organised commerce for a bloc of politically
independent business men in Parliament.   These are all
unmistakeable signs of a growing revolt against
existing party political divisions.

The second front on which the assault was conducted was
that of the alleged 'naturalness' and impartiality of
South Africanism.   Whereas South Africanism's early
battles had been with the mining, British, ideology, and
had accordingly been developed to emphasise its patriotic,
nationalistic and anti-imperial characteristics, its
battles in the early 1930s were with nationalists more
patriotic and anti-imperial than themselves.
'Irrationality' was the concept developed to cope with
this fact.   It made it possible for South Africanism,
like many ideologies of national capital, to place itself
'between extremes', to emphasise its non-ideological
components, and to show up the 'extreme' and 'ideological'
concerns of those on either side of it.   Thus
intellectuals had found a means of transforming the

ideology from a radical to a conservative one, while
preserving the identification of 'capital' with 'nature'.
Thus we find the ideologist developing the secular side of
South Africanism in these years, and establishing it as an
ideology divested of overtly political content, identified
with rationality, pragmatism, common sense, and 'good
business'.   In these terms, the government was irrational
in so far as it failed to embrace these values, and
persisted with the 'old', 'racialist' politics of pre-
protection South Africa.   When the government refused to
leave the gold standard, and Hertzog claimed that this had
been for nationalistic, political reasons, the 'Commercial
Bulletin' responded: 'The structure of sound economic
reasons for adhering to gold crumbled away and was
replaced by a fetish.' (98)

Hertzog, it was claimed, had made the gold standard
controversy into a 'political' issue, and by doing so had
failed to transcend the old racialist mould.   South
Africanism, on the other hand, embodied a more rational
nationalism:

> True and lasting economic independence can be achieved
> only by both races coming together to bury the hatchet
> once and for all, and to work shoulder to shoulder to
> make South Africa what it should be - the most
> prosperous of all the Dominions. ... There are no
> Uitlanders in South Africa today.   It is the home and
> heritage and pride as much of the English-speaking as
> of the Dutch-speaking citizen.   The former have proved
> their patriotism by supporting governments composed
> ever since Union almost exclusively of Dutch-speaking
> South Africans.   The differences, prejudices and
> barriers are the creation of the politicians, and the
> country is sick and tired of it.

Hertzog was, however, doing nothing more than operating
within an old and corrupted system of political life.
South African politics as a whole was uniquely cursed by
the irrationalities of race and ideology: (99)

> as a result of the increasing tendency to approach
> every economic problem from the angle of party
> politics.   The political system has often been
> criticised in this and other countries, and, apart from
> Bolshevism and Dictatorship, nothing has been found to
> take the place of government by groups or parties.
> But in South Africa the admitted drawbacks of the party
> system have been accentuated by racialism, and by a
> blind determination to subordinate the interests of the
> country to the fetish of party loyalty.

Thus, during the crisis, ideologists were able to
identify the actual institutions of South Africa's polity

with the ideological content of South Africanism.   Never
before had it been possible to relate the interests of
capital to the specific political institutions to which
the general public held allegiance.   The new legitimacy,
which had previously been articulated in specific,
interest-based contexts, could now be posed as an
alternative to the old, in the wider society, amongst the
politicised and often disillusioned public.   The process
of 'externalisation' described in chapter 5, which was to
do with the interests of capital in incorporating the
white working and middle class, could now be linked to the
process of public legitimation.   Paradoxically, the
'non-political' 'non-ideology' was given the opportunity
of becoming a popular political ideology.

The third sphere was that of the extension and
consolidation of consultative hegemony.   During the
crisis, the consultative relationship which had been built
up over the past fifteen years was seriously threatened.
The government's adherence to the gold standard against
industrial and commercial advice was a rejection of
consultation, and this was exacerbated by the conscious
policy of the Hertzog government to ignore any attempts
made by businessmen to restore and extend consultative
structures.   Ideologists reacted passionately to this
rift between state and industry.   The gold standard
crisis became, as the Wage Act had been in the late
1920s, a symbol of state autonomy.

At the same time, from the state's point of view,
Chambers of Commerce and Industry were also regarded with
suspicion, because of their close association with the
South African Party during the 1920s.   This was another
indication of the continuing inadequacy of the
consultative relationship.   For hegemony to be
sustained neither the party affiliations of the hegemonic
class nor the particular party in power at any one time
should affect the structures of consultation.   This was
patently not so during the depression.   Chambers of
Commerce in particular, were called by Nationalist
ministers 'South African Party agents', or 'the heavy
artillery of the SAP'.   The 'Bulletin' said that: (100)
    until quite recently, the Government has tacitly
    refused to recognise the Associated Chambers of
    Commerce and has insisted in regarding that body as a
    party political organisation.   In this way, a barrier
    had been created which to all intents and purposes
    closed the only channel of communication between
    commerce and the Government.   Consultation become a
    dead letter, and resolutions submitted to the
    Government, as the outcome of much research and

> consideration, were politely, and not always even
> politely, ignored.   Until only a few months back,
> there was a general feeling that organised commerce was
> being boycotted, and that it was a sheer waste of time
> to hold congresses.

As is suggested by this quotation, this rift in
consultation did not last long.   But during the months
that it did persist, commercial and industrial ideologists
gave a clearer indication than ever before of their ideas
about the nature of consultative hegemony.

In September 1931, before the gold standard crisis had
developed, the chairman of Assocom gave some indication of
the extent to which the desirable amount of consultation
had expanded.   In his ideal 'Parliament of businessmen',
the cardinal principles of a policy of reconstruction and
development would be: the placing of railways under a
board of business directors, instead of a Minister;   the
holding of a national convention to discuss the
Provincial Council system, and provincial finance;   the
appointment of a customs tariff commission, to review the
Union's tariff policy;   the appointment of a standing
committee of parliament to check government expenditure;
the reorganisation of the Board of Trade and Industries,
its composition and function;   the development of markets
and negotiation of treaties;   the 'acceptance of the
principle of giving notice of all legislation';   the
revision of wage legislation and wage determinations 'in
the light of recent economic developments', and the 'more
general adoption of the Industrial Conciliation Act in
preference to the arbitrary fixing of wages';   less
government trading;   and the limiting of free education
facilities to the poor. (101)

Businessmen wanted to have more to do with state
legislative and administrative activities than ever
before, particularly in those fields in which the
government had recently made innovations, or over which
politicians still possessed a great deal of control, such
as railways, or legislation itself. (102)   The depression
and crisis made the need for consultation even more
urgent.   In times of crisis, the deficiencies in social
structures are revealed, and calls for something to be
done about them increase: (103)

> Cannot we as a people look facts squarely in the face,
> and without regard to political or personal prejudices,
> see if we cannot thresh out major policies which will
> lay sure foundations upon which to build a national
> superstructure which will stand firm in the new world
> which is in the making?

Both the state and the new bourgeoisie regarded

consultation in these months to be a clear *alternative* to politics. Commerce urged the government to appoint an 'Economic Advisory Commission, composed of the best brains in the country, and entirely free from party political influences,' (104) while it regretted that the government sometimes tended to confuse the two aspects of the relationship:

> We cannot and do not believe that it is the deliberate policy or intention of the Government to alienate the co-operation and support of that great section of the community which commerce represents, and to which the state has to look for nearly fifty per cent of its revenue. It is all the more unfortunate, therefore, that such an impression should be created. It certainly does not apply to the permanent Government staff, nor to the heads of state departments with whom, despite the inevitable differences of opinion which must inevitably arise from time to time, the most friendly relations are maintained.

Politics, in the eyes of the business ideologist, could almost be defined as 'ineffective consultation', and itself became 'non-politics' once the issues with which it had been concerned were institutionalised. The ideologists were anxious to communicate this view of things to the state: (105)

> [commerce] is no respecter of governments, whatever their political leanings may be ... all we ask is that criticism should be made and taken in the right spirit. ... It is discouraging ... to find an increasing tendency on the part of the Government to resent and view with suspicion any form of criticism as being biased or influenced by political considerations. This is no doubt partly due to the fact that there is no connecting link between the Government and commerce, such, for instance, as the Board of Trade in Britain, a strictly non-political body, with a Minister of the Crown at its head. It follows that public bodies are frequently thrown back on one or other of the political parties to make their views heard. As long as this state of affairs exists, misunderstandings are bound to arise.

The process of re-establishment and extension of consultation began when Hertzog invited representatives of commerce to advise him on South Africa's best approach to the Ottawa world economic conference: 'It was felt, and is felt today, that the barrier had to a great extent been removed, and that the Government no longer regarded the Associated Chambers as a body working in the interests of any particular political party.' (106) The Ottawa

reconciliation was regarded by commerce as one of the most
significant happenings of that year, (107) and was
followed by other approaches by the state to both commerce
and industry.   Oswald Pirow became the state's spokesman
on consultation, and when in 1932 he made a speech to the
FCI on 'The State and Private Enterprise' he said
that: (108)

> we shall probably, in the course of time, be compelled
> to travel much further along the road [to state
> interference] than the most autocratic Minister or
> would-be Minister will today admit to himself.   That
> is a prospect which we will have to face.   With it,
> any Government of the day will have to face this
> further certainty: that state interference is bound to
> overreach itself unless coupled with most extended
> consultation with the interests to be affected.   Your
> Annual Conferences provide a basis for such
> consultation in respect of all matters affecting
> industries,

while later he announced his 'complete conversion to the
principle of Government consultation with interested
parties'. (109)

Before the gold standard crisis was over, therefore,
both the state and the new bourgeoisie had developed their
concepts of consultation in new directions.   Consultation
did not reach the low level of 1931 and 1932 again, and
ideologists were never again provoked into making this
aspect of their hegemony explicit.   Only after 1948, with
the coming to power of the National Party, did it
become again an important aspect of bourgeois ideology,
but by then it was the ideology of an established ruling
class, not of an aspirant one.   Until then consultation
faded from the ideological picture of the 1930s and 1940s,
while it continued to exist as an ongoing structural
basis for bourgeois hegemony.

The final response of ideologists lay in the explicitly
political field.   Political ideology was a continuation
of the identification between party, state, capital and
nature examined earlier in this chapter.   Working from
this, industrial and commercial thinkers proposed a
transcending political solution which incorporated
consultation, and went beyond it, to the ongoing problem
of hegemony.

Early ideological responses to the depression were on
traditional lines.   Businessmen should stand for
parliament, or form their own, separate commercial and
industrial party, said the 'Bulletin'. (110)

> Commerce, regarded in the widest sense, has a part to
> play in the government of the country, a part which

cannot always be denied to it.   If the politicians
must keep the game to themselves commerce can at least
give them a definite lead by enumerating the cardinal
principles of a policy of reconstruction and
development. (111)

However, in the light of the vastly increased
politicisation of the population and the other problems
created by the depression, it began to seem to ideologists
that their ideas about the identification of party, state
and the natural will of the people could perhaps be put
into practice.   The time seemed ripe for the organisation
of politics in new forms, and the assertion of new
ideological patterns throughout the society.

Besides the politicisation of the people, this
possibility was made more likely by the increasing
identification between commerce, industry, and the third
vital interest, agriculture.   The depression and the
crisis had reinforced the sense of interdependence between
these sectors.   In 1932, it was reported how this had
been reflected organisationally: (112)

It is encouraging to note that in the country districts
there is every indication that Chambers of Commerce are
entering upon a new lease of life.   They were badly
hit by the depression, but few of them went under.
They form a most important link between the farming
community and commerce, and it has been a wise move on
the part of some of the country chambers to encourage
the farmers in their district to join at a nominal
subscription.   We hope that this movement will spread,
and that there will be a general linking of
agriculture, industry and commercial interests
throughout the country.

With commercial ideologists emphasising the need for a
transcending political solution, and manufacturing
ideologists emphasising the need for the spread of a
'national spirit', a concerted attempt was made by both
interests to advocate and assist the organisation of a new
political party.   This party would, it was envisaged,
embody South Africanism; it would transform the political
system and allow the will of the people to be expressed.
Commerce, at first, proposed it somewhat
tentatively: (113)

The outstanding national problems of the moment can
never be satisfactorily solved on party political
lines, and this applies with equal force to the native
question, education, the Provincial Council system and
the gold standard. ... A National Convention might
conceivably lead to a National Government, national in
the true sense of the term, and bringing together those
who should never have drifted apart.

This solution was seen as being 'better than a
General Election'.   So taken was commerce with this idea
that in 1932, the Association of Chambers of Commerce took
it to Hertzog, but it was rejected outright. (114)
Nevertheless, the idea grew and spread.   Percy Wenban,
President of the Cape Town Chamber of Commerce, called for
business to 'organise itself as to give a lead and express
public opinion, which cannot much longer be
stilled'. (115)   A movement was set afoot to form not
only the businessman's party, which had long been proposed
by ideologists, (116) but a National, or Coalition,
government: (117)

> it is perhaps almost an open secret that, outside the
> official organisation of the Chambers of Commerce,
> informal discussions have taken place between leading
> citizens of the Union, with a view to considering what
> concerted action could be taken to give definite
> expression to the growing volume of public opinion in
> favour of the formation of a National or Coalition
> Government.   The difficulties to be faced were not
> underestimated, but everywhere there was evidence that
> the great bulk of the electorate was ready and waiting
> for a lead in that direction.

A 'Coalitionist Movement' was actually formed at that
time, as if to confirm commerce's conviction that the
public would support such a move. (118)
Throughout the remaining months of the crisis, it was
Commerce that led a vigorous campaign for a national
government.   It was proposed as the best means of
solving virtually every problem of the time: (119)

> we are profoundly convinced that such a Government
> would have an electrifying effect in restoring
> confidence, that, with the support of a vast majority
> of both races in the country, it could embark on a
> national programme of development which neither party
> could carry through alone, and that it would put an
> end, once and for all, to party political divisions
> based on racialism.   We are convinced, too, that there
> are leaders in both parties big enough and patriotic
> enough to make whatever personal sacrifices which might
> be involved.   That, after all, is the true test of a
> Nation's greatness and independence.

This national government was conceived of more as a
movement than as a party.   The word 'movement' was
frequently used.   The fact that a need for such a
movement arose at all lay, of course, in the inadequacy of
the previous political system:

> It is not a question of blaming the Government, or one
> or other of the political parties.   The evil is much

more deep-seated, and it is the people of the country
who will ultimately have to shoulder responsibility if
they are willing to let things drift as the politicians
are doing today. ... It is not suggested for a moment
that all the best or soundest politicians are in one or
other of the political parties.   They may be fairly
evenly distributed, but the trouble with most of them
is that, in the nature of things, vote catching and
party interests come before everything else.   This
tendency ... is no doubt intensified here as a result
of race prejudices and individual political jealousies,
which, if allowed to continue unchecked, will make true
statesmanship impossible.

As an alternative to this ineffective system, the new
movement would have for its object: (120)

the bringing together of all the best elements in the
political life of the country to work together for the
common good.   Whatever the politicians may think, the
mass of the electorate have come to realise that in
this lies the country's only hope of salvation.

This was a movement that would require 'statesmanship',
a 'national spirit', (121) courage and sanity. (122)   It
would, ultimately, mean the 'end of politics', even the
'end of ideology'.   For these reasons, according to
commercial ideologists, business was best suited to lead
the movement: 'Organised commerce, entirely detached as
it is from party politics, is undoubtedly in a position to
give a definite lead on these lines.'   Even more
explicitly: (123)

Is the time ripe for such a movement, and can it best
be led and organised by the business community?   Yes
to both.   If the business community, holding itself
entirely aloof from the political game, and acting
solely in the interests of the country, cannot succeed
in giving a very definite lead in this matter, then the
position may well be regarded as hopeless.

When eventually the Hertzog government left the gold
standard and formed a coalition with the South African
Party, in 1933, ideologists claimed the victory for South
Africanism and its industrial and commercial creators.
'Party political sanity has been restored', wrote the
'Bulletin'.   Everywhere in South Africanist media, the
'new era' was greeted.   The economy revived;   capital
returned, and while most other countries continued to
suffer from the depression, South Africa was able to rely
on its gold-mining industry to provide a basis for the
coming industrial boom.   The coalition was seen as the
result of the 'groundswell of public opinion' in favour of
a National government, of the ineptitude of the

Nationalist Party and of the ultimate truth of the South
Africanist vision.   Looking back on the preceding
months, the 'Bulletin' painted a vivid picture of the 'old
politics' which makes it easier to understand what
bourgeois hegemony must have meant during the
crisis: (124)

> During the last eighteen months, since Great Britain
> abandoned the Gold Standard, the Parliament of the
> Union ceased to function normally as a legislative
> body giving expression to the views of the electorate.
> The controversy on the all-important and vital gold
> standard policy was rapidly reduced, almost from the
> outset, to a battle of wits, not between the
> financiers, bankers and economists, but between the
> party political leaders, with a single eye to the party
> **advantages to be secured** at the next general election.
> Native Policy, the Provincial Council system, work-
> men's compensation legislation, and other matters of
> supreme national importance were approached from the
> same angle, resulting in a position of absolute
> stalemate.   Consultation and co-operation had become
> impossible.   Important public bodies such as the
> Agricultural Unions, the Chamber of Mines, and the
> Associated Chambers of Commerce, the views of which in
> other countries would have carried considerable weight,
> were muzzled and silenced and they had gradually
> retired from the field of controversy.   The
> professional and trained economist ceased to carry any
> weight, except insofar as his views coincided with
> those of a particular political party.   The rising
> generation in our universities looked in vain for
> guidance.   The man in the street had ceased to take
> even the remotest interest in the fate of the political
> parties.

By contrast, the coalition was a victory for the
entirely opposite state of affairs.   Ideologists could
not have been more anxious to emphasise the popular and
grassroots basis for the coalitionist achievement.   While
the 'statesmanship' they had pleaded for undoubtedly had
played its part, it was with the people, with 'public
opinion' that the credit for the victory of South
Africanism rested.   'Commercial Bulletin' criticised the
popular press for its tendency to emphasise statesmanship
rather than the people in its interpretations of the
events leading to coalition - a critique which could well
apply to historians of the same period and issue: (125)

> The press has variously ascribed this eleventh hour
> salvation of the country to brilliant or self-
> sacrificing statesmanship on the part of individual

political leaders, to the pressure of world conditions,
and less insistently to the intervention of Mr.
Tielman Roos.   No doubt there is a substance of truth
and foundation for all these explications of the
'miracle'.   They are not, however, quite so
convincing to the business man, who for many years past
has been a passive and harassed spectator to the
political morass into which the countryside drifted.
The business community, as represented by the
Associated Chambers of Commerce, and which owed
allegiance to no political party, has in season and out
of season urged that no solution of our economic
problems could be found so long as the largely
artificial and racial divisions, influenced and kept
alive by politicians, were allowed to continue. ...
The dramatic entry of Mr. Tielman Roos into the
political arena undoubtedly precipitated the crisis -
as it was deliberately intended to do.   It is
impossible to escape from the conclusion that Mr. Roos
from the very fact that he had been detached from
politics for several years, had his hand on the pulse
of public opinion far more closely than had any of the
active political leaders.   He knew that behind him he
had thousands of others in all sections of the
community, agricultural, commercial and industrial, who
thought precisely on the same lines.
Commerce and industry regarded the time of the
depression as having been revolutionary from their point
of view.   At the end of 1933, the 'Bulletin' said that
'it is doubtful whether the full significance of the
revolutionary change in the political and economic life of
South Africa during 1933 has yet been fully realised,
even in this country', (126) while in retrospect the FCI
President for 1935 could say that: 'The past year has
provided conditions favourable to solid progress, and
industry has been in a position to reap benefit from these
conditions, because purged by the cleansing processes of
a depression, it is in a healthier, better state'. (127)
   With a new confidence and economic and political
strength, the manufacturing and commercial bourgeoisie
was able to cope with the remainder of the decade - the
period of South Africa's 'take-off' in Rostowian
economic terms - in spite of the new spate of problems
with which it confronted them.   Although the problems of
consultation, conciliation, political ideology and
hegemony were not of the type that could ever be finally
settled, the crisis years had made it possible for firm
ideological and structural bases for their ongoing
solution to be built.   South Africa and South Africanism
had both undergone some sort of transformation: (128)

The fact remains that South Africa has sprung suddenly
from a position of acute depression and financial
embarrassment to one of prosperity and wealth to which
the political differences which tore the country
asunder are gradually and surely sinking into the
background.   And herein lies our greatest strength and
hope for the future. ... The country has indeed entered
upon a new era.

CONCLUSION

At the beginning of chapter 4 mention was made of the
difficulties involved in explaining large-scale, complex
social changes.   We have now reached the point where the
various elements in the explanation we have attempted of
the change in hegemony in South Africa from imperial to
national capital, need to be drawn together and assessed,
and some of the theoretical and historical insights we
have gained to be stated.
    The first of our stated aims was to conduct our
explanation on more than simply one level.   We set out
to discover the workings of hegemony on the three levels
on which it exists - the political, the ideological and
the economic.   This divided approach has borne fruit.
Not only is 'hegemony' better understood this way, but it
would seem that the particular change in hegemony that
concerns us cannot be understood *other* than on three
separate levels.   Had our explanation been pursued simply
on the economic level we might have come to believe that
national capital had achieved hegemony by the time it had
grown to become a major economic force after the First
World War.   Had it been conducted on the ideological
level, we might have thought that the spreading of South
Africanism during the 1920s indicated that national
capital prevailed;   while had we confined ourselves to
'the political' we might have thought (as several authors
have done) that the 1925 Tariff Act indicated the capture
by national capital of the state apparatuses.   Moreover,
all of these times and dates would have had a somewhat
arbitrary character to them.   How can we decide whether
national capital's *real* economic flourishing was after the
First World War, or after the depression?   Can we be
confident in stating that the *real* spread of South
Africanism was in the 1920s, rather than the 1940s?   Was
the Tariff Act the *real* indicator of national capital's
political hegemony, or should we rather place it at the
time of the setting up of Iscor, or the beginnings of the
taxation of the gold-mining industry?   A change in

hegemony does not lend itself to quantitative or mono-causal explanations of this type.

The overall thrust of our more complex and historical explanation is that this particular change in hegemony can be pinned down to neither a date, nor an event. Instead it was a *process* or a series of processes which took place in a particular sequence.   The first process was that of class formation.   Perhaps this could be designated the 'economic' level although the label is not quite accurate.   For a variety of reasons national capital grew in size, importance and self-consciousness, while imperial capital declined, during and after the First World War.   Simultaneously there took place a growth and spreading of its class ideology - 'South Africanism'.   Perhaps this could be designated the 'ideological' level, although this, too, is rendered a somewhat crude term since ideologies only 'spread' if the class structure has changed in some way to make this possible.   The third major change could perhaps be termed 'social' - for it involved the growth and development of a structure of working and middle classes around the burgeoning of national capital;   it involved the 'ideological' level too, for capital's intellectuals developed South Africanism to cope with this growth.

Thus we find that by 1924 a number of important changes in South African society on the economic and ideological levels had taken place, against whose background this final chapter was written.   And here we have tried to show that it was only on the basis of these changes that the final change - that occurring on the 'political' level - could take place.   What we hope to have demonstrated was that imperial hegemony was deeply undermined by the mid-1920s;   but that imperial interests continued to hold sway over the 'narrow' state apparatuses.   When in 1924 the Pact government came to power, imperial control over the state was not completely destroyed, but it was considerably weakened.   The Pact government could introduce legislation which ran against imperial interests.

Capital's ideologists at first thought this meant their total hegemony had been ensured.   But this was not so. The negative side of the weakness of imperial control over the state lay in the fact that the party now in control - the Pact - could begin to introduce legislation which ran against national capital's interests too.   National capital's hegemony had not replaced that of imperial capital and a hiatus in the system of power could be exploited by a white-worker dominated government.   It is

this fact that has led some to believe that the Pact
government represented a 'workers' state', and our
evidence would seem to suggest that for a short period,
before the national bourgeoisie was able to assert
itself, this may have been the case.

Capital thus began to perceive that the achievement of
political hegemony was more complicated than the passing
of legislation or the coming of particular political
parties to power.   To control the narrow state meant to
limit its autonomy, and to confine its activities to those
in the interests of capital.   This it set about doing in
three different ways.   First, it sought to establish
consultative mechanisms whereby the voice of capital in
general, under the sway of national capital in particular,
was given a special place in the state.   But the narrow
state is not so narrow as to be understood only on the
level of its legislative and administrative apparatuses.
The state is embedded in the system of 'political
practices' - the party system, the electorate, and the
ideology of representation.   It was with this fact in
mind that capital developed an ideology suited to
controlling the autonomy of the state, in which the state,
capital, the party, and the people were all identified
with one another and with nature;   where capital's rule
was postulated as the natural social form.   Furthermore,
it attempted to create a new system of political
representation and to mobilise the electorate, in these
terms.   With their newly 'secularised' and now-
conservative South Africanist ideology, capitalists wished
to transform the very form of the old imperial state.

That this transformation was able to take place was a
result of the fact that the economic, ideological and
social face of South African society had changed
fundamentally, so that by the time of the gold standard
crisis and depression a deep rift had developed which the
old imperial state form proved unable to bridge.   This
was national capital's opportunity to clinch the process
of hegemonic change, through providing massive support
for the new party system and riding on the crest of the
wave of 'public opinion'.   The political revolution in
this case came last.   Only now was capital able to fulfil
all its ambitions for the narrow state.   Consultation was
secured;   the state's autonomy was curbed;   the electorate
was mobilised under a quite clearly South Africanist
banner;   while political ideologies and organisations
which ran against the interests of national capital were
deemed to be irrational.

It should be pointed out that these victories of the
bourgeoisie need to be understood in a two-fold manner.

In the sphere of party politics, victory was short-lived, since soon after Fusion between the South African and National Parties, the 'purified' National Party, under Malan, broke away, destroying the facade of total white unity.   But to focus only on this level is to mistake political power for social hegemony, and to miss the underlying relationships between state and capital which are here shown to have been established.   We have seen capitalists consciously setting out to create these relationships, moreover - they have not come about simply through the operation of abstract, mechanical social laws. The new 'state form' suited bourgeois interests more than had the old one; and although the struggle between social classes and sectors of capital (including that between the remnants of 'imperial capital' and the new bourgeoisie) continued, and new contradictions emerged to replace the old, the bourgeoisie had had a decisive hand in shaping the institutions within which struggles were to take place and contradictions were to be resolved.   In spite of the challenge to this new order presented by black and Afrikaner movements in subsequent years, no major struggle seems to have taken place outside of the terms set by the ruling class, and social debate appears to have been contained within the flexible and adaptable South Africanist paradigm for some time.   These issues are further raised in the Conclusion.

Conclusion

This study began by observing the need for improving our
understanding of the relationships between the political
and ideological features of particular capitalist
societies; and the economic system prevailing within
them. In the South African example, the concrete case
through which these rather more abstract concerns were
pursued, 'racism' was pointed to as one such feature, the
most vivid and obvious one, whose relationship to
'capitalism' was in need of further elaboration and
explanation.

However, it has become clear that there is a great deal
more to the political and ideological manifestation of the
rule of capitalism in South Africa than the racist
exclusion of blacks from participation in the state, from
residence in the cities, or even from equality with white
members of the working class. For the owners of the
means of production themselves are deeply divided in
various complex ways between and across sectors and even,
it has been argued, into different classes; the
exceptionally complex mix of classes and modes of
production that preceded the 'mining revolution' of the
late nineteenth century gave rise to important ideological
and political forms not easily incorporated into the
concept of 'race'; while important changes over time took
place within the 'white' state. Indeed the 'racism'
articulated and practised by particular sections of the
ruling class was embedded in an overall, broader, ideology
and strategy, whose nature was not determined simply by
the nature of the relationships between black and white.
While the racist character of South Africa's ruling class
seems beyond doubt, it appears that the key to the
explanation of its form and character does not lie simply
within a one-to-one connection between 'capitalist
interests' on the one hand, and 'racist ideology and

258

practice' on the other.   Racism is an important and
central characteristic of the overall system of capitalist
domination, but it cannot be understood without an understanding of the origins, form and internal structure of
that system as a whole.   Thus the 'racism' of the mineowner was a part of the hegemony which he brought into
being, whose character was determined by his relationships
with a range of classes, modes of production, ideological
and political forms, and other forms of capital, and not
simply by his relationship with black workers and
peasants;   and it differed from the 'racism' of the
manufacturer to the extent that all of these variables
differed.

In the introduction, three broad approaches to the
understanding of the relationships between such categories
as 'race' and 'nationalism' on the one hand, and such
categories as 'class' and 'capitalism' on the other, were
outlined: that based on the nature of the process of
accumulation as a whole;   and those based on the needs of
particular sections of capital on the one hand;   and on
specific problems within the accumulation process on the
other.   The implication of our findings is that no one of
these approaches is adequate on its own.   The needs of
the bourgeoisie as a whole should be understood as an
expression of the needs of one or more of its particular
sections at particular times;   and conversely no need of
any of these particular sections can be properly understood without an understanding of the needs of the whole
class.   Furthermore, no single aspect of the process of
accumulation can be understood separately from the overall
process, while finally, and most importantly, no single
facet of the system of domination and 'hegemony' can be
understood separately from the overall system of
domination of which it is a part.   'Fractions of
capital' or 'problems of accumulation' are thus, it
appears, a necessary but not sufficient condition for
understanding how ruling classes rule.

This plea for a more integrated approach applies,
therefore, as much to the interpretation of the political
and ideological expressions of ruling class domination as
it does to its economic foundations.   The 'political
nature of a ruling class' cannot be understood through
piecemeal and partial approaches but must be viewed in the
context of the entire political economy in which it is
formed.   Certain of the ideological and political
peculiarities of South African capitalism - in particular,
the expression of relations of domination and
subordination in terms of 'race', 'Britishness',
'English-speakingness', 'Afrikanerdom', 'black', or

'white' have powerful structural roots in the periods
during which South Africa's ruling classes were in the
process of formation, and in the interplay of classes,
modes of production and economic systems that took place
in those periods, and it is the overall character of these
periods that we must now seek to understand.

1 THE FRAMEWORK OF CLASS FORMATION

The analysis undertaken here has demonstrated
that the bourgeoisie has a 'political nature' which, while
it rests upon and is a product of its economic nature, has
a distinct form of its own, to be interpreted through the
use of distinct conceptual and theoretical notions.   A
knowledge of the economic nature of capital, of its place
in relation to the means of production and the process of
accumulation, is a necessary but not sufficient condition
for understanding how it embeds itself in particular
social formations, and, indeed, transforms them in its own
image.   The search for the undoubtedly vital and complex
differences between the economic interests of the various
forms of capital - whether merchant, industrial, imperial
or national - alone will not lead towards an understanding
of their political and ideological interests.   Instead,
in fact, it may lead towards ever more abstract, or
perhaps deterministic, discussions of the economic roots
of political systems, which may lend density rather than
light to the matter.
     In the introduction to this study the core of the
system whereby capital's economic interests were
translated into political and ideological realities, was
described.   The organic intellectual, it was suggested,
was situated within the network of intra-class
communication so as to be able to view the economic
interests of the emerging capitalist class from a social
point of view.   And it has been demonstrated in
considerable detail how he functioned to translate for his
bourgeois audience, economic necessities into concrete
political possibilities.   We saw how such 'economic'
matters as the obtaining of capital, the cheapening of
the cost of labour, the mechanisation of production, the
creation of markets, the distribution of goods, or the
price of gold, gave rise to layer upon layer of political
problems for the bourgeoisie, ranging from the need to
subordinate indigenous modes of production, to the attempt
to create 'consumerism' amongst whites.
     The processes whereby the bourgeoisie, through its
system of interest-translation, reached solutions to these

problems, and developed ideological formulae capable cf
communicating and encapsulating them in meaningful imagery
have been synthesised here as the process whereby it came
to be formed as a fully-fledged class, with developed
relationships on all three levels of social reality. And
hopefully it was demonstrated that the formation of the
capitalist class was not a neutral process, but one
distorted by the facts of domination and subordination.
The bourgeoisie was locked in unequal struggle with other
classes, and the story of its formation is the story cf
its attempts to subdue them. What we now need to ask is
how these attempts may be characterised in a systematic
way, and by what broad parameters they are shaped. For
if the process of accumulation which is the basis of
capitalism possesses a certain systematicity and
coherence, so must the political and ideological struggles
which arise out of it. Class formation took place
within a certain framework whose dimensions now need to
be stated.

According to the definition of 'class' used here there
existed in South Africa in the period under discussion,
not one but two bourgeoisies. While of course it is true
that only one category of people constitutes the owners of
the means of production and the prime movers in the
accumulation process, at least within each social
formation, our definition of class went beyond the purely
economic realm, giving great weight to the political and
ideological character of classes. This has proved to be
extremely useful heuristically. For one thing, a concept
of class which allows us to see two classes of capital in
South Africa in these years has enabled us to put forward
an explanation of the 'change in hegemony' in the 1920s
and 1930s which is perhaps more convincing than those
which depend upon the concept 'fraction'. But it has
also facilitated the development of our understanding of
the consistent, overarching pattern of the process of
class formation, for we have two examples to examine and
compare. And indeed in each case, it seems, a similar
series of experiences was undergone by the class in the
process of formation. Each underwent the process in
four distinct, overlapping spheres (each sphere operating
on all three levels of social reality - the economic, the
political and the ideological), whose main features were
strikingly similar. It is the combination of these
spheres of class formation that provides the framework
within which the emerging system of hegemony, of which
'racism' is but one part, may be understood.

It is important to point out that this framework
class formation does not constitute a static, synchronic

'model', an a-historical structure.   Above all it is as a
dynamic process, a part of the movement of history, that
it must be seen.   The political nature of the ruling
class must be seen as the evolving product of a process
which takes place in four, moving, dynamic and over-
lapping spheres.

a)   The need for class unity

While economic relationship to the means of production
constitutes the essential defining characteristic of any
particular class, it alone does not constitute class.   It
is for this reason, it would seem, that organic
intellectuals became important to capitalists soon after
they had consolidated their own economic position in the
case of both mineowners and manufacturers.   At that
stage, the capitalist 'class' in each case consisted
merely of a number of separate owners of the means of
production, distribution and exchange.   As such it was
unable to realise any of its class interests;   thus
revealing the innate contradiction between the individual
capitalist and the interests of the class to which he
belongs.   The rise of the organic intellectual to a
position of prominence within the bourgeoisie at a
certain point in time may be seen as its method of
resolving this contradiction.   The intellectual was
there to ensure that the individual owner of the means of
production knew what his class, as opposed to his
individual, interests were and that the former must
prevail over the latter.
     But this was complicated by the fact that capital was
not a monolith, but consisted of a number of different
sectors.   It was not only the individual capitalist's
interests that contradicted those of his class.   There
was also a difference between the interests of certain
sections of the bourgeoisie and the bourgeoisie as a
whole.   Furthermore, it would seem that some sections of
the capitalist class had interests that accorded more with
those of the bourgeoisie as a whole, than did others.
Within imperial capital, for example, merchants had no
interest in revolution;   within national capital, farmers
had no interest in white working-class conciliation.
Thus the organic intellectual's role in the solving of the
problems this created must also be explored.
     What seems to have happened in the examples we have
examined, is that the organic intellectual was attached
not to the whole capitalist class, but to one of its
sections.   This seems to have been the 'leading' section,

the section whose interests matched those of the whole
class most closely.   In the case of imperial capital this
leading section consisted of mining capital after the
discovery of gold, while in the case of national capital,
it consisted of manufacturing capital early on, and of
commerce later on.   Incidentally it is this kind of
change in leading sections that Poulantzas has mislead-
ingly called a 'change in hegemony', leading several
analysts of the South African case into a confusion
between changes in dominance of one section *within* a
class of capital; and changes such as the large-scale
one documented here in the very dominant class itself.
Some of the analytical defects which have resulted from
this confusion in terms were discussed in the body of this
work.

The functions of the organic intellectual in this
sphere were to articulate the interests of the leading
section, and at the same time to promote an identification
with those interests by other sections.   Mineowners'
interests were expressed as being universal;
manufacturers' interests as those of all whites.   This
too, then, was a class-forming function.   It promoted
the unity of capital as a whole over the divisions within
it, while preserving the control of whichever section was
leading at any one particular time.   Furthermore, the
intellectual made it easier for the lead to be taken by
the 'right' section.   In other words, the fact that one
or another section became dominant at any one time was not
simply a matter of chance, or merely the result of
'voluntaristic' struggles between sections.   It was
itself a result of the overall path taken by the class
interests of the capitalist class as a whole.   It was
shown how commerce came to lead national capital at a time
when national capital's overall interests rendered
leadership by the owners of the means of distribution and
exchange necessary.   The organic intellectual was poised
to cope with this fact and indeed to promote the
interests of rising sections.   It may be suggested that
'fractional' analyses of the South African case have
failed to observe this fact, and have instead tended
towards a certain degree of voluntarism.   While, of
course, it would be crudely deterministic to argue that
political struggles between sections of capital played no
part in the capacity of one or another section to realise
its interests, the overall path of the development of the
system should not be ignored.

Intellectuals thus built unity between individual
capitalists, and sections of capital.   As a concomitant
of this process, they sketched the basic outline of a

class ideology whose first (but not only) purpose was to
promote awareness by its members, both individual and
corporate, that the bourgeoisie's interests were
synonymous with their own.   A rudimentary class
consciousness was created during the very first stages of
class formation in the cases of both early imperial and
early national capital.   It was built upon the
historical characteristics of capitalists themselves in
the first instance.   Imperial ideology, for example,
had its roots in the post-mercantile, British, mining,
monopoly, nature of capital's leading section - mining -
in the 1890s, while the later bourgeois ideology was
marked by the 'English' petty-bourgeois, anti-imperial,
competitive and weak character of national capital's
leading section - manufacturing - in the early 1900s.

In summary we may say that the first sphere of class
formation took place on three levels: on the economic
level, the bourgeoisie constituted itself as a class with
a particular relationship to the means of production;   on
the political level it created unity between its
individual and corporate members;   and on the ideological
level, it created a crude class ideology which was based
upon its historical place, its internal structure and
economic form.

The second, third and fourth spheres of class formation
were shaped by the first.   With their unity and class
consciousness forged, capitalists were now in a position
to set about realising their many and varied interests.
This was where the role of the organic intellectual became
crucial.

b)   The need for hegemony over preceding classes and
modes of production

The translation of capital's objective, innate economic
interests in the process of accumulation into political
realities and ideological formulae, seems to have taken
place in two distinct spheres - spheres two and three of
the framework of class formation.   The first was that of
the system of hegemony over preceding systems;   the second
that of the system of labour exploitation in pursuit of
accumulation itself.   The reason why capital's interests
needed realising in these two spheres, rather than simply
in the latter, more commonly acknowledged sphere, was that
in the cases of both industrial imperial capital, and
national capital, those interests were of a
fundamentally revolutionary nature.   That is to say that
their realisation was impossible without a transformation

of the social formation on all three levels; capital's
basic business of extracting surplus value from labour
could not be pursued in a sustained manner over a period
of years, or decades, until the social formation had been
shaped in a certain way.   In the case of imperial
capital, this might well have been because of the
exceptionally precarious profitability, the extremely
large scale, and the crucial position in the world
economic system, of the gold-mining industry.   It might
well be the case, in other words, that industrial imperial
capital of an extractive nature does not *normally* possess
revolutionary interests, but that it might in other
situations be able to survive (like mercantile imperial
capital) in a social formation only partially transformed
in its own image.   In the case of national capital,
however, the revolutionary nature of its interests seems
to be innate, a function of its need to sell as well as
to produce goods internally.

Both forms of capital which we have examined,
therefore, needed to undergo a process of mutual
adaptation to the existing social formation as a whole,
before their profitability could be secured, but for
different reasons.   The fact that the need for hegemony
preceded the securing of profitability in theoretical
terms should not be taken to mean that the latter followed
the former in historical terms, however; the precise
strategies through which capital secured both of these
aims are discussed separately.   For the moment, we are
concerned with the logical sequence of the process of
capital's formation as a fully-fledged class, and for
purposes of exposition and understanding, hegemony must
precede profitability.

The realisation of the bourgeoisie's interest in
hegemony over the old system began when intellectuals set
about distinguishing for the fledgeling class its allies
and its enemies in the existing social formation.
Behind these crude political distinctions lay more subtle
ones.   For again the identification of friends and
enemies was not arbitrary or 'voluntaristic', but based
on the existence of contradiction or harmony between
capital's interests and those of the group concerned.
The best way of interpreting these forces seems to have
been in terms of the form taken by the existing system of
dominance or hegemony.

Thus the system with which mining capital had to
contend was that of mercantile hegemony.   The form it
took was such that it bred for mining capital few allies
and a large number of enemies.   Merchant capital's
interests had not been revolutionary.   Indeed, far from

it - they had required the active promotion of the pre-
capitalist economic and political systems that existed in
the region.   The forces and relations of production were
not transformed in the ways required by mining capital;
the system of mercantile imperialism had failed to impose
ideological unity on the region as a whole, while
political systems of some considerable strength had not
only survived but been strengthened and shaped in new
ways.   Merchant capital's rule thus eluded mining
capital's grasp.   Having itself not required a vast
sub-continental revolution, merchant capital had not
created the kind of system able to carry one through.
Mercantile hegemony permitted the persistence of a
variety of classes able to resist proletarianisation,
retard the capitalisation of agriculture, or set up local
industries in competition with imperial importers.   And
yet it offered to mining capital no central apparatuses
through which this fragmented social formation could be
united and transformed.

It was on this basis that the identification of mining
capital's friends and enemies was undertaken by its
ideologists.   And it was on this basis that a truly
revolutionary ideology was forged.   For mining capital,
it was postulated, had few allies of any substance.
Most pre-existing classes and modes of production before
1900 were to a greater or lesser extent incompatible with
mining's interests, and most had therefore to be either
destroyed, subordinated or radically altered.   It was
only diamond-mining capital that was treated at all
sympathetically, for it had provided gold-mining capital
with a mercantile-based precedent in several fields;   but
it does not seem as if an actual alliance was at any stage
proposed between the two forms of capital, at least on the
political or ideological levels.

Thus the fragmentation and intangibility of merchant
capital's hegemony forced mining capital into a
revolutionary mould.   National capital by contrast, was
confronted by a social order which in many respects was
entirely compatible with its interests.   Indeed what is
important about the rise of national capital (a point to
be discussed in more detail below) is that its revolution
had in a number of senses already been carried out for it,
by mining capital.   This weak and struggling class was
thus freed of the necessity to carry out such fundamental
processes as proletarianisation, the subordination of old
modes of production, or the initial setting up of narrow
and wide states.   This would again seem to provide
confirmation that mining capital in South Africa was not
in the classic mould of imperial capital.   Whereas most

national bourgeoisies in underdeveloped systems are too weak to implement some of their basic class needs, most of which have been inhibited by imperialism, South Africa's admittedly weak national bourgeoisie had had a number of its interests realised already.

However, this did not mean that national capital did not require changes in mining hegemony in a large number of spheres.   The mining system of dominance had indeed to be revolutionised.   But the combination of its own weakness, and the extent of the compatibility between mining's rule and national capital's aspirations, forced this revolution into a reformist mould.   Partly, reform was possible, moreover, because here intellectuals could seek and find allies for their audience almost to the same extent as they could enemies.

Furthermore, mining imperialism was not a stable form of rule.   Contradictions within the world imperial system in general (manifested by the upheaval of the First World War) and in South Africa in particular (manifested by the labour upheavals of the 1918-22 period) combined to weaken the economic hold of imperial capital in South Africa, as well as the stability of the imperial state itself. National capital was for this reason able to adopt a policy of gradualism, of political opportunism, in seeking to carry out its revolution.   Its reformism was imbued with pragmatism, while both were couched in ideological terms which expressed the need and wish of national capital for a revolution based on co-operation between supportive and allied classes and sub-classes.

Finally, the terms in which the contradictions between imperial and national capital were expressed were those of the conservative nationalism of the English-speaking white petty-bourgeoisie.   The resulting 'white dominionism' formed the third arm of the emerging bourgeois ideology.

In summary, the second sphere of the process of class formation took the form of identifying the contradictions between the existing hegemonic order and the desired one; of developing political strategies for changing the one to the other which were practicable and necessary;   and of enlarging the class ideology of capital to incorporate the conceptual implications of these facts.

c)   The need for hegemony over the working class

The next sphere of class formation centred on the problem of accumulation itself.   Capital's own class nature was now assured;   and its relationship to older social forms

decided.   The realisation of its central interest in the
accumulation of capital through the exploitation of wage
labour took place in terms determined by spheres one and
two of class formation, on the one hand, and by the
economic, political and ideological nature of the
potential or actual working class, on the other.

Once again the unique pattern of relationships at the
interface between mercantile and industrial imperial
capital was highly important.   The intellectuals of
mining capital working on this interface had to translate
their audience's interest in a particular kind of working
class into terms which would suit the circumstances of
South Africa at the time.   The remarkable size and
nature of mining required that the proletariat be large,
cheap and mainly unskilled, but its capital intensity and
the peculiarities of the mining labour process also
required a smaller but skilled section of the working
class to be created.   Furthermore, the enormous capital
investment in mining, coupled with its crucial place in
the world monetary system, required that the proletariat
be obtained in an exceptionally short period of time.
The intellectual's task here was again threefold.   In the
first place, he had to assess not only the extent of the
need for an unskilled, semi-skilled and skilled workforce.
He then had to devise strategies whereby this need could
be fulfilled.   The large, cheap, unskilled labour force
was a matter for crude, straightforward strategy.
Mining's revolution, the need for which had already been
determined, must be orientated towards the destruction of
pre-capitalist domestic modes of production on a
sufficiently wide scale so as to produce a proletariat.
At the same time, certain of the weaknesses which both
merchant capital and their own internal structures had
lent to these domestic modes of production should be
exploited to the full, so that the proletariat arising
from them would not be able to attain the political,
economic and ideological strength which normal working
classes have attained in the past.   These weaknesses and
the proletariat which was partly their product, were
conceptualised in terms of the ideological category of
'race'.

The small but essential skilled workforce complicated
this pure cotermination between class and race.
Intellectuals had to make capitalists aware that much as
it would have been a desirable state of affairs, not all
of the proletariat could be black.   The racial
distinctions that had prevailed in the Transvaal in
particular, and the Southern Africa region in general, the
exigencies of the international labour market, and the

urgency of the mining industry's need, had combined to
place workers with white skins, important skills, and
considerable political power, in firm control of the
skilled labour sector.   This fact represented one of the
most serious contradictions in the order which imperial
capital was trying to create.   For mining capital's only
interest concerning labour was its ability to produce
surplus value.   It needed no market, no consumers, no
embourgeoisement.   Expensive labour was anathema to
mining capital.   The remainder of its intellectual's
activities in this sphere concerned the evaluation of
various complex political mechanisms whereby this expense
could be reduced while at the same time class conflict
could be kept to a minimum.

Capital, in the process of its own formation as a
ruling class, thus set about controlling the formation of
the classes subordinated to it.   The hierarchical system
of labour-capital relationships which was finally proposed
as the most rational method of realising capital's
interests must be distinguished from the more clearly
racial system which later capitalists were to introduce.
It is not often recognised that mining capital made no
attempt to postulate the existence of a white consensus,
clearly demarcated from the black populace.
Differences between white classes were almost as clear
as those between white and black races.   Used as we are
to the mystifications of a more bourgeois order, we are
unable to comprehend the explicit nature of capital's rule
in that time, the open acknowledgment of class differences
and class domination.   Instead of being mystified and
obscured, the hierarchical order was exalted.   Ideology
did not operate to blur distinctions but to elevate them
to an equivalent status with nature.   This capitalist
ideology had a pre-capitalist character.

When national capital in turn came to challenge this
order of things, it did so without disturbing the
fundamental structure of the hierarchy.   Capitalists
preserved the system whereby blacks were on the lowest
rung of an economic, political and ideological ladder - a
situation that suited their interests in almost every
sense.   And as intellectuals were quick to point out, the
need for a consumer market could be satisfied first
through the embourgeoisement of the already expensive
white working class.   Nevertheless, intellectuals made
sure that the system of exploitation did not run against
national capital's interests by failing to win the support
of white labour for the new, industrialising system, or by
preventing the increasingly skilled and settled black
proletariat and growing petty-bourgeoisie from expressing

its own interests in systematised and controlled ways.
What could perhaps be called a hierarchy of incorporation
was proposed through which the ongoing hierarchy of
exploitation could be not only obscured, but also
prolonged, perhaps more effectively than under the
unstable and highly contradictory system which mining had
operated.

This, then, the third sphere of class formation,
involved the identification by intellectuals of the extent
and nature of capital's interest in one or another kind of
working class; the proposal of strategies whereby it
might be actually created, if it did not exist, or pressed
into a particular mould if it did, in ways that not only
ensured that profitability would be maximised, but also
that class conflict would be minimised; and the putting
forward of an ideological framework in which the stability
of the resulting system could be preserved and sustained.

d) The narrow and the wide states

The fourth and final sphere in which the formation of the
ruling class proceeded was that in which it sought to
secure and preserve the sets of structures that had
evolved from the preceding three spheres through an
overarching system. Capitalists sought to rule the
whole social formation and required that some system
existed whereby their rule could be entrenched on a
society-wide scale, while at the same time all of the
interests identified during the first three stages of
class formation could be realised; and all of their
political and ideological implications made concrete.

The resulting proposals by organic intellectuals
constituted what may be called the 'state'. For the
process of class-formation implies the process of state-
formation when the class concerned is a ruling one.
However, the concept of 'the state' is highly complex, as
we have suggested in the course of this work. We need
first to outline some of the problems involved in
conceptualising it.

In the Introduction it was pointed out that several
writers on 'the state' have extended the concept to
include not simply the system of government, or of
repression, but the wider system of class domination
itself. And in our example the state, it emerged, was
indeed usefully categorised into two parts - called, in
the absence of any other terms, the 'narrow' and the
'wide' states. While through the narrow state direct
power over other classes was exerted through the

enactment and enforcement of legislation, the exertion of
direct repression, and the channelling of conflicts
through a system of political representation, none of
these things could have taken place in ways which suited
capitalists without the prior creation of the wide state.
This was the arena in which the bourgeoisie not only
exerted power over other classes, but actually shaped
their very class nature and position. Not only did it
enact and implement legislation, but it designed the very
system for which that legislation would be suited; not
only did it work through a party system, but it created
the kinds of political and ideological divisions and
allegiances within the population that would ensure that
the party system was compatible with its own continuing
dominance. The acquiescence of the governed was thus, in
an abstract sense, obtained before the government was set
up! It was the consent of the subordinated, whose
inevitable protest against their own subordination was
skilfully pre-empted and dealt with in a hundred ways.
It is probably a fair statement of our findings to say,
therefore, that while the narrow state was the instrument
of bourgeois *power*, the wide state was the instrument of
bourgeois *hegemony*, in the sense in which Gramsci has used
the term, of its dominance over the entire social
formation on the economic, political and ideological
levels, including the level of the narrow state itself.

What we summarised in our discussion of the first three
spheres of class formation were the processes whereby
capitalists determined the nature of the hegemonic order
they wished to impose. However, how they actually
imposed it has not yet been discussed. In fact, their
intellectuals guided them towards seeking out the best
strategy to adopt in this respect no less than in any
others.

In the case of mining, ideologists proved incorrect in
their early assessment that through the existing Transvaal
'narrow state' far-reaching changes in the overall social
formation could be introduced. At the same time the
revolutionary nature of their interests *and* of their
necessary strategy, plus the immediacy of their demands,
meant that capitalists soon became impatient with attempts
to alter the 'wide state' first, through the operation of
their own, admittedly extremely powerful, agents. While
the industry was capable of undermining black modes of
production, for example, it could not co-ordinate its
proletarianising assaults on them in a satisfactory
manner; while the mining bourgeoisie could topple
kingdoms and destroy classes, it could not singlehandedly
alter the fact that mercantile rule was fragmented and

regionalised, and in this sense contradicted its interests
directly.

Throughout the 1890s intellectuals sought out ways of
overcoming this problem;   it was only towards the end of
that decade that the key ideologists of capital began to
realise that the wide state lay out of their grasp unless
and until they could gain control of a narrow state
capable of centralising their assaults on the system of
mercantile dominance.   The Jameson Raid was in these
terms not only premature (since leading sections of the
bourgeoisie were at that stage still concerned to work
within the existing Kruger regime) but directed at what
later events were to prove to be too restricted a target.
The Transvaal state alone - even had it been totally
subordinated to mining needs - could not have carried
through a Southern African revolution of the type needed.

The Anglo-Boer War may thus be seen as an attempt to
create a new state in Southern Africa, of the narrow
variety.   Through the capture of the hostile Transvaal
and Free State 'Boer' states, and the co-opting of the
mercantile Natal and Cape states, the new imperialists
sought to conduct their revolution in a Leninist fashion -
through the transformation of the political before all
else.   Victory for the British in the war meant that in
the early 1900s capitalists could rely on what amounted to
a revolutionary impetus for the carrying out of their
long-awaited transformations of the 'wide state'.   Over
the following decade or more, imperial capital became a
ruling class in every sense of the term;   its long-term
profitability was secured, and its hierarchical system of
exploitation set up;   its definition of the terms in which
class struggle was to be conducted prevailed, while the
narrow state apparatuses operated to preserve these things
on an ongoing basis.

It was this hegemonic order that national capital in
turn sought to overthrow;   but in this case the
intellectuals of this second class of capitalists were
obliged by the nature of the interests of capital as
already outlined, to work in a somewhat less sudden and
violent fashion.   Furthermore, there was little chance
that bourgeois capital would ever be powerful enough to
capture the narrow imperial state, while it was in any
case doubtful that the kind of revolution that it needed
could be imposed from above.   These various factors, and
others, led national capital towards a different strategy
towards the state.   Capitalists in this case went for the
wide state first, directing all their efforts towards
exploiting what contradictions had arisen in the
foundations of imperial system as a result of the First

World War. Intellectuals concerned themselves with
problems of class formation, protectionism, the creation
of alliances with the disaffected (from mining) white
working class, and with disaffected sections of
agriculture and commerce; and the propagation of
ideology. In contrast with mining, time was on their
side - for the longer they waited, the more secure would
be their economic and ideological base, and the more shaky
the shattered post-war imperial system. When the third
blow to imperial capital within two decades came - in the
form of the world depression (the other two being the
world war and the post-war labour conflict) - national
capital had undermined the foundations of its hegemony
over the wide state to such an extent that the toppling of
its control over the political apparatuses was relatively
easy.

The slow and painful rise of national capital in South
Africa provided us with an opportunity to explore one of
the problems to which this study has addressed itself,
namely, that of the nature of the narrow and wide states
under capitalism, and the relationships between them and
the bourgeoisie, which mining capital's rapid and violent
procedures denied to us. For capital's strategy in
capturing both states had to be based on a solid
assessment of their purposes. Capital had to dissect and
expose both states, while the obstacles it encountered in
each are themselves indicative of their natures.

The purpose of the narrow state under mining hegemony
seems to have been markedly different from that which
national capital envisaged. Political parties closely
paralleled the class and interest structure, so that the
'mining party', or the 'white labour party' could be
identified quite clearly; while the actual operation of
the state apparatuses seems to have been strongly
orientated towards administration of the law. Capital
did not seem to have demanded a highly complex narrow
state in the years of class formation - it had seemed to
be satisfied with a set of administrative apparatuses
subordinate to its interests, with a political system
capable of reconciling differences within capital, and
exercising coercive and controlling functions over
subordinate classes. What ideological apparatuses there
were, were organs of simple propaganda rather than the
elaborate structures that develop in industrialised
systems. From the little information we have, therefore,
it would seem, ironically, in the light of our criticisms
of this concept as metaphorical, that the narrow state
could in some senses have in fact been termed the
'executive committee of the bourgeoisie' in this
particular historical period.

Perhaps this may be explained in terms of the nature of
the wide state required by mining capital. For we saw in
some detail the relative simplicity and starkness of
capital's rule over subordinate classes in this period,
and the absence of highly obscure and mystifying
ideologies. The hierarchy of exploitation required a
crude, coercive state apparatus to preserve it. Moreover, it had originally been forged in a period of
military victory and possessed the legitimacy of conquest.
In addition, the enormous physical and military power of
imperial capital in the first few decades of its existence
in Southern Africa rendered elaborate systems of non-
coercive control superfluous.

However, these very factors were the ones that lent a
certain brittleness to the imperial state. Once the
revolutionary impetus of the Anglo-Boer War had waned, the
brute power of imperial capital had been weakened, and the
acquiescence of labour in the system of hierarchy had been
undermined, the narrow state's lack of flexibility and
resilience was exposed. Perhaps this explains why the
victory of the Pact government in 1924 proved such a
disproportionate blow to imperial capital. The narrow
state had not been designed with a substantial working
class political movement in mind, let alone one whose
interests accorded in certain respects with another,
increasingly powerful form of capital.

While much of what we know of the imperial state form
is sketchy, the contrast it provides with that set up by
national capital is most illuminating. Here was a class
that envisaged its period of rule to be long and filled
with contradictions. It set out to build a narrow state
that would protect it in spite of its own weakness,
against other forms of capital as well as against labour.
It eschewed simple coercion in favour of a more complex
structure of controlling devices, ranging from
conciliation for white workers to limited incorporation
for certain blacks. Most importantly, however, it set
out upon a mammoth task of mystification.

The most important characteristic of this narrow state
was its effective mystification of the nature and extent
of bourgeois rule. While on the one hand, capitalists
set out to enlarge the scope of the state far beyond that
which it had held under imperial rule, on the other hand,
they set out to make it appear as if the state as such had
virtually disappeared, while the hand of capital in
shaping it was nowhere to be seen. Just as had been the
case with imperial capital, these features of the new
narrow state were also a function of the nature of the
wide state. For the essence of the wide state was its

conciliation and incorporation of whites into a
'consensus' through the operation of particular political
and ideological devices, while it needed the co-optation
and co-operation of blacks in the industrialising system
increasingly over the years.   Another feature of the wide
state was the nature of the ruling class itself, for here
was a bourgeoisie whose lateness, weakness and
peripherality rendered it virtually dependent on 'narrow
state' assistance in bringing about the industrialised
system.   The ideology of mystification, if we might call
it that, served the functions, therefore, of channelling
class conflicts into harmless directions;   ensuring the
co-operation of subordinate and intermediate classes in
capitalism;   and controlling the autonomy which the state
might otherwise develop.

A further point about the narrow and wide states
concerns the nature of hegemony.   What has this analysis
revealed about the ways in which hegemony operated, its
scope and pervasiveness?   While on one level we have
already pointed out that hegemony is a useful term to
describe the entire economic, political and ideological
system through which capital exerts its dominance - the
wide state - this is a somewhat abstract formulation and
we need to ask what it means in real terms to inhabitants
of a real social system.

While the narrow state was highly visible, a great deal
of the wide state remained invisible and intangible.
Undoubtedly 'ideological state apparatuses' played a part,
probably a major part, in its operation.   But it would
seem to accord more with the kinds of matters discussed
here to describe hegemony as something which operated in
unseen and unrecognised ways as much as through concrete
institutions.   To an inhabitant of the society,
particularly one attempting to change it fundamentally, it
must have appeared as a twisted, invisible and enclosing
web that rendered all opposition futile by its false
assertions of the nature of reality.   Furthermore, it
was fragmented.   To a 'Boer' in the 1900s, capital's
hegemony might have been experienced as the dominance of
British culture over his own;   to an English white worker
it might have been experienced simply as the dominance of
capital over labour;   or it might have appeared as the
growing threat of cheap black worker competition;   and to
the Afrikaner workers of the depression years (and indeed
to Afrikaners of all classes), as a new form of English-
speaking domination.   Perhaps most important of all is
the fact that under both forms of hegemony blacks would
have tended to see their domination only in terms of white
racism.

'Hegemony' seems thus to have been multi-faceted.   It could mean different things to different subordinate groups.   However, this does not mean it operated purely on the level of ideology.   For the perception of the nature of the subordination of each group corresponded to reality, to their objective place in the social formation, as much as it was a reflection of capital's control over class and class consciousness.   The paradox is that whatever their understanding of their oppression, all of these groups were experiencing some common oppression, for all were subordinate to capital in one form or another. Objectively, therefore, hegemony was a whole, it was one system of dominance.   But its form was such as to obscure this wholeness of oppression.   In fact, that was its very function for capital, for not only did it divide oppressed groups from one another in terms of their subjective perception of the nature of their subordination, but it created, and exploited, objective divisions between them, as long as these did not thwart its own interests.

Once the wide state, the system of hegemony, had been shaped, and the process of forming the ruling class had been completed, it appeared as given and unalterable, as if its social categories were natural ones, and the system of domination the result of the evolution of a social contract of some sort.   The 'narrow' state was then thrown into relief by the apparently fixed nature of the wide state, so that societal changes seemed to be possible only through the political apparatuses, and within the definition of reality, capital itself had designed.

This pessimistic picture of the scope and extent of capital's power should not be thought to mean that no changes and no contradictions are possible in any one system of hegemony.   In fact we have seen how capital's rule gave rise to its own contradictions, allowing different classes to become the ruling ones.   However, what it does imply is that change is a far more complex matter than inhabitants of particular systems might, by their own subordination to the hegemony of capital, believe;   and that capital usually is in a position to pre-empt other groups aspiring to dominate by virtue of its entrenchment in the narrow and wide states, its previous experience of dominance and its monopoly of ideas and historical understanding.

2   SOUTH AFRICA'S FOUR-DIMENSIONAL REVOLUTION

Many of the issues concerning the uniqueness or ordinariness of South African capitalism have been raised already in this study and pursued in this conclusion. The question of the relationships between economic systems and their political and ideological manifestations has now been explored at length; while the ways in which the ruling classes were formed and their hegemony secured in South Africa have been discussed and conclusions drawn about them. Much of the evidence has supported the argument that by the mid-1930s the South African state could be characterised as a capitalist rather than a colonial one, and a great deal of our discussion has concerned the ways in which the transition from the 'imperial state form' to the capitalist one took place.

However, what we have not yet systematically examined are the reasons for the capacity of the South African system to undertake this transition from 'imperialism' to 'capitalism'. A great deal has been said about how the transition, the 'change in hegemony', took place, but very little about why. What factors in the South African experience placed it in a position to make a partial but significant break from its subordination to imperial domination, while other African countries, for example, which were also subjected to domination by imperial capital in the late nineteenth century, remained, and in many cases still remain, under its sway?

It seems that it was the extraordinarily far-reaching and complex four-dimensional mining revolution at the turn of the century that constituted the major single historical determinant of South Africa's subsequent unique political and economic path. Of primary significance in this revolution, and indeed, it should be reiterated, at the heart of the racist form of the modern South African state, was the onslaught made by mining capital on weakened and fragmented non-capitalist 'black' modes of production in this era. It is true that the preconditions for black subordination to late nineteenth-century imperial capital were laid by the encroachments and deformations wrought upon black societies by the preceding decades of mercantile penetration and military conquest. In this sense the continuities between the mercantile and mining eras of imperial domination are of course vitally important. But there are important discontinuities too, which we have attempted to clarify here. For example, some writers have assumed that it was the hegemony of mining, with its preservation of the remnants of what were once non-capitalist modes of production in the black rural areas, that is comparable with the hegemony of imperial capital in Latin America, or indeed the old American South, where 'feudal' or 'slave' modes of production survived and sometimes thrived under

imperial domination. (1)   But others have made clear that
the comparison is far more pertinent in the case of
nineteenth-century, mercantile-dominated Southern Africa
than in the twentieth century.   In the earlier period,
some non-capitalist modes of production seem to have been
genuinely preserved, in some cases even created, albeit
under the underdeveloping and ultimately destructive
burden of imperial domination. (2)   This was surely not
what the relationship of mining capital was to non-
capitalist modes?   Indeed, it was their systematic
destruction that was at least the stated aim of the
intellectuals of the late nineteenth-century bourgeoisie;
only later was it planned to reconstruct them so as to
ensure the cheap reproduction of the proletariat and the
accommodation of a large reserve army.

This suggests that South Africa's experience of
imperial underdevelopment may not be entirely comparable
with that of other colonies in the same period.   Kay has
argued that in most underdeveloped systems today, it is
the surviving non-capitalist modes of production that act
as the most serious brake upon sustained local
accumulation; and has suggested that ironically it is
thus because the underdeveloped countries have not been
'exploited enough', in that their non-capitalist relations
of production have not been destroyed, that they have
failed to undertake an industrial revolution. (3)   The
implication of this is that to the extent that imperial
mining capital in South Africa destroyed non-capitalist
systems rapidly and effectively, this brake was thus
removed, and accumulation could proceed; evidence exists
that this may have indeed become the case by as early as
1920. (4)

Thus although it has been shown in detail in this work
that the immediate interests of mining capital
contradicted those of national capital, its revolutionary
assault on non-capitalist modes of production may well
have provided one important objective basis upon which
national capital was able to achieve a place of dominance,
and indigenous accumulation could take place without
hindrance from older social forms.   But what of the other
necessary ingredients of a capitalist revolution - the
existence of a wage labour force freed from ties to the
land, and the capacity of that labour force to meet with
'capital' in the market place?

To understand the ways in which these two factors
operated, it is important to remember that the mining
revolution had not been a two-dimensional one, a clash
between weakened 'black' systems, and incoming imperial
forces, but a four-dimensional one.   And the other two

forces - those of the 'Boer' societies, and that of
merchant capital itself - also played significant roles
in the creation of the modern industrialising South
African system.

The 'Boer' semi-feudal systems were stronger, if not
economically then at least politically, than many African
societies, and their presence in the region lent great
complexities and contradictions to the emerging social
formation.   The 'Boer' social and economic systems too
were subordinated to the interests of imperial capital;
indeed their own transition to capitalism was nipped in
the bud.   But whereas most blacks became
proletarianised, the processes of rural accumulation and
struggle which emerged from imperial domination over the
'Boer' systems gave rise to two distinct classes: a
white Afrikaner proletariat on the one hand, and an
Afrikaner rural, and increasingly urban, bourgeoisie on
the other.

Sustained accumulation is impossible unless capital and
labour are able to come together in the market place.   Of
course a large black proletariat was created in South
Africa during the mining revolution;   but it may be
argued that this black working class was more important to
the mining industry than it was to the manufacturing
sector;   and of course labour-coercive laws and
mechanisms existed to keep it so.   Thus it is important
to recognise that the indigenous industrial bourgeoisie
did not at first rely primarily on a black working class,
but rather on a white one, an Afrikaner one, a class
thrown off the land by changes which had come about
through imperial penetration and conquest. (5)   This
class, as we have shown, was rejected by the mining
industry, and in its resulting destitution prepared not
only to labour in the new manufacturing enterprises, but
to act as a political ally to local capital.   The
importance of the availability of this 'free' wage labour
force to local capital cannot be underestimated;   while we
have shown how its political alliance with non-mining
forces was of great importance in the weakening of the
imperial state.

With a proletariat having been produced from the
destruction of 'Boer' as well as 'black' societies, and
non-capitalist relations of production having been
systematically undermined, two of the conditions for the
development of local capitalism had thus been fulfilled
by processes arising out of the mining revolution.   A
third condition - that of the necessity for a class of
local capitalists willing and able to undertake and lead
the ousting of imperial capital and the initiation of

local capital accumulation - also was fulfilled during the early years of mining development.

Some of the small capitalists we examined seem to have arisen from the fourth 'dimension' of the mining revolution - that of merchant capital.   Significantly, it was these small businessmen who were most capable of fulfilling the ideological and political functions of a national bourgeoisie rather than a comprador one;   for many larger entrepreneurs and capitalist farmers found their political and ideological interests, together with many of their economic ones, locked in with those of mineowners;   they found it difficult to develop a coherent 'national' world-view.

Furthermore, as economists have argued, the capacity of this national class to accumulate to the extent that it did was predicated upon the creation by the imperial mining industry of a large market for a remarkably wide range of goods.   One of the many ironies of the situation was that this market was given a significant boost by an event not unconnected with the interests of imperial capital - the Anglo-Boer War.   During this vast conflict local producers flourished and afterwards they made signi- ficant advances in the spheres of economic consolidation, political alliances and ideological developments.   The very war which saw the entrenchment of imperial domination sowed the seeds of a major element in its future decline.

We have thus emphasised some of the ways in which South African history was shaped by its initial capitalist imperial revolution, concentrating on the effects thereof, on its capacity to break free from the pattern of under- development.   Perhaps in conclusion it is appropriate to point out some of the other ways in which the first revolution affected subsequent developments, with special regard to its effects on the creation of the present South African state and society.

All classes emerging from the 'Boer' modes of production - even those owning the means of production on the land and in the cities - were subjected to the hegemony of imperial capital;   they suffered economically, politically and ideologically, and their subordination was experienced as subordination to 'British South African' interests.   This might itself have led to considerable complexities in the subsequent South African social formation.   An emerging Afrikaner bourgeoisie, resentful of its subordination, might have successfully challenged imperial hegemony in nationalist terms, with the support of the white working class, with whom it would ally on the basis of 'national' oppression.   However, what is interesting, and what the common view of South African

history fails to take into account, (6) is that this
challenge, which indeed did begin to emerge during and
after the First World War, and did begin to become a
serious one, was in fact pre-empted.   Just as it
appeared that an emerging Afrikaner bourgeoisie (in the
form of the Nationalist Party), with a white working-
class ally (in the form of the Labour Party) appeared to
have ousted imperial control over the state by winning
the election of 1924, so it began to become clear that
their victory was to be short lived.   A national
capitalist class, which was no more Afrikaner or 'Boer'
than had been the imperial mining industry, was, through
a complex series of processes described in detail in this
study, to become the new ruling class.   All that the Pact
alliance had achieved had been the weakening of the
imperial state, which had simply facilitated the rise of
the new bourgeoisie to a position of dominance.

Afrikaners of all classes were thus subjected to a
second form of hegemony, a second subordination, this time
by an English-speaking South African bourgeoisie.   The
new class sought to entrench itself partly through the
forging of alliances with agriculture and white workers;
but its alliances were on its own political terms, and
were framed in the South Africanist ideology, which was
in part an expression of the superior position of the
English-speaker over the Afrikaner.

Thus both the Afrikaner bourgeoisie and the Afrikaner
working class found themselves allied with, or subjected
to the domination of, the bearers of a new, English,
hegemonic order.   And like British South African hegemony
before it, this new system was to exclude them from
political and economic power, either on grounds of
class or of nationality.   The material disadvantages
of this to both classes were considerable.   Afrikaner
farmers, for example, found their economic interests were
severely threatened by the burgeoning labour demands of
the more affluent industrial sector which drew their cheap
black labour off the land; (7) Afrikaner businessmen
found their capacity to accumulate was curtailed by the
overpowering English bourgeoisie; (8) while Afrikaner
workers found themselves not only in the exploited
condition of all workers, but in the same vulnerable
position that white workers in South Africa had always
experienced, where cheaper black labour presented a
constant threat to their security.   The ground was laid,
thus, for a new expression of resistance by Afrikaners,
rich and poor, to the new system of capitalism which
emerged in the 1930s.   And indeed these groups did
articulate their material grievances most clearly in these
years.

However, the ideological dimension of the suppression and subordination of Afrikaners of all classes should not be forgotten in the face of the important economic disadvantages they suffered.   Economic grievances may be necessary to the explanation of why Afrikaners began to oppose the new order of the 1930s;   but they are not sufficient to explain why this opposition was expressed in the form of a virulent nationalism, with an overriding ideological component.   It may be suggested that it was not simply their subordination to the *economic* interests of English capital that bred the new Afrikaner nationalism of the 1930s, but their subordination to English hegemony as a whole, that form of domination which as we have argued at length, expressed itself on every social level.

The objective meaning of the rise of Afrikaner nationalism must surely lie in the experience of all Afrikaners to a form of subordination which, while it was itself a result of the particular way in which capitalism developed in South Africa, was not expressed simply in economic class terms.   If the use of the concept of 'hegemony' is capable of allowing us to perceive and understand this, without leading us into 'idealist' explanations of a social phenomenon, such as 'nationalism', then perhaps it has taken us a step further in advancing our understanding of the profound conflicts of the 1930s, and of their subsequent resolution in the creation of the post-1948 South African state.

Notes

INTRODUCTION

1   See Martin Legassick, South Africa: Capital
    Accumulation and Violence, 'Economy and Society',
    vol. 3, no. 3, 1974.
2   F.A. Johnstone, 'Class, Race and Gold', London, 1976.
3   H. Wolpe, Capitalism and Cheap Labour Power In South
    Africa: From Segregation to Apartheid, 'Economy and
    Society', vol. 1, no. 4, 1972.
4   J.E. Borain, Presidential Address to the 1929 Annual
    Convention of the FCI, in '12th Annual Report of the
    FCI', 1929; see also pp. 174-5.
5   See A. Gramsci, 'The Modern Prince and other
    writings', New York, 1957, particularly the chapter
    on The Formation of Intellectuals, pp. 118-25. The
    long extract from that chapter which introduces this
    book contains Gramsci's most suggestive and
    illuminating formulation of the concept 'organic
    intellectual'.
6   C. Geertz, Ideology as a Cultural System, in D.E.
    Apter (ed.), 'Ideology and Discontent', New York and
    London, 1964, pp. 47-76.
7   Ibid.
8   G.A. Williams, The Concept of 'Egemonia' in the
    Thought of Antonio Gramsci: Some Notes on Interpre-
    tation, 'Journal of the History of Ideas', vol. 21,
    no. 4, 1960, p. 587.
9   A. Gramsci, 'Selections from the Prison Notebooks of
    Antonio Gramsci', London, 1971, pp. 181-2.
10 L. Althusser, Ideology and Ideological State
    Apparatuses, in 'Lenin and Philosophy', London,
    1971, pp. 123-73.
11 N. Poulantzas, 'Political Power and Social Classes',
    London, 1973.

12 R. Miliband, 'The State in Capitalist Society',
    London, 1969.
13 See, for example, their published controversy in
    R. Blackburn (ed.), 'Ideology in Social Science',
    London, 1972.
14 For a recent statement of this position see R. Davies
    et al., Class Struggle and the Periodisation of the
    State in South Africa, 'Review of African Political
    Economy', 7, September-December 1976.   See also p.
    142.
15 See S. Clarke, Capital, 'Fractions' of Capital and the
    State: Neo-Marxist Analyses of the South African
    State, 'Capital and Class', 5, Summer 1978.
16 See B. Bozzoli, Capital and the State in South Africa,
    'Review of African Political Economy', 11, January-
    April 1978.

1 THE MINING REVOLUTION

  1 It is thus unfortunate that the two major works
     devoted specifically to the South African gold-mining
     industry start in 1910 and 1911 respectively, by which
     time the mining ideology and many of the structures
     which the industry established had already been formed.
     See: F.A. Johnstone, 'Class, Race and Gold', London,
     1976, and Francis Wilson, 'Labour in the South African
     Gold Mines, 1911-1969', Cambridge, 1972.   But the
     lack of discussion on the details of the mining
     revolution is partly compensated for by the theoreti-
     cal and conceptual richness of recent studies such as
     that of Johnstone (above); Martin Legassick, South
     Africa: Capital Accumulation and Violence, 'Economy
     and Society', vol. 3, no. 3, 1974, and C. van Onselen,
     'Chibaro', London, 1976.   These three studies have
     made the structured analysis of the mining ideology
     possible.
  2 The work of Southern African imperial historians in
     general, such as Mawby, LeMay or Robinson and Gallagher
     concerning the political role of mining in the Trans-
     vaal tends to emphasise the role of 'great men' and to
     become almost obsessively concerned with the individual
     characteristics of mineowners, and with what conspira-
     cies they may or may not have collaborated.   This
     approach, while it may be worthwhile in its own terms,
     is incapable of generating or stimulating any debate
     which goes beyond those terms.   See, amongst others,
     for the debate occurs within an ongoing tradition in
     South African history: D. Denoon, 'Capitalist influence'

and the Transvaal Crown Colony Government, 'The
Historical Journal', 1969, and 'A Grand Illusion',
London, 1973; A.A. Mawby, The Transvaal Mineowners
in Politics, 1900-1907, paper delivered at the
Institute of Commonwealth Studies, University of
London, May 1972; R. Robinson and J. Gallagher,
'Africa and the Victorians', London, 1961; and
G.H.L. Le May, 'British Supremacy in South Africa',
London, 1965. By contrast, G. Blainey, Lost causes
of the Jameson Raid, 'Economic History Review', 1965,
and I.R. Phimister, Rhodes, Rhodesia and the Rand,
'Journal of Southern African Studies', vol. 1, no. 1,
1974, attempt to show the extent to which individuals
were inseparable from the particular economic
interests they upheld, thus criticising the
'individualist' tradition from 'within'.

3 The 'South African Mining Journal' ('SAMJ'), ran for
eight years, and after a break during the Anglo-Boer
War was reconstituted as 'South African Mines, Commerce and Industries' ('SA Mines'). It was an almost
perfect example of the kind of source journal on
which this work is based, and upon which any study of
ideologies in their living and creative context
should be built. Like the other journals used here
('South African Commerce and Manufacturers' Record',
'Commercial Bulletin', etc.) it combined the
independence of the 'forum' with the restraint of
the 'mouthpiece', so that ideologists writing in it
were able and required both to lead their audience
and to represent it.

4 Rathbone's South Africanness is evidenced by his
roles as founder of the S.A. Association of
Engineers, co-founder of the important Mine Managers'
Association, drafter of early mining regulations,
Inspector of Mines under the Kruger administration,
and co-founder of the St John's Ambulance
Association, the Rand Pioneers, and the Statistical
Society of South Africa, and a number of other
activities. For a brief biography of Rathbone see
'SA Mines', 19 May 1906. Later the journal came
under the editorship of a man called Tainton, who was
followed by C.D. Webb. Both editors continued the
Rathbone tradition of ideological creation.

5 The non-mining 'audience' of the journal included
commercial, industrial, white labour and farming
interests; and, in the absence of any firm and
satisfactory relationship between mining and the
state, the Transvaal government itself.

6 The timespan 1891-1907 was determined by the fact

that the role of the journal as a mouthpiece-forum
declined after 1907, by which time the formative
ideological battles of the mining industry had been
fought and won, and the need for a highly
concentrated forum such as the 'SAMJ' had declined.
Ideology could be, and was, sustained and articulated
on a more diffuse plane after this time.   The
journal continued to be seen, however, as the most
reliable 'voice' of the industry, and is treated as
such by, for example, Johnstone, op. cit.

7 F.A. Johnstone, op. cit.

8 M. Williams, An Analysis of South African Capitalism:
Neo-Ricardianism or Marxism?, 'Bulletin of the
Conference of Socialist Economists', February 1975,
p. 7.

9 During the 1890s wages were an extraordinarily high
proportion of overall costs.   FitzPatrick, in his
evidence to the 1897 Commission of Enquiry, claimed
that of Eckstein and Co.' costs white labour
constituted 28 per cent, black 23 per cent,
explosives 10 per cent and coal 8 per cent.   The
Secretary of Rand Mines Ltd, Frank Raleigh, claimed
that white labour constituted as much as 36 per cent
of costs on one mine.   It was generally accepted
that, together, white and black labour constituted
about 50 per cent of overall costs.   The extent to
which this affected profitability is revealed in the
report of the commission of 1897, in which it is
claimed that in 1896 of 183 mines in the Transvaal,
79 produced gold and of these only 25 declared
dividends which amounted to only £1.7m.   High costs
were blamed for this.   See Supplement to 'SAMJ',
7 August 1897.

10 Some analysts, of an 'idealist' bent, have assumed
that the modern forms of segregation 'evolved' out of
the earlier ones.   See, for example, David Welsh,
'The Roots of Segregation: Native Policy in Colonial
Natal, 1845-1910', Cape Town, 1971.   Legassick's formulation is more to the point when he writes: 'Both
the character of the institutions of colonial conquest
and its incompleteness, combined to permit ideologies
of racial difference and institutions of racial dis-
crimination to be utilised in creating the social
relationships of capitalism as a dominant mode of
production in South Africa', op. cit., p. 259.

11 See Stanley Trapido, Liberalism in the Cape in the
19th and 20th Centuries, in 'Collected Seminar
Papers', no. 17, University of London, Institute of
Commonwealth Studies, 1972-3.

12   The analysis of the diamond industry which follows is
     based largely on: Hedley A. Chilvers, 'The Story of
     De Beers'', London, 1939; Theodore Gregory, 'Ernest
     Oppenheimer and the Economic Development of Southern
     Africa', Cape Town, 1962; Duncan Innes, The Exercise
     of Control in the Diamond Industry of South Africa:
     Some Preliminary Remarks, in T. Adler (ed.),
     'Perspectives on South Africa', Johannesburg, 1977;
     and H.J. and R.E. Simons, 'Class and Colour in South
     Africa, 1850-1950', Harmondsworth, 1969.
13   Innes, op. cit., p. 205.
14   For a description (and justification) of the
     establishment of the closed compound system see
     Chilvers, op. cit., pp. 39-40.   See also H.J. and
     R.E. Simons, op. cit., pp. 42-3.   For a discussion
     of the place of the compound system in the overall
     Southern African system of labour control see van
     Onselen, op. cit.
15   See H.J. and R.E. Simons, op. cit., pp. 44-5, and
     Chilvers, op. cit., pp. 101-2.
16   H.J. and R.E. Simons, op. cit., pp. 40-2.
17   The Glen Grey Act of 1894 served the twin functions
     of individualising Cape African land tenure and
     proletarianising those rendered landless or deprived
     by its provisions.
18   See J.S. Marais, 'The Fall of Kruger's Republic',
     Oxford, 1961, pp. 3-4, who names the most important
     capitalists in control of the mines by the mid-
     1890s as: Wenher, Beit, Rhodes, Robinson, Barnato,
     Farrar, Neumann, Goerz, Albu, Marks and Bailey.
19   'SAMJ', 12 November 1892.
20   See Blainey, op. cit.   Other divisions within the
     industry were often regionally based: Barberton had
     a separate Chamber of Mines which sometimes took an
     independent line, while the Klerksdorp Mine
     Managers' Association too distinguished itself from
     the larger organisation.   See 'SAMJ', 27 April 1895,
     and 13 June 1896.
21   The Association of Mines broke away from the Chamber
     of Mines after the Jameson Raid.
22   See, for a variety of examples, the issues of 22 July
     1893, 9 December 1893, 24 February 1894, 12 May 1894,
     and many others.
23   Marais, op. cit. gives a good impression of this in
     his chapter 1.   See also C.T. Gordon, 'The Growth of
     Boer Opposition to Kruger 1890-95', Cape Town, 1970,
     whose discussion of the period 1890-5 is testimony to
     the wide-ranging effects which the mining industry
     had in those early years.

24   C.W. de Kiewiet, 'A History of South Africa: Social
     and Economic', Oxford, 1957, pp. 122-3.
25   Marais, op. cit., p. 1, gives a breakdown of the
     origins of the Uitlander population: United Kingdom,
     16,265;   Cape Colony,   15,162;   Natal, 1,242;
     Russian Jews, 3,335;   Germans, 2,262;   Australasians,
     992;   Netherlanders, 819;   Americans, 754;   French-
     men, 402, and some others.
26   'To the Kruger regime, the gold mining industry ...
     was a liability because the *uitlander* community was a
     potential Trojan horse.   The cultural gulf between
     the urban, individualistic and materialistic
     uitlander community and the rural, socially
     integrated, and Calvinistic *burger* community was deep
     and the problem of an accommodation extremely
     difficult.   The *burgers* recalled that the British
     element in the Transvaal had played a significant
     role in the events leading to the annexation of the
     Republic in 1877, and their suspicions of the
     political implications of the growth of Johannesburg
     were confirmed by the arrogant behaviour of many
     uitlanders.'   Leonard Thompson, Great Britain and
     the Afrikaner Republics, 1870-1899, in Monica Wilson
     and Leonard Thompson (eds), 'The Oxford History of
     South Africa', vol. II, 'South Africa, 1870-1966',
     Oxford, 1971, p. 309.
27   Denoon, 'A Grand Illusion', p. 5.
28   For one of the many descriptions of the perceptions
     by the 'Boers' of the Uitlanders, see Eric A. Walker,
     'A History of Southern Africa', 3rd Edition, London,
     1957, pp. 433-6.
29   'Race', in the ideology of the times, almost
     invariably referred to the differences between the
     British and the Afrikaners, and not to the
     differences between blacks and whites, which were so
     clearly defined in hierarchical terms that the
     concept of 'race' was not only unnecessary, but even
     implied a degree of similarity and competitiveness
     supposedly, although not actually, absent from black-
     white relationships.   This may be contrasted with
     the use of the term in British colonies, such as those
     in Central Africa, to refer to blacks, the difference
     perhaps being attributable to the fact of South
     Africa having so substantial and powerful a white
     population.   See H.A.C. Cairns, 'Prelude to
     Imperialism', London, 1965.
30   L. Reyersbach, for example, spoke of how the 'labour
     problem' in South Africa was not only exacerbated by
     the attitude of white labour, but by the 'prejudices

of the British people, who in their wisdom have
decreed that the aboriginal shall be considered and
treated as a ward in Chancery, and that he is
entitled to far greater help and assistance from the
law than his less fortunate white superiors in the
great manufacturing and mining centres in Europe',
Rand Mines Ltd, '9th Annual Report for the year
ending 31st December 1903', Chairman's Address,
Annual General Meeting, 23 March 1904.

31   In a synthesis of writings on the Anglo-Boer War,
Bransky describes the alliance thus: 'In the end the
British Government and mineowners found common cause
in fighting for a White South Africa under a British
flag'; see D. Bransky, The Causes of the Boer War:
Towards a Synthesis, unpublished paper delivered to
the workshop on Southern African Studies, Oxford,
1974, p. 22. However, the view of a British
Government and mineowning capitalist alliance which
both Bransky and A.H. Jeeves in his paper on The
Administration and Control of Migratory Labour on the
South African Gold Mines: Capitalism and the State
in the Era of Kruger and Milner, in P.L. Bonner (ed.),
'Working Papers in Southern African Studies',
Johannesburg, 1977, put forward, tends to by-pass the
problem of hegemony and to treat the state as an
autonomous entity.

32   'SAMJ', 17 December 1892. It is probably the case
that the journal and the Mine Managers' Association
were seen by Rathbone as twin methods of launching
an assault on the Chamber of Mines, the one
ideological, the other more in the nature of a
pressure group. Thus, in only the 6th issue of the
journal, he proposed the formation of a Mine
Manager's Association ('SAMJ', 7 November 1891).
Contemporary work has found it difficult to
acknowledge the extent to which mine managers were
independent and powerful figures in the mining
industry, in many ways more important to the actual
running of the mines than the Directors or mineowners, many of whom lived in England, and whose
concerns in any case were with the obtaining of
financial backing, the dividends of shareholders, and
other more elevated issues. As the discussion of
the ideology shows, the MMA and the 'SAMJ' between
them constituted a formidable pressure on the
industry's upper stratum of ownership to recognise,
act upon and legitimate its own interests.

33   Report of Committee of the Mine Managers' Association
on the Native Labour Question, 'SAMJ', 23 September
1893.

34 Ibid.
35 Ibid.
36 Report of the first Annual General Meeting of the
    Mine Managers' Association, 8 January 1894; 'SAMJ',
    13 January 1894.
37 Editorial, 'SAMJ', 30 November 1895.
38 Ibid.
39 Ibid.
40 Anon. article, Compound Management, 'SAMJ', 7 April
    1894.
41 Anon. article, The Compound Manager, 'SAMJ',
    24 August 1895.
42 For a detailed discussion of the concessions policy
    see Gordon, op. cit., pp. 35-57; D.A. Etheridge,
    The Early History of the Chamber of Mines,
    University of the Witwatersrand, MA thesis, 1949,
    discusses the dynamite monopoly in particular, while
    C. van Onselen, The Randlords and Rotgut, 1886-
    1903, 'History Workshop Journal' 2, Autumn 1976,
    discusses the liquor concession. See also Marais,
    op. cit., pp. 25-45.
43 H.J. and R.E. Simons, op. cit., pp. 61-2. Although
    evidence of this has been adduced by many writers on
    the subject, no systematic study has yet been
    attempted of Kruger's industrialising aims; see
    C.T. Gordon, op. cit., chapter 2; J.S. Marais, op.
    cit., chapter 2; and D. Bransky, op. cit., who
    makes Kruger's national capitalist policy a central
    factor in his reinterpretation of the Anglo-Boer War.
44 30 November 1895; see also 26 December 1896, where
    the plea was reiterated.
45 Comment on the Report of the 1897 Commission of
    Enquiry, 'SAMJ', 7 August 1897.
46 Walker, op. cit., p. 435.
47 See, for example, Editorial, 'SAMJ', 14 July 1894,
    and Editorial, 'SAMJ', 27 June 1896.
48 Editorial, 'SAMJ', 16 June 1894.
49 Editorial, 'SAMJ', 29 December 1894.
50 In one letter to the journal, a white miner declared
    that it was 'a good thing for the white miner that
    the Government recognises the difference between the
    Kaffir and his white brother, as you are pleased to
    call him, and for which they will have the support of
    all the working men on the Rand, especially the white
    miners. I make no doubt the miners would have been
    working for starvation wages long before this if the
    capitalists of Johannesburg had their own sweet
    will', 'SAMJ', 25 May 1895. See also 'SAMJ', 16
    July 1898, when it was reported that in the Volksraad

complaints were made of the exorbitant salaries of
mine managers.

51   Education and the Mines, anon article, 'SAMJ', 19
      October 1895.

52   'SAMJ', 21 November 1896.

53   Most historians of the period emphasise these
      attempts, and Jeeves, op. cit., summarises them
      coherently, in making his case that state-mining
      relationships both before and after the war were on a
      level of 'alliance' and 'collaboration' on some
      issues, non-alliance and conflict on others.
      Because of the apparent (relative) willingness of
      Kruger's government to assist mining in certain
      ways, many analysts of the roots of mining hostility
      to the regime have been hard put to explain capital's
      support for the war, and the destruction of the
      state.   H.J. and R.E. Simons, op. cit., as we have
      seen, assert that the war was 'neither inevitable nor
      necessary to modernise the republic'.

54   Partly, no doubt, because they would necessarily be
      badly administered.   For a description of the pass
      laws considered most desirable by ideologists see
      Editorial, 'SAMJ', 18 August 1894.   For reports and
      discussions on the passing and content of the new
      pass laws, see 'SAMJ', 6 December 1894, and 19
      January 1895.   The initial response to these laws
      was one of hope and relief, since they accorded so
      closely with what had been requested.   But before
      the end of 1895, a general dissatisfaction with the
      Transvaal administration's willingness or ability to
      implement them had set in, and by 1896 it was
      accepted that the pass laws were 'ineffective' and
      'badly administered'.   See Editorial, 'SAMJ', 3
      November 1895 and 'SAMJ', 5 September 1896, and many
      other examples occurring during that year.   For a
      brief analysis which does examine the structural
      reasons for the inability of the Transvaal state to
      satisfy mining see S. Trapido, South Africa and the
      Historians, review article, 'African Affairs',
      October 1972.

55   Of the many accounts of these events the most
      succinct is that of de Kiewiet, op. cit., chapter V.

56   See, for example, the 'SAMJ', 1 February 1896:   'The
      mines were violently shaken from the equable groove
      into which constant and vigilant supervision and
      organisation had placed them, and there is no
      promise that they will regain this groove for many
      months.   The employees, particularly the natives,
      are unsettled and the compound managers find it

difficult to induce them to return to regular habits
of work.'

57   For the background to this issue, see Blainey, op.
     cit.   The 'Association of Mines' was the breakaway
     body from the Chamber, and was supported by the
     Volkstem, because it was said to have in it people
     who were not enemies of the ZAR.   The split lasted
     just over a year.   By January 1897, it had become
     clear to the Association of Mines that its aim in
     breaking away - the obtaining of concessions from the
     government which the Chamber could not get - was
     unattainable, and negotiations had begun for a
     reunion, which in fact only took place in November of
     that year.   It is interesting to note that the
     Association acted together with the Chamber and the
     AMM on the issues of the formation of a Native Labour
     Bureau, compound administration and 'native wage
     reductions', perhaps confirming that it was on the
     issue of the desirable attitude of mining towards the
     state at that time, rather than the nature of the
     industry and the overall class structure of the
     society, that the split occurred.   Moreover, the
     neutral attitude of the journal at the time, and the
     subsequent development of its undivided support for
     the violent overthrow of the Transvaal state, seem
     also to indicate that it was the prematurity rather
     than the lasting inappropriateness of the type of
     action involved in the Jameson Raid that was the real
     issue at stake.   In 1896, some mineowners still
     thought the Transvaal to be manipulable.   By 1899,
     very few did.   See the 'SAMJ' on these matters
     during 1896 and 1897, in particular, 2 May 1896;   22
     August 1896;   30 January 1897;   1 May 1897;   and 20
     November 1897.

58   See C. van Onselen, Reactions to Rinderpest in
     Southern Africa: 1896-1897, 'Journal of African
     History', vol. XIII, no. 3, 1972, from which it
     emerges that although the short-term reaction of
     blacks to the disease and to the wage reductions may
     have been to stay away from the mines, the long-term
     effect of the epidemic was to increase and hasten
     their proletarianisation.

59   This view, empirically valid for the period before
     Africans had been proletarianised, held that all
     black workers were 'target' workers, who worked to
     obtain a certain amount of money;   if the time taken
     to gain that amount was lengthened, through the
     lowering of wages, then workers would stay on the
     mines that much longer.   This approach attained the

status of ideology and was used to justify lower
wages even when many of the workers had become
proletarianised.

60   See 'SAMJ', 2 May 1896, where the first suggestions
of wage reductions were put forward; 27 June 1896,
where it is reported that the Mine Managers'
Association had decided to 'reduce wages, as it were,
by force and at the point of the Bayonet' on 1 August
in spite of warnings by the journal and by Grant not
to go too hastily; and 5 September 1896, when it is
reported that the wage reductions had taken place on
1 September.

61   See 'SAMJ', 8 August, 22 August, 5 September,
3 October, and 17 October 1896.

62   See 'SAMJ', 17 October 1896.

63   'SAMJ', 7 November 1896.

64   Ibid.   See also 'SAMJ', 28 November 1896.

65   These complaints were common throughout 1896.   For
specific examples, see 'SAMJ', 5 September 1896 and
9 January 1897.

66   See 'SAMJ', 13 February 1897.

67   As C. van Onselen, in his 'Randlords and Rotgut', has
made clear, the liquor concession was not a matter of
simple opposition between state and mining since
eminent mineowners themselves were involved in the
liquor industry.   It was the expression of a
contradiction within mining capital as well.

68   See 'SAMJ', 24 April 1897 for details about the
petition and the conference.   See 'SAMJ', 7 August
1897 for a report of an article in the 'Journal of
Finance' by Walter W. Wall saying that South African
mining was not worth investing in because of
inefficiency.

69   See the evidence to the Commission as it appeared in
supplements to the 'SAMJ' during April, May, June,
July and August of 1897.

70   Evidence of George Albu, supplement to the 'SAMJ',
24 April 1897.   Albu was a leading member of the
breakaway Association of Mines, and it is striking
the extent to which this piece of his statement
reveals that the issue of means and not ends divided
his view of the state from that of other more hostile
men.   That the state and industry should ultimately
be in accord was not in doubt; but it was his view
that they should 'grow' and not be forced, together.

71   Evidence of James Percy Fitzpatrick, supplement to
the 'SAMJ', 1 May 1897, who declared that the Pass
and Liquor laws would be acceptable if they had been
carried out, but that since the introduction of the

pass law, the Robinson Company had had over 1,600
deserters of whom not a single one had been 'caught'.
See also evidence of William Dalrymple, supplement to
'SAMJ', 8 May 1897, who reported that on one mine,
the New Kleinfontein, 245 deserters had left during
six months, and not one had been returned, and, most
striking evidence of all, that of C.S. Goldmann, 8
May 1897, who declared that figures from 33 companies
showed that a total of 14,000 Africans had deserted
between April 1896 and March 1897 from a monthly
complement of 19,000, and not one was brought back.
The Chamber of Mines Annual Report, 'SAMJ', 28
January 1899, reported that 5,000 men deserted each
month; they were said to be going to other
employers.   The aim of the pass laws was to
'establish a complete system of control over the
natives at the mines, so that they could be traced
from place to place from the date of their arrival on
the fields to that of their departure'.

72 'SAMJ', 28 August 1897 and 23 October 1897.
73 See Editorial, 'SAMJ', 1 October 1898.
74 In a controversial Chairman's address to the George
Goch Amalgamated Company on 11 January 1899, Albu
pursued his advocacy of the peaceful transformation
of the state, condemning the South Africa, or
National, League for planning to sow strife in 'this
otherwise peaceful country, and to disturb everything
that was calculated to forward the welfare of the
people of the country' and whose 'only object in this
country was to oust the present Government and get
the English flag waving here'.   The journal for the
first time utterly condemned this view.   See 'SAMJ',
14 January 1899.
75 Speech to the Rand Mines Ltd Annual Meeting, 25 March
1903, supplement to 'SA Mines', 28 March 1903.
76 See 'SA Mines', 11 July 1903.
77 Contracts worth £2m within a mile of Johannesburg
were reported, and in the suburbs, contracts worth
£1/4m; 'SA Mines', 5 December 1903.
78 See 'SA Mines', 19 December 1903.
79 White average wages were lowered by the replacement
of skilled and expensive white workers by unskilled,
unorganised and cheaper, whites.   See 'SA Mines',
30 May 1903, when it was reported that the average
white wage had fallen from £26.10.11 to £24.10.9
between 1898 and 1902.
80 The Acting Mining Commissioner's Report in 1904 said
that although the number of black workers had fallen
by 39 per cent between 1899 and 1902, output had only

decreased by 30 per cent.   This increase in average
output per worker was attributed to a variety of
factors including the absence of drunkenness, the
increased white/'native' ratio and improved mechanical
techniques.   See 'SA Mines', 9 January 1904.

81   The old pass law administration had been replaced by
a far more efficient administration, said H. Ross
Skinner, in his address to the Annual Meeting of the
AMM, 'SA Mines', 18 February 1905.   Furthermore, he
pointed to the lower costs of stores, greater
efficiency of labour, and 'the general tendency to a
gradual improvement in the handling and management
of our mines'.

82   Editorial, 'SA Mines', 4 March 1905.

83   Here we concur with D. Denoon, 'A Grand Illusion',
where he argues that the Milner administration
was decisively and significantly under
the influence of the mining industry.   Jeeves, op.
cit., supports this argument.   As we have said,
however, both studies lack a concept of hegemony
within which to explore the relationship between the
two, and are forced to approach the state through
the mechanisms of law-making, staff appointment and
administration.   It is because the debate is
conducted in these terms that A.A. Mawby, op. cit.,
for example, is able to criticise their findings.
Just as evidence may be adduced of the specific cases
in which mining men communicated sympathetically with
the state, so evidence of the opposite may be found,
since the operation of the state apparatus cannot be
explained simply by referring to the actions of
individuals working for it.

84   See, for example, Editorial, 'SA Mines', 8 September
1906.

85   Editorial, 'SA Mines', 13 October 1906.

86   Cairns, op. cit., p. 30.

87   Cairns, op. cit., p. 34.   This is in contrast to the
imperialisms of extermination which occurred in
German South West Africa, Australasia and elsewhere.

88   Cairns, op. cit., pp. 102-19.

89   Martin Legassick, in The Frontier Tradition in South
Africa Historiography, unpublished seminar paper,
University of Sussex, 1970, gives an outline of these
differences.

90   Legassick, South Africa: Capital Accumulation and
Violence, p. 10.

91   L. Reyersbach, Chairman's address to the Rand Mines
Ltd, Annual General Meeting, 23 March 1904, op. cit.

92   Evidence of F. Perry, Chairman and Managing Director

of the Witwatersrand Native Labour Association
(Wenela), to the Transvaal Labour Commission, 1903.

93   'SA Mines', 11 February 1905.

94   G. Farrar, Retiring Presidential Address, Annual
meeting of the Chamber of Mines, reported in 'SA
Mines', 20 February 1904.

95   'SAMJ', 30 November 1895 - an important issue from
which several extracts have been taken.

96   The frequency with which this assertion is made would
seem to indicate that it needs to be taken more
seriously than usual and the precise relationship of
the sexes in the political economy of non-capitalist
societies established, not only for purposes of
understanding those societies themselves, but for
purposes of reaching a fuller understanding of the
way in which proletarianisation was able to be forced
upon them.

97   Farrar, op. cit.   The use of the term 'raw' was and
is common in Southern Africa; it implies not only
savagery and 'native' backwardness, but naiveté and
lack of sophistication in an industrial setting.
See also 'SAMJ', 21 April 1894.

98   Anonymous article, 'SAMJ', 19 September 1896.

99   The exceptions to this were in the Cape, where
certain blacks were included, through the qualified
franchise, in the polity; and the Transvaal, where
certain whites, the Uitlanders, were not permitted
full political participation under Kruger.   Neither
of these cases was of great import to the
incorporation and non-incorporation of the working
class under capitalism; the Cape system was
developed so that wealthy and/or educated black
peasant farmers and professionals could be
incorporated; while the Transvaal's exclusion of
whites was more to do with the conflict between the
old 'Boer', and the new, capitalist, modes of
production, than with the lines of incorporation
between black and white groups.

100 For discussion of the growth of this peasantry in the
Cape and Natal, see Colin Bundy, The Emergence and
Decline of a South African Peasantry, 'African
Affairs', October 1972, and Henry Slater, The
Changing Pattern of Economic Relations in Rural
Natal, 1938-1914, unpublished seminar paper,
Institute of Commonwealth Studies, University of
London, January 1972.   That a similar process of the
growth of a relatively wealthy class of African
farmers was taking place in the Transvaal at the time
too is suggested by the Transvaal Landowners'

Association, which in its 'Report for 1906'
complained that the 'natives' owned the largest
herds of cattle in the Transvaal.
101   'SAMJ', 30 November 1895.
102   Ibid.
103   'Locations' was used to mean rural areas to which
      Africans were confined by law, for which the word
      'reserves' is used today.   It could sometimes be
      extended to mean the urban or periurban areas to
      which Africans were also confined by law, which is
      its modern usage.
104   'SAMJ', 30 November 1895.
105   Ibid.
106   Ibid.
107   See 'SAMJ', 12 May 1894, 16 June 1894 and 18 August
      1894.
108   Anonymous pamphlet on The Native Labour Question,
      reported in the 'SA Mines', 16 June 1906.
109   Evidence of C.S. Goldmann, supplement to 'SAMJ', 8
      May 1897.   The converse of this purifying aspect of
      labour was that it could also corrupt.   See chapter
      2, for a discussion of this aspect of the ideology.
110   As reported in the 'SA Mines', 14 March 1903.
111   Evidence of George Albu, supplement to the 'SAMJ', 24
      April 1897.
112   See, in particular, the evidence of James Hay, to the
      1897 Commission of Enquiry: 'Do you think it would
      be desirable to get forced labour?' - 'Yes.'
      'Against fair pay?' - 'Of course.'
113   The Report on the 1897 Commission of Enquiry issued
      by the Aborigines Protection Society in 1901, was one
      attempt to establish that forced labour was being
      used, but generally the case has not been
      systematically proved in detail, although it is clear
      from a variety of primary and secondary sources that
      forced labour was an integral part of the industry's
      system of labour supply.   See, for example,
      Johnstone, op. cit.   The precise definition of the
      term 'forced labour' is a subject for debate, since
      it is clearly not desirable that it should be implied
      that labour forced off the land by taxation or other
      laws is in any way less 'forced' than labour which is
      actually physically taken to places of work.   Indeed
      the very opposite is argued here.   Some distinction
      between the two is obviously necessary, and here the
      term 'forced labour' is generally used to refer to
      the latter process, and that of 'proletarianisation'
      to the former.   See G. Arrighi, Labour Supplies in
      Historical Perspective: A Study of the

Proletarianization of the African Peasantry in Rhodesia, 'The Journal of Development Studies', vol. 6, no. 3, April 1970, for an analysis and development of this concept in the Southern African context.

114 van Onselen, in 'Chibaro', documents the various methods of forcing labour to the Rhodesian mines used in this period; even the 'SAMJ' itself complained that some of the recruiting methods used were too 'harsh' and drove Africans away from the Transvaal, particularly in the pre-war period.

115 See Johnstone, op. cit., pp. 35-8, where the systems of loan advancement and debt-inducement used are described.

116 'SAMJ', 30 November 1895.

117 Ibid.

118 It was repeated in an almost identical form in 1897, for example, see 'SAMJ', 9 January 1897. Later the advocacy of the destruction of polygamy declined. The Intercolonial Customs Conference in 1903, for example, included in its resolutions a declaration that polygamy had had less influence on the labour supply than had been supposed. This does not, however, diminish the significance of the statements of the 1890s, whose purpose was to legitimate the necessary radical and irreversible changes in pre-capitalist societies in the interests of mining. In the journal in the 1900s several letters were published from interested members of the industry repeating the ideas of destroying polygamy, however. See, for example, 'SA Mines', 13 April 1907. By this time it had become part of the debate over whether or not black labour should be fully, or only partially proletarianised, a debate which is discussed more fully in chapter 2.

119 'SAMJ', 30 November 1895.

120 Ibid.

121 'SAMJ', 22 February 1896.

122 'SA Mines', 30 May 1903: 'If mealies were to be distributed to indolent Kaffirs we should soon be face to face with a "poor black" question. Even the question of relief to the infirm, old women and children of natives requires to be approached with caution'.

123 'SAMJ', 1 May 1896.

124 'SAMJ', 16 June and 18 August 1894.

125 'SAMJ', 30 November 1895.

126 Ibid.

2 THE HIERARCHY OF EXPLOITATION

1 The term 'extra-economic' coercion has been applied
   to these mechanisms by Johnstone and others. This
   term is misleading because it implies the absence of
   political and ideological coercion in the case of
   'normal' Western working classes. The more valid
   distinction suggested here would be one between
   interventions in the relations of production (as in
   the South African case) and coercion exercised outside this realm, through the state.

2 See F.A. Johnstone, 'Class, Race and Gold', London,
   1976, pp. 26-34 for an analysis of the 'exploitation
   colour bars' which capital set up over black workers
   including the 'monopolisation of labour recruiting'.
   C. van Onselen, 'Chibaro', London, 1976, develops the
   analysis of such a labour recruitment system in the
   Rhodesian case far beyond anything that has been done
   for South Africa, although A.H. Jeeves, The
   Administration and Control of Migratory Labour on the
   South African Gold Mines: Capitalism and the State
   in the Era of Kruger and Milner, in P.L. Bonner
   (ed.), 'Working Papers in Southern African Studies',
   Johannesburg, 1977, does explore some of the detailed
   material concerning labour recruitment in South
   Africa; see also S. Moroney, Industrial Conflict in
   a Labour Repressive Economy, Black labour on the
   Transvaal Gold Mines, 1901-1912, University of the
   Witwatersrand, BA Hons Dissertation, 1976.

3 'Report of the Mine Managers' Association on the
   Native Labour Question', 'SAMJ', 23 September 1893.
   Other proposed measures included the elimination of
   labour 'touts', the abolition of the practice of
   offering work to miners who 'will bring boys', and
   the stricter enforcement of existing pass laws. The
   first two of these seem to suggest not only that
   forced labour was being supplied to the mines but
   that an extensive entrepreneurial system had built up
   in the business of 'supplying natives'. The MMA
   opposed this system because it was haphazard and
   above all tended to force the price of labour up
   through competition between companies.

4 Black wages during the 1890s must have been the
   highest real wages ever paid to black mine workers.
   As W.Y. Campbell said in a speech at a special
   meeting of the Chamber of Mines, on 30 November 1893,
   mine-workers earned three times the wages paid to
   Cape or Natal 'natives', and 'the wages paid here
   were not based on the value of the labour, but on the

pressure of competition by the Companies', 'SAMJ',
9 December 1893.   According to the Chairman of the
MMA, J.H. Johns, average wages in 1894 were 58s per
month ('SAMJ', 24 February 1894), and in spite of
regular attempts to reduce them, the wages remained
at this relatively high figure until the universal
forced reduction effected by the British
administration during the Anglo-Boer War.

5 The weapon of planned and systematic desertion as a
method of establishing worker bargaining power on
South African mines was first explored by C. van
Onselen, Worker Consciousness in Black Miners:
Southern Rhodesia, 1900-1920, 'Journal of African
History', vol. XIV, no. 2, 1973, whose Rhodesian
examples may be supplemented by examples in South
Africa such as that of the 100 black miners at the
Worcester Company who deserted together in protest
against a new system of fines ('SAMJ', 7 April 1894),
and by the frequent criticisms of compound managers
by the journal editor for mistreatment of black
workers since this, it was said, would give their
mine a bad reputation on the black workers' 'grape-
vine', and reduce their work-force.   See 'SAMJ',
7 April and 21 April 1894.

6 J.H. Johns, Chairman's Address, Mine Managers'
Association monthly meeting, reported in 'SAMJ', 24
February 1894.

7 They left the Mine Managers themselves to draft and
adhere to an agreement, based on their own 1893
report.   The Chamber objected to the agreement since
it included a compulsory deposit of £200 by each
company - clearly in those early years they were not
prepared to pay for the establishment of a ration-
alised labour supply system.   See 'SAMJ', 18
November 1893, and 24 February 1894.

8 'SAMJ', 6 April 1895.

9 Ibid.

10 The stated aims of the original association were to
'acquire' or 'fetch' natives 'by whatever means as
shall be deemed expedient', through the erection of
depots, the acquisition of all other recruitment
organisations, the prevention of the form of 'gangs
of natives' going to one employer, and the making of
supply contracts with mine managers.   See 'SAMJ',
22 August 1896.   At the same meeting, a decision was
made to introduce a 'uniform method of conducting
compounds', the establishment of a pay-gradation
system for blacks, and a general reduction in pay of
20 per cent.

11 'SAMJ', 6 April 1895.
12 Evidence of Sir Percy FitzPatrick, 'Report of the
   Transvaal Labour Commission', together with minority
   report, minutes of evidence and proceedings,
   Johannesburg, 1903.
13 'SAMJ', 30 November 1895.
14 'SAMJ', 28 November 1896. See also 'SAMJ', 1
   February 1896.
15 F. Strange, Chairman's Address, 1st Annual Meeting of
   the Rand Native Labour Association, reported in
   'SAMJ' 28 January 1898.
16 Anonymous article, 'SAMJ', 19 September 1896.
17 'East Coast Natives' were workers from Mozambique,
   whose poverty and harsh experiences of colonialism
   had indeed rendered them less capable of resisting
   the forced labour system.
18 Editorial, 'SAMJ', 12 November 1892.
19 Ibid. It is not entirely clear what exactly the
   housing arrangements were for black workers during
   the 1890s, some mines apparently having built
   compounds virtually identical to those used today,
   others depending on labour from the nearby black
   'location'. But in virtually all cases, the
   completely closed Kimberley-type compound was not
   used, partly because of the power of the commercial
   lobby which objected to the elimination of the market
   usually open to them which would follow the closing
   of compounds.
20 Anonymous article, The Compound Manager, 'SAMJ',
   24 August 1895.
21 E. Goffman's 'Asylums', London, 1961, has influenced
   several studies of compounds, including van
   Onselen's 'Chibaro', op. cit.; Robert Gordon,
   'Mines, Masters and Migrants', Johannesburg, 1977;
   T. Dunbar Moodie, The Perceptions and Behaviour
   Patterns of Black Mineworkers on a Group Gold Mine,
   mimeo, Johannesburg, 1976; and Patrick Pearson,
   The Social Structure of a South African Gold Mine
   Hostel, University of the Witwatersrand, BA Hons
   Dissertation, 1975.
22 'SAMJ', 21 April 1894.
23 'SAMJ', 22 September 1894, comment on a pamphlet by
   W. Grant, the Native Commissioner.
24 J.H. Johns, address to the monthly meeting of the
   AMM, recorded in 'SAMJ', 24 February 1894.
25 L. Reyersbach, Chairman's Address, Annual General
   Meeting, Rand Mines Ltd, 23 March 1904; in 'Ninth
   Annual Report', Rand Mines Ltd, for the year ending
   31 December 1903.

26   M. Legassick, South Africa: Capital Accumulation and
     Violence, 'Economy and Society', vol. 3, no. 3, 1974
     and H. Wolpe, Capitalism and Cheap Labour Power in
     South Africa: from Segregation to Apartheid, 'Economy
     and Society', vol. 1, no. 4, November 1972, have
     between them been able to give an idea of the nature
     of the rural agricultural sector at this time and its
     relationship to the demands of capital, although
     Wolpe's assertion that the pre-capitalist forms were
     'preserved' is perhaps misleading.   Perhaps the
     terms 'destruction' and 're-construction' would leave
     no doubt that the 'pre-capitalist' modes of production
     were utterly subordinated to capital's revolutionary
     demands, and that the capitalist mode of production
     penetrates and transforms all other modes once it
     attains dominance.

27   The 1913 Land Act, designed partly to force black
     workers off the land, had begun to have such great
     success by the end of the First World War that laws
     began to be contemplated to stop or regulate the
     'flow' of blacks to the towns.   This is but one
     aspect of a growing body of evidence which suggests
     that Wolpe, op. cit., was incorrect in his assertion
     that the disintegration of the pre-capitalist modes
     of production took place during the 1930s and 1940s
     and could be clearly linked to the rise of the
     Apartheid system.

28   Indeed so successful is this ideological conceptuali-
     sation of one structure of South African society that
     it forms the basis of those analyses which postulate
     a 'dual economy'.

29   Once more the analysis by Johnstone provides the foun-
     dations from which this study of white workers is
     pursued.   See particularly pp. 49-64.   In H.J. and
     R.E. Simons, 'Class and Colour in South Africa, 1850-
     1950', Harmondsworth, 1969, a great deal of detailed
     information is available on the position of the white
     working class in this period;   in particular see their
     chapter 4, White Labour Policies;   while R. Davies,
     Mining Capital, the State and Unskilled White Workers
     in South Africa, 1901-1913, 'Journal of Southern
     African Studies', vol. 3, no. 1, October 1976, has
     been useful too.

30   The cost of living on the Rand at the turn of the
     century, and hence the necessary wage of workers, was
     extremely high.   In his evidence to the 1897
     Commission of Enquiry, W.H. Hall, an American-born
     mine manager, gave figures in which he estimated that
     it was 22-27 per cent higher than that in the average
     American city for the average white miner and his

family, and 80-90 per cent higher for middle-class
accountants; these were figures calculated with
cultural and class variables very much in mind, but
nevertheless they have objective validity, and are of
use in our attempt to understand the white working
class's own perceptions.   See the supplement to the
'SAMJ', 12 June 1897.   See also evidence of Robert
Barrow, foreman at Jumpers Deep, Ltd (supplement to
'SAMJ', 15 May 1897), who said that the same amount
of milk, butter, meat, vegetables, bread, groceries,
rent and doctor's fees, came to £5.3.0 in England,
and £20.12.6 in the Transvaal and that the average
married worker with a family of five could 'barely
live' on the pay of £23.16.8.   See also evidence of
Alec Buchan Fyffe, representative of the Mine Workers
Union (supplement to the 'SAMJ', 22 May 1897), in
which many of the grievances of white workers were
systematically and passionately expressed.

31   See, amongst others, evidence of Fyffe, op. cit.

32   Mine Management, 'SAMJ', 22 April 1899, says that
'frequent changes are made in the technical staff
whenever a man takes up a new appointment.   Men
follow him from the old to the new mine, so men at
the latter are displaced. ... When men are uncertain
of retaining their positions beyond a few months it
is scarcely to be expected that they will take
sufficient interest in their work to do their best.'
See also The Housing of Workmen, 'SAMJ', 20 April
1895: 'The continual changing from place to place is
one of the worst features of the conditions of labour
here', and 'SA Mines', 31 March 1906: 'to be
successful in a search for work as miner, shift boss,
or mine overseer, one must speak in the vernacular
of the county from whence came the manager or
overseer.'

33   Edgar P. Rathbone, letter to 'SA Mines', 28 April
1906.

34   'SAMJ', 7 December 1895.

35   'SAMJ', 8 May 1897.

36   'SAMJ', 20 October 1896.

37   'SAMJ', 20 May 1899.

38   Reported speech by George Farrar, 'SAMJ', 20 July
1895.

39   'SAMJ', 1 October 1898.

40   See H.J. and R.E. Simons, op. cit., pp. 53-4.

41   'SAMJ', 22 April 1893.

42   The Housing of Workmen, 'SAMJ', 20 April 1895.

43   For example, Farrar, in the speech already quoted;
see also Education and the Mines, 'SAMJ', 19 October

1895, and 11 March 1899: 'Surely there is no need
for us to enlarge on the responsibilities of the
companies to the children of their workmen and to the
children of those poor men who have done so much to
make dividends possible', wrote the editor in
response to a call by FitzPatrick and Julius Wernher
for the establishment of elementary schools.

44 Farrar, 1895 speech, op. cit.
45 'SAMJ', 7 December 1895.
46 Ibid.
47 According to the evidence of C.S. Goldmann to the
1897 Commission, a sample of 53 companies employed
3,620 white workers, of whom 470 were married with
families on the property, 195 married with families
away, and 1,955 were single.
48 According to Fyffe, op. cit., white workers were
often on contracts providing for twenty-four hours'
notice, while black workers were theoretically,
though probably not practically, supposed to receive
one month's notice.
49 Fyffe, for example, spoke of how 'there is simply no
provision made for enjoyment or pleasure of any kind
for employees. A man is supposed to rise in the
morning, take his breakfast and go to work, work till
dinner and go to work again till teatime, and then
there is nothing left for him but to go to his room -
which in some cases is hardly fit for a kaffir - to
spend the rest of the evening.'
50 In the 'SAMJ', the formation of the Mine Workers'
Union, and the Randfontein strike against wage
reductions in 1897; the formation of the albeit
moderate Society of Mill and Cyanide Men, and the
meetings held by Bain in 1898; and the strikes and
'restlessness' which preceded the war in 1899 were
all reported with growing concern.
51 'SAMJ', 29 July 1893.
52 'SAMJ', 22 July 1893.
53 Ibid.
54 Government Report on Mining Economics, 'SA Mines',
12 December 1903.
55 'SAMJ', 29 July 1893.
56 Ibid. See also 'SAMJ', 7 November 1891; Compound
Management, 'SAMJ', 7 April 1894, etc.
57 'SAMJ', 22 July 1893.
58 Leading article: White Miners on the Rand, 'SAMJ',
4 May 1895.
59 See 'SAMJ', 22 February 1896 which regrets 'the
neglect of the white overseers to properly
supervise the gangs under their care, causing the
boys to become careless and lazy'.

60   This was first made explicit at the time of
     rinderpest when the 'SAMJ' (17 October 1896) claimed
     that whites were 'tampering' with natives because of
     fear that their own wages may be dropped: 'it is
     obviously in their interest to foment discontent
     amongst the boys.'
61   Strike, 'SAMJ', 11 May 1907.
62   A substantial debate is growing around the issue of
     whether white workers produce surplus value or not,
     based on the influential, but in South African terms,
     somewhat inappropriate article by G. Carchedi, On the
     Economic Identification of the New Middle Class,
     'Economy and Society', vol. 4, no. 1, 1975.   See
     H. Wolpe, The 'White Working Class' in South Africa,
     'Economy and Society', vol. 5, no. 2, May 1976, and
     R.H. Davies, 'Capital, State and White Labour in
     South Africa 1900-1960: An Historical Materialist
     Analysis of Class Formation and Class Relations',
     Brighton, 1979.
63   'SAMJ', 21 April 1894.
64   William Grant, pamphlet on the 'management' of
     'natives', described but not named in the 'SAMJ',
     22 September 1894.
65   'SAMJ', 21 April 1894.
66   Leading article: White Miners on the Rand, 'SAMJ',
     4 May 1895.   See also a letter in the 'SAMJ', 25
     May 1895, from a Cornish miner, six years in South
     Africa, who claimed that 'The mines, becoming better
     organised, have dispensed with some labour formerly
     needed, and kaffirs are also being trained to do work
     formerly called white man's work.   I have had
     kaffirs under me who could thoroughly explain the
     working of an engine and even knew the use of the
     fusible circuits in electric plants, etc. ... They
     will become serious competitors, though that will be
     resisted by the whites.'
67   'SAMJ', 21 April 1894.
68   Leading article: Classification of Labour, 'SAMJ',
     25 May 1895.
69   Evidence of Hennen Jennings, supplement to the
     'SAMJ', 5 June 1897.
70   M.E., letter to 'SA Mines', 13 April 1907.
71   Evidence of George Albu, supplement to the 'SAMJ',
     24 April 1897.   See also George Farrar, Presidential
     Address, Chamber of Mines Annual Meeting, reported in
     the 'SAMJ', 20 February 1904.
72   Reported extract from a petition drafted after a
     conference between representatives of all mining
     groups, to be submitted to the Volksraad, 'SAMJ', 24

April 1897.   See also Reyersbach, Chairman's
Address, 'Rand Mines Annual Report', 1903, op. cit.
73 Evidence of this is to be found in the Report of the
1897 Commission of Enquiry into the mining industry,
where mine managers giving evidence alluded to their
own 'permanent' locations.
74 Ibid.
75 I am grateful to Martin Legassick for making
available to me his material on this subject, and for
valuable discussions concerning it.
76 Rand Mines Ltd, '7th Report and Accounts' for the
three years ending 31 December 1901.
77 Speaking at the Annual General Meeting of the
Johannesburg Consolidated Investment Co. Ltd, Mr
Emrys Evans, a director, added that 'it is abundantly
evident that Africa cannot give us enough native
labour and it therefore becomes both a necessity and
a duty to import unskilled labour from abroad.   The
competition for natives will be less than when native
labour is the only labour obtainable, and the farmer,
instead of competing with those who pay 2-6d to 3-6d
a day may secure his labour in the country at rates
which should place the farming industry on a proper
footing and enable this country to permanently
produce the grain which it consumes.'   Supplement to
'SA Mines', 21 November 1903.
78 See D. Dencon, The Transvaal Labour Crisis, 'Journal
of African History', vol. 7, 1967.
79 For the background to this see the 'Report of the
Transvaal Indigency Commission, 1906-08', T.G.
13'08, Pretoria 1908:   'even before the outbreak of
war in 1899, a great portion of the agricultural
population was declining into indigency.   The
evidence shows that the more advanced farmers within
the reach of the markets of the Rand were prosperous,
and that many owners of the larger undivided farms
were well off.   But the majority of the small
farmers, those who owned small shares in sub-divided
farms, and the bywoners, living on sufferance on the
farms of other men, were gradually drifting from bad
to worse' (pp. 11-12).   Thus the war did not 'cause'
indigency, but accelerated the processes already
under way.
80 Editorial, 30 September 1899.
81 'SAMJ', 7 October 1899.
82 See Davies, Mining capital ..., op. cit.
83 See 'Report on the "Compound System"' submitted to
P. FitzPatrick by the Commission of Compound Managers
and Engineers, reprinted in the 'SA Mines', 25 April

1903, which referred to Kimberley compounds as a
'Kaffir Valhalla', and said that 'At Kimberley, Mr.
Gardner Williams reigns supreme.   Whilst the
different Rand houses have been arguing over wages,
introduction of white and coloured labour etc. Mr.
Williams, who has no one to gainsay him, sent his
labour agents to recruit, and the result is that
today De Beers' compounds are full.'

84   See 'SA Mines', 4 April 1903, for reports of several
proposals for the importation of indentured Chinese
labour, particularly one made by Farrar.   But in 'SA
Mines', 18 February 1905, a grass-roots ideologist -
the Chairman of the AMM - was given credit for the
idea.

85   The Housing of Mine Employees, part of a speech by
FitzPatrick at the Annual Meeting of Rand Mines Ltd,
25 March 1903.

86   The Inter-Colonial Conference, held in Bloemfontein in
1903 on the 'native question', proposed residential
locations for black workers.   For a comment on this
see 'SA Mines', 21 March 1903.

87   'SA Mines', 3 October 1903.   Little is known about
the use of Italian labour on the mines, but it is
certain that they were introduced often to undercut
British workers, in this decade.   In one letter to
the 'SA Mines', 1 December 1906, 'A Miner' described
how British workers had been sacked to make way for
cheap Italians on one mine saying 'It was a
distinctly unfriendly act on the part of the
capitalist towards the British miners ... there is
today hardly a mine without its Italian colony of
miners.'   This was 'part of the underhand, cunning
anti-British-miner policy of the capitalist'.

88   'SA Mines', 14 November 1903, reported that someone
had suggested bringing 100,000 Russian Jews to South
Africa.

89   See Davies, Mining capital ..., who gives great emphasis to this economic factor, dismissing Johnstone's
emphasis on the 'political freedom' of white workers.

90   Speech to Rand Mines.

91   Editorial, 'SA Mines', 28 November 1903.

92   Carl Hanau, Presidential Address to the 1903 Annual
Meeting of the Johannesburg Consolidated Investment
Company, Ltd.

93   C.D. Rudd, Director of Gold Fields Ltd, memorandum to
'Transvaal Labour Commission, 1903'.

94   Letter to the 'Transvaal Labour Commission,
1903', op. cit., from Percy Tarbutt, Director of
Gold Fields Ltd, Chairman of Village Main Reef mine.

95 George Farrar, speech at Driefontein, op. cit., 1903, reprinted in the 'Report of the Transvaal Labour Commission, 1903', op. cit., as well as in 'SA Mines', as above.

96 Objections to the importation of Russian Jews are set out in 'SA Mines', 14 November 1903.

97 Editorial, 'SA Mines', 15 August 1903.

98 'SA Mines', 5 September 1903.

99 Editorial, 'SA Mines', 12 September 1903.

100 Carl Hanau, Presidential Address, 1903.

101 'SA Mines', 5 December 1903, reported that the Chamber had decided by a majority to urge the importation of Chinese labourers, but that a minority still supported the idea of cheap white workers.

102 Ibid.

103 Editorial, 'SA Mines', 12 December 1903.

104 Transvaal Labour Importation Ordinance of 1904. (Ordinance 17, 1904, Article 9, Schedule I.)

105 Editorial, 'SA Mines', 9 January 1904.

106 This list, therefore, constituted the first comprehensive systematised 'job colour bar' and has been seen by Johnstone as having 'set a precedent for the extension of the job colour bar in coming years', Johnstone, op. cit., p. 67.   According to 'SA Mines', 30 January 1904, the list of prescribed jobs was drawn up by Farrar.

107 Fourteen 'Boer' leaders signed a protest against the use of Chinese labour in February 1904 which they submitted, to no avail, to the High Commissioner. It was probably motivated by a concern that unskilled Afrikaner workers would be replaced by the Chinese. Black 'representatives', such as Chief Linchwe of the Bakhatla, also objected, but could be treated some- what more highhandedly.   See 'SA Mines', 21 November 1903.

108 'SA Mines', 23 July 1904, mentioned 'malicious attempts' in the press to show that the Chinese, who had by then begun to arrive on the mines, were not a success, and mentioned that 'discipline in the compounds' was 'improving', and that 'matters are gradually settling down and less difficulty is experienced in handling the boys there.'   Desertions were mentioned.   They were referring to black worker 'unrest'.   In September black desertions were continuing: 'SA Mines', 10 September 1905.

109 'SA Mines', 4 March 1905.   Moreover, recruitment figures for black workers were also said to have gone up: 'During the half-year, each succeeding month a fresh high water mark has been recorded in the annals of Rand labour getting.'

110   F.D.P. Chaplin, President of the Chamber of Mines for
      1905 calculated that for a comparable period of three
      years, the Chinese worker cost £14 10s to acquire,
      while the black worker cost only £10 15: 'Nor is
      there any question of recouping this expenditure by
      the provision of inferior food or the payment of
      lower wages. ... At the Simmer and Jack Proprietary
      Mine the average cost of feeding the Chinese works
      out at 11d per head per day as compared with 5d per
      head per day in the case of Kaffirs.'   The Chinaman
      as Mr Chaplin has Found Him, 'SA Mines', 11 March
      1905.
111   Ibid.   See also 'SA Mines', 18 March 1905, where it
      was claimed that the number of whites had risen from
      12   to 14,873 since the Chinese had come.
112   Dr F.C. Sutherland: How the Mines care for Unskilled
      Labour: Minimising Disease and Increasing
      Efficiency, 'SA Mines', 15 April 1905.
113   'SA Mines', 8 July 1905.
114   'SA Mines', 16 December 1905.
115   'SA Mines', 8 July 1905, mentioned, but did not
      describe in detail, the 'disturbances' on mines using
      Chinese.   The two main disturbances seem to have
      occurred on the 'Wit Deep' mine; and the 'Croesus'
      mine.   At the former, there was a riot.   By 22 July
      of that year the journal reported that so many
      'disturbances' were occurring on mines where Chinese
      were employed, that the Chamber of Mines had
      recommended the moving of armed forces from the
      country to mining areas in case the police were not
      enough.   This was done; on 26 August of that year
      the journal said that 'extra precautions' were needed
      to prevent Chinese 'desertions', since Chinese
      workers were said to have been found 'roaming in
      large gangs'.
116   'SA Mines', 20 May 1905.
117   The speech was by Major Collins, a 'prominent leader
      of the industry', 'SA Mines', 8 July 1905.
118   Ibid.   He concluded 'properly handled, a Chinaman is
      worth two Kaffirs'.
119   1903, speech to Rand Mines, op. cit.
120   See 'SA Mines', 22 October 1905, amongst other
      references to this matter.
121   The Inflation of Working Costs by Inefficient Labour,
      'SA Mines', 24 March 1906, reported that 50 unskilled
      whites per week applied for jobs on one mine alone.
122   See for example, the Editorial, 'SA Mines', 20
      October 1906.
123   Editorial, 'SA Mines', 24 November 1906.

124   Editorial, 'SA Mines', 2 February 1907.   Solomon was
      called a 'negrophilist'.
125   On 14 April 1906 the journal proclaimed success since
      its efficiency campaign had as yet been 'unrefuted'
      by spokesmen for mining; by 2 June 1906, it could
      claim that the existence of 'inefficiency' was now
      'generally conceded'.
126   Is Mining Labour Becoming Less Efficient, 'SA Mines',
      17 February 1906.   The article gave figures of
      'employees per stamp' which indicated the 'organic'
      nature of production and the changing proportions of
      different coloured workers:
      Employees per stamp, 1899-1905

Date	Whites	Coloured (black)	Chinese	Total
July 1899	1.89	16.5	-	18.4
June 1902	2.3	11.8	-	14.1
November 1903	2.1	11.88	-	13.9
June 1904	2.09	12.87	-	14.9
June 1905	1.9	13.1	5.1	20.1
November 1905	1.9	11.3	5.5	18.7

127   Editorial, Wanted - Efficient Miners, 'SA Mines',
      24 February 1906.
128   Our Mining Results Compared with Westralia's, 'SA
      Mines', 3 March 1906.
129   The Inflation of Working Costs by Inefficient Labour,
      'SA Mines', 17 March 1906.
130   Editorial, 'SA Mines', 7 April 1906.
131   Ibid.
132   'SA Mines', 28 April 1906.   Rathbone was not the
      editor at the time.
133   Is Native Labour Cheap?, 'SA Mines', 16 June 1906.
134   H.J. and R.E. Simons, op. cit., p. 87.
135   'SA Mines', 13 October 1906.   The white rock
      drillers had met and sent a deputation in protest,
      saying that the system would make them unemployed,
      their pay would not increase but the physical strain
      involved would.
136   H.J. and R.E. Simons, op. cit., p. 87.
137   See 'SA Mines', 4 May, 11 May, 18 May and 25 May
      1907, and throughout the months of June and July, for
      material on this strike.
138   'SA Mines', 18 May 1907.
139   'SA Mines', 25 May 1907.
140   Ibid.
141   Editorial, 'SA Mines', 22 June 1907.
142   'SA Mines', 29 June 1907.
143   In 'SA Mines', 18 May 1907, it was suggested that:
      'Clean compounds, the regulation cubic air space,

blankets, short hours and good food are not enough to
keep the native.   He must have his patch of ground,
his wife and family with him, and all he now goes
home for.'   These ideas were reiterated in the
issues of 25 May, 1 June, 20 July and others.   In
addition, E.P. Rathbone supported this campaign in
Britain, having already written an article in the
journal 'Nineteenth Century', August 1906, entitled
The Problem of Home Life in South Africa, in which he
advocated the full proletarianisation of blacks and
their settlement near the mines and towns.

144 Johnstone, op. cit., pp. 2-3.   (As will have been
made clear, in this analysis the distinctions between
'white' and 'non-white' workers have been made on the
basis of a larger number of factors than just
political freedom.)

3   THE SEEDS OF A NATIONAL BOURGEOISIE

1 'Standard and Diggers' News', 30 November 1893;   I am
grateful to Charles van Onselen for making available
to me his material from the 'Standard and Diggers'
News' and other sources on this and other subjects
during the 1890s.

2 See 'The Critic', 20 April, 22 June and 19 October
1894 for articles on The Ring in Mining Machinery.
A complex system of interlocking directorships,
involving Howard Farrar and his brother, mining
magnate George Farrar, Julius Wernher, Alfred Beit,
the British firms of F.A. Robinson and Co. and
Fraser and Chalmers Ltd, and a number of other
individuals and companies, preserved the supply of
mining machinery for firms approved of by mining.

3 'Standard and Diggers' News', 5 April 1894.

4 'SA Mines', 19 December 1903.

5 Ibid., Report on a Bluebook on South African Trade,
by Birchenough.

6 As far as the secondary literature is concerned,
those studies written outside of the recent liberal
tradition in South African historiography tend to
give more emphasis to the development of early
manufacturing than do liberal writers;   see, for
example, such studies as M.H. de Kock, 'Selected
Subjects in the Economic History of South Africa',
Cape Town, 1924, chapter 10;   L.C.A. Knowles, 'The
Economic Development of the British Overseas
Empire', vol. 3, London, 1936, pp. 297ff;   and D.M.
Goodfellow, 'Economic History of South Africa',

London, 1931, all of which precede the era of high
liberalism.   See also B. Bozzoli, The Origins,
Development and Ideology of Local Manufacturing in
South Africa, 'Journal of Southern African Studies',
vol. 1, no. 2, April 1975.   The reasons for this
are complex.   Centrally, they lie in the fact that
the liberal tradition is heavily evolutionist, and
prefers to perceive manufacturing as the next stage
after mining; see, for example, the evolutionist,
Rostowian interpretations of D. Hobart Houghton,
'The South African Economy', 2nd edition, Cape Town,
1967, or R. Horwitz, 'The Political Economy of South
Africa', London, 1967.

7   According to Laite, of the whole value of industrial
produce, gold and diamonds were worth 34 per cent,
manufacturing 33 per cent, agriculture 17.2 per cent
and 'pastoral' 9.8 per cent.   See W.J. Laite, 'The
Union Tariff and its Relation to Industrial and
Agricultural Development: The Case for
Manufacturers', Cape Town, 1913, pp. 11-12.   This
was a figure commonly referred to by manufacturers
themselves, as demonstrating the fact that a 'false
appreciation of the country's economy' existed; see
for example, Report of the Congress of the South
African Manufacturers' Association, Chairman's
Address, in 'South African Commerce and Manufacturers'
Record' (hereafter known as 'SAC'), 3, 31, November
1909, where manufacturing produce was again said to
be worth 33 per cent of the total.

8   The Census of 1904 gave the proportions as follows:

Colony	Number of institutions		Value of machinery and plant		Value of material used		Value of articles produced	
	No.		£		£		£	
Cape	2,527	53.0	2,280,336	39.0	5,843,593	52.0	9,040,579	47.0
Natal	749	15.0	1,408,342	25.0	1,892,408	17.0	3,683,608	19.0
Transvaal	1,353	28.0	1,920,471	32.5	3,247,611	29.0	6,289,402	32.5
ORC	149	3.0	197,129	3.5	223,211	2.0	279,101	1.5
Total	4,778	100	5,806,278	100	11,206,823	100	19,292,690	100

9   The average value of machinery and plant was
£1,200 per factory in 1904.

10   'In too many cases, their time, capital and energies,
have been devoted to keeping their concerns from
disaster, and they have had little inclination for
public affairs', according to John Rothes, The Truth
About Protection of Colonial Industries, 'SAC', 1,
4, August 1907.

11   In 1883, 1891 and 1904 Cape manufacturing industries
had been considered important enough to warrant

committees of enquiry into them - significantly, all
three were depression years - while one was held in
Natal in 1905 and another, the Customs and Industries
Commission, in the Transvaal in 1908.   See Rothes,
op. cit., and, for the Natal case, S. Marks,
'Reluctant Rebellion', Oxford, 1970, p. 49.   In
1899 a conference of manufacturers was held in
Grahamstown and an unsuccessful petition presented to
Schreiner, Prime Minister of the Cape, asking for a
revision of the Customs Tariff.   According to the
'Transvaal Leader', 18 August 1899, Schreiner said in
reply that 'he was convinced that South Africa would
never be largely a manufacturing country'.

12   'Colonial Industries; Being an Enquiry into their
Progress and Present Condition and the Effects of the
Customs Tariff Upon Them', reprinted from the 'Cape
Times', 1906.

13   'SAC', 1, 2, June 1907.

14   The 'SAC' was the central journal of manufacturing in
these early years.   Like the 'SAMJ' and 'Commercial
Bulletin', it aimed to reflect and express the views
of members of its section and to provide a forum for
ideological creativity.   The opening issue
proclaimed that it was 'a monthly journal devoted to
the furtherance of the interests of Manufacturers and
Merchants, and circulating in every part of South,
East and West Africa, and all Corresponding houses in
Europe and America' 'SAC', 1, 1, May 1907.

15   This was a union of MPs and public men of the Bond,
Progressive and Independent Parties, under the
leadership of F.S. Malan and George Duncan and was a
powerful pro-South Africanist and protectionist
pressure group which published its own pamphlets,
journal and yearbook, held many meetings, and
mobilised support amongst farmers.   It is
unfortunate that so little is known about this early
voice of capitalist farming.   See 'SAC', 1, 6,
October 1907; the SANU Journal, 'The Official Organ
of the South African National Union' (circa 1908-10);
SANU pamphlets 1-47; SANU 'Annual', 1910-11 etc.,
and SANU 'Annual Reports', 1914-28.

16   This too was under the Presidency of F.S. Malan and
had the support of men such as W.P. Schreiner, George
Duncan, J.A.C. Graaff, C.W.H. Kohler, as well as
many prominent manufacturers.   In 1907 it held its
first meeting in Cape Town and the 'SAC' reported
that it was 'well-received by a large audience'.
See 'SAC', 1, 7, November 1907, and 'SAC', 1, 8,
December 1907, for reports of this Association, about
which, like SANU, all too little is known.

17 Based in Port Elizabeth, this combined manufacturers and white workers, through such organisations as the Master Builders and Allied Trades Association, the Typographical Society, the Carpenters' and Joiners' Union, and the Trades and Labour Council, as well as the 'Grocer's Association', and the 'South East Farmers' Co-operative'.   There is no mention of it, however, besides 'SAC', 1, 5, September 1907.
18 Editorial, 'SAC', 1, 5, September 1907.
19 See 'SA Mines', from 5 August to 23 December 1905.
20 Rothes, op. cit.
21 For biographical details about Laite see Harold J. Laite, 'Portrait of a Pioneer: The Life and Work of William James Laite, 1863-1942', Cape Town, 1943.
22 These details are from: 'SAC', 11, 121, May 1917.
23 See 'SAC', 3, 29, September 1909.   Other 'pioneers' were, for example, Captain H.A.P. Burmeister, by 1909 owner of South African Candle Works, who was German born and went to sea before coming to South Africa in 1881; W. Ruthven-Hall, who was said to have been 'born amongst the tanneries of South East London', and whose father was a builder, but who had somehow obtained a university education and was by 1910 manager of a harness-making firm; or Thomas Kirk, by 1910 Manager and Director of Buffalo Roller Mills of East London, who had started as an eight-year-old half-time worker in worsted mills in Britain, and by thirteen had become a full-timer. See, for further examples, the series Pioneers of Industry run in the 'SAC' during 1909-10.
24 Many examples of this appeared in descriptions of manufacturers in the journal. See, for example, Laite's editorial, 'SAC', 1, 1, May 1907, in which he said that besides 'perseverance', manufacturers needed 'business aptitude, merit, the determination to create a market ... and co-operation with the dealer and consumer'. Rothes, op. cit., referred to similar required qualities, as did G.J. Bruce, in Manufacturers and the Regulation of Wages, 'SAC', 1, 1, May 1907.
25 E.J. Hobsbawm describes how in Britain 'The capitalist manufacturers of the first phase of industrial revolution were - or saw themselves as - a pioneering minority seeking to establish an economic system in an environment by no means entirely favourable to it. ... The epics of the rise of the Victorian Middle class, as preserved in the works of Samuel Smiles, looked back to an often quite mythical era of heroes of self-help. ... What is equally to

the point, they were themselves men formed by their
past - all the more so as they lacked scientific
education and prided themselves above all on
empiricism' ('Industry and Empire', Harmondsworth,
1969, p. 121). See also David Rogers and Ivar E.
Berg, Occupation and Ideology: The case of the Small
Businessman, 'Human Organization', vol. 20, 1961-2.

26 In September 1908, the 'SAC' announced that there was
a 'scheme afoot' to unite all the manufacturers'
associations; and in December of that year reported
that this scheme had in fact succeeded. However the
Transvaal Association later broke away from the
larger, national association, and proper unity was
not restored until 1917.

27 Transvaal industries resented Cape ones for their
stability and their access to 'cheap coloured
labour'. See 'SAC', 1, 2, June 1907 for a report on
the formation of the Transvaal Association and the
speech by its President, E.E. Hart, who hoped it 'was
possible, while still remaining within the (customs)
Union, to devise a means of protecting the local
industries and producing interests, not only against
overseas competition, but also against the longer
established industries of a kindred nature at coastal
ports, who were mainly carried on by the use of
skilled coloured labour. He felt sure that
manufacturers in the Transvaal were capable of
holding their own against Colonial competition, where
the economic conditions were similar; but they did
object most strongly to compete on the same basis
with the skilled coloured labour of the other
Colonies. They could not compete with coloured
races, whose standard of living was immeasurably
inferior to their own, whose working hours were
longer, whose wants were less, and whose wages were
very much lower than what they pay to their own
employees.' For more detail on the problems of
customs tariffs in this pre-union era, see L.M.
Thompson, 'The Unification of South Africa, 1902-
1910', Oxford, 1960, especially pp. 59-60, and
Knowles, op. cit., chapter 13, Trade Relations. So
deep did this conflict go that in 1907 the Transvaal
denounced and left the Intercolonial Customs
Convention claiming it was designed to disadvantage
Transvaal Industries. See W. Smale-Adams, The
Transvaal and the Customs Convention, 'SAC', 1, 3,
July 1907, and other reports in that issue.

28 Editorial', SAC', 3, 34, February 1910.

29 'The Commission on Trade and Industries', U.G. 10,
1912.

30 In this sense the commission's report reflected
     accurately the balance of interests and power on the
     issue of industrialisation at the time, in the whole
     society.
31 W.J. Laite, op. cit.
32 The wavering of Smuts on the issue came to be some-
     thing of a *cause célèbre* in manufacturing circles.
     He appeared, from his budget speech of 1914,
     according to the 'SAC', to have 'turned a complete
     economic somersault' from being in favour of
     protection at an earlier stage, to opposing or
     doubting it now.   See 'SAC', 7, 85, May 1914.
     Later, he became one of the most ardent
     protectionists in the South African Party.
33 Part of this smoothing-over process was performed by
     referring to the local conflicts between the Cape and
     Transvaal as 'petty jealousies' or 'parochialism'.
     By implication, 'rationality' lay in Union.
34 This division was at its clearest in the Transvaal,
     where two completely distinct commercial
     associations were formed in the 1890s.   The
     Johannesburg Mercantile Association, on the one
     hand, represented 'local' commerce; while on the
     other, the Chamber of Commerce was said by observers
     to be 'in league' with the Chamber of Mines.   See
     the 'Standard and Diggers' News', 24 January 1894 for
     discussions of this.   But similar splits must have
     existed all over the country.   Even in the earliest
     years of their development, manufacturers would refer
     to local commercial associations and groups which
     supported them, distinguishing them from their
     primary enemy, the large importing houses.
35 Reported in 'SAC', 3, 28, August 1909.
36 One of the 'SAC' 'Pioneers of Industry', D. Isaacs,
     had begun as an importer, but by 1909 was owner of a
     furniture factory, Isaacs and Co. Ltd; H. Holt, in
     1909 Manager and Chairman of United Tobacco Co. (SA)
     Ltd, had also begun as a tobacco trader.   See 'SAC',
     3, 27, July 1909, and 3, 28, August 1909.
37 Rothes, op. cit.
38 See, for example, T.G. Trevor, The Industrial
     Development of South Africa: a Historical Sketch:
     Part One, 'South African Journal of Industries', vol.
     4, no. 2, February 1921, in which he describes how he
     wanted to start a blanket factory but was told by
     local storekeepers that the houses to which they were
     bound would not allow them to trade in locally-
     produced goods.   Rothes, op. cit., also describes
     this system, while an anonymous article in 'SAC', 5,

49, May 1911, described how in the early years
manufacturers had had to distribute their own goods,
because merchants had refused to do so; this had led
manufacturers to establish relationships directly
with retailers.

39   W.J. Laite, op. cit., p. 30.
40   Editorial, 'SAC', 1, 7, 1907.
41   Rothes, op. cit.
42   W.J. Laite, op. cit., p. 8 and more generally, pp.
     7-10.
43   Editorial, 'SAC', 4, 41, September 1910: 'The
     constitution of the two great Parties who today are
     contending for power, is an insult to the intelligence
     of all right-thinking people. ... The great principle
     of Protection, which has split in twain the electors
     of every civilised country in the world, finds
     supporters under both existing party umbrellas,
     whilst adherents to the worn-out creed of so-called
     Free Trade claim brotherhood in the ranks of both
     Unionists and Nationalists'; this was another
     example of the early 'ideology of non-ideology'.
44   W.J. Laite, op. cit., p. 38.
45   Ibid., 'Manufacturers were hardly regarded as
     respectable people; bank managers were sceptical of
     their bona fides, and traders turned away from their
     wares', p. 37.   No manufacturer appeared in 'Who's
     Who', or on the membership lists of the elitist
     social clubs of the Rand or Cape Town.
46   W.J. Laite, op. cit., pp. 50-1.
47   The Gospel According to Samuel Evans, 'SAC', 5, 55,
     November 1911.   Samuel Evans campaigned unceasingly
     for Free Trade right into the 1920s by which time it
     had become a distinctly less fashionable issue; see
     S. Evans, Public Expenditure and Taxation in South
     Africa; Whither are we Drifting? The Coming Crises,
     'The Star', 16 March 1926.   For an earlier statement
     of his views see S. Evans, Free Trade and Protection
     in South Africa: Rhodes v. Cullinan, 'SA Mines',
     September 1912.
48   Evidence of O'K. Webber and E. Farrar to the
     'Commission on Trade and Industries, 1912' (Cullinan
     Commission), quoted in W.J. Laite, op. cit., p. 50.
49   Anon. article, 'SAC', 1, 9, January 1908.
50   Editorial: The Miners' Strike, 'SAC', 1, 2, June
     1907.
51   Editorial, 'SAC', 4, 39, July 1910.
52   Rothes, op. cit.
53   Editorial, 'SAC', 7, 82, February 1914.
54   Lessons of the Strike, 'SAC', 7, 76, August 1913.

55 Quoted in H.E. King, The South African National
    Union: Its Part in Development, 'South African
    Journal of Industries', February 1919.
56 'By establishing industries using imported raw
    materials, a market is created, and new opportunities
    arise for farmers and other producers', wrote W.J.
    Laite, op. cit., p. 5, while A.B. Reid, prominent
    member of SANU and manufacturer, spoke in 1913 of how
    there was an 'identity of interest' between farmer
    and manufacturer based on the fact that both needed
    domestic trade more than foreign trade, while farmers
    needed more consumers if they were to develop.
57 'SAC', 4, 42, October 1910.
58 Editorial: The Rise of Labour, 'SAC', 7, 84, April
    1914.
59 Dr (?) Schlesinger, speech to the first annual
    general meeting of the Transvaal Chamber of
    Industries, August 1908; reported 'SAC', 2, 17,
    September 1908.
60 Laite frequently extolled the virtues of 'work'.
    See for example, his editorial,'SAC', 2, 18, October
    1908 on 'the value of work', and another in 'SAC',
    4, 42, October 1910.
61 'SAC', 7, 85, May 1914, and also the editorial,
    'SAC', 5, 51, July 1911.
62 H.P. Gordon, The Labour Party and the Bloemfontein
    Platform, 'SAC', 6, 59, February 1912.
63 Schlesinger, speech, op. cit., and W.J. Laite, op.
    cit., p. 5.
64 See The Opinion of the Ladies, 'SAC', 2, 19,
    November 1908, in which is expressed a somewhat
    peevish resentment that it was women whose
    preferences determined whether or not local goods
    sold in the face of overseas competition: 'There is
    something delightfully feminine in the complaint that
    candles are quite as dear as the imported, and we
    have an idea that this is at the bottom of much of
    the boycott to which colonial manufacturers have been
    subjected.   There has existed a hazy conception in
    the minds of many of our lady friends that Colonial
    goods cannot be as good as the imported, and
    consequently ought to be cheaper.'
65 Bruce, op. cit.
66 See, for example, The Influence Behind the Worker,
    'SAC', 9, 101, September 1915, in which the role of
    the nuclear family in encouraging this belief, is
    discussed.
67 Bruce, op. cit.
68 Anon. article, Loyalty in Business, 'SAC', 9, 99, July
    1915.

69   'SAC', 5, 51, July 1911.   See also H.P. Gordon, A
     Wages Board and a Minimum Wage, 'SAC', 5, 55,
     November 1911:   'The white eage-earner is being so
     rapidly displaced by the coloured wage-earner in
     certain trades and occupations that unless a minimum
     wage is made a matter of compulsion not only will
     white skilled workers leave South Africa, but no
     workmen from overseas will be likely to come here
     and chance their luck in competition with a low-waged
     coloured proletariat.'
70   A Grave Outlook, 'SAC', 1, 3, July 1907.
71   This and the subsequent extracts are from Lessons of
     the Strike.
72   The Rise of Labour, op. cit.   This was written in
     1914 after the Labour Party had made electoral gains.
73   Editorial, 'SAC', 1, 12, April 1908.
74   Archibald Campbell, Arbitration and Conciliation,
     'SAC', 3, 26, June 1909.   He was supported by Laite
     in that month's editorial.
75   H.P. Gordon, a Wages Board, op. cit.   At the 1911
     Annual Meeting of the South African Manufacturers'
     Association, a resolution was passed advocating that
     'the best method of avoiding future industrial
     disputes, strikes and lockouts is the formation of
     conciliation and Wages Boards';   'SAC', 5, 45,
     January 1911.
76   Strike, 'SAC', 6, 82, 1914.
77   'SAC', 1, 8, December 1907.
78   Op. cit.
79   Anonymous notes, 'SAC', 4, 46, February 1911.
80   Editorial, 'SAC', 4, 46, February 1911.
81   Editorial, 'SAC', 4, 47, March 1911.
82   One article referred to the 'woven business network'
     that covered South Africa, an entirely different, and
     characteristic, metaphor which contrasts with the
     mining 'centre-periphery' concept.   See 'SAC', 2,
     14, July 1908.
83   C.W.H. Kohler, The Truth about the Wine Industry,
     'SAC', 2, 14, July 1908.   For a later example see
     anon., The Native as Market, 'South African Journal
     of Industries', II, 2, February 1919.   The entire
     issue of the market is discussed at length in chapter
     5.
84   Editorial, 'SAC', 7, 69, January 1913.
85   'SAC', 1, 9, January 1908.   In striking contrast to
     the ideologists of mining, manufacturing ideologists
     expressed disapproval of the system of 'isibalo' or
     forced labour prevalent in Natal;   see 'SAC', 4, 43,
     November 1910.
86   Editorial, 'SAC', 1, 4, August 1907.

87 'SAC', 5, 55, November 1911, where it is claimed that
    'In Germany they know what Protection is and should
    be.   They don't worry over there about trusts and
    combinations, except to encourage and help them in
    order to secure the advantages of capital.   They
    don't complain of the cost of living, as they
    recognise that a Protective Tariff provides work for
    their masses, and contentment always follows well-
    paid and regular labour.   There are no "tariffs-for-
    revenue purposes" in Germany; no section of the
    mercantile community losing sleep because they think
    the manufacturer is making a little profit.   Neither
    does Germany handicap her farmers by letting in
    cheaper products without paying duties. ... There are
    many things in Germany's economic and industrial
    policy which might with advantage be studied and
    imitated in South Africa', etc.
88 See Rothes, op. cit.; W.J. Laite, op. cit., and many
    other examples of ideologists referring to these
    countries for comparative insights into their own
    needs and requirements, from the details of
    protection, to the broad principles, and details as
    well, of industrial legislation.   Rothes wrote with
    resentment that South Africa was the only British
    possession 'of any consequence enjoying responsible
    government which is not fostering and building up
    local industries by a settled policy of protection.
    Nowhere else in the world, where the vigorous races
    of Europe have settled permanently, have they made so
    little progress in the arts and industries of
    civilisation.'
89 J.M. Buckland, speech at first annual general meeting
    of the Transvaal Chamber of Industries, August 1908;
    'SAC', 2, 17, September 1908.
90 A.B. Reid, Chairman's Address to the South African
    Industrial Parliament, reported in 'SAC', 6, 61,
    May 1912.
91 A.B. Reid, Chairman's Address to the annual meeting
    of the South African Manufacturers' Association,
    January 1911.
92 See 'SAC', 2, 19, November 1908, and The Opinion of
    the Ladies.
93 A.H. Moore, speech reported in 'Industrial South
    Africa', 17, 187, November 1922.
94 A.B. Reid, 1911 address, op. cit.
95 'SAC', 5, 45, January 1911.
96 'SAC' (comment on the formation of the South African
    National Alliance), 1, 6, October 1907.
97 The Commercial Aspect of Closer Union, op. cit.

98   'SAC', 3, 34, February 1910.
99   Ibid.
100 'SAC', 4, 42, October 1910.
101 Hiram Strong, Wanted: A National Party with a
     National Policy, 'SAC', 1, 5, September 1907.
102 Ibid.   Calls for a 'national party' were to become a
     hallmark of South Africanism in later years, as this
     study shows; while at this early stage they were
     linked to the demand for total Union between colonies
     and for ties between members of that union that would
     prevent secessions. See, for further examples, The
     Commercial Aspect of Closer Union, and 'SAC', 3, 34,
     February 1910 for a discussion of the reasons why a
     National Party had not materialised and could not at
     that stage.
103 Laite also urged manufacturers in the 1910 elections
     'to give their wholehearted support to those
     candidates who are prepared to pledge themselves to a
     policy of industrial expansion and who are willing to
     place principle before party'.   'SAC', 4, 41,
     September 1910.
104 A.B. Reid, 1911 Address, op. cit.
105 E. Chinoy, 'Automobile Workers and the American
     Dream', Boston, 1965.

4 THE EMERGING CONTENDER

  1 There have been several papers written on this topic,
     including D. Kaplan, Capitalist Development in South
     Africa: Class Conflict and the State, M. Fransman
     and R. Davies, The South African Social Formation in
     the Early Capitalist Period Circa 1870-1939: Some
     Views on the Question of Hegemony, both in T. Adler
     (ed.), 'Perspectives on South Africa', Johannesburg,
     1977, and most recently, R. Davies, D. Kaplan,
     M. Morris and D. O'Meara, Class Struggle and the
     Periodisation of the State in South Africa, 'Review
     of African Political Economy', 7, September-
     December 1976, all written in terms of Poulantzas's
     conceptions of hegemony and periodisation.
     Critiques of this approach have been made in S.
     Clarke, Capital, 'Fractions' of Capital and the
     State: 'Neo-Marxist' Analyses of the South African
     State, 'Capital and Class', 5, Summer 1978 and B.
     Bozzoli, Capital and the State in South Africa,
     'Review of African Political Economy', 11, January-
     April 1978.
  2 Editorial,'South African Commerce and Manufacturers'
     Record' (hereafter 'SAC'), 8, 89, September 1914.

3   For these and other statistics see 'Union Statistics
    for Fifty Years', Jubilee Issue, 1910-60, Pretoria,
    1960.   However, as is pointed out on p. 150 *infra*
    the amount of local raw materials used was still
    comparatively low.   For other indications of the
    growth during the war see D. Hobart Houghton and
    J. Dagut (eds), 'Source Material on the South African
    Economy, 1860-1970', vol. 2, 1899-1919, Cape Town,
    1972, pp. 214ff.   See also E.G. Saunders, Industry
    and Labour in South Africa, 'Industrial South
    Africa' (hereafter 'ISA'), 13, 139, November 1918,
    which contains a description of the effects of the
    war on one industry – the match industry: 'Prior to
    1906 a match factory established in Natal imported
    manufactured splints, boxes and packing cases;   all
    it did was to tip the matches, pack them in boxes and
    despatch them in the cases.   Step by step the under-
    taking passed from this easy form of assembling to
    actual manufacture.   In 1906 a splint factory was
    opened for which wood was imported direct from
    Russia.   In 1910 the making of boxes was started,
    again from imported wood. ... As a result of further
    progress in self-support, the importation of timber
    was, from 1915, stopped altogether and supplies of
    native wood were purchased. ... It is almost
    unnecessary to emphasise the fact that the existence
    of a local source of supply has been of great value
    under war conditions.'   This gives some small
    indication of the qualitative as well as quantitative
    nature of the changes during the war.
4   Some regional autonomy was allowed to persist within
    this early organisation, but it did represent the
    first indication that the ideologists' slow task of
    forging unity within the manufacturing fraction had
    at last borne fruit.
5   'SAC', 11, 127, November 1917.
6   Editorial, 'SAC', 10, 116, December 1916.
7   'ISA', 13, 136, August 1918.
8   'ISA', 13, 140, December 1918.
9   'SAC', 10, 114, October 1916.
10 According to the editorial in the 'SAJI', VI, 12,
    December 1923, 'commercial men' were 'becoming more
    interested in industrial development';   the President
    of Assocom for that year, R. Stuttaford, had pointed
    out that at its congress of that year there had been
    a 'much more noticeable disposition' towards the
    acceptance of 'production as a thing South Africa
    would depend on in future'.
11 'Commercial Bulletin' (hereafter 'CB'), XI, 129,
    October 1933.

12 At the 1934 Bulawayo conference of Assocom,
commercial and industrial interests were represented
'for the first time ... on an official and personal
scale', 'CB', XII, 139, August 1934. Commercial and
industrial representatives attended meetings of each
others' organisations, and a merger between them was
proposed about this time.

13 See, amongst many examples, J.W. Mushet, Presidential
Address to the 33rd Annual Congress of Assocom, 1931;
or H.C. Gearing, Presidential Address to the 1936
Convention of the FCI.

14 J.E. Borain, Presidential Address to the FCI Annual
Convention, 1929.

15 H.C. Gearing, Presidential Address to the FCI Annual
Convention, 1927.

16 Thus when Smuts introduced a protective tariff in
1923 it catered for the interests of this group.
See editorial, 'ISA', 18, 192, April 1923: 'With the
exception of the Footwear and Confectionery
Industries, the Board has confined its efforts to the
study of conditions affecting a number of small
propositions in which the importing community are not
particularly interested.' More is said about this
in chapter 6.

17 See C.H. Malan (Minister of Railways), speech to the
Annual Convention of the FCI, 1930, 'Industrial and
Commercial South Africa' (hereafter 'ICSA'), 25, 282,
October 1930: 'This attitude [towards the Board of
Trade and Industries] contrasts very favourably with
that of sections of the commercial community who, I
regret to observe, have gone out of their way to
belittle the value of the proposed enquiry'; as late
as 1934, conflict between commerce and industry over
the degree of protection erupted: see 'Commercial
Bulletin', XII, 138, July 1934, for example, for
details of this conflict, and 'ICSA', 29, 326, June
1934, where an article on The Leopard's Spots pointed
out that 'The anti-industrial policy of the Chambers
of Commerce, after slumbering uneasily for some time
has again awakened into activity', and after a
scathing review of the 'Commercial Bulletin''s
support for this 'anti-industrial policy', concluded
that, 'If the article in the Bulletin really reflects
commercial opinion, it is to be feared that [the]
suggestion that Commerce and Industry should link up
in one organisation is likely to be received with a
certain amount of scepticism.'

18 'CB', X, 115, August 1932.

19 Ibid.

20 Editorial, 'CB', X, 121, February 1933.
21 Ibid.
22 J.E. Borain, Presidential Address, 1929, op. cit.
23 Ibid.
24 See editorial, 'SAC', 10, 116, December 1916.
25 Frank Gibaud, speech to the Cape Manufacturers'
    Association, reported in 'ISA', 17, 177, January
    1922.   See also A.H. Moore, speech reported in
    'ISA', 17, 187, November 1922, and other examples.
26 Reported in 'SAC', 11, 125, September 1917.
27 For example, at an agricultural congress in
    Bloemfontein in November 1922, farmers agreed to
    support manufacturers in their demand for protection.
    See 'ISA', 17, 187, November 1922.
28 For an outline of the growth of SANU, see H.E. King,
    The South African National Union: Its Part in
    Development, 'SAJI', II, 2, February 1919.
29 Mentioned in 'ISA', 18, 192, April 1923.
30 See 'ISA', 18, 189, January 1923.
31 'ISA', 18, 192, April 1923: 'A little while ago Mr.
    Martin, in addressing a meeting of agriculturalists,
    expressed his surprise - and if we remember rightly,
    his abhorrence - at the action of the South African
    Agricultural Union entering into a working
    arrangement with the Chamber of Industries.   He even
    went so far as to state that such a policy would
    prove detrimental to the farmer, as their best policy
    was to cultivate exports and to get closer to the
    mercantile community who had the handling of their
    products.'
32 S.H. Frankel, 'The Railway Policy of South Africa',
    Johannesburg, 1929.   See below, note 44.
33 See D. Hobart Houghton, op. cit., p. 115; in the
    early 1930s, South African materials constituted just
    over half in value of the total materials used in
    manufacturing.   See 'ICSA', 32, 365, September 1937:
    of £55.7m used, £30.5m in value was South African in
    1933-4; and of £66.0m used, £34.5m was South African
    in 1934-5.
34 'Union Statistics for Fifty Years', op. cit.
35 E.G. Saunders, Mining and Manufacturing, op. cit.,
    for example, said that 'Gold mining can no longer be
    regarded as an avenue for employment of any large
    number in excess of those now at work.   On the
    contrary, the mines are gradually being worked out,
    and it is only a question of time for this to happen,
    so that the tendency must be for mine workers to be
    forced to seek employment in other spheres.'
36 Industry and Labour in South Africa, 'ISA', 13, 139,
    November 1918.

37   Interview with Frank Gibaud, President of the FCI,
     'ISA', 17, 177, January 1922.
38   'SAC', 11, 128, December 1917.
39   This is discussed in F.A. Johnstone, 'Class, Race and
     Gold', London, 1976, pp. 93-104.
40   E.G. Saunders, Mining and Manufacturing, 'ISA', 19,
     211, November 1924.
41   Its 1911 position was indicated by the evidence of
     O'K. Webber and E. Farrar to the 'Commission on Trade
     and Industries, 1912' (Cullinan Commission).
42   Gold Producer's Committee, Transvaal Chamber of
     Mines: 'Party Programmes and the Mines: A Business
     Statement', Johannesburg, 1924, pp. 8-9.
43   'Our First Half Century', says that early engineering
     was handicapped not only by the high wages of its
     artisans, but by the fact that 'finance', which would
     have had to be obtained overseas, was not forth-
     coming, since nobody in Europe was interested in
     spoiling 'a lucrative export market', and that right
     up until 1939, most engineering works were 'jobbing'
     for the mining industry: 'the industry wisely
     confined itself to articles which allowed a measure
     of mass production. Many of these "industries" were
     really not much more than artisans who ventured into
     the field of industrial manufacture. The five years
     before the outbreak of World War 2 can with some
     justification be termed the age of the artisan
     entrepreneur. Their business experience was
     limited, and their capital resources more often than
     not ridiculously small. Working in the shop by day
     and in the office by night, they were determined to
     overcome the odds ... which they had to face.' This
     suggests that engineering was maintained for many
     years by imperial interests at the level of petty-
     commodity production which had prevailed in other
     sectors of manufacturing far earlier, in the 1900s,
     and which by this time had begun to disappear.
     Those engineering firms that did exist were in fact
     incensed by the mining industry's power to stop their
     local development, and after the protective tariff of
     1924 started their own journal which is discussed
     below.
44   S.H. Frankel's book, 'The Railway Policy of South
     Africa', drew criticism from the manufacturing
     fraction for being overwhelmingly 'biased'
     against industries and in favour of mining
     on the matter of railway tariffs; see Railway
     Policy: Dr Frankel's Challenging, But Biased Book
     Reviewed, 'ICSA', 24, 270, October 1929; Saunders, in

Mining and Manufacturing, 'ISA', 19, 210, October
1924, had claimed in 1924 that 'the gold industry
being the most wealthy in the country has an
organisation at its command which can be and is
undoubtedly made use of through the press of the
country and politically.' The chief exception to this
anti-protectionism was provided by Lionel Philips,
who in 1921 was one of the men behind the formation
of the Industrial Development Company, and who in
other ways encouraged industrialising ideas and
actions. His views remained those of a minority
within the industry; the early IDC, for example,
failed after only a few years, as we shall see
below. See A.P. Cartwright, 'Golden Age', Cape
Town, 1968, and 'Our First Half Century', op. cit.,
for further discussion of Philips.

45 T.G. Trevor, The Industrial Development of South
Africa: An Historical Sketch, 'SAJI', IV, 2,
February 1921, says that 'a school of Mines was
started [recently] in connection with the South
African College, and the staffs of the mines, from
the manager downwards, now consist of quite 50% South
African born men'. This, however, is contradicted
by Cartwright, op. cit., who claims that 'It was one
of the anomalies of the twenties that, although the
mining industry had been in existence for thirty five
years, there were comparatively few South African
born mining engineers, and even fewer South African
born directors. It was still the custom to send
young Englishmen to Johannesburg, and train them for
executive positions in the company', p. 164.
However, the ownership statistics support Trevor.
In 1922 R.A. Lehfeldt, 'The National Resources of
South Africa', Johannesburg, 1922, pointed out that
'during the last three or four years many gold mining
shares have been purchased by residents in this
country, and in the case of some of the new mines on
the Far Eastern Rand, which have turned out very
profitable, a good part of the original capital was
subscribed here. It is stated on good authority
that more than half of the dividends from gold mines
now go to South Africans; although in fact, in
1917-18 one is probably safe in saying that quite 60%
of the dividends left the country.' Whatever the
precise figures, it would seem true to say that the
industry was at least becoming localised; quoted in
D. Hobart Houghton and J. Dagut, op. cit., p. 221.

46 For example, editorial notes, 'SAJI', IV, 1, January
1921, discussed Smuts's new protectionism, and the

fact that he had claimed that the gold mines 'are
going to run out', so that new industries would be
required to support the population. This was
generally a popular view of the matter in the early
1920s.

47 'Customs Tariff Commission', 1934: statement of
evidence by the Gold Producers' Committee of the
Transvaal Chamber of Mines.

48 A.H.L. Burmeister, Presidential Address to the 1937
Convention of the Federated Chamber of Industries,
'ICSA', 32, 367, November 1937.

49 'British Trade Review', article quoted in 'SAC', 10,
122, June 1917.

50 I am grateful to Philip Bonner for valuable
discussions concerning this strike. See his paper
The 1920 Black Mineworkers' Strike: A Preliminary
Account, in B. Bozzoli (compiler), 'Labour, Townships
and Protest', Johannesburg, 1979.

51 Interview with F. Gibaud, op. cit., January 1922.

52 For example, the Unemployment Commission of 1922
('Final Report of the Unemployment Commission',
Cape Town, 1922, U.G. 17/22) maintained that it was
the lack of manufacturing industries which caused
unemployment in these years of high unemployment and
depression, much to the delight of manufacturers.
See, for example, editorial, 'ISA', 16, 171, July
1921, which comments on the 'First Interim Report of
the Commission', issued that year; and editorial,
'ISA', 16, 173, September 1921.

53 Smuts, for example, in a speech in Johannesburg in
December 1921 said that 'By industrial stability and
expansion the area of employment will be enlarged,
and unemployment will be prevented'. Quoted in
'ISA', 17, 177, January 1922.

54 See, for example, E.G. Saunders, Mining and
Manufacturing, op. cit.

55 Foreword, 'SAC', 11, 117, January 1917.

56 'ISA', 13, 138, October 1918.

57 Editorial, 'ISA', 13, 140, December 1918.

58 Interview with Gibaud, op. cit., January 1922.

59 Ibid. See also F. Gibaud, Address to the Cape
Manufacturers' Association, January 1922.

60 Speech by L.E. Lintott, 'Transvaal Chamber of
Industries Journal', vol. 1, no. 8, March 1927.

61 I. Wallach, speech to a meeting of the Pretoria
branch of the Transvaal Chamber of Industries,
'Transvaal Industrialist', vol. 2, no. 4, November
1927.

62 W. Seals Wood, Presidential Address to the Annual

Convention of the FCI, 'Transvaal Industrialist',
vol. 2, no. 12, July 1928.

63 Editorial, 'SAJI', vol. IV, no. 1, January 1921.

64 Workers and Producers, 'SAJI', vol. III, no. 11,
November 1920.

65 H. Warington Smyth, Secretary for Mines and
Industries, speech to the National Conference of
Employers and Employees, 1919. In this and other
examples, state ideologists addressed themselves
consciously to industrialists.

66 Editorial, 'SAJI', vol. III, no. 11, November 1920.

67 H. Warington Smyth, speech to FCI Annual Convention,
1918.

68 Parliamentary Speech, 17 September 1919. He tended
to refer to the relationship between industrialism
and patriotism: 'The greatest and most patriotic
service we can render to South Africa today is to
devote all our attention and energies to the great
problems of development which be at our door and
clamour for solution', he was quoted as saying by the
'SAJI', vol. IV, no. 1, January 1920.

69 See, for further examples, speech by F.S. Malan,
opening the National Conference of Employers and
Employees, 1919, reprinted in 'SAJI', vol. II, no.
10, December 1919, and that by Warington Smyth to the
same conference, op. cit.

70 Bernard Price was perhaps the most 'scientific' of
these. See, for example, a reported statement of
his in 'ISA', 12, 138, October 1918, and later
speeches such as his Presidential Address to the
Associated Scientific and Technical Societies of
South Africa, 20 February 1946 (I am grateful to Mr
Roger Price for his permission to use this and other
material from his father's papers). See also, for
evidence of this ongoing 'scientific' tradition
within South Africanism, the speeches of H.J. van
Eck — for example, The Potential of Industrial
Development in South Africa, Bearing in Mind
Limitations in Natural Resources, address delivered
to the Annual Convention of the FCI, 1952, and Some
Trends in Industrial Development, address to the
Rotary Club, Johannesburg, 1952. Ideologists such
as Fremantle and Caldecott are discussed at other
places in this work.

71 H.E. King, The South African National Union: Its
Part in Development.

72 Sir Evelyn Wallers, quoted in 'SAJI', vol. II, no. 4,
April 1919.

73 The Industrial Outlook from the Labour Point of View,
quoted in 'SAJI', vol. II, no. 7, July 1919.

74 For example, Prof. R. Leslie, Government Assistance to Industrialists, 'SAJI', vol. III, no. 2, February 1920; and T.G. Trevor, op. cit.
75 These were the words actually used in the journal; see 'SAJI', vol. IV, no. 1, January 1921.
76 Warington Smyth, op. cit.
77 Gold Producers' Committee, op. cit.
78 Theodore Gregory, 'Ernest Oppenheimer and the Economic Development of Southern Africa', Cape Town, 1962, p. 19.
79 Ibid., p. 22.
80 Ibid., pp. 96ff.   See also Hedley A. Chilvers, 'The Story of De Beers', London, 1939, pp. 223ff.
81 Gregory, op. cit., p. 9.
82 See the Annual Reports of the Johannesburg Chamber of Commerce, 1893-1908, for example, which display Free Trading ideas but are overwhelmingly technical in their content.
83 'CB', XI, 130, November 1933.
84 'CB', IX, 103, August 1931.
85 'CB', X, 109, February 1932.
86 'CB', X, 115, August 1932.
87 A similar argument may be found in Hamza Alavi, The State in Post-Colonial Societies: Pakistan and Bangladesh, 'New Left Review', 74, 1972.

5   THE FOUNDATIONS OF THE WHITE STATE

1 J.E. Borain, Presidential Address to the 1929 Annual Convention of the FCI, in '12th Annual Report of the FCI', 1929.
2 H.J. and R.E. Simons, 'Class and Colour in South Africa, 1850-1950', Harmondsworth, 1969, p. 220.
3 Edmund Hastings, The Tailors' Strike in Cape Town: Some Industrial Lessons Resulting from the Dispute, 'South African Commerce and Manufacturers' Record' (hereafter, 'SAC'), 11, 128, December 1917.
4 See Anon., The Industrial Outlook: Some Suggestions for Achieving Settled Conditions, 'Industrial South Africa' (hereafter, 'ISA'), 13, 145, May 1919.
5 Ibid. For a description see H.J. and R.E. Simons, op. cit., p. 222, and for a more general view of the period, see their chapter 11, Class Struggles Resumed.
6 Anon., The Industrial Outlook, op. cit.
7 Ibid.
8 H.J. and R.E. Simons, op. cit., for example, although they are concerned to condemn the extent to which white and black workers were mutually hostile, in

fact give examples of substantial collaboration
between the two groups.   See pp. 224ff.   The
anonymous article, The Industrial Outlook, op. cit.,
made it quite clear that employers felt this was
where the problem for them lay.

9 Editorial, 'ISA', 16, 171, June 1921, for example,
says that: 'It is not an uncommon remark that
manufacturers are taking advantage of the state of
depression and unemployment to force wage
reductions', and defends this in terms of 'mutual
interdependence': 'the fact is that depression and
unemployment exist because the industrial situation
is out of balance, and there is no remedy except such
readjustment of wages and prices as will restore the
balance and enable the various industries to exchange
products on a fair basis.'

10 See the 'South African Mining and Engineering
Journal' during the years 1919-22, for an indication
of the sterility which had pervaded this previously
creative forum, in spite of the fact that these years
were the most conflict-ridden the industry had
experienced since the 1890s and 1900s.   The
impression is that the journal was expressing the
views of an established interest and not creating
structures of ideas to accompany the process of class
formation and the establishment of structures of
exploitation.   At the same time it was quite clearly
the mining ideology that the journal continued to
express - it did not adopt South Africanist ideas in
any significant editorials or articles.   It had
become the reproducer and disseminator of a fully-
formed and ongoing ideology.

11 Edmund Hastings, op. cit.

12 Patrick Duncan, South African Industrial Legislation,
'ISA', 12, 136, August 1918.   This Act, which was
discussed earlier in this study, was inadequate for
industry's purposes since it had originally been
designed to serve the mining industry's limited need
for conciliation.

13 Hastings, op. cit.

14 Anon., Labour Unrest: A Suggested Method of Bringing
About Industrial Peace, 'ISA', 13, 143, March 1919.

15 Anon., The Industrial Outlook, op. cit.

16 Editorial, 'ISA', 17, 187, November 1922, expressed
support for unemployment insurance, whether
controlled by the state or the employers: 'The
honest, capable and willing worker is not responsible
for such fluctuations in trade conditions - they are
beyond his control - therefore in equity he should
not be compelled to suffer, if a remedy can be found.'

17   Editorial, 'ISA', 15, 153, January 1920.
18   H.E.S. Fremantle, Industrial Destiny of the Union:
     The Way to Production: Our Great Resources but
     Inadequate Population, 'ISA', 18, 192, April 1923,
     for example, said that 'very little has been done to
     give labour the voice in regard to the direction f
     industry which labour is everywhere also demanding,
     and it is not to be thought of that this question can
     long leave industry in this country without being
     answered. For this the leaders of industry must
     prepare themselves.'
19   See, for example, some of the comments in Black and
     White Labour in Industries: Interesting Comments by
     Industrialists and Others, 'ISA', 19, 207, July 1924;
     or the editorial already quoted, in 'ISA', 15, 153,
     January 1920.
20   See, for example, Laite's editorial in 'ISA', 14,
     141, January 1919: 'The interests of Capital and
     Labour are identical, but under the old system there
     have grown up armed camps, each determined to beat
     the other. I have no hesitation in saying that
     these should find some method of union. These two
     classes must stand together in their own interests.
     There must be a meeting ground where antagonisms and
     suspicion shall not dwell. ... Capital, on the one
     hand, must realise the duty of caring for the welfare
     of all those associated in industry, and Labour must
     be ready to co-operate to the fullest possible extent
     in a spirit of helpfulness.' A more explicit
     statement not only of the conciliatory intentions of
     capital, but of the contrast between the old and new
     forms, would be difficult to find.
21   Whereas, as we saw, before the war manufacturers were
     almost completely opportunistic in relation to
     political parties, supporting whichever offered to
     press hardest for protection, the new post-war
     climate encouraged them to enter the fold of the SAP
     so that by the time of the 1921 General Election,
     Laite was urging industrialists to support 'Smuts and
     the Constitution versus the Republicans', while the
     1922 strike action by Smuts was, as is described
     above, vigorously supported by the manufacturing
     sector. See 'ISA', 15, 164, December 1920.
     Nevertheless, manufacturing always maintained a
     characteristic aloofness from the Party until its
     capture by bourgeois interests in the 1930s.
22   'Our First Half Century: 1910-1960, Golden Jubilee
     of the Union of South Africa', Johannesburg, 1960,
     p. 93.

23 Simon Collier, Is a Permanent Industrial Peace
    Possible?, 'ICSA', 22, 245, September 1927.
24 See, for example, the 'Native Economic Commission,
    1930-32', in which it is stated that between 1911 and
    1921, the number of women in the towns increased by
    around 50 per cent while that of men increased by
    only about 7 per cent.
25 'ISA', 15, 154, February 1920.
26 Editorial, 'ISA', 15, 157, May 1920.
27 'ISA', 15, 162, October 1920.
28 'ISA', 15, 164, December 1920.
29 'ISA', 15, 163, November 1920.
30 E.G. Saunders, The Industrial Situation, 'ISA', 14,
    147, July 1919.   See also his Mining and Labour,
    'ISA', 19, 211, November 1924.
31 The work of Martin Legassick on this subject is of
    crucial relevance.   See for example, British
    Hegemony and the Origins of Segregation in South
    Africa, 1901-1914;   The Making of South African
    'Native Policy' 1903-1923:   the Origins of
    Segregation;   and The Rise of Modern South African
    Liberalism: its Assumptions and its Social Base, all
    delivered at the University of London Institute of
    Commonwealth Studies 1972-3, as well as Liberalism,
    Social Control and Liberation in South Africa,
    unpublished paper, 1975, and Race, Industrialisation
    and Social Change in South Africa: The Case of RFA
    Hoernle, 'African Affairs', vol. 75, no. 299, April 1976.
32 In fact, Frankel was ambiguous, sometimes supporting
    manufacturing, and others mining.   The 'ICSA', in
    fact, pointed this out in its review of the book
    'Coming of Age' when it said that Frankel 'seems to
    run with the hare of industrial development and hunt
    with the hounds of mining and importing'.   See, The
    Right and Wrong Way of Governing South Africa,
    'ICSA', 26, 289, May 1931.   As will emerge below,
    however, on the matter of the black population,
    Frankel unequivocally criticised the older liberals
    and mining ideologists, and identified with the
    industrialisers.
33 S.H. Frankel, The Position of the Native as a Factor
    in the Economic Welfare of the European Population in
    South Africa, part 1, 'ICSA', 22, 240, April 1927;
    for part 2, see 'ICSA', 22, 241, May 1927.   It is
    from these two articles that the subsequent
    quotations of Frankel's work are taken.   It is
    interesting to note how Frankel forms a
    communicative link between industrialists and
    liberals such as MacMillan, Reinhallt-Jones, etc.

34 Comment, 'ICSA', 33, 379, November 1938.
35 See P. Bonner, The Decline and Fall of the ICU: A
   Case of Self Destruction, 'South African Labour
   Bulletin', vol. 1, no. 6, September-October 1974.
36 For one of many examples, see the editorial in the
   'Commercial Bulletin', XI, 129, October 1933: 'the
   vital issue at the moment is the limitation of the
   markets for our secondary products, for which the
   overseas markets are and must remain a closed door.'
37 See, for example, F.S. Malan's speech to the FCI
   Annual Convention 1920, 'SAJI', vol. III, no. 7,
   July 1920; Smuts's speech, a year later, quoted in
   'SAJI', vol. IV, no. 1, January 1921, etc.
38 Fremantle, Industrial Destiny of the Union, op. cit.
39 For example as early as 1915, Laite had toured the
   West African Coast, in search of markets for South
   African goods, and stated that 'Portuguese Angola
   was a natural market for South African goods' and
   that 'commercially speaking, Angola should form part
   of South Africa. In the sub-continent the line of
   economic and industrial advance has for centuries
   been from the south and not from the north, and there
   is no obvious reason, except the existence of a
   temporary hostile tariff, why Angola should be the
   exception.' See 'SAC', 9, 104, December 1915.
40 In October 1925, Laite's journal announced its re-
   naming as 'Industrial and Commercial South Africa'
   ('ICSA'), and said that the object of the journal
   twenty years ago had been 'to create interest in, and
   public demand for, the creation of manufacturing
   industries as a secondary development to agriculture
   in a national policy of development, so that as the
   great mining industry declined in the ordinary course
   of nature, there would be substituted for it another
   form of wealth production so necessary to the state
   and the employment of its people. That object has
   been achieved.' It also pointed out that the three
   great future concerns of manufacturers would be
   production, distribution and exporting, the
   'development of markets'. To that end, an export
   edition of 'ICSA' was to be published and sent to the
   Rhodesias, East and West Africa, Australia, New
   Zealand, Canada, Great Britain, the United States,
   France, Germany, Italy, Holland, Switzerland,
   Denmark and India for foreign buyers, and the journal
   would become 'an organ designed to disseminate trade
   news and to play its part in promoting a real and
   lasting national and international trade activity'.
   See 'ICSA', 20, 222, October 1925. For the state's

role in expanding exports, see the same editorial,
and the survey in the address to the 1933 Annual
Convention of the FCI by A.P.J. Fourie, Minister of
Commerce and Industries, 'ICSA', 28, 318, October
1933.

41 Morris Kramer, Presidential Address to the 1930
Annual Convention of the FCI, 'ICSA', 25, 282,
October 1930.

42 C.H. Malan (Minister of Railways), The Industrial
Policy of the Union Government, 'ICSA', 25, 282,
October 1930. The Minister of Railways seems to
have been able to give a unique and penetrating
survey of the state of industries at this time,
perhaps because of the importance of railways, and
the tariff structures relating to them, to the
strategy of development in a country such as South
Africa with its peculiar geography and uneven
development. For more on the markets of Africa see
H.J. Choles, The Trade Possibilities of Africa,
'SAJI', vol. VI, no. 5, May 1923; and H.E. King, The
South African National Union: Its Part in
Development, 'SAJI', vol. II, no. 2, February 1919.

43 Anon., The Union and Rhodesia, 'ICSA', 30, 333,
January 1935, mentions a statement made by Smit,
Rhodesian Minister of Finance, to the Salisbury
Chamber of Industries: 'The trade of Rhodesia, if
the present conditions continued', he said, 'would
gradually be done by travellers from Union factories,
and Union wholesale houses. The effect of this on
trade and commerce in Rhodesia was obvious, but it
would have another effect. Gradually Rhodesia's
importations from the United Kingdom and other parts
of the Empire would be replaced and eliminated by
competition from the Union. It was absolutely
essential for Rhodesia to look for other markets than
the Union for her primary products.' For a further
discussion of Rhodesia see G. Arrighi, 'The Political
Economy of Rhodesia', The Hague, 1967, particularly
pp. 19-35 on the pre-Second World War economic and
political structures. This is one of the few
Southern African works that treats ideologies in the
context of the economic history and structures of
society.

44 J.W. Mushet, Presidential Address to the 1931
Congress of Assocom, 'CB', IX, 104, September 1931.

45 Ibid. The concept of 'political interference' is
the subject of a detailed discussion in chapter 6.

46 Editorial, 'CB', XII, 136, May 1934.

47 See The Native and His Blanket, 'ICSA', 29, 322,
February 1934.

48 See 'Our First Half Century', for a survey of the
    history of the woollen textiles industry, pp. 494-9.
49 H.E. King, The South African National Union: Its
    Part in Development.
50 See, for example, H.J. Choles, op. cit., who
    estimated the total wage-earning capacity of
    'natives' as £25m.
51 Quandell, The Native Considered as Customer, 'CB', X,
    117, October 1932. The article continues: 'He may
    slip back into the ways of the kraal when he goes to
    visit his family; but gradually the habits acquired
    in contact with civilisation will take a firm hold.
    White South Africa cannot at will and in its own
    interest either preserve or destroy the simple
    customs and the primitive standard of living of the
    black population. The most that can be done is
    either to accelerate by encouragement or retard by
    discouragement ... its tendency to reach out towards
    a higher standard of living', and went on to mention
    that 'If chairs and tables became as essential to the
    furnishing of a Native hut as they are to the
    furnishing of a white man's cottage, there would be
    an enormous amount of additional work for furniture
    makers', and continued to discuss the entire range of
    problems related to the matter of raising the
    necessary means of subsistence of the black worker.
52 See Choles, op. cit.
53 Ibid. As 'Quandell' said, 'If a number of Natives,
    sufficient to give all-the-year-round employment to
    one white worker in the footwear industry, learned to
    wear shoes regularly, it would not appreciably
    increase their essential happiness, and might,
    indeed, diminish it if, after acquiring the habit of
    wearing shoes, and consequently allowing the soles of
    their feet to grow tender, they found a difficulty in
    earning sufficient to keep themselves in shoes.'
54 See D. Hobart Houghton, 'The South African Economy',
    2nd edition, Cape Town, 1967, p. 256, where it is
    said that average annual earnings in 1935 for blacks
    in South African mining were R61, while in
    manufacturing they were R84. However, these figures
    did not include benefits in kind in mining.
55 'ICSA', 27, 300, April 1932.
56 Anon., The Natives and South African Industries,
    'ICSA', 27, 305, September 1932.
57 Evidence to the Wage and Industrial Legislation
    Commission, 'CB', XII, 139, August 1934.
58 Anon., The Problem of African Native Labour: How it
    may affect the Union, 'ICSA', 23, 250, February 1928.

59 See B. Bozzoli, Managerialism and the Mode of
Production in South Africa, 'South African Labour
Bulletin', vol. 3, no. 8, October 1977. See Choles,
op. cit., for example, who said that since most
'native needs' such as food, tobacco, metal goods,
blankets, clothing and leatherware, could be supplied
from within the Union, small factories should be
replaced by larger ones, and mass production should
be introduced.

60 In manufacturing, Laite himself had long expressed an
interest in the ideas of 'efficiency' in industry,
particularly with reference to the white working
class. In the mid-1930s, a journal called 'South
African Business Efficiency' was started, in Cape
Town, and was clearly a part of the Scientific
Management movement, deriving its ideas directly from
those of Ford, Taylor and other apostles of the
movement. However, a truly indigenous South African
managerial ideology along similar lines did not
emerge until much later, and was directed at black
workers.

61 See, for example, 'ISA', 14, 143, March 1919. It is
no coincidence that this institute was formed at the
time of great labour 'unrest' after the war; in its
own advertisements the Efficiency Institute
proclaimed its ability to 'bridge the gap between
Capital and Labour'.

62 See, for example, 'ISA', 17, 183, July 1922 and
subsequent issues for a great deal of material on
Scientific Management, and for specific references to
the work of Ford, Taylor, Gilbreth and others.

63 Editorial, 'SAC', 8, 91, November 1914.

64 See 'SAC', 9, 93, January 1915; and 'SAC', 10, 109,
May 1916.

65 'Transvaal Chamber of Industries Journal', vol. 1,
no. 7, February 1927.

66 W. Seals Wood, Problems of South African Industrial
Development, Presidential Address to the FCI Annual
Convention, 1928.

67 J.E. Borain, Presidential Address to the FCI Annual
Convention, 1929.

68 Editorial, 'CB', XII, 138, July 1934. This
statement is doubly interesting since it suggests a
link between political power and consumer status.

69 A.P. Cartwright, 'Golden Age', Cape Town, 1968, p.
222.

70 Ibid., p. 224. See also 'ISA', 14, 147, July 1919,
where it says that Lever Brothers, Cadbury's,
Rowntrees, Armstrongs and 'many others' had 'model'

housing schemes and other structures 'bearing upon
company partnership, co-operation, technical
education, apprenticeship and good housing, which
were real incentives to manufacturers'.

71 Resolution passed at the 1919 Convention of the FCI,
'SAJI', vol. II, no. 8, August 1919.   In April 1920,
the 'SAJI' mentioned that employees frequently
opposed this sort of housing plan since it gave
employers the right to evict the worker if he was
striking or if he had been dismissed, and workers
therefore wanted the right to buy.

72 R. Beattie, Inspector of Factories in the Transvaal
and OFS, Factory Buildings and Factory Hygiene: The
Welfare of the Worker, 'SAJI', vol. VI, no. 11,
November 1923.

73 'ICSA', 32, 362, June 1937.   As will be gathered
from the context, by 'middle class' was meant 'white
working class'.

74 'Our First Half Century', pp. 473-4.

75 Prof. R. Leslie, Government Assistance to
Industrialists, 'SAJI', vol. III, no. 2, February
1920.

76 Anon., The Development of the Financial Structure of
the Union since 1910, in 'Our First Half Century'.
See also D.G. Franzsen and J.J.D. de Villiers,
Economic Growth and Capital Accumulation in South
Africa 1870-1955, paper presented at the 5th
Conference of the International Association for
Research in Income and Wealth, August 1957;   and
Hobart Houghton, op. cit., chapter 9.

77 Anon., The Development of the Financial Structure of
the Union, op. cit.

78 Ibid.   See also Hobart Houghton, op. cit., pp. 262-
3, tables 25-6 on the liabilities and assets of the
Reserve and Commercial Banks 1938-65.

79 'Memorandum Representing the Views of the Association
of Chambers of Commerce of South Africa', submitted
to the Select Committee of the House of Assembly on
the Gold Standard, 1932.

80 'CB', X, 117, October 1932.

81 'CB', IX, 104, September 1931.

82 'CB', IX, 103, August 1931.

83 A subtle distinction between the orientation of, for
example, the press in the era of mining hegemony and
that of bourgeois hegemony is discernible in this
respect;   whereas newspapers at that time tended to
play the role of 'mouthpieces' for specific
interests, in later years they acquired the more
generalised functions of expressing 'public opinion'.

The parallel phenomenon in the journals used in this study has already been pointed out, when it was observed above how the South African mining and manufacturing journals tended to be interest-orientated to the exclusion of other concerns, and the later journal, 'Commercial Bulletin', was externally-orientated.

84 King, op. cit.

85 H.E. King, Why is South Africa not Progressing More Rapidly?, 'SAJI', vol. VII, no. 1, January 1924.

86 Morris Kramer, Presidential Address to the 1930 Convention of the FCI, 'ICSA', 25, 282, October 1930.

87 Editorial, 'CB', X, 115, August 1932.

88 L.E. Neame, 'Today's News Today: The Story of the Argus Company', Johannesburg, 1956, p. 231.

89 In 1928, for example, the 'Star' was selling 50,000 copies daily.

90 This and the following quotations are taken from Neame, op. cit.

91 Ibid.

92 See the report in 'CB', XI, 135, April 1934.

93 S.F. Waterson, MP, Speech to a Junior Chamber of Commerce meeting in 1935. These meetings were reported in the 'CB'. See, for this example, 'CB', XII, 145, February 1935.

94 'SAJI', IV, 8, September 1921.

95 Quandell, From an Onlooker's Armchair, 'CB', XI, 131, December 1933.

96 'SAJI', vol. IV, no. 8, September 1921.

97 N. Poulantzas, 'Political Power and Social Classes', London, 1973, p. 217.

6   A SECOND REVOLUTION

1 H. Warington-Smyth, speech entitled Problems for the Future, at the National Conference of Employers and Employees, Pretoria, 3 November 1919, reported in the 'South African Journal of Industries' (hereafter, 'SAJI'), vol. III, no. 1, January 1920.

2 Prof. R. Leslie, Government Assistance to Industrialists, 'SAJI', vol. III, no. 2, February 1920.

3 See, for example, Smuts' speech in the House of Assembly, 17 September 1919, and a speech of his reported in the 'South African Commerce and Manufacturers' Record' (hereafter, 'SAC'), 17, 177, January 1922.

4 Reported in 'SAC', 10, 108, April 1916.

5   H.E. King, The South African National Union: Its
    Part in Development, 'SAJI', vol. II, no. 2,
    February 1919.

6   In April 1923, H.E.S. Fremantle could say that 'It is
    hardly too much to say that there is something like a
    national movement, in which the Government is taking
    its share, in regard to the establishment of several
    great key industries, each of which draws several
    distinct subordinate, but highly important industries
    in its train, as for instance galvanised iron and
    wire may be expected to follow the establishment of
    the iron industry ...', in his article Industrial
    Destiny of the Union: The Way to Production: Our
    Great Resources, but Inadequate Population,
    'Industrial South Africa' (hereafter, 'ISA'), 18,
    192, April 1923.   However, Sammy Marks had
    established his Union Steel Corporation in 1910.
    But according to one authority, this industry did not
    do more than re-process scrap metal, and probably did
    not possess the capital to venture into the
    processing of South African iron ore.   For a useful
    discussion of the history of the industry see Anon.,
    Iscor: Backbone of the Union's Industries, in 'Our
    First Half Century: 1910-1960: Golden Jubilee of
    the Union of South Africa', Johannesburg, 1960.

7   In 'SAJI', vol. II, no. 1, September 1917, it was
    reported that Alex Aiken was the Managing Director of
    the Industrial Development Company, Ltd, formed in
    that year 'by a few financial institutions', for 'the
    purpose of assisting financially in the development
    of manufacturing industries in South Africa'.
    However, this seems to have had little effect on
    manufacturing, and Laite's journal pleaded throughout
    1918 for more capital.

8   See 'ISA', 13, 136, August 1918, which reported that
    there was a resolution to that effect passed at the
    FCI congress in July of that year.

9   E.C. Reynolds, Financial Resources of South Africa
    available for Industrial Expansion, 'SAJI', vol. II,
    no. 7, July 1919.

10 Editorial, 'SAC', 11, 126, October 1917.   See also
    H.E. King, The South African National Union: Its
    Part in Development, in which a plea was made for the
    state's income to be increased through broadening the
    basis of taxation.

11 The 'SAC' waged a consistent campaign for the 'Closer
    Union' of South Africa.   See Anon., The Commercial
    Aspect of Closer Union, 'SAC', 2, 14, June 1908, in
    which it was claimed that 'The Colonial boundaries

are purely artificial in their arrangement, and the
existence of separate Governments is due to a series
of historical incidents which were largely
accidental, as well as to lack of foresight by those
who exercised political power in the past.   The
present division of South Africa is a monument of
apathy, negligence and vacillation of the British
Ministries of the last century in regard to Colonial
Development.   The people of this sub-continent are
in fact bound together most intimately in their
commercial and personal relationships. ... All who
are interested in trading or industrial concerns have
ample grounds for realising the disadvantages and
drawbacks of the present conditions.'
12   'SAC', 9, 104, December 1915.
13   'SAC', 17, 185, September 1922.
14   See editorial, 'SAC', 15, 153, January 1920, in which
it was claimed that 'what we need is education of the
workers ... in regard to the fundamental principles
underlying production and distribution', in the light
of recent labour unrest: 'Never before have so many
futile schemes for living without work been hatched
in the muddled brains of the fanatic.   Instead of
getting down to bedrock producing for the "good of
the State", they are only concerned with attempts to
force up wages in an unsuccessful endeavour to over-
take the increased cost of living.'
15   See the important speech by C.H. Malan, Minister of
Railways, to the 1930 congress of the FCI, entitled
The Industrial Policy of the Union Government,
'Industrial and Commercial South Africa' (hereafter,
'ICSA'), 25, 282, October 1930.
16   See J.F. Borain, Presidential Address, Federated
Chamber of Industries Annual Convention, 1929, '12th
Annual Report of the South African Federated Chamber
of Industries', 1929, in which he said that: 'Today
the chemist and engineer are important factors in
industries. ... Governments are assisting in this
work with the idea of investigating methods tending
to improve quality, reduce costs and eliminate waste
... whilst we may, as we often do, feel aggrieved at
the greater interference by Government in business,
we must, I think, in fairness, allow that this is
offset to some extent by the valuable assistance
which is rendered to all forms of production and
distribution by Government encouragement in many
directions.'
17   Editorial, 'SAC', 16, 173, September 1921.
18   In 1917, the Industries Advisory Board was reported

to have been authorised to appoint a 'Tariff Committee', 'to prepare for the next tariff revision', while the 'SAC' claimed that 'An attempt is to be made to remove existing anomalies and to prepare a tariff suitable to the needs of a developing country', 'SAC', 11, 126, October 1917. When in 1923 it appeared that the SAP government had relented on the principle of protection, 'Industrial South Africa' wrote 'For the first time in the history of the country, a responsible Government, through its mouthpiece the Minister of Finance, has definitely declared its adherence to the policy of Protection. ... For what we have received, as manufacturers, we are grateful.' Editorial, 'ISA', 18, 192, April 1923. The limitations to this concession are discussed below.

19 See 'SAC', 11, 128, December 1917 for a report that 'Wages Boards are being considered'; and July 1921 for a discussion of the Wages Board Bill.

20 See the Select Committee into Industrial Conciliation. An Industrial Conciliation Bill was actually drafted in 1923, but dropped then rendered redundant by the subsequent Act of 1924.

21 See 'SAC', 16, 171, July 1921.

22 See editorial, 'SAC', 10, 113, September 1916.

23 This pleased manufacturers; see 'SAC', 11, 122, June 1917.

24 The earlier 'Scientific and Technical Committee' was incorporated into the Advisory Board.

25 Once more, this pleased manufacturers. See 'ISA', 15, 162, October 1920.

26 Ibid.

27 See for example, H.E.S. Fremantle, Industrial Destiny of the Union ....

28 Other articles of interest and note included H.E. King, The South African National Union ...; E.C. Reynolds, Financial Resources ...; S.E.T. Ewing, The Economic and Natural Factors Affecting Factory Location in South Africa, vol. II, no. 10, October 1919; Prof. R. Leslie, Government Assistance ...; a series of articles by Prof. G.H. Stanley on Iron and Steel in South Africa during 1920; a series of articles in early 1921 by T.G. Trevor on The Industrial Development of South Africa: An Historical Sketch; and one by H.E.S. Fremantle in April 1924 on The Outlook for industrialism in South Africa.

29 See 'Our First Half Century', op. cit., for the background to this.

30   See 'ISA', 17, 185, September 1922.
31   'SAJI', vol. III, no. 7, July 1920, reported that six
     films had already been made by Killarney film studios
     in collaboration with the Department of Industries,
     and that twenty more were planned.   They could, said
     the journal, also be used for educational purposes,
     such as for showing to children.
32   Anon., Growth of Electricity Supply Industry in the
     Union, in 'Our First Half Century'.
33   See H.E. King, The South African National Union.
34   In 'ISA', 18, 192, April 1923, it was said that 'Dr.
     van der Bijl was chosen by the Government, and in
     order to help the country of his birth, sacrificed a
     very lucrative appointment in the United States, to
     answer the call from General Smuts.   Since his
     return to South Africa he has done much to forward
     industrial progress.'
35   'Report of the Committee Appointed by the Minister of
     Mines and Industries', reproduced in 'SAJI', vol.
     VII, no. 5, May 1924.
36   'SAJI', vol. VII, no. 5, May 1924.
37   In its editorial of April 1923, op. cit., the 'ISA'
     described the protectionist 'victory' as follows: 'it
     has been a long up-hill fight;   the forces arrayed
     against us have been powerful and well-organised;
     and it is only the righteousness of our cause which,
     after years of patient effort, has enabled us to
     prevail.   But the whole victory is not yet ours.
     The Board of Trade and Industry has not attempted to
     deal with the large labour-employing industries, and
     in consequence the Government is unable to introduce,
     this Session, such tariff adjustments as are
     necessary to ensure the stability of market, and the
     consequent increasing avenues of employment, which
     must result from the imposition of protective duties
     upcn the goods which are the product of our
     Engineering establishments, our Furniture Factories,
     the Printing and Allied trades, Manufactured Joinery,
     Pottery Works, Motor Body Building, the Wholesale
     Clothing Industry, Manufacturing Chemists, and many
     others.'   All of these were still excluded from
     protection.   The writer went on: 'With the
     exception of the Footwear and Confectionery
     industries the Board has confined its efforts to the
     study of conditions affecting a number of small
     propositions, in which the importing community are
     not particularly interested.   To the operators
     therein, these small industries are of vital
     importance, but as affecting labour employment, and

the general development of our industrial life, the
majority of them are negligible!'
38 Manufacturers, pleased as they were to have such a
prominent supporter, were always cynical about
Smuts's alleged commitment to industries:
'Manufacturers are beginning to feel that they have
played the role of political Cinderella quite long
enough.   For years their demands have been met by
promises - and the appointment of Boards and
Commissions.   Ministers have pledged themselves to
tariff revision and industrial development and today
we have a very large number of the Prime Minister's
supporters who are determined ... to see these
pledges fulfilled.   No doubt a further attempt will
be made to evade the issue by pleading that the Board
of Trade and Industry ... has not yet had time to
master the problems facing it, but this will not do.'
'ISA', 17, 178, February 1922.   In 'ISA', 17, 177,
January 1922, Laite said that the problem lay in the
fact that 'an influential section of the Cabinet is
opposed to Protection through the tariff'.
39 'ISA', 16, 169, May 1921.
40 Frank Gibaud, speech to the annual meeting of the
Cape Province Manufacturers' Association, December
1921, reported in 'ISA', 17, 177, January 1922.
41 See editorial in 'SAC', 10, 113, September 1916,
when, on the initial formation of the board, the
journal urged that it be extended beyond its
'Advisory' capacities and be given greater powers as
in Germany.
42 'ISA', 18, 192, April 1923.
43 Editorial, 'ISA', 14, 150, October 1919.   The
failure was said to have been due to the lack of
'debate', and the 'uncompromising' attitude of
labour.
44 'Our First Half Century'.
45 According to Hobart Houghton, even though the
establishment of the Reserve Bank was seen as 'the
first major development' in the banking structure of
the Union, it was, at its inception, 'relatively
weak ... especially in relation to the powerful and
long established commercial banks'; it was in 1927,
under a different government, that 'the transference
to it of the government accounts ... considerably
enhanced its prestige', and in 1925 that the Chamber
of Mines agreed that it should become the channel for
the sale of South African gold.   See D. Hobart
Houghton, 'The South African Economy', 2nd edition,
Cape Town, 1967, pp. 183-90.

46   Houghton, op. cit., points out that while in the
     1920s mining taxation averaged £4m, during the 1930s
     it reached £15m.
47   H.E. King, The South African National Union.
48   Recorded in 'SAJI', vol. VII, no. 5, May 1924.
49   Editorial, 'SAJI', vol. VII, no. 8, August 1924.
50   With the exception of the Engineering Industry, every
     major South African industry was protected under the
     new law; 'ICSA' considered this an advance so
     significant that it could say that 'The need for
     propaganda work, as understood in the past, has
     therefore ceased', in October 1925.
51   It was this Board that determined and directed the
     path the new protective policy of the state should
     take.   See editorial, 'SAJI', vol. VII, no. 10,
     October 1924.
52   'Our First Half Century'.
53   '13th Annual Report of the South African Federated
     Chamber of Industries', Presidential Address by
     Morris Kramer, 1930.
54   The 'Commercial Bulletin of South Africa' (hereafter,
     'CB'), VI, 68, September 1928.
55   Commentary, in 'The Transvaal Chamber of Industries
     Journal', 1, 4, November 1926, reported that a
     special FCI Convention had been called to discuss the
     recent recommendations of the Wage Board.
56   Ibid.
57   Union Wage Legislation: Mr. Gundelfinger's Grave
     Warning, 'ICSA', 23, 260, December 1928.
58   See 'ICSA', 25, 282, October 1930; 27, 308, December
     1932; 28, 317, September 1933; and 28, 318,
     October 1933, all of which contained criticisms of
     the Wage Board.
59   Editorial, 'CB', VI, 68, September 1928.
60   T.W. Cullinan (son of Sir Thomas), Presidential
     Address to the Transvaal Chamber of Industries,
     recorded in 'Transvaal Industrialist', 2, 1,
     August 1927.
61   Editorial, 'CB', XI, 131, December 1933.
62   South African Banking in 1931, by 'our Financial
     Correspondent', 'CB', IX, 110, March 1932.
63   See, for example, H.C. Gearing, Presidential Address,
     1927 Annual Convention of the FCI, recorded in the
     '10th Annual Report of the South African Federated
     Chamber of Industries'.
64   Editorial, 'CB', VI, 68, September 1928.
65   Ibid.
66   H.C. Gearing, Presidential Address, 1927.
67   Editorial, 'ISA', 16, 170, June 1921.

68 W. Seals-Wood, Presidential Address, FCI, 1928, '11th
    Annual Report of the South African Federated Chamber
    of Industries'.
69 J.E. Borain, Presidential Address, FCI, 1929, '12th
    Annual Report of the South African Federated Chamber
    of Industries'.
70 H.C. Gearing, Presidential Address, 1927 Annual
    Convention of the FCI, recorded in its '10th Annual
    Report'.
71 Anon., 'ICSA', 24, 272, December 1929.
72 L.E. Lintott, speech to Engineers and Founders
    Association, 'Transvaal Chamber of Industries
    Journal', 1, 8, March 1927.
73 Editorial, 'ISA', 13, 140, December 1918.
74 Laite had stood as an independent against Jagger in
    the 1915 General Election and was defeated, in Cape
    Town Central.   He claimed that because he had
    attempted to make the issue of the election
    'Protection' vs 'Free Trade', the 'Magnate Press'
    had got to work, asserting that he would support
    Botha if it suited him, but change to Hertzog if he
    offered him a better tariff policy.   Editorial,
    'SAC', 9, 103, November 1915.   By the time of the
    1920 election, Laite's journal urged manufacturers to
    support Smuts.
75 'SAC', 9, 101, September 1915.
76 Editorial, 'SAC', 9, 98, June 1915.
77 Editorial, 'ISA', 13, 140, December 1918.
78 Editorial, 'CB', VI, 68, September 1928.
79 Editorial, 'CB', IX, 103, August 1931.
80 J.W. Mushet, Presidential Address, Assocom Congress,
    East London, 1931, reported in 'CB', IX, 104,
    September 1931.
81 'ICSA', October 1930.
82 J.W. Mushet, Presidential Address, 1931.
83 Memorandum Representing the Views of the Association
    of Chambers of Commerce of South Africa, submitted to
    the Select Committee of the House of Assembly,
    reproduced in 'CB', X, 113, June 1932; see also an
    editorial of that year, which claimed that at first,
    both the Chamber of Mines and Assocom supported
    government policy: 'CB', IX, 108, January 1932.
84 W. Seals-Wood, The Industrial Outlook: Real States-
    manship and Political Expediency, 'ICSA', 27, 308,
    December 1932.
85 Presidential Address (no name given), '15th Annual
    Report, South African Federated Chamber of
    Industries, 1932', indicates that there was some
    division within industry on this issue, but that by

that time the majority view had become in favour of
leaving gold.

86 Memorandum, op. cit.

87 'Hertzog made it a political issue by saying at
Smithfield that what mattered was maintaining South
Africa's independence', according to the 'CB', IX,
108, January 1932.

88 Memorandum, op. cit.

89 R. Islip, Presidential Address, 34th Annual Congress
of the Association of Chambers of Commerce, October
1932.

90 Ibid.

91 Presidential Address, FCI, 1932.

92 Editorial, 'CB', IX, 108, January 1932.

93 Ibid.

94 Editorial, 'CB', IX, 109, February 1932.

95 'CB', X, 112, May 1932.

96 Editorial, 'CB', X, 113, June 1932.

97 Ibid.   Most interesting of the proliferating
coalitionist movements of this time was the extreme
South Africanist organisation formed in Natal around
the journal 'The Industries of South Africa'.   Its
creed, unlike the new South Africanism of the 1930s,
was unashamedly ideological and political, and in no
sense could be said to have tried to obscure its
purpose in legitimating capitalism.   For this, and
other, reasons, it appeared to be quasi-fascist.
Its chief platforms were strict bilingualism; the
urging of all South Africans to 'buy South African',
and thereby give employment to their fellow citizens;
the consolidation of industries, by 'bringing home to
every section that their interests are identical',
the mutual support of industrialists and white
workers; the incorporation of the black working
class; and the encouragement of the realisation
amongst South Africans that 'loans floated
promiscuously overseas are nothing more nor less than
an inducement to import goods into South Africa,
irrespective of whether such goods are, or can be,
made in South Africa.'   Most of these prescriptions
seem familiar enough.   However, in 'The Industries
of South Africa' they were couched in nationalist,
antisemitic and right-wing phraseology.   The
proclaimed aim of the movement was the mobilisation
of farmers, workers and industrialists to unite
against Jewish and foreign imperialism.   See for
example, 'The Industries of South Africa', November
1932.   The journal was supported by several
prominent Natal industries including African

Explosives and Industries Ltd; Bakers Ltd; Buffalo
Paints, Ltd; Fisons, Durban; Greatrex; Hulett and
Sons; Lever Brothers (SA); Nestlé (SA); SA
Breweries; and many others. Related to this
movement, and sometimes indistinguishable from it,
was the Douglas Social Credit movement, which claimed
that all the problems which faced capitalist systems
in times of crisis could be traced to the inadequacy
of the financial system. Supporters of Douglas
Social Credit, a system which seems to have
originated in North America, and which gained
considerable support in Canada in particular, spanned
the entire range of English-speaking political
organisations in South Africa. Social Credit was
advocated by liberals, by the right wing South
Africanists, and by writers, for, and readers of,
Laite's journal; for this reason it could be said to
symbolise the South Africanist idea, since those
sympathetic to it were the constituency which South
Africanist ideologists sought. Its critique of the
'financial system' was organic, resembling the
analogy quoted above between capital and human blood:
'a country which is suffering from loss of capital
and bad circulation has no more hope of being healthy
and vigorous than has a human being suffering from
bad circulation and an extensive loss of blood'.
See, for example, the articles by E.G. Tomalin,
Overproduction, Unemployment and Poverty: The Modern
Triangle of Financial Impotence, 'ICSA', 26, 286,
February 1931; and An Alternative to Economic Chaos:
The Douglas Social Credit Proposals, 26, 287, March
1931, in which the main proposal of the scheme was
set out, i.e. the abolition of money, and its
replacement by 'social' as opposed to 'financial'
credit: 'The general effect would be instantly to
raise the destitute above the poverty line, and
proportionally improve the condition of every class
above them: thereafter progressively to increase the
relative prosperity of the poor - with the willing
assent of the rich'; the populism and social concern
of the scheme are both features of a particular brand
of South African petty-bourgeois ideology during the
1920s and 1930s. Both of these movements indicated
how thin was the dividing line between liberals,
capitalists, and petty-bourgeois 'fascists'. In
addition, there arose in these years the 'National
Non-Party Government League', which was started by a
'group of business men'; public interest in the
Ottawa Conference on the world economy; and other

similar indications of the rise in public consciousness and participation. See, for example, 'CB', X, 121, February 1933.

98 Editorial, 'CB', IX, 108, January 1932.
99 Editorial, 'CB', X, 119, December 1932.
100 Editorial, 'CB', X, 122, March 1933.
101 J.W. Mushet, Presidential Address.
102 On the issue of railways, for example, F. Islip, Assocom President in 1932 said in his Presidential Address for that year that he hoped 'railways may be divorced from the blighting influence of political control, and may be administered by a Railway Board consisting of men whose first qualifications for the appointment shall be a practical knowledge of railway and business administration, rather than a blameless record of faithful party political services.'
103 J. Neil Boss, Presidential Address, FCI, 1931.
104 Editorial, 'CB', X, 123, April 1933.
105 Editorial, 'CB', X, 112, May 1932.
106 Editorial, 'CB', X, 119, December 1932. Several other ideologists emphasised the extent to which they perceived Ottawa as a 'breakthrough'.
107 See, for example, R. Islip, Presidential Address, amongst others.
108 '15th Annual Report, Federated Chamber of Industries of South Africa', 1932.
109 'Government Consultation with Industries': Important Pronouncement by the Hon. the Minister of Justice, '15th Annual Report', FCI.
110 Editorial, 'CB', IX, 103, August 1931.
111 Editorial, 'CB', IX, 104, September 1931.
112 Editorial, 'CB', IX, 108, January 1932.
113 Ibid.
114 Ibid.
115 As recorded in 'CB', X, 119, December 1932.
116 Editorial, 'CB', X, 120, January 1933.
117 Ibid.
118 It is probable that this was the 'National Non-Party Government League', referred to by the editor and 'Quandell', in 'CB', X, 121, February 1933.
119 Editorial, 'CB', IX, 109, February 1932.
120 See the December 1932 editorial, op. cit.
121 Is the Cloud of Depression Lifting: An Interesting Symposium, 'ICSA', 28, 313, May 1933.
122 Today Black Depression, Tomorrow Golden Sunshine: Courage and Sanity in these difficult times are urged by prominent business men, 'ICSA', 27, 299, March 1932.
123 'Government Consultation with Industries': Important

Pronouncement by the Hon. the Minister of Justice,
'15th Annual Report', FCI, op. cit.
124 Editorial, 'CB', X, 122, March 1933.
125 Ibid.
126 Editorial, 'CB', XI, 131, December 1933.
127 The Wage Question: Mr. S. Craig Bain's Presidential
     Address to the Convention, 'ICSA', 30, 344,
     December 1935.
128 Editorial, 'CB', XII, 143, December 1934.

CONCLUSION

  1 H. Wolpe has made this comparison in his Capitalism
     and Cheap Labour Power in South Africa: from Segre-
     gation to Apartheid, 'Economy and Society', vol. 1,
     no. 4, 1972.
  2 See, for example, S. Trapido, Aspects in the
     Transition from Slavery to Serfdom: The South
     African Republic, 1842-1902, University of London,
     Institute of Commonwealth Studies, Seminar Paper,
     June 1975.   Several studies of African systems are
     to be included in a forthcoming collection on
     nineteenth-century Southern Africa, edited by
     S. Marks.
  3 G. Kay, 'Development and Underdevelopment: A Marxist
     Analysis', London, 1975.
  4 P. Bonner, for example, has argued that the 1920
     black mineworkers' strike was in part a response to
     the virtual disintegration of the reserve economies;
     see his The 1920 Black Mineworkers Strike: A
     Preliminary Account, in B. Bozzoli (compiler),
     'Labour, Townships and Protest', Johannesburg, 1979.
  5 An example of this is the garment industry, where
     accumulation clearly took place through the use of
     white, Afrikaner, female labour.
  6 Much of the 'factionalist' literature on this subject
     makes the assumption that 'national' capital and the
     Afrikaner bourgeoisie were synonymous.   See, for
     example, R. Davies et al., Class Struggle and the
     Periodisation of the State in South Africa, 'Review
     of African Political Economy', 7, September-December
     1976.
  7 See M. Morris, The Development of Capitalism in South
     African Agriculture: Class Struggle in the Country-
     side, 'Economy and Society', vol. 5, no. 2, 1976.
  8 See D. O'Meara's suggestive analysis in his The 1946
     African Mineworkers' Strike and the Political Economy
     of South Africa, 'Journal of Commonwealth and
     Comparative Politics', vol. XIII, no, 2, July 1975.

Select bibliography

1 JOURNALS AND OTHER MEDIA SUBJECTED TO CONTENT ANALYSIS

'The South African Mining Journal' (a weekly periodical),
    vol. 1: September 1891-March 1892, vols 2-8: October
    1892-October 1899.
'South African Mines Commerce and Industries'
    (incorporating the 'South African Mining Journal'), vols
    1-5: March 1903-July 1907, and other subsequent issues
    during 1912 and 1919-22.
Barlow Rand Archives, Johannesburg, Annual Reports and
    Chairman's Addresses of Rand Mines, Ltd, 1894-1904.
Johannesburg Chamber of Commerce, 'Annual Reports', 1893-
    4, 1898-9, 1905-8.
Rand Pioneers, 'Annual Reports', 1904, 1907-9.
Transvaal Landowners Association, 'Annual Reports', 1906,
    1911-12, 1934.
'The Official Organ of the South African National Union',
    a monthly periodical, August 1908-October 1910.
'South African Commerce and Manufacturers' Record', a
    monthly periodical, vols 1-11, May 1907-December 1917.
'Industrial South Africa' (incorporating 'South African
    Commerce and Manufacturers' Record'), vols 13-20,
    August 1918-September 1925.
'Industrial And Commercial South Africa' (incorporating
    'Industrial South Africa'), vols 20-33, October 1925-
    December 1938.
'The South African Journal of Industries', a monthly
    periodical, vols 1-8, September 1917-December 1925.
'Annual Reports' and Chairman's Addresses, of the South
    African Federated Chamber of Industries, 1918 and 1927-
    40 inclusive.
'The "Official Labour Gazette" of the Union of South
    Africa', a monthly periodical, vol. 1, no. 1, April
    1925-no. 5, August 1925.

'The South African Labour Gazette' (incorporating the
    'Official Labour Gazette'), vol. 1, no. 5, August 1925-
    vol. 2, no. 1, January 1926.
'The Social and Industrial Review' (incorporating the
    'South African Labour Gazette' and the 'South African
    Journal of Industries'), vol. 2, January 1926-December
    1926.
'The Transvaal Chamber of Industries Journal', a monthly
    periodical, vol. 1, August 1926-July 1927.
'The Transvaal Industrialist' (incorporating the
    'Transvaal Chamber of Industries Journal'), vol. 2,
    August 1927-July 1928.
'Commercial Bulletin of South Africa', a monthly
    periodical, vol. 6, no. 68, September 1928, vols 9-14:
    August 1931-April 1937.
'The Industries of South Africa', a monthly periodical,
    vols 1-3, November 1932-December 1934.
'The Rota', November 1923-November 1925.
'South African Business Efficiency', 1935-9.
'Progress', official organ of Junior Chambers of Commerce,
    attached to 'Commercial Opinion', February 1937-8.

2 GOVERNMENT PUBLICATIONS

'Evidence and Report of the Industrial Commission of
    Enquiry', with an Appendix, compiled and published by
    the Witwatersrand Chamber of Mines, Johannesburg,
    South African Republic, 1897.
'Report, Minority Report, Minutes of Proceedings and
    Evidence of the Transvaal Labour Commission',
    Johannesburg, 1903.
'Report, Minutes of Proceedings and Evidence of the South
    African Native Affairs Commission' (SANAC), 1903-5,
    Johannesburg, 1905.
'Report of the Transvaal Indigency Commission, 1906-08',
    Pretoria, 1908.
'Report of the Commission Appointed to Inquire into the
    Conditions of Trade and Industries, 1912' (Cullinan
    Commission), Pretoria, 1912.
'First Interim Report of the Unemployment Commission',
    Cape Town, 1921.
'Report of the Native Economic Commission', Pretoria,
    1932.

3 ARTICLES, PAMPHLETS AND PAPERS

ALAVI, H., The State in Post-Colonial Societies: Pakistan and Bangladesh, 'New Left Review', 74, 1972.
ARRIGHI, G., Labour Supplies in Historical Perspective: A Study of the Proletarianization of the African Peasantry in Rhodesia, 'The Journal of Development Studies', vol. 6, no. 3, April 1970.
ASSOCOM, Memorandum Representing the Views of the Association of Chambers of Commerce of South Africa, submitted to the Select Committee of the House of Assembly on the Gold Standard, 1932.
BALBUS, I.D., The Concept of 'Interest' in Pluralist and Marxian Analysis, 'Politics and Society', vol. 1, no. 2, 1970.
BALBUS, I.D., The Negation of the Negation: Theory of Capitalism within an Historical Theory of Social Change, 'Politics and Society', vol. 3, no. 1, 1972.
BALBUS, I.D., Ruling Elite Theory versus Marxist Class Analysis, 'Monthly Review', vol. 23, no. 1, May 1971.
BERGER, P. and PULLBERG, S., Reification and the Sociological Critique of Consciousness, 'History and Theory', vol. IV, no. 2, 1965.
BLAINEY, G., Lost Causes of the Jameson Raid, 'Economic History Review', 2nd series, 18, 1965.
BLUMER, H., Industrialisation and Race Relations, in G. Hunter (ed.), 'Industrialisation and Race Relations', London, 1965.
BONNER, P.L., The Decline and Fall of the ICU – A case of self-destruction?, 'South African Labour Bulletin', vol. 1, no. 6, September–October 1974.
BONNER, P.L., The 1920 Black Mineworkers' Strike: A Preliminary Account, in B. Bozzoli (compiler), 'Labour, Townships and Protest', Johannesburg, 1979.
BOZZOLI, BELINDA, The Origins, Development and Ideology of Local Manufacturing in South Africa, 'Journal of Southern African Studies', vol. 1, no. 2, April 1975.
BOZZOLI, BELINDA, Managerialism and the Mode of Production in South Africa, 'South African Labour Bulletin', vol. 3, no. 8, October 1977.
BOZZOLI, BELINDA, Capital and the State in South Africa, 'Review of African Political Economy', 11, January–April 1978.
BRANSKY, D., The Causes of the Boer War: Towards a Synthesis, paper delivered to the Workshop on Southern Africa, Oxford, 1974.
BUNDY, COLIN, The Emergence and Decline of a South African Peasantry, 'African Affairs', October 1972.
CAPE TIMES, Colonial Industries: An Enquiry into their

Progress and Present Condition and the Effects of the
Customs Tariff upon Them, 1906.
CARCHEDI, G., On the Economic Identification of the New
Middle Class, 'Economy and Society', vol. 4, no. 1, 1975.
CLARENCE-SMITH, W.G. and MOORSOM, R., Underdevelopment and
Class Formation in Ovamboland 1845-1915, 'Journal of
African History', vol. VI, 1975.
CLARKE, S., Capital, 'Fractions' of Capital and the State:
'Neo-Marxist' Analyses of the South African State,
'Capital and Class', 5, Summer 1978.
CONNOLLY, W.E., On 'Interests' in Politics, 'Politics and
Society', vol. 2, no. 4, 1972.
DANZIGER, K., Ideology and Utopia in South Africa: A
Methodological Contribution to the Sociology of Knowledge,
'British Journal of Sociology', vol. 14, 1963.
DAVIES, R., Mining Capital, the State and Unskilled White
Workers in South Africa, 1901-1913, 'Journal of Southern
African Studies', vol. 3, no. 1, October 1976.
DAVIES, R. et al., Class Struggle and the Periodisation of
the State in South Africa, 'Review of African Political
Economy', 7, September-December 1976.
DENOON, D., The Transvaal Labour Crisis, 'Journal of
African History', vol. 7, 1967.
DENOON, D., 'Capitalist Influence' and the Transvaal Crown
Colony Government, 'The Historical Journal', 1969.
FOX, ALAN, Managerial Ideology and Labour Relations,
'British Journal of Industrial Relations', vol. 4, no. 3,
November 1966.
GOLD PRODUCERS' COMMITTEE, Transvaal Chamber of Mines,
Party Programmes and the Mines: A Business Statement,
Johannesburg, 1924.
HAUPT, H.-G. and LEIBFREID, S., Marxian Analysis of
Politics or Theory of Social Change? Toward a Marxian
Theory of the Political Domain, 'Politics and Society',
vol. 3, no. 1, 1972.
JEEVES, A.H., The Administration and Control of Migratory
Labour on the South African Gold Mines: Capitalism and
the State in the Era of Kruger and Milner, in P.L. Bonner
(ed.), 'Working Papers in Southern African Studies,
Johannesburg, 1977.
JOHNSTONE, F.A., White Prosperity and White Supremacy in
South Africa Today, 'African Affairs', April 1970.
LAITE, W.J., 'The Union Tariff and its Relation to
Industrial and Agricultural Development: The Case for
Manufacturers', Cape Town, 1913.
LEGASSICK, MARTIN, The Frontier Tradition in South African
Historiography, University of Sussex, seminar paper, 1970.
LEGASSICK, MARTIN, Development and Underdevelopment in
South Africa, University of Sussex, seminar paper, March
1971.

LEGASSICK, MARTIN, The Making of South African 'Native Policy', 1903-1923: The Origins of 'Segregation', University of London, Institute of Commonwealth Studies, seminar paper, 1972.

LEGASSICK, MARTIN, The Rise of Modern South African Liberalism: Its Assumptions and its Social Base, University of London, Institute of Commonwealth Studies, seminar paper, 1972.

LEGASSICK, MARTIN, British Hegemony and the Origins of Segregation in South Africa, 1901-1914, University of London, Institute of Commonwealth Studies, seminar paper, 1973.

LEGASSICK, MARTIN, 'Class and Nationalism in South African Protest: The South African Communist Party and the 'Native Republic' 1928-34', Syracuse, 1973.

LEGASSICK, MARTIN, Legislation, Ideology and Economy in Post-1948 South Africa, 'Journal of Southern African Studies', vol. 1, no. 1, 1974.

LEGASSICK, MARTIN, South Africa: Capital Accumulation and Violence, 'Economy and Society', vol. 3, no. 3, 1974.

LEGASSICK, MARTIN, Liberalism, Social Control, and Liberation in South Africa, unpublished paper, 1975.

LEGASSICK, MARTIN, Race, Industrialisation and Social Change in South Africa: The Case of RFA Hoernle, 'African Affairs', vol. 75, no. 299, April 1976.

MAWBY, A.A., The Transvaal Mineowners in Politics, 1900-1907, University of London, Institute of Commonwealth Studies, seminar paper, 1972.

MILIBAND, R., Reply to Nicos Poulantzas, in R. Blackburn (ed.), 'Ideology in Social Science', London, 1972.

MOODIE, T.D., The Perceptions and Behaviour Patterns of Black Mineworkers on a Group Gold Mine, mimeo, Johannesburg, 1976.

MORRIS, M., The Development of Capitalism in South African Agriculture: Class Struggle in the Countryside, 'Economy and Society', vol. 5, no. 2, 1976.

OLLMAN, B., Marxism and Political Science: Prolegomenon to a Debate on Marx's 'Method', 'Politics and Society', vol. 3, no. 4, 1973.

O'MEARA, DAN, The 1946 African Mine Workers' Strike and the Political Economy of South Africa, 'Journal of Commonwealth and Comparative Politics', vol. XIII, no. 2, July 1975.

PHIMISTER, I.R., Rhodes, Rhodesia and the Rand, 'Journal of Southern African Studies', vol. 1, no. 1, 1974.

POULANTZAS, NICOS, On Social Classes, 'New Left Review', vol. 78, 1973.

POULANTZAS, NICOS, The Problem of the Capitalist State, in R. Blackburn (ed.), 'Ideology in Social Science', London, 1972.

PRICE, BERNARD, Some Aspects of the Union's Economic
Development Policy, Presidential Address to the Associated
Scientific and Technical Societies of South Africa, 1946.
PRICE, BERNARD, Some Trends in Industrial Development,
address to the Rotary Club, Johannesburg, 1952.
RATHBONE, E.P., The Problem of Home Life in South Africa,
Nineteenth Century', August 1906.
REX, JOHN, The Compound, The Reserve and the Urban
Location: The Essential Institutions of Southern African
Labour Exploitation, 'South African Labour Bulletin', vol.
1, no. 4, July 1974.
ROBERTSON, H.M., 150 Years of Economic Contact Between
Black and White: A Preliminary Survey, 'South African
Journal of Economics', vol. 2, no. 4, December 1934 and
vol. 3, no. 1, March 1935.
ROGERS, D. and BERG, I.E., Occupation and Ideology, The
Case of the Small Businessman, 'Human Organisation', vol.
20, 1961-2.
SHILS, EDWARD, The Concept and Function of Ideology,
reprinted from the 'International Encyclopedia of the
Social Sciences', New York, 1968.
SILVER, ALLAN, Social and Ideological Bases of British
Elite Reactions to Domestic Crisis in 1829-1932, 'Politics
and Society', vol. 1, no. 2, 1970.
SKINNER, QUENTIN, Some Problems in the Analysis of
Political Thought and Action, 'Political Theory', vol. 2,
no. 3, August 1974.
SLATER, HENRY, The Changing Pattern of Economic Relations
in Rural Natal, 1838-1914, University of London, Institute
of Commonwealth Studies, seminar paper, January 1972.
STADLER, A.W., The Afrikaner in Opposition, 1910-1948,
'Journal of Commonwealth Political Studies', vol. VII,
no. 3, 1969.
STANLEY, MANFRED, The Structures of Doubt: Reflections on
Moral Intelligibility as a Problem in the Sociology of
Knowledge, in G.W. Remmling (ed.), 'Towards the Sociology
of Knowledge', London, 1973.
STONE, ALAN, How Capitalism Rules, 'Monthly Review', vol.
23, no. 1, May 1971.
THOMPSON, E.P., Time, Work Discipline and Industrial
Capitalism, 'Past and Present', vol. 38, 1967.
TRAPIDO, STANLEY, Political Institutions and Afrikaner
Social Structures in the Republic of South Africa,
'American Political Science Reivew', vol. 57, no. 1,
March 1963.
TRAPIDO, STANLEY, Labour Movements and Power in South
Africa, University of London, Institute of Commonwealth
Studies, seminar paper, 1967.
TRAPIDO, STANLEY, South Africa in a Comparative Study of

Industrialisation, 'The Journal of Development Studies', vol. 7, no. 3, April 1971.

TRAPIDO, STANLEY, The South African Republic: The Role of the State in Capital Formation, 1850-1900, University of London, Institute of Commonwealth Studies, seminar paper, March 1972.

TRAPIDO, STANLEY, South Africa and the Historians, 'African Affairs', October 1972.

TRAPIDO, STANLEY, Liberalism in the Cape in the 19th and 20th Centuries, 'Collected Seminar Papers', 17, 1972-3, University of London, Institute of Commonwealth Studies.

TRAPIDO, STANLEY, Aspects in the Transition from Slavery to Serfdom: The South African Republic, 1842-1902, University of London, Institute of Commonwealth Studies, seminar paper, June 1975.

TRAPIDO, STANLEY, The Long Apprenticeship: Captivity in the Transvaal, 1843-1881, paper presented to the Southern African Labour History Conference, University of the Witwatersrand, 1976.

VAN ECK, H.J., The Potential of Industrial Development in South Africa, Bearing in Mind Limitations in Natural Resources, address delivered to the 35th Annual Convention of the South African Federated Chamber of Industries, September 1952.

VAN ECK, H.J., Some Trends in our Industrial Development, address delivered to the Rotary Club of Johannesburg, October 1952.

VAN ONSELEN, CHARLES, Reactions to Rinderpest in Southern Africa, 1896-1897, 'Journal of African History', vol. XIII, no. 3, 1972.

VAN ONSELEN, CHARLES, The Role of Collaborators in the Rhodesian Mining Industry 1900-1935, 'African Affairs', vol. 72, 1973.

VAN ONSELEN, CHARLES, Worker Consciousness in Black Miners: Southern Rhodesia 1900-1920, 'Journal of African History', vol. XIV, no. 2, 1973.

VAN ONSELEN, CHARLES, The 1912 Wankie Colliery Strike, 'Journal of African History', vol. XV, no. 2, 1974.

VAN ONSELEN, CHARLES, Black Workers in Central African Industry: A Critical Essay on the Historiography and Sociology of Rhodesia, 'Journal of Southern African Studies', vol. 1, no. 2, April 1975.

VAN ONSELEN, CHARLES, The Randlords and Rotgut, 1886-1903, 'History Workshop Journal', 2, Autumn 1976.

VAN ONSELEN, CHARLES, The Witches of Suburbia: Domestic Service on the Witwatersrand between 1890 and 1914, paper presented to the History Workshop, University of the Witwatersrand, February 1978.

VAN ONSELEN, CHARLES, 'The Regiment of the Hills': South

Africa's Lumpen-proletarian Army, 1890-1920, 'Past and Present', no. 80, August 1978.
WILLIAMS, G.A., The Concept of 'Egemonia' in the Thought of Antonio Gramsci: Some Notes on Interpretation, 'Journal of the History of Ideas', vol. 21, no. 4, 1960.
WILLIAMS, M., An Analysis of South African Capitalism: Neo-Ricardianism or Marxism?, 'Bulletin of the Conference of Socialist Economists', February 1975.
WOLPE, HAROLD, Capitalism and Cheap Labour Power in South Africa: From Segregation to Apartheid, 'Economy and Society', vol. 1, no. 4, 1972.
WOLPE, HAROLD, Pluralism, Forced Labour and Internal Colonialism in South Africa, paper presented at the Conference on South Africa, York University, 1973.
WOLPE, HAROLD, The 'White Working Calss' in South Africa, 'Economy and Society', vol. 5, no. 2, 1976.

4 BOOKS AND THESES

ADAM, HERIBERT (ed.), 'South Africa: Sociological Perspectives', London, 1971.
ADLER, T. (ed.), 'Perspectives on South Africa', Johannesburg, 1977.
AMPHLETT, G.T., 'History of the Standard Bank of South Africa Ltd., 1862-1913', Glasgow, 1914.
ALTHUSSER, L., 'Lenin and Philosophy', London, 1971.
APTER, DAVID E. (ed.), 'Ideology and Discontent', New York and London, 1964.
ARRIGHI, G., 'The Political Economy of Rhodesia', The Hague, 1967.
BARAN, PAUL A. and SWEEZY, PAUL M., 'Monopoly Capital', Harmondsworth, 1968.
BARKER, H.A.F., 'The Economics of the Wholesale Clothing Industry of South Africa 1907-1957', Johannesburg, 1962.
BARTHES, ROLAND, 'Mythologies', London, 1963.
BENDIX, REINHARD, 'Work and Authority in Industry: Ideologies of Management in the Course of Industrialisation', New York, 1956.
BERGER, P.L. and LUCKMANN, T., 'The Social Construction of Reality', Harmondsworth, 1967.
BONNER, P.L. (Ed.), 'Working Papers in Southern African Studies', Johannesburg, 1977.
BOZZOLI, BELINDA (Compiler), 'Labour, Townships and Protest', Johannesburg, 1979.
BRAVERMAN, H., 'Labour and Monopoly Capital', New York and London, 1974.
BRAYSHAW, B.C., 'The I.D.C.: Its Work and Influence, 1940-65', Johannesburg, 1965.

BROWN, DOUGLAS, 'Against the World: A Study of White
South African Attitudes', London, 1966.
CAIRNS, H.A.C., 'Prelude to Imperialism', London, 1965.
CARTER, G.M., 'The Politics of Inequality: South Africa
Since 1948', 2nd edition, London, 1959.
CARTWRIGHT, A.P., 'The Dynamite Company', London, 1964.
CARTWRIGHT, A.P., 'Golden Age', Cape Town, 1968.
CHILVERS, HEDLEY A., 'The Story of De Beers'', London,
1939.
CHINOY, ELY, 'Automobile Workers and the American Dream',
Boston, 1965.
COMMERCIAL EXCHANGE OF SOUTHERN AFRICA, 'A History of the
Commercial Exchange of Southern Africa, 1905-1955',
Johannesburg, 1955.
COSER, LEWIS, 'Men of Ideas: A Sociologist's View', New
York, 1965.
CURTIN, PHILIP D., 'The Image of Africa: British Ideas
and Action, 1780-1850', London, 1965.
DAVENPORT, T.R.H., 'South Africa: A Modern History',
Johannesburg, 1977.
DAVIES, R.H., 'Capital, State and White Labour in
South Africa, 1900-1960: An Historical Materialist
Analysis of Class Formation and Class Relations',
Brighton, 1979.
DE KIEWIET, C.W., 'A History of South Africa: Social and
Economic', Oxford, 1957.
DE KOCK, M.H., 'Selected Subjects in the Economic History
of South Africa', Cape Town, 1924.
DENOON, D., 'A Grand Illusion', London, 1973.
DOBB, M., 'Studies in the Development of Capitalism',
London, 1963.
DOUGLAS, MARY, 'Purity and Danger', Harmondsworth, 1970.
DOXEY, G.V., 'The Industrial Colour Bar in South Africa',
Cape Town, 1961.
DOYLE, BERTRAM W., 'The Etiquette of Race Relations: A
Study in Social Control', New York, 1971.
DUMONT, LOUIS, 'Homo Hierarchicus', London, 1970.
EASTON, D., 'A Systems Analysis of Political Life', New
York, 1965.
ETHERIDGE, D.A., The Early History of the Chamber of
Mines, University of the Witwatersrand, MA thesis, 1949.
FANON, FRANTZ, 'A Dying Colonialism', Harmondsworth, 1967.
FANON, FRANTZ, 'The Wretched of the Earth', Harmondsworth,
1967.
FRANKEL, S.H., 'The Railway Policy of South Africa',
Johannesburg, 1929.
GENOVESE, E., 'The World the Slaveholders Made', New York,
1969.
GLYN, A. and SUTCLIFFE, BOB, 'British Capitalism, Workers
and the Profits Squeeze', Harmondsworth, 1972.

GOFFMAN, E., 'Asylums', London, 1961.
GOLDMANN, LUCIEN, 'The Human Sciences and Philosophy',
London, 1969.
GOODFELLOW, D.M., 'Economic History of South Africa',
London, 1931.
GORDON, C.T., 'The Growth of Boer Opposition to Kruger,
1890-1895', Cape Town, 1970.
GORDON, R.J., 'Mines, Masters and Migrants',
Johannesburg, 1977.
GRAMSCI, ANTONIO, 'The Modern Prince and other writings',
New York, 1957.
GRAMSCI, ANTONIO, 'Selections from the Prison Notebooks of
Antonio Gramsci', London, 1971.
GREGORY, THEODORE, 'Ernest Oppenheimer and the Economic
Development of Southern Africa', Cape Town, 1962.
HANCOCK, W.K., 'Smuts: The Sanguine Years, 1870-1919',
London, 1962.
HELLMAN, ELLEN (ed.), 'Handbook on Race Relations in South
Africa', London, 1949.
HENRY, J.A., 'The First Hundred Years of the Standard
Bank', London, 1963.
HESSIAN, B., An Investigation into the Causes of the
Labour Agitation on the Witwatersrand, January to March
1922, University of the Witwatersrand, MA thesis, 1957.
HOBART HOUGHTON, D., 'The South African Economy', 2nd
edition, Cape Town, 1967.
HOBART HOUGHTON, D. and DAGUT, J. (eds), 'Source Material
on the South African Economy 1860-1970', vol. 2, Cape
Town, 1972.
HOBSBAWM, E.J., 'Industry and Empire', Harmondsworth,
1969.
HOBSON, J.A., 'Imperialism: A study', London, 1902.
HOROWITZ, IRVING LOUIS, 'Philosophy, Science and the
Sociology of Knowledge', Springfield, Illinois, 1961.
HORWITZ, R., 'The Political Economy of South Africa',
London, 1967.
HUDSON, W., JACOBS, G.F. and BIESHEUVEL, S., 'Anatomy of
South Africa', Cape Town, 1966.
JOHNSTONE, F.A., 'Class, Race and Gold', London, 1976.
KAY, G., Development and Underdevelopment: A Marxist
Analysis', London, 1975.
KNOWLES, L.C.A., 'The Economic Development of the
British Overseas Empire', vol. 3, London, 1936.
LAITE, H.J., 'Portrait of a Pioneer: The Life and Work of
William James Laite, 1863-1942', Cape Town, 1943.
LAURENCE, JOHN, 'The Seeds of Disaster', London, 1968.
LEACH, EDMUND, 'Levi-Strauss', London, 1970.
LE MAY, G.H.L., 'British Supremacy in South Africa',
London, 1965.
MANDEL, E., 'Marxist Economic Theory', London, 1962.

MANDEL, E., 'Late Capitalism', London, 1975.
MANNHEIM, KARL, 'Ideology and Utopia: An Introduction to the Sociology of Knowledge', London, 1936.
MARAIS, J.S., 'The Fall of Kruger's Republic', Oxford, 1961.
MARKS, S., 'Reluctant Rebellion', Oxford, 1970.
MARQUARD, LEO, 'The Peoples and Policies of South Africa', 3rd edition, London, 1962.
MARX, KARL, 'Capital: A Critique of Political Economy', vols I-III, London, 1972.
MARX, KARL, 'Grundrisse', Harmondsworth, 1973.
MARX, KARL and ENGELS, FREDERICK, 'Literature and Art', New York, 1947.
MARX, KARL and ENGELS, FREDERICK, 'The German Ideology', London, 1970.
MAWBY, A.A., The Political Behaviour of the British Population of the Transvaal 1902-1907, University of the Witwatersrand, PhD thesis, 1969.
MILIBAND, RALPH, 'The State in Capitalist Society', London, 1969.
MILLIN, SARAH GERTRUDE, 'The People of South Africa', London, 1951.
MITCHELL, JULIET, 'Woman's Estate', Harmondsworth, 1971.
MOORE, BARRINGTON, 'Social Origins of Dictatorship and Democracy: Lord and Peasant in the Making of the Modern World', Harmondsworth, 1967.
MORONEY, S., Industrial Conflict in a Labour Repressive Economy: Black Labour on the Transvaal Gold Mines 1901-1912, University of the Witwatersrand, BA Hons Dissertation, 1976.
MUELLER, CLAUS, 'The Politics of Communication: A Study in the Political Sociology of Language, Socialisation and Legitimation', New York, 1963.
NEAME, L.E., 'Today's News Today', Johannesburg, 1956.
NEAME, L.E., 'The Rand Club, 1887-1957', Johannesburg, 1957.
NICHOLS, THEO, 'Ownership, Control and Ideology', London, 1969.
O'MEARA, DAN, Class and Nationalism in African Resistance: Secondary Industrialisation and the Development of a Mass Movement in South Africa, 1930-1950, University of Sussex, MA dissertation, 1973.
'Our First Half Century: 1910-1960, Golden Jubilee of the Union of South Africa', Johannesburg, 1960.
PATON, ALAN, 'Hofmeyr', London and Cape Town, 1964.
PEARSON, P., The Social Structure of a South African Gold Mine Hostel, University of the Witwatersrand, BA Hons dissertation, 1975.
POULANTZAS, NICOS, 'Political Power and Social Classes', London, 1973.

POULANTZAS, NICOS, 'Fascism and Dictatorship', London, 1974.

REMMLING, GUNTER W. (ed.), 'Towards the Sociology of Knowledge: Origin and Development of a Sociological Thought Style', London, 1973.

REUNERT, T., 'Diamonds and Gold in South Africa', London, 1893.

ROBERTSON, J., 'Liberalism in South Africa, 1948-63', Oxford, 1971.

ROBINSON, R. and GALLAGHER, J., 'Africa and the Victorians', London, 1961.

ROUX, EDWARD, 'Time Longer than Rope', Madison, 1964.

SACHS, E.S., 'Rebels Daughters', London, 1957.

SHORTEN, JOHN R., 'The Johannesburg Saga', Johannesburg, 1970.

SIMONS, H.J. and R.E., 'Class and Colour in South Africa, 1850-1950', Harmondsworth, 1969.

STADLER, A.W., The Party System in South Africa, 1910-1948, University of the Witwatersrand, PhD thesis, 1970.

THOMPSON, A.G., 'The Years of Crisis: A Record of the Work of the Metal Industries During the War Years 1939-1944', Johannesburg, 1944.

THOMPSON, L.M., 'The Unification of South Africa, 1902-1910', Oxford, 1960.

TRANSVAAL CHAMBER OF INDUSTRIES, 'The Transvaal Chamber of Industries 1910-1960: An Historical Review', Johannesburg, n.d.

VAN ONSELEN, C., 'Chibaro', London, 1976.

WALKER, ERIC A., 'A History of Southern Africa', 3rd dition, London, 1957.

WELSH, D., 'The Roots of Segregation: Native Policy in Colonial Natal, 1845-1910', Cape Town, 1971.

WILSON, FRANCIS, 'Labour in the South African Gold Mines, 1911-1969', Cambridge, 1972.

WILSON, MONICA and THOMPSON, L.M. (eds), 'The Oxford History of South Africa', vol. II, 'South Africa 1870-1966', Oxford, 1971.

WOLFF, R.P., MOORE, B. and MARCUSE, H., 'A Critique of Pure Tolerance', London, 1969.

Index

academics: relationship to capital, 148, 164

Acts: Electricity, 220; Factory, 152; Glen Grey, 32, 287n; Industrial Conciliation (1924), 158, 180-1, 219, 226, 246; Iron and Steel (1928), 223, 227, 230-1; Iron and Steel Encouragement (1922), 219, 222; Land (1913), 302n; Regulation of Wages (1918), 178, 180; Tariff (1923), 323n; Tariff (1925), 110, 158, 172, 223, 254; Transvaal Nos. 21-4 (1895), 42; Transvaal Industrial Disputes, 178; Wage (1921), 219; Wage (1926), 158, 180, 225-6, 228, 231, 234, 245

advertising, 161

Advisory Board of Industries and Science: establishment of, 219-20; limits of, 221-2, 342-3n; South Africanism in, 163

AE and CI, 201

African National Congress, 189

African societies, see precapitalist modes of production

Afrikaners: in agriculture, 123, 204, 279; as businessmen, 280-1; challenge pre-empted, 281; emergent bourgeoisie, 279-81; and English-speakers, 135, 139, 204, 237-8, 280-2; experiences of hegemony, 275, 280-2; as manufacturing working class, 279, 281; in mine working class, 37-8, 83, 89, 97, 280-1; as nationalists, 237-8, 241, 244, 281-2; as poor whites, 42, 97, 306n; proletarianisation of, 89, 97, 151, 279; as racial category, 38; as subordinate, 105, 280-1; in 1907 strike, 100-1

Agricultural Union, see South African Agricultural Union

agriculture: as Afrikaner, 123; as ally of manufacturing, 121-3, 136, 150, 249, 318n; after Anglo-Boer War, 59, 63, 88, 90, 306n; capitalist, 12, 121-3; and commerce, 249; in depression, 242, 249; divisions in, 121-3, 149,

For Product Safety Concerns and Information please contact our EU
representative GPSR@taylorandfrancis.com
Taylor & Francis Verlag GmbH, Kaufingerstraße 24, 80331 München, Germany

www.ingramcontent.com/pod-product-compliance
Lightning Source LLC
Chambersburg PA
CBHW060134280326
41932CB00012B/1518

9 781032 899336